Through the Heart of Dixie

CIVIL WAR AMERICA

Gary W. Gallagher
Peter S. Carmichael
Caroline E. Janney
Aaron Sheehan-Dean
editors

This landmark series interprets broadly the history and
culture of the Civil War era through the long nineteenth century
and beyond. Drawing on diverse approaches and methods, the series
publishes historical works that explore all aspects of the war,
biographies of leading commanders, and tactical and campaign
studies, along with select editions of primary sources.
Together, these books shed new light on an era that
remains central to our understanding of
American and world history.

Through the Heart of Dixie

Sherman's March and American Memory

ANNE SARAH RUBIN

The University of North Carolina Press Chapel Hill

*This book was published with the assistance of the Fred W. Morrison Fund
for Southern History of the University of North Carolina Press.*

© 2014 The University of North Carolina Press

Set in Charter by codeMantra

Manufactured in the United States of America

The paper in this book meets the guidelines for permanence and
durability of the Committee on Production Guidelines for Book Longevity
of the Council on Library Resources.

The University of North Carolina Press has been a member
of the Green Press Initiative since 2003.

Jacket illustration: Columbia in flames, February 17, 1865.
Sketched by William Waud. *Harper's Weekly*, April 8, 1865.

Library of Congress Cataloging-in-Publication Data
Rubin, Anne S.
Through the heart of Dixie : Sherman's March and American memory / Anne Sarah Rubin.
pages cm. — (Civil War America)
Includes bibliographical references and index.
ISBN 978-1-4696-1777-0 (cloth : alkaline paper) — ISBN 978-1-4696-1778-7 (ebook)
1. Sherman's March to the Sea. 2. Sherman, William T. (William Tecumseh),
1820–1891. I. Title.
E476.69.R83 2014
973.7'378—dc23
2014008431
18 17 16 15 14   5 4 3 2 1

For Jack and Lucas

In war you lose your sense of the definite,

hence your sense of truth itself,

and therefore it's safe to say that in a war story

nothing is ever absolutely true.

—Tim O'Brien, *The Things They Carried*

CONTENTS

MAPS AND ILLUSTRATIONS

ACKNOWLEDGMENTS

Sherman's March took just over six months; my work on this project has taken considerably longer. I have my own army of supporters without whom this work could not have been finished, and I apologize in advance if I leave anyone out. First and foremost, I owe a debt of thanks to the American Council of Learned Societies whose Digital Innovation Grant allowed me to do the bulk of my research and begin building the Mapping Memory website. The University of Maryland, Baltimore County's College of Arts, Humanities and Social Sciences Research Fellowship allowed me to write most of my manuscript. I especially want to thank Dean John Jeffries for his support and contributions.

I could not ask for better, more congenial, and more supportive colleagues than the ones I have in the UMBC History Department. I'm especially grateful to Kate Brown, Amy Froide, Marjoleine Kars, Kriste Lindenmeyer, Denise Meringolo, and Michelle Scott. Drew Alfgren in Reference, Tom Beck in Special Collections, and the staff of Interlibrary Loan at UMBC's library all made researching easier. Dan Bailey and Lee Boot at UMBC's Imaging Research Center have not only played important roles in shaping the website but also in helping me frame my larger arguments. Dan deserves special thanks for putting me and Kelley Bell together. Kelley's enthusiasm for this project and our many conversations about the stories of Sherman helped this book immensely.

I did most of my research at the Library of Congress, and I am grateful to members of the staff there for their assistance. I also want to thank the staff of the Atlanta History Center's Kenan Research Library. While retracing Sherman's March I met several people who shared their knowledge and stories, including the staffs of the Old Capitol Museum and Old Governors Mansion in Milledgeville, Georgia; James Dailey of Clyde, Georgia; and Pastor Jerry DuBose of the Church of the Holy Apostles in Barnwell, South Carolina.

Over the years, I have presented parts of this project at conferences, roundtables, and symposia. Thanks are due to the following people for their comments, suggestions, and friendship: Kevin Adams, Steve Berry, Fitz Brundage, Jackie Campbell, Kathleen Clark, Catherine Clinton, Michael Fellman, Matt Gallman, Judy Giesberg, Joe Glatthaar, Kevin Levin, Bill Link,

Anne Marshall, Jim Marten, Jeff McClurken, Becky McIntyre, Brian Craig Miller, Megan Kate Nelson, Rob Nelson, Scott Nesbit, Christopher Phillips, Josh Rothman, Megan Taylor Shockley, Nina Silber, Diane Miller Sommerville, Richard Starnes, and Will Thomas.

Ed Ayers has continued to offer wise advice and support long after he officially needed to. Gary Gallagher and Karen Cox both suggested improvements to my manuscript that strengthened it considerably. At UNC Press, David Perry cultivated this project for years, and waited patiently to see it through. His encouragement means the world to me. Mark Simpson-Vos took over and shepherded the manuscript in its final stages, for which I am grateful. Ellen Bush encouraged me to blog about my trip to the Carolinas. I also want to thank Caitlin Bell-Butterfield and Ron Maner for their assistance.

I have been extraordinarily fortunate in finding a professional sisterhood that has marched with me on this project. The dinners, commiseration, and celebrations that I have shared with Sarah Gardner, Lesley Gordon, Amy Murrell Taylor, and Susannah Ural have sustained me through writer's block and crises of confidence. I could not have written this book without them.

My greatest thanks, however, are to my family. Deborah Rubin's enthusiasm for this project never flagged. Victoria Wilson made it possible for me to research, write, and travel. Lodge, Lucas, and Jack Gillespie allowed Sherman to invade our home for years. Lodge has been my best friend, cheerleader, and sounding board for over twenty years. I should take his advice more often than I do. His wit and wisdom have enlivened my life. Lucas and Jack have been my comic relief and welcome distractions. They never doubted that I would finish the book, and for that I thank them with all my heart. This book is for them.

Through the Heart of Dixie

Marching through Metaphors

Forty-one times a year, twenty-three hundred miles from Atlanta, the legacy of Sherman's March comes alive on the windswept prairies of Calgary, Alberta, Canada. There, thousands of people regularly brave below-freezing temperatures and head to the Scotiabank Saddledome to cheer on their beloved Calgary Flames of the National Hockey League. Does the name refer obliquely to Calgary's petroleum industry? To the Calgary Fire of 1886? No. It's the last remnant of Atlanta's short-lived NHL franchise, the Atlanta Flames (1972–80). The very fact that Atlanta could glibly memorialize what was arguably the worst moment in its history tells us something about the powerful hold of memories of the American Civil War.[1]

"Sherman's March." The name conjures up a host of images and references, myths and metaphors for Americans. They think of Clark Gable and Vivian Leigh, silhouetted against the flames in *Gone with the Wind*; of lone chimneys standing sentinel, all that remained of destroyed plantations; of soldiers stealing hams and silver, chickens and jewelry; of "war is hell," and "forty acres and a mule"; of the birth of total war. It is, I would argue, the most symbolically powerful aspect of the American Civil War, one that has a cultural dominance perhaps disproportionate to its actual strategic importance. It has come to stand for devastation and destruction, fire and brimstone, war against civilians, and for the Civil War in microcosm. Sherman's March has been memorialized in fiction and film, been used to explain both America's involvement in Vietnam and one man's search for romance. It has been employed as a metaphor for the burned out South Bronx of the 1970s and the gerrymandering of electoral districts.[2] Sports teams talk about enacting a Sherman's March on their opponents.[3] Opponents of video poker liken it to the scourge of the March.[4] Insects provide a particularly common metaphorical partner; the destruction wrought by the March has been variously compared to that of army worms, fire ants, the boll weevil, and the "Sherman bug" (official name: the harlequin bug).[5] One legend holds that the line of Sherman's March can be traced in the growth of daisies across the South, as their seeds arrived in the horses' fodder; another makes a similar argument about the proliferation of wild chives in Savannah; a third claims that the tradition of eating black-eyed peas on New Year's Day stemmed from the Yankees leaving only black-eyed peas behind.[6] The largest tree in the world, measured by volume, is the General Sherman, in Sequoia National Park, so named in 1879 by a naturalist who had participated in the March.[7] Storytellers often claim that the March's physical scars on the landscape are still visible, making it seem as though the earth itself was one of Sherman's victims. Certainly, the March obliterated physical structures, broke down fences, chopped down trees, ruined fields. But these effects were temporary, and can no longer be seen.[8]

William Tecumseh Sherman himself is a figure of profound contradictions. Excoriated by white Southerners as a heartless butcher, one who was, in Henry Grady's classic phrase, "a bit careless with fire," Sherman was a firm believer in a "soft peace" and offered surrender terms so generous that his own government rejected them. Hailed by many African Americans as a liberator, he opposed emancipation and was certainly no supporter of racial equality. Future generations would castigate him as the originator of "total war," even though he was not the only Union general to treat civilians harshly, nor did his way of making war involve wholesale slaughter of non-combatants (as would twentieth-century wars).

Just as Sherman could be painted as a hero or a villain, so too could his men. Sherman's soldiers were and are still roundly condemned as thieves and pillagers, men who ran roughshod over Southern whites and blacks, whose baser impulses could not be controlled. But unlike later generations of soldiers who found themselves struggling with having fought wars against civilians, Sherman's men seem remarkably untroubled by their weeks on the March. Many of them adopted the initially pejorative term "bummers" as their own, reminiscing good-naturedly about days spent chasing chickens or stealing hams. They believed that they ended the war, and that the end justified their means. For many of these men, the war and the March were the central events of their lives, and they felt no shame about the part they played.

Sherman's soldiers of course came into contact with white Southerners, and the vast majority of civilians they met were women, often alone or with children. While in the immediate aftermath of the March women were frequently portrayed as helpless victims, powerless in the face of the Yankee horde, with the passage of time their image seems to shift to that of brave resisters. Women are shown turning back soldiers with guns and fireplace pokers, holding on to their valuables by sewing them into their dresses, and shaming men into leaving them unmolested. This intertwining of Sherman's

March with gender roles and questions of both masculinity and femininity continued into the twentieth century.

African Americans experienced the March from a unique vantage point. Whatever Sherman thought about emancipation and the use of black troops in the Union army (he opposed both), his army was an agent of liberation for the thousands of African Americans along its path. Thousands of so-called contrabands left their homes and followed Sherman's men, where they were sometimes put to work, sometimes harmed and cruelly treated. In the worst instance, Sherman's men pulled up a bridge they had used to cross a river, leaving hundreds of African Americans to drown or face capture by Confederates. While Sherman clearly felt an affection for the white South he helped to destroy, he also was the architect of an early plan for Reconstruction in the Sea Islands that would have given former slaves land of their own, a plan that, had it been fully put into effect, might have changed the course of Reconstruction.

The contradictions and tensions extend even to the name "Sherman's March" itself. In common parlance "Sherman's March" is often taken to mean the March to the Sea, from Atlanta to Savannah in November and December 1864, also known as the Georgia campaign. Savannah was not Sherman's final destination; rather it was a chance for the army to rest and recover, to consolidate before heading north again. Savannah represents a metaphorical, if not absolutely geographic, halfway point of the March. In late January 1865 the army commenced its Carolinas campaign, marching north toward Grant's army outside of Petersburg. This campaign ended in late April near Durham, North Carolina, with Confederate general Joseph Johnston's surrender. But the men made one final march, to Washington, D.C., to take part in the Grand Review of the Armies on May 23 and 24, 1865. This book explores the stories of the entirety of the March, through three states, sixty-three counties, and scores of towns and villages.[9]

The March was explicitly designed to show "the World, foreign and domestic," that Jefferson Davis's Confederacy was powerless to resist Union military power. Sherman candidly explained his reasoning: "This may not be war, but rather Statesmanship, nevertheless it is overwhelming to my mind that there are thousands of people abroad and in the South who will reason thus—'if the North can march an Army right through the South, it is proof positive that the North can prevail in this contest,' leaving only open the question of its willingness to use that power."[10] And Sherman was quite willing to use that power, attacking the Confederacy militarily, materially, and spiritually.

The March undoubtedly achieved Sherman's military and material goals. The army faced little opposition on its inexorable movement through Georgia and the Carolinas, and in the latter stages prevented Johnston's army from being able to reinforce Lee in Virginia. The devastation wrought along the March's route was extraordinary: Sherman famously claimed to have destroyed $100 million of property in Georgia alone, and one could easily assume similar numbers for the Carolinas. The March's impact on Confederate morale, however, was more mixed than I believe Sherman would have liked. While clearly it frightened Southern civilians, and left a legacy of hunger, homelessness, and discomfort, it also engendered considerable anger, and from that anger came a sense of defiance or resistance.

Sherman is often credited with—or blamed for—being the originator of "total war." While the March was arguably the most dramatic Civil War example of the explicit targeting of civilian supplies and possessions, it was hardly the first. The Union had turned to a so-called hard-war policy by 1862, using tough tactics against guerrillas in Missouri. By 1864 it was committed to breaking the will of Confederate civilians by destroying their property and crops. Philip Sheridan's spring 1864 campaign in the Shenandoah Valley provides a textbook example of this hard war, months before Sherman's March began.[11]

SHERMAN'S MARCH has been an evergreen subject for students and scholars of the Civil War. Dozens of historians have written about various aspects of Sherman's March—the military and strategic, the impact of the war on female civilians, the role the March played in spreading the news of emancipation, the lives of Sherman's soldiers, and of course, William T. Sherman himself.[12] *Through the Heart of Dixie: Sherman's March and American Memory* takes a different approach. Rather than retell the story of the March, this project explores the myriad ways in which Americans have retold and reimagined Sherman's March. It looks at the March from a range of perspectives—from the participants themselves, including white Southerners, African Americans, Union soldiers, to a mosaic of sources: travel accounts, memoirs, music, literature, films, and newspapers. *Through the Heart of Dixie* unpacks the many myths and legends that have grown up around the March, using them as a lens into the ways that Americans' thoughts about the Civil War have changed over time.[13]

I originally conceived of this project as one describing the memory of Sherman's March, both as expressed by those who lived through it and the broader "social memory."[14] Over time, however, I have come to see this project as more about stories than memories. This may seem to be a purely semantic issue, but I think there is something more to it. Historical studies of memory have often focused on the creation of false or inaccurate narratives,

The popular view of Sherman's March is depicted in this 1868 engraving, after an illustration by F. O. C. Darley. It features African American refugees, a burning building, and soldiers tearing down telegraph wires and tearing up railroad tracks. The sense of chaos is palpable. (Library of Congress, http://www.loc.gov/pictures/item/2003679761/)

privileging one version over another. This book tries not to do that. Instead, I look at the different stories told about the March, at the ways that they overlapped or contradicted each other. At times the stories may seem ahistorical. Some attitudes and opinions change over time and generations, others seem more fixed. One anecdote might be repeated multiple times, in multiple sources, gaining the force of ubiquity. Others might be more fleeting, but no less powerful.

CHAPTER 1, "STORIES OF THE GREAT MARCH," provides a relatively brief narrative of the Georgia and Carolinas campaigns. Unlike the other seven chapters which draw on sources written or otherwise produced after the Civil War, this one uses contemporary sources—letters, diaries, and official military reports—as well. As the March moves across Georgia, South Carolina, and North Carolina, we meet both Southern white women and Union soldiers, seeing the March from multiple vantage points.

The next three chapters of this book delve into postwar stories of the March from the perspectives of white Southern civilians, African Americans, and Union veterans, respectively. In chapter 2 white Southerners' stories of Sherman tend to fall into one of two camps: either accounts stressing victimization in order to justify long-lingering anger and resentment, or tales of outwitting or defying Union soldiers, which serve as face-saving expressions of Southern pride. Finally, the chapter also examines tales of Yankee kindness, which exemplify pro-reunion and reconciliation sentiment designed to bind the sections together.

Chapter 3 turns to African Americans' contradictory experiences of the March. While the March certainly made emancipation a reality along its path, Sherman's soldiers were frequently uncomfortable with their role as liberators and treated as many African Americans with cruelty as with kindness. This chapter begins with African American memories of the March, describing both positive and negative interactions with Sherman's soldiers: watching troops pass, being emancipated, seeing their own property destroyed, and following along the length of the March. From there we move to a discussion of Southern white tales of faithful slaves, which serve to both condemn Yankees and present an image of Southern race relations as relatively benign. Next this chapter looks at the ways that Union soldiers felt about African Americans, including a discussion of the drowning of African Americans at Ebenezer Creek in Georgia and the origins of Sherman's Special Field Orders No. 15. This chapter concludes with an exploration of the relationship between collective memories of the March and the 1960s civil rights movement.

Chapter 4 shifts perspective to that of the common soldier. The popular image of Sherman's soldiers is that of "bummers": basically thieves and vagabonds, lacking all military discipline. The troops on the March saw themselves differently, however, and they quickly turned the pejorative "bummer" into a point of pride and framed the March as a lark or a picnic. From their perspective, it was a time of lighthearted fun, lots to eat, and relative safety. There is also an element of defensiveness in many of their writings, and their stories often featured examples of kindness toward Southern whites (and occasionally blacks as well). Sherman's men saw themselves as having won the war and would accept no criticism of their actions. They believed that they did what they had to do and that Southerners deserved what they got.

Chapter 5 focuses on Sherman the man. The traditional narrative features him as a figure of consummate cruelty and coldness, but this chapter seeks to complicate this picture, in part by showing that Sherman was not uniformly hated in the South. It also looks at examples of Sherman memorialization and the national outpouring of grief upon Sherman's death in 1891. Sherman's March is often mischaracterized as the birth of total war, as though one could draw a line connecting it with World War II and the Vietnam War. The second half of this chapter unpacks those notions, first looking at the March in the context of nineteenth-century theories or laws of war, and then tracing how opinions changed over time through World Wars I and II and the Vietnam War.

The final three chapters take the variety of images of Sherman and the March and explore how they have been presented, both on the landscape of tourism and in American culture, including songs, poems, photographs, fiction, and films. Chapter 6 hones in on travel and tourism along the path of the March, beginning with travelers in the immediate postwar years. This chapter also tells the story of Sherman's son, Father Tom Sherman, who sought to retrace the March at the turn of the twentieth century. During the 1980s and 1990s men like James Reston and Jerry Ellis used their trips along the line of the March as voyages of self-discovery, exploring themes of masculinity and violence. It also addresses the Civil War Centennial and the way that various states dealt with Sherman's March against the backdrop of the civil rights movement.

Chapter 7 opens with songs written about the March even as it continued across the Carolinas. Songs like "Marching through Georgia" and "Sherman's Bummers" kept the March alive well into the twentieth century. George Barnard's 1866 *Photographic Views of Sherman's Campaign*, with its pictures of Atlanta and Columbia in ruins helped shape and disseminate popular imagery of the March. Contemporary artwork also presents a particular image of Sherman and his men. Poems written in the nineteenth and twentieth centuries detail the March's enduring emotional pull.

Sherman's March has also been featured in dozens of novels and films, often used as a symbol of the harsh depravity of war or as a romantic device to get two people together. Considered in Chapter 8, this material looks, of course, at *Gone with the Wind*, but it also examinees both nineteenth-century novels and more recent works (like E. L. Doctorow's *The March*), as well as other films and documentaries. Many of the themes explored in the earlier chapters come together in this one, as we look at which stories are told and which are ignored or omitted.

THE STORIES I WANTED TO TELL about the March could not all be contained or best be expressed between the covers of a book. To that end, for the past several years, I have been working with Kelley Bell and the University of Maryland, Baltimore County's Imaging Research Center to build a visually arresting interactive exploration of Sherman's March. We call it *Sherman's March and America: Mapping Memory*. It uses a combination of maps and brief artistic and interpretive videos to tell stories of the March from a range of perspectives. I encourage you to take some time to explore the site at http://www.shermansmarch.org.

CHAPTER ONE

Stories of the Great March

Most of the chapters in this book delve deep into the stories of one place or another; they tell them from different perspectives and at different times. The purpose of the thematic chapters is to explore the common threads that bind together one place and another; they are not generally designed to weigh in on accuracy or veracity. They are impressionistic and episodic in nature. The stories of the March have a certain repetitive cadence to them, a kind of metaphorical tramp, tramp, tramp. The marchers came, they frightened, they stole, they burned, they moved on. From the soldiers' perspective they marched, they foraged, they camped, they celebrated, and then they did the same thing the next day. Each day was different, each encounter governed by the personalities and circumstances involved, yet they fall into patterns and tropes. This book explores those patterns, finding meaning in the stories. That these various stories and meanings coexist and overlap is important to keep in mind. For all the multiple perspectives and disputed accounts, there is a common story of the March, one that draws on common accounts and well-respected histories. This chapter is designed to briefly outline the course of the March and touch on the major battles, skirmishes, and encounters—in a sense to give a common vocabulary to the rest of the book.

BY THE FALL OF 1864 Sherman was already one of the best-known Union generals, famed for his support of Ulysses S. Grant during the Vicksburg campaign, and his relentless push toward Atlanta during the spring and summer of 1864.[1] He and his men took control of the city on September 1–2, 1864. The last thing Sherman wanted was to permanently occupy the city of Atlanta. On October 1 he requested authorization to destroy Atlanta and march to the coast, to either Savannah or Charleston, "breaking roads and doing irreparable damage." While his proposal was unenthusiastically discussed in Washington, Sherman prepared his men and assembled the few supplies they would carry with them. Not wanting his men to be distracted by either Confederate operatives or women and children or being forced to leave any of his men behind to hold the city, he ordered the evacuation of civilians, Unionist and Confederate. Accused of being unduly harsh and punitive by both the mayor of Atlanta and John Bell Hood, Sherman replied simply that "war is cruelty and you can not refine it."[2]

Sherman divided his sixty-thousand-man army into two wings, each one comprising two corps: the XV and the XVII in the right wing, the XIV and the XX in the left wing. General Oliver O. Howard commanded the right wing, with Peter J. Osterhaus leading the XV Corps and Francis Preston Blair Jr. the XVII Corps. General Henry W. Slocum took charge of the left wing, with Jefferson C. Davis (no relation to the Confederate president) leading the XIV Corps and Alpheus S. Williams the XX Corps. Sherman would ride with the left wing. Almost five thousand cavalrymen under Judson Kilpatrick would weave back and forth. Although Sherman's March was famous for its dictate that the soldiers should live off the bounty of the countryside, that did not mean that they traveled without supplies. The soldiers started out accompanied by twenty-five hundred wagons and six hundred ambulances, thousands of horses, mules, and cattle. They traveled lighter than they might have otherwise, but this was not pure living off the land.[3]

Sherman had studied maps and 1860 census data to plan his route. Although both wings headed for Savannah, the left wing initially did so in the direction of Augusta and the right via Macon, although neither city was visited by the troops. The distance between the two wings ranged between twenty and forty miles apart. The two wings were further subdivided, so in general the men marched in four columns. Thus, the distance from the edge of one column of one wing to the furthest of the other could be as much as fifty miles, but not a solid fifty miles. Rather than imagining the March as mowing down everything in its path, it is better to think of it as rows of stitches, with untouched spaces in between. Confederate opposition was light and sporadic: eight thousand cavalrymen under Joseph Wheeler and some companies of the Georgia state militia.

Before setting out Sherman tried to set some ground rules. His Special Field Orders No. 120 ordered his men to "forage liberally on the country" and "to destroy mills, houses, cotton-gins, etc.," but within limits. The foraging parties were supposed to be regularized and under the control of "discreet" officers; soldiers were not supposed to enter homes; should the army be left "unmolested" Southern property was also supposed to be left alone. Significantly, Sherman also ordered that when seizing livestock, his men ought to discriminate "between the rich, who are usually hostile, and the poor and industrious, usually neutral or friendly." As for African Americans, Sherman was willing to permit commanders to put "able-bodied" men who could "be of service" into pioneer corps, but he urged them to be mindful of their limited supplies. Well aware of his logistical limitations, Sherman wanted his officers to leave the newly freed women and children behind.[4]

Most of these rules were honored more in the breach than in reality, but their very existence gave Sherman (and, to an arguably lesser extent, his men) a degree of moral cover. They certainly allowed for a certain elasticity—harsher treatment of some people in some places, leniency elsewhere.

Before leaving Atlanta, Sherman ordered that anything of military value in the city be burned. This included not just supplies like ammunition and trains, but also machine shops and roundhouses. While this was supposed to be accomplished under the control and direction of Colonel Orlando M. Poe, many Union soldiers took their own initiative to torch vacant buildings. In addition, sparks from burning ammunition ignited neighboring buildings, and before the fire was out it had spread around the city. Despite stories to the contrary, however, the entire city was not destroyed—four hundred buildings (about 70 percent of the city), most of them private homes, remained. Civilians moved back, many of them living in railcars that could no longer be used, as Sherman's men had ruined the tracks.[5]

During the Georgia phase of the March, and for much of the Carolinas campaign, Sherman was cut off from communication with the North. Grant did not know what was happening day to day, nor did Lincoln, nor did the Northern press. Northern newspapers were occasionally able to piece together reports, but they were spotty. Georgia still had several newspapers publishing, but much of their reporting was misinformed or just plain wrong. The best sources were the people living through the March.[6]

Right Wing

The right wing moved out of Atlanta, beginning with a feint toward Jonesboro, a railroad town that had already endured hard fighting in late July.[7] With apparently little left to take or destroy, the troops marched through quickly.[8] "Item: Had my first drink of milk since the 26th of December, 1863," recorded Charles Wright Wills of the 103rd Illinois on his first day out. Subsequent diary entries noted the unusually wide variety of fare available to soldiers, including eggs, pork, potatoes, peach brandy, and, on one notable occasion, opossum.[9] On November 16 Wright and his fellow soldiers entered the town of McDonough. From McDonough the right wing moved on, crossing the Ocmulgee River on pontoon bridges, some men marching on through

These images from Harper's Weekly *detail the devastation that was left when Sherman's men marched out of Atlanta (Library of Congress, http://www.loc.gov/pictures/item/00652832)*

Monticello and Blountsville, Haddock and Fortville, others through Hillsboro and Clinton.

One Union soldier found the town of Jackson, in Butts County, "beautiful . . . and evidently occupied by the most prosperous people of the region." Jackson's beauty did not protect it, however, for the soldier reported that, after the soldiers passed through, the town was left "a little sadder, if not a wiser community." "Nothing remained," artillery officer Thomas Ward Osborn recalled, "but a few civilians and their houses." Osborn told of Sherman's men impressing horses and mules to replace their own exhausted mounts, and killing those deemed not serviceable, as many as a thousand. Residents of a nearby home, the Johnsons, told of soldiers drinking their milk, eating their dried fruit, and stealing (and presumably butchering) the children's pet turkey. Dead horses choked the road for a half a mile on either side of their home, leaving a vivid reminder of the March, and one that would appear again and again in Georgia and the Carolinas.[10]

So it went on November 18, 19, and 20 as the right wing moved south and east through Monroe and Jasper and Jones Counties, still feinting toward Macon, but never reaching it. The soldiers marched ten to twenty miles a

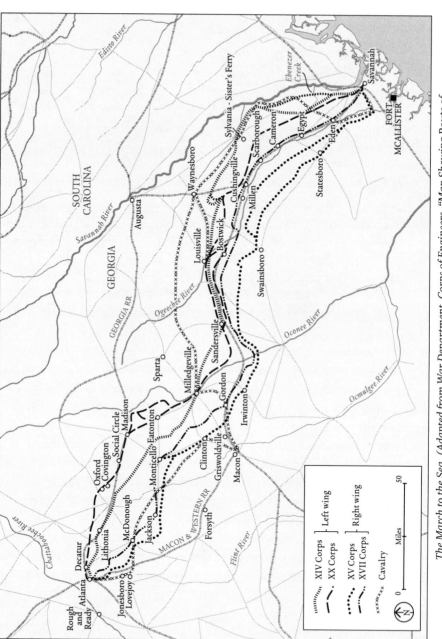

The March to the Sea. (Adapted from War Department, Corps of Engineers, "Map Showing Route of Marches of the Army of Genl. W. T. Sherman from Atlanta, Ga., to Goldsboro, N.C." [1865])

day. Thomas Osborn watched a large textile factory on the banks of the Oc-mulgee River burn and its enslaved workers volunteer to serve in the Union pioneer corps. He could see the smoke from dozens of fires all over the countryside. Local accounts featured stories of torched gin houses and cotton bales, ransacked homes and frightened women, and slaughtered livestock.[11]

Unlike most military campaigns, Sherman's March did not feature many true battles, pitting one massive army against another. There were countless skirmishes, especially involving Kilpatrick's cavalry, but the infantrymen and artillerymen rarely found themselves engaged against men in Confederate uniform. These conditions make a broad overview of the March difficult to construct, because while the men were moving in the same *general* direction, the particulars of their experiences tended to vary depending on where they might halt and forage. They also demonstrate the degree to which this was a lopsided endeavor: soldiers versus civilians, for the most part.

Circumstances were different, however, for the men who found themselves engaged at Griswoldville. Because there were so few traditional engagements, this small fight, with fewer than four thousand men engaged on each side, has taken on outsize importance.[12] On November 21, near the village of Griswoldville, inexperienced Georgia militiamen attacked a Union brigade in the rear of the XV Corps. The Union men were able to throw up some quick entrenchments, and as the lines of Georgians moved across an open field, they were cut down in droves. When the smoke cleared, 51 Georgia militia men were dead and 472 wounded, versus 13 dead and 79 wounded for the Union. Seasoned veteran Charles Willis "was never so affected at the sight of wounded or dead before" and found himself disturbed by what he found on the field: "Old grey-haired and weakly-looking men and little boys, not over 15 years old, lay dead or writhing in pain. I did pity those boys, they almost all who could talk said the Rebel cavalry gathered them up and forced them in. . . . I hope we will never have to shoot at such men again. They knew nothing at all about fighting, and I think their officers knew as little."[13]

From Griswoldville, the right wing kept moving. The men marched into Wilkinson and Washington Counties. "When the Yankees came into Tombsboro," recalled one witness many years later, "it was not slowly and orderly over one road. They came on horseback, in wagons, on foot, riding steers, and three . . . were driving a fat, beautiful milk cow to a buggy—the entire harness properly fitted to the cow." And when they left the men were laden down with jewelry and other valuables.[14] Survivors lamented the near-starvation that followed in Sherman's wake, with residents picking up leftover fodder for the horses and eating it. At the same time, however, survivors also conceded that the path of destruction was relatively narrow, for they ultimately received "provisions in abundance" from elsewhere in the state.[15]

The right wing halted briefly at the Oconee River, stopped by swamps and Confederate cavalry, but they eventually crossed at Balls Ferry on pontoon bridges and flimsy rafts. By November 26, eleven days after setting out, they were across the river, and with it the geographic fall line. Now they were moving through the sandy soil, pine forests, and cypress swamps of southeastern Georgia. Thomas Osborn noted that the maps bore lines that "purport to be roads," but they were really no more than trails.[16] They swept through towns like Tennille and Riddleville, Swainsboro and Canochee, Midville and Scarboro.

The stories told by civilians in southeastern Georgia had a certain similarity. The soldiers rushed in, took whatever they could, and moved on. Mrs. F. S. Williams, whose farm was bisected by the Bulloch and Bryan county line, related the oft-told tales of fire and vandalism, cut-up feather beds and stolen food, but also reflected that "those who had opposed secession before the war seemed to fare better than the others." This slight kindness was extended to her family, for her husband had voted against secession, before "[doing] his full part as a soldier."[17]

On December 4, the March reached Statesboro, the Bulloch County seat, where the initial foragers were scattered by Confederate cavalry. The Federals then regrouped and ran them out of the small town—really just a courthouse and a few boardinghouses and private homes. The courthouse record book for the time included the following notation:

Statesboro, GA, Monday December 5th 1864
This being the day set apart by law for holding the court of the
Ordinary; but the Yankees was here and have burned the court house
and there will be no court held today.
(signed) David Beasley, Ordinary

Clearly, this was not written in the courthouse; rather the books must have been saved and hidden, as happened in Irwinton and Milledgeville, among other places.[18]

Over the next few days the right wing crossed both the Ogeechee and the Canoochee Rivers, closing in on the coast. The closer they got to the ocean, however, the less food and fodder there was for men and horses. Too, the Confederates had realized that Sherman was aiming for Savannah, and they had begun to prepare for the onslaught that was sure to come.

Left Wing

The movements of the left wing are much better documented and much better known than those of the right, perhaps because Sherman traveled with it initially, perhaps because the well-known memoirs by Henry Hitchcock and George Nichols focus on the left.[19] Sherman and his men rode out of Atlanta and headed east. Just as the right wing was feinting toward Macon, the left was moving toward Augusta, confounding the Confederates as to the real target. Sherman traveled with the XIV Corps, the last group to leave Atlanta.

On the first day, they passed through Decatur and by Stone Mountain, spending the night in the village of Lithonia. The men burned gins and barns, and the campfires that Sherman gazed on approvingly were made from fences and railroad ties.[20] The following day Sherman and the marchers passed through Covington and Oxford, Social Circle and Rutledge. Sherman remembered Covington as a "handsome" town, but his main recollection of the visit was the jubilation with which African Americans received him. He described a conversation with an older black man about the need for African Americans to stay in place, even as he was being greeted as "the angel of the Lord." Sherman also recalled stopping a young soldier who appeared to be foraging a bit too liberally on the countryside.[21] These anecdotes, focused around Sherman, are nowhere to be found in Southern postwar recollections and county histories.

From Covington the XIV Corps turned south toward Milledgeville, Georgia's capital. The XX Corps approached Madison, the seat of Morgan County. As residents of a pretty little town, once described as "'the wealthiest and most aristocratic village' between Charleston and New Orleans," Madisonians were understandably concerned about what the invaders might leave in their wake. It was November 20, and the men of the left wing had already torn up seventy-five miles of railroad track. The soldiers marched into Madison and torched the courthouse, the railroad depot, and, in the most symbolical action, the town slave pen. Private homes were spared through the intercession of former U.S. senator Joshua Hill. Hill had been a Unionist, and a longtime friend of William T. Sherman's brother, Senator John Sherman. (He had met William Sherman outside of Atlanta earlier in the year, while searching for the body of his son.) The presence of Hill saved private homes from being burned by Slocum's men, although they were ransacked as much as any place else. Certainly Hill's prewar Unionism didn't stop Union soldiers from stabling their horses in the brick-floored basement of the First Baptist

Church, or from stealing the silver service from the Presbyterian church (later returned by General Slocum).[22]

Nine miles from Covington, Dolly Lunt Burge frantically prepared for the arrival of the rumored marchers. "What shall I do? Where to go—," she lamented on the night of November 17. But the following day she sprang into action, arranging for livestock to be hidden, hiding a barrel of salt in an enslaved woman's garden, and packing up clothes in case she needed to flee. On November 19, as the first Union soldiers approached she steeled her nerves, told her slaves to hide, and walked out "to claim protection & a guard." To her dismay,

> like Demons they rush in. My yards are full. To my smoke house, my Dairy, Pantry, kitchen & cellar like famished wolves they come, breaking locks & whatever is in their way. The thousand pounds of meat in my smoke house is gone in a twinkling my flour my meal my lard butter, eggs, pickles of various kinds, both in vinegar & brine. My eighteen fat turkeys, my hens, chickens, and fowls. My young pigs are shot down in my yard & hunted as if they were the rebels themselves.

Her remaining livestock—horses, mules, and pigs—were rounded up, and her young male slaves (Burge calls them her boys) were forced to leave with the army. Money and clothing, belonging to both Burge and her slaves, was taken, coffee pots and flour sifters, ovens and skillets, all seized.[23]

All of this appeared to have happened even though Burge's home was being guarded, at least nominally. Perhaps the presence of Union guards (one of whom knew Burge's brother who lived in Chicago), helped to save her home, for the soldiers torched her cotton as they left. To her great pleasure the cotton did not go up in flames entirely. The following morning she fixed breakfast for her guards, using their coffee ration in her teakettle (as she no longer had any coffee pots). At last they all passed by leaving her "poorer by thirty thousand dollars . . . and a much stronger rebel." For all the terror that Burge endured, she surely fared better than many neighbors did, for she had managed to hide some provisions: potatoes, flour, syrup, and a bit of meat. In the days that followed, a few cows wandered home, and she even happened upon the still edible carcass of one of her hogs, near the family's unmolested graveyard.[24]

As soldiers from both corps of the left wing headed for Milledgeville, they needed to pass through Putnam County, where they burned tanyards, a shoe factory, and the Eaton Manufacturing Company in Eatonton. In Denhamville soldiers of the XX Corps were ordered to burn bales of cotton but used it for bedding instead. The soldiers also passed by Turnwold Plantation, a few miles outside of Eatonton. The plantation was the home of Joseph Addison Turner, and also the site of his newspaper print shop and a small hat factory. Turner employed a teenage typesetter, Joel Chandler Harris.[25]

Almost thirty thousand Union soldiers marched into Milledgeville on November 22, 1864, to the cheers of local African Americans. While obviously uninvited and unwelcome, they were not unexpected. On November 19, the Georgia state legislature met in the statehouse on Capitol Square, voted to institute a draft of all Georgia (white) men between sixteen and sixty-five. Governor Joe Brown pardoned most of the convicts in the state penitentiary, provided they joined the militia. They thanked him for this by setting fire to the prison almost immediately. The legislature proceeded to evacuate, sending important papers into southwestern Georgia for safekeeping and hiding other valuables and the Great Seal around town. Governor Brown also fled, loading furniture, carpets, curtains, and provisions from the governor's mansion onto the last train to Macon.[26]

Sherman spent the night of November 22 a few miles out of town, on a plantation. Not until he had already set up his camp did he realize that it was "Hurricane," the home of Howell Cobb, a well-known politician, who had served as Speaker of the House of Representatives and secretary of the U.S. Treasury during the 1850s. Cobb had also served as president of the Provisional Confederate Congress, and by 1864 was commanding Georgia state troops. Cobb's healthy slaves and livestock had been moved off the plantation already, but the Union soldiers found fifty African American women, children, and old men, more than one thousand bushels of peas, and substantial stockpiles of corn, beans, and sorghum. Sherman ordered the food confiscated and the property destroyed—except for the slave cabins, which were to be left untouched. The slaves were also given any food that was not consumed that night by the army. In contrast to the revenge brought down on the Cobb property, Sherman also ordered guards be placed (to prevent foraging) at the home of Andrew Banks, a known local Unionist.[27]

Major James A. Connolly of the 123rd Illinois Infantry was among the men who spent the night at Hurricane. He and his companions found three new iron kettles (used for boiling sorghum) and took action: "Poe picked up an axe and with a few blows shivered one of them into atoms. Buttrick took the axe and shivered the second one. I then took the axe and paid my respects to 'Ginral Cobb' by shattering the third one." Connolly's depiction of destruction was striking for its straightforward tone. No regrets, no explanation. Just the facts.[28]

Sherman arrived in Milledgeville on November 23 and set up his headquarters in the Governor's Mansion, using his campaign furniture. His men swept through the town like the proverbial hurricane: they plundered the state house, blew up the arsenal, and burned the central depot and bridge over the Oconee River. St. Stephen's Episcopal Church was damaged in the arsenal explosion and had its pews torn out for use as firewood. But the ultimate insult came when the Yankees poured molasses into all of the organ pipes. Despite a thorough cleaning after the troops left, it never worked perfectly again. Only three or four homes in town were burned, including that of Judge Iverson Harris. His residence was targeted because he had urged local planters to burn their property in advance of the arrival of the March, to prevent the foragers from having their pick. One civilian died in Milledgeville: Patrick Kane, an Irish-born overseer shot while defending his employer's plantation.[29]

While plenty of buildings in Milledgeville were destroyed, the Georgia Statehouse was not among them. Rather, about one hundred New York and Wisconsin members of the XX Corps took advantage of the empty state capitol building to hold their own legislative session, eventually deciding to lead Georgia "back like a conquered child into the Union" and appointing a committee to kick Governor Brown and President Davis "at their most accessible point." One Indiana infantryman found it "very amuseing" to hear the Northerners "carr[y] it on in regular Southern fire eating stile." The men then adjourned for more destructive revelry, dumping flour and meal throughout the halls, and scrawling obscenities on the walls. They broke windows and furniture, and threw books out the windows to the ground below, where they were trampled by horses. A group of soldiers went on to hold a mock funeral for Georgia governor Joe Brown, using a box of pikes as a coffin, and leading a winding procession through town to the Baptist church.[30]

While James Connolly witnessed much of the mayhem in Milledgeville, his only recorded complaint involved the pillaging of the state library. "Public libraries should be sacredly respected by all belligerents," he proclaimed with disgust, going on to explain his personal moral code: "I don't object to stealing horses, mules, niggers, and all such *little things*, but I will not engage in plundering and destroying public libraries. Let them alone, to enlarge and increase for the benefit of the loyal generations that are to people this country long after we shall have fought our last battle and gone into our eternal camp."[31] It seemed that it would be some time before Milledgevillians could worry about the loss of the state library, however. Eliza Frances Andrews had fled to Macon in advance of Sherman's March but did pass through Milledgeville a few weeks later, and was shocked by the detritus left in the Yankees' wake. She saw families wandering around the former campgrounds, searching for food and "even picking up grains of corn that were scattered around where the Yankees had fed their horses." Rumor had it that the field was once full of discarded valuables, but by the time that Andrews passed by "little now remained except tufts of loose cotton, piles of half-rotted grain, and the carcasses of slaughtered animals, which raised a horrible stench."[32]

On November 24 the soldiers moved out of Milledgeville, embarking on what Henry Hitchcock called "the second Act of the drama," abuzz with news of Kilpatrick's raids.[33] Kilpatrick and his cavalry were en route to Millen in order to liberate Union soldiers held in a newly constructed prison, Camp Lawton. The XX Corps under Slocum, with Sherman, was headed for Sandersville and would reach it on November 26, but not without incident.

Ella Mitchell was nine years old in November 1864, and she lived with her family on the Old Louisville Road, which ran from Milledgeville through Sandersville, and finally to Savannah. On the night of November 25, some of Wheeler's Confederate cavalry captured thirteen Union soldiers and hid twelve of them in a store in the town of Sandersville. That night they were taken out of the store, perhaps by deserters, perhaps by soldiers, taken to a field outside of town, and executed. The thirteenth man proved lucky—he was wounded and cared for by a minister. Mitchell's father, who had been home recovering from a collapsed lung, was among a group of men who hearing of this went and buried the bodies. They feared, not without some justification, that Sherman would demand revenge and burn the town.[34]

At first, it seemed that this would come to pass. Sherman not only learned of the killings but also saw Confederates torching their own fields and houses, in order to deny the fodder and food to Sherman's marchers. What actually happened to save the town (though not some individual properties) is a matter of dispute. In his memoirs, Sherman (who did not mention the executed men) explains that he warned some local citizens that if they continued to destroy food along his route, "I would most undoubtedly execute to the letter the general orders of devastation made at the outset of the campaign." This appeared to solve the problem to the general's satisfaction.[35]

Sandersville residents told a different story, namely that the Methodist minister, Rev. J. D. Anthony personally appealed to Sherman to spare the town. Some versions of that story had Anthony appealing to Sherman as a brother Mason (although Sherman appears not to have been a Mason in fact), while others had him invoking the need to protect innocent women and children. Henry Hitchcock had still another explanation: that the ladies of the town begged Sherman directly, and he relented, agreeing to burn only the courthouse and public buildings.[36] The different versions illustrate the difficulty of pinning down one narrative of the March. We can place people on the landscape, but we cannot re-create the interactions and emotions.

Ella Mitchell's memories of terror and fear are representative of many other Georgians. She described the blue-coated forces filling her house as a "surging mass," sweeping up the food, china, silver, and even the tablecloth. The soldiers dug up graves, ripped down fences, butchered cows and hogs, and set fire to barns, the jail, the courthouse, all in full view of crying women and screaming children. "Pandemonium reigned," she noted, and then went on to complain about slaves running away with the Union army, "arrayed in their mistresses' dresses . . . on their favorite horses." Sherman and his men stayed over a weekend in Sandersville and the surrounding area:

> From Saturday morning until Monday, many inhabitants had neither
> food nor water. It seems beyond belief that not a chicken was left, not
> a hog, and only a few cows, no meal nor flour, the ground was strewn
> with food, carpets were drenched with syrup and then covered
> with meal. Negro soldiers entered private homes and searched for
> valuables. My mother refused to unlock her bureau drawers, but a
> soldier placed his bayonet at her back and forced her to march in
> front of him. Father was helpless from a terrible hemorrhage brought
> on by excitement, to save him she obeyed the Yankee's command,
> then he helped himself to all valuables that she had overlooked when
> hiding some treasures.[37]

The impact of the March lingered. For five years, Mitchell lamented, whites and blacks struggled with deprivation, coping with the lack of livestock and supplies. While this might have been an overstatement, or a conflation of postwar difficulties with wartime hardships, Sandersville's home county was harder hit than most. In addition to the left wing, the right wing passed through the area around Tennille, leaving the twisted iron rails known as "Sherman's neckties" in their wake.[38]

For their part, many soldiers' mentions of Sandersville are unremarkable. James Connolly described the local landscape in vivid detail, down to the types of forage available and the quality of the soil. William Bluffton Miller and his compatriots came upon a deserted storehouse full of wine and "helped ourselves as usual and made ourselves perfectly at home." Other soldiers recalled it as a locale with exceptionally good food to be foraged.[39]

On November 27, Sherman went from Sandersville to Tennille, leaving the left wing behind and joining up with the right. The columns were converging on Millen and passing through Burke County. Why Millen? Because just outside the town was the Confederacy's largest prison camp, and Sherman and his men wanted to liberate it. Camp Lawton was hastily built during the fall of 1864, thrown up to handle overflow from the notorious Andersonville prison. Georgians also worried that once Sherman moved out of Atlanta he might head for Andersonville. Camp Lawton was in an ideal location—the forty-acre stockade straddled the free-flowing Magnolia Spring, which provided water for both drinking and sanitation; had a hilly area for defensive earthworks; and was close to a railroad. Camp Lawton's first prisoners arrived on October 10, 1864, and within weeks the stockade housed more than ten thousand Union men. As many as seven hundred men died of disease and exposure in a few short weeks.[40]

A mere six weeks after it opened, with Sherman's men heading for Millen, Camp Lawton was evacuated, with the prisoners scattered around Georgia and South Carolina. The marchers found an empty camp, but the obviously horrible conditions within the stockade—few huts, men forced to live in holes dug out of the earth, and the fresh graves—sickened and enraged the Union men. They, whether under orders or in spite of them, went on a frenzy of burning in nearby Millen, torching the railroad depot and the town hotel, the latter because of rumors that it had refused to sell food to the prisoners.[41]

From Millen the soldiers continued to move through Burke County. Near the town of Girard, previously known as Liberty Hill, Southern whites tried to protect their homes by burning the bridge across Briar Creek. They also claimed to be trying to protect Augusta, which we now know was never in danger.[42] Kilpatrick's cavalry raided Bellevue Plantation, burning the outbuildings but not the main house. Perhaps Kilpatrick, a well-known ladies man, spared the house because it was filled with women and children. The home still has bullet holes in it from a brief skirmish.[43] That wasn't the only souvenir Kilpatrick and his men left behind. One wall of the Cheedy-Coleman house in Shoals (Hancock County) bears the graffiti

> May all the names engraved here
> in the golden book appear

over the signatures of Kilpatrick and his staff.[44] On December 4, 1865, Kilpatrick's cavalry fought Wheeler's Confederates in the Battle of Waynesboro and were able to slow the March's progress toward Savannah, but not for long. Wheeler's men were eventually pushed out, and the Union soldiers continued via the town of Alexander.[45]

A runaway slave named Henry led marchers to the Thomas plantation in Burke County, much to the dismay of his former mistress, Gertrude Thomas. Once there, Henry showed them where the horses were hidden and received a stolen suit of clothes and one of the Thomas's prized horses in return. The soldiers burned the Thomas's gin house, cotton, and corn cribs "and committed other depredations." Thomas praised most of her slaves for remaining "faithful," but astutely recognized that Henry perhaps felt more inclined to leave because he "had no ties to bind him to the plantation and has been a runaway from childhood." While Thomas was not present for the March (she received her news in a letter from her husband), her absence did nothing to quell her anger at Sherman and the March. Even while Sherman was in Savannah she continued to worry that he would move on Augusta, her current residence. And in January, she penned a long entry in which she ruminated on the sufferings of Southern white women and her desire to see Northern women miserable as well. She vented particular spleen on the wives of Generals Kilpatrick and Sherman. She went so far as to write a letter to Mrs. Sherman, blaming her for supporting her husband in his war on women and children. Interestingly, Thomas ascribed emancipationist aims to the Shermans and spun out a fantasy of Sherman having affairs with black women (she does the same with Kilpatrick). Thomas closed with sardonic pity for Mrs. Sherman having to be married to such a brutal and dishonorable man. Thomas never sent the letter, however, for she was moved by the news of the death of the Shermans' infant and chose not to pile on a grieving mother.[46]

Just as Henry left the Thomas plantation to try his luck with the army, so too did thousands of other African Americans. Everywhere the marchers went, they were followed by African Americans who were eager to put their newfound freedom to the test. Sherman and his generals tried constantly to dissuade black families from traveling with them, believing that they slowed down and distracted the columns, although they were willing to take on able-bodied young men as a pioneer corps. This tension between Union commanders and Georgia freedmen came to a head on December 9, as the XIV Corps drew ever closer to Savannah.

The army needed to cross the deep, wide, and icy waters of Ebenezer Creek, a river that ran through tangled cypress swamps before it joined the Savannah River. Brigadier General Jefferson C. Davis (no relation to the Confederate president) ordered his troops to set up pontoon bridges. They crossed swiftly, mindful that Confederate raiders were close behind.

Thousands of freedpeople, who were afraid of being captured by the Confederate troops, were told to wait to cross until all the soldiers and wagons were over. After the soldiers had crossed, though, they pulled up and dismantled the bridges, leaving the African Americans stranded, trapped between the frigid water and Confederates firing upon them. Many of the soldiers who witnessed this were horrified, watching men, women, and children drown before their eyes. Other African Americans were captured by Wheeler's cavalry, and presumably reenslaved.

The evidence indicates that Brigadier General Davis planned to rid himself of his African American followers several days before the event. In no way could the deaths be excused as the product of a quick decision. How many African Americans were left behind is impossible to know, but estimates are about five thousand, made up primarily of old men, women, and children (able-bodied men were working for the Union army and would have already crossed).[47] James Connolly witnessed the cruelty at Ebenezer Creek first hand and was outraged. First, he vented his anger on General Davis's staff officers, but once he reached Savannah he wrote a letter to his congressman (and gave a copy to another general), detailing the mistreatment of African Americans. The letter had the desired effect: its contents were published in Northern newspapers, and a copy of it reached Secretary of War Stanton. Stanton, in turn, would come to Savannah to investigate.[48]

While Sherman took the deaths of African American civilians in stride, he reacted quite differently to the deaths of his own men. On December 8, a young officer traveling with Sherman had his horse killed, and his own leg blown off by a hidden torpedo. "This was not war, but murder and it made me very angry," Sherman recalled. In response, he called for Confederate prisoners to be brought up to the front and ordered them to march along the road testing for further mines. While Sherman "could hardly help laughing" at their gingerly pace, one can imagine that the prisoners were terrified. Fortunately, they did not find any other hidden explosives.[49]

As devastating as much of the March was, its impact was still localized and inconsistent. Thus, residents of Screven County, near Savannah, recalled that the marchers "passed through in good order, following Sherman's orders forbidding random destruction." Screven's white population had been frightened by reports coming from elsewhere in Georgia and expected their homes and hamlets to be burned to the ground. When that did not happen, one local historian noted wryly that "every family seemed to be compelled in later years to devise some explanation as to why its home was spared."[50]

Savannah

By December 10 the army's left wing had reached Savannah, meeting with the right wing as its columns arrayed themselves a few miles outside the city. In twenty-four days they had traveled about three hundred miles. But Savannah was protected by a combination of swamps and salt marshes, bridges, and a network of forts and floodgates. The Confederates, under General William J. Hardee, had about ten thousand men guarding Savannah. Sherman faced a further problem, in that the area around Savannah did not have nearly as much for his men to eat as central Georgia did, and he worried about his men running out of supplies. His best chance for reopening a supply line and taking Savannah itself was to focus his men's energies on Fort McAllister, south of the city where the Ogeechee River entered Ossawbaw Sound.[51]

A division of the right wing attacked the fort on December 13, eventually overwhelming its defenses and taking control with minimal loss of life. The Union men captured around 250 Confederates and, more importantly, their heavy guns. The capture of Fort McAllister also allowed Sherman to open up a supply line (via the water). His men received mail for the first time in a month, which delighted them. Now that he was back in contact with the Union, Sherman decided to wait out Savannah, rather than attack it immediately.[52]

Even as they waited, Sherman's marchers continued to forage and raid. William Bluffton Miller marched south through the swamps and at first complained that there was no foraging to be found—only rice, which he hulled with his bayonet in a tin cup. On his second day out, he and his fellow soldiers found a plantation that belonged to "an old Rebel by the name of Collins." In addition to a hog (which Miller shot) and some hams and yams, the regiment loaded dozens of wagons with corn to take back to the main army. On the third day out, December 18, they moved toward Riceville, Georgia, where they seized 150 barrels of salt. Overall, Miller was less impressed with the coastal countryside, complaining that "they don't raise any thing but rice and alligators and there is plenty [of] boath."[53] Like Miller, George F. Cram of the 105th Illinois initially lamented the lack of food compared to the richness of the early days of the March. Fortunately, he noted, they discovered a large rice plantation and several herds of cattle and "have lived quite comfortably one week."[54]

Soldiers might complain about the lack of plantations on which to forage, but Southern civilians felt the presence of the Yankees acutely. Agitated letters flew among the extended Jones family of Liberty County, Georgia, during December 1864. At Arcadia Plantation, Mary Jones worried abstractly about her family and more concretely about how to prepare for the impending marchers. "Ought the furniture to be removed? Books etc.?" she wrote to her sister on December 9.[55] Her niece Laura Buttolph detailed her own preparations, closing with a sweet suggestion from her young son: "Let us give the Yankees some of our little things, and then they will love us and not kill us."[56] A few days later, while moving items from one home to another, Mary Jones ran right into a group of Union soldiers, who briefly stopped her. Although she made her way home without further incident, a few days later several groups of Union soldiers arrived. After seizing the family's horses and mules and its whiskey, they commenced searching the house for valuables, opening drawers and boxes, strewing the contents about the rooms. They demanded food from the Jones women (Mary's daughter Mary Mallard was there as well), and even went through trunks in the attic. Interestingly, the Jones women stood their ground against the soldiers. As elite plantation mistresses, they were accustomed to giving orders and being obeyed and, at least according to Mary Mallard's journal, were able to shame the Union soldiers into leaving at least a few valuables behind. They left the horses and mules as well, because they were too old to be of much use to the army on the move.[57]

But the encounters between the Jones women and their Yankee enemies were not over. The following day, December 16, the Jones women heard "the clash of arms and the clatter of horsemen," and rushed into their pantry and kitchen to find forty or fifty men tearing the place apart, ripping into smoked meats, demanding whiskey and flour. They seemed less moved by Mary Jones's remonstrances, threatening to take every bit of food and starve the family to death, leaving only a little rice and some spilled corn meal. The possessions that the first day's soldiers had left were rifled and taken by this more out-of-control group. Mary Mallard, justifiably, seemed much more frightened of these later raiders:

It is impossible to imagine the horrible uproar and stampede through the house, every room of which was occupied by them, all yelling, cursing, quarreling, and running from one room to another in wild confusion. Such was their blasphemous language, their horrible countenances and appearance, that we realized what must be the association of the lost in the world of eternal woe. Their throats were open sepulchers, their mouths filled with cursing and bitterness and lies. These men belonged to Kilpatrick's cavalry. We look back upon their conduct in the house as a horrible nightmare, too terrible to be true.

In these two experiences—one relatively controlled, one terrifyingly unchecked—the Jones women experienced what so many other women did. Sometimes, their gender and social privilege protected them; sometimes it did not.

Indeed, following their terrifying encounter with Kilpatrick's raiders, the Jones women awoke to find a Union guard posted outside. He left their personal property alone but took more of the remaining food: turkeys, syrup, one small pig, and, in the final insult, filled the family carriage with chickens. They called for some of the Jones slaves to drive the mule and horse cart filled with food and then left. Each day for the next several days, the Jones plantation was visited by at least one squad of foragers, including some repeat visitors. Cornelia Jones Pond, a neighbor of Mary Jones, experienced similar repeated visitations. Her mother was especially troubled by having her underclothes repeatedly rifled through, and she hid them in a locked trunk.[58] The next group of Union soldiers to come through simply picked the lock. It seems amazing that either family had anything left at all, and by the time it was over, all of the slave cabins had been raided as well. The later raiders claimed to be searching for weapons or hidden Confederate soldiers. "My mind is made up," wrote an angry Mary Jones, "not to leave my house until the torch is put to it." Fortunately for her, it never came to that.[59]

The Jones women's saga began before Sherman had even entered Savannah. On December 17, Sherman wrote to Confederate general Hardee, demanding a surrender. In addition to the metaphorical stick of this demand, he also left a carrot—an escape route out of the city. Sherman did not want to have to fight a pitched battle for Savannah; rather he wanted to terrorize the city enough so that the soldiers gave up. For his part, Hardee rejected the December 17 demand. But after three more days of bombardment, which resulted in the destruction of more ordnance and ships, Hardee ordered his men to slip out across the Savannah River to the relative safety of South Carolina. On December 21 Sherman rode into the city, and on December 22 he sent a witty telegram to Washington:

His Excellency
Prest. Lincoln

I beg to present to you as a Christmas gift the City of Savannah with 150 heavy guns & plenty of ammunition & also about 25,000 bales of Cotton.

W. T. Sherman

Major General

Lincoln thanked him warmly for the gift in his reply and praised him for the success of the operation, about which Lincoln felt "anxious if not fearful."[60] Sherman had marched across Georgia and taken Savannah, losing less than two thousand men.[61] By any measure, it was a stunning achievement.

In Savannah, Sherman was greeted by a jubilant African American population and a nervous white one.[62] Local politicians visited him; Confederate generals and officers who had fled left their wives under Sherman's protection. Charles Green, a British banker and cotton merchant and the richest man in Savannah, offered his lavish mansion on Madison Square to Sherman, which he accepted. According to one story, Green was not motivated by any sort of latent Unionism; rather "Mr. Green wanted to save some other citizen the humiliation of having his house taken as the enemy's headquarters." Reportedly, the Reverend C. F. McRae, rector of St. John's Episcopal Church next door, had lived in Green's home for years but moved out immediately upon Sherman's arrival.[63] Sherman used the Green House as his headquarters and for Christmas and New Year entertaining, gradually softening the attitudes of white Savannahans toward him.

Sherman's relationship to Savannah's African Americans was equally complicated. The incident at Ebenezer Creek continued to resound in Washington, and not to Sherman's benefit. His continued support of General Jefferson C. Davis, along with his long-avowed opposition to commanding black troops, led many to believe that Sherman in General Halleck's words "manifested an almost *criminal* dislike to the Negro."[64] Sherman's attitude towards African American refugees can best be described as paternalistic. He seemed to take pride and pleasure in the streams of black men and women, young and old, who came to see him at the Green house, shaking their hands, and Sherman couldn't understand why so many people in Washington disapproved of his conduct and felt that it needed to be corrected.[65]

Thus Sherman was displeased when Secretary of War Edwin Stanton came to Savannah to chastise him. Stanton arrived on January 9, 1865, and, after meeting privately with Sherman, arranged for a meeting with about twenty of Savannah's leading African American men, many of them ministers. Stanton asked the African Americans about Sherman's dealings with local blacks; they replied that they had always been treated fairly, which satisfied Stanton. A few days later, Sherman issued his Special Field Order No. 15, setting aside land abandoned by whites for black settlement.[66]

Savannah also afforded Sherman's officers the chance to catch up on their paperwork, impossible to do on the constantly moving march across Georgia. Thus, dozens of them, from generals to captains put pen to paper during late December and early January, filing reports describing their experiences over the prior weeks. Of these reports, 130 were later compiled in the *Official Records*; taken together, they paint an extraordinarily detailed portrait of troop movements and frequent skirmishing. Of course, they also vary considerably. Some track a regiment's movements day by day, going on for pages. Others are quite brief, providing only the barest of facts. Many contain detailed statistics for food and livestock collected, distances marched, places camped, rivers crossed, and miles of track destroyed. What they tended not to capture, however, was the personal dimension of the encounters between soldiers and civilians. Nor did the reports describe the many excesses of the March in any detail, leaving the stories of Sherman's bummers to more personal sources.[67]

As for the bummers, the men spread themselves out all over Savannah, camping in the city's famous squares and even pitching tents in cemeteries. In general, they behaved with more decorum than during the March itself—perhaps because they could not simply move on from whatever havoc they wreaked. They tended to pay for the food they consumed in Savannah, rather than just take it. That's not to say that nothing was destroyed. In particular, Union soldiers who camped in Colonial Park Cemetery vandalized tombstones, crossing out dates of birth and death and writing in new ones. Soldiers rummaged through burial vaults in search of valuables, and sometimes moved into the more spacious ones. They also knocked over and scattered dozens of headstones, many of which could never be matched with their original locations.[68]

The Swamps of South Carolina

Secretary Stanton left Savannah on January 15, promising to send supplies to Sherman as quickly as possible. While the time in Savannah had been a respite from the road, one certainly enjoyed by the men who marched miles each day, Sherman felt "quite impatient to get off myself, for a city-life had become dull and tame, and we were all anxious to get into the pine-woods again." James Connolly had much the same complaint in a letter to his wife, telling her that "our beds should be at the roots of the cypress trees in Carolina instead of the luxurious couches of Savannah." In large part, Sherman (and perhaps Connolly as well) had tired of the administrative burdens of "rebel women asking for protection and of the civilians from the North who were coming to Savannah for cotton and all sorts of profit." It was time to enter South Carolina. While Sherman's next major destination was the capital of the Palmetto State, Columbia, he once again obscured his intentions, hoping to trick the Confederates into believing that he was headed for Augusta or Charleston instead.[69]

The army retained the same basic structure of left and right wings, further subdivided. The troops of the left wing (XX Corps) began crossing the Savannah River in early January and by the middle of the month were encamped outside of Hardeeville. At the same time, the XVII Corps (right wing) traveled by boat up the coast to Beaufort, South Carolina, all the better to seem to be threatening Charleston. On January 21, Sherman himself boarded a steamer in Savannah, and after a brief stop in Hilton Head, he arrived in Beaufort on January 23.[70]

The March through South Carolina would differ from the one through Georgia in some significant ways. First, it would be much harder going, especially in the first few weeks. The region between the coast and the capital was sandy and swampy, cut through by numerous rivers and creeks. Winter rains turned the few roads through the region into mud so deep that it could swallow wagons and mules almost entirely. Soldiers slogged at half their normal pace. Camps flooded, and buildings that in Georgia would have been destroyed for sport now were needed as shelter. The men spent hours corduroying roads and tearing up railroads. Even the pontoon bridges were of limited use initially, for they were vulnerable to being washed away. Pickets sometimes stood guard in boats rather than on the ground.[71]

The other difference, somewhat surprisingly, was soldiers' attitudes toward the local populations. It seems hard to believe that Union soldiers could exhibit more anger, resentment, and vengeance than they did in Georgia, but in fact they did. In general, Sherman's men blamed South Carolina for starting the war, and they were determined to punish the citizens for that transgression. Sherman himself recalled, somewhat disingenuously, that

> somehow our men had got the idea that South Carolina was the cause
> of all our troubles; her people were the first to fire on Fort Sumter,
> had been in a great hurry to precipitate the country into civil war; and
> therefore on them should fall the scourge of war in its worst form. . . . I
> saw and felt that we would not be able longer to restrain our men as
> we had done in Georgia . . . and I would not restrain the army lest its
> vigor and energy should be impaired.[72]

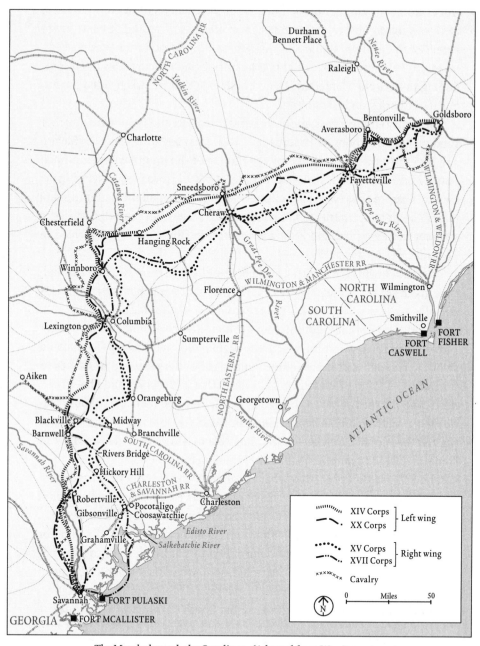

The March through the Carolinas. (Adapted from War Department,
Corps of Engineers, "Map Showing Route of Marches of the Army of Genl.
W. T. Sherman from Atlanta, Ga., to Goldsboro, N.C." [1865])

This would prove to be all too true. Whereas most of the damage in Georgia was confined to barns and gin houses, smokehouses and chicken coops, more homes were targeted in South Carolina. James Connolly told his wife that the men burned everything they could in South Carolina, "not under orders, but in spite of orders. The men 'had it in' for South Carolina and took it out in their own way."[73]

And so the men moved on, inexorably, leaving a trail of smoke and rubble behind them. Several towns in South Carolina, particularly those along the railroad were left in ruins during the first two weeks of February: McPhersonville, Hickory Hill, Brighton, Purysburg, Hardeeville, Robertsville. Much of the blame for this falls on Kilpatrick and his cavalry who took a particular delight in tormenting their enemies. In Barnwell, they held a party with newly freed slaves in the hotel as the town burned, quipping that that the town should be called "Burnwell." Only a few homes remained standing.[74] The local Episcopal Church of the Holy Apostles, an unusual gothic structure built of pine with a stained glass window given to it by James Henry Hammond also survived, though not without a degree of desecration. The window had been removed and buried; the church silver had been hidden in a well, so those were reinstalled after the war. General Kilpatrick stabled his horses in the sanctuary, and, until a recent renovation, hoofprints could be seen in the floor. The horses drank from the baptismal font.[75]

The Sheldon church in Hardeeville was not so fortunate. A group of soldiers set to work tearing it apart, pulling out the pulpits and seats, then ripping off the siding. Finally, using axes the men hacked away at the corner posts, "the building tottered, the beautiful spire, up among the green trees, leaned, for a time several degrees out of the perpendicular, vibrating to and fro." The men chopped down a tree that was helping hold up the steeple and then used poles to shake the building back and forth, until "with a screeching groan the spire sunk down amidst the timbers which gave way beneath." As the building crashed to the ground, one Union soldier called out, "there goes your damned old gospel shop." This was personal, not strategic.[76]

As in Georgia there were few true battles along the road to Columbia. One occurred on February 2–3, 1865, at a Salkehatchie River crossing known as Rivers Bridge. About fourteen hundred Confederates under Lafayette McLaws tried to hold off members of the right wing at the crossing point. Union soldiers worked feverishly, building bridges through the swamps in order to bypass them. On February 3, two brigades waded through the swamp and flanked McLaws's men, forcing them to withdraw to Branchville. In the end, although the battle has been hailed as one of the "last stands" against Sherman and his men, it delayed them for only one day and cost them about forty men killed and a hundred wounded.[77] Like Griswoldville, it seems to show the futility of resistance this late in the war.

South Carolina's noted poet, William Gilmore Simms, lived on Woodlands Plantation near Orangeburg. In addition to the value of the land and home and furnishings, Simms also boasted a library of ten thousand books, many of them irreplaceable gifts from fellow European and American writers. After hearing of the March's approach, Simms fled to Columbia, but his absence did not stop the soldiers from learning who was the master of Woodlands. They also knew that he had been a great supporter of secession and, in an echo of the happenings at Howell Cobb's home, chose to punish him for it. Some bibliophilic Union soldiers tried to save the library, and at least a few books survived as "souvenirs," or "mementos," but in the end, Woodlands burned, along with its library.[78]

The marchers continued toward Columbia, tearing up miles of railroad track as they went. From across the Edisto to Orangeburg, where Sherman recalled visiting and provisioning an orphanage filled with young refugees from Charleston, to the banks of the Congaree they went.[79] By February 15, Sherman was on the outskirts of Columbia, and writing new orders for his marchers.

Rumors flew around South Carolina throughout January and February. Southern civilians knew the marchers were coming, and it seemed only a question of when and where they would appear. Dread and apprehension filled letters and diaries, and parcels and wagons full of people and valuables traversed the state. On January 19, Lizzie Smith wrote that "the people in Columbia are on the verge of a panic, the slightest thing will set them off." She professed no fear, conceding, "I am very thankful I have neither silver or negroes to take care of." Mary Chesnut left Columbia, headed first to Camden, South Carolina, but ultimately ending up in Lincolnton, North Carolina. Grace Elmore stayed behind, but her family had sent so much away that they had only "champagne glasses to drink from and not enough forks for dessert." Nevertheless, she concluded, they had better eat as much as they could before the "rascals" came and took what they had.[80]

Columbia

Sherman's General Order No. 26, written "on the nearest dry ground behind the little Congaree," on February 16, 1865, ordered General Howard's

XV Corps to cross the Saluda and Broad Rivers and enter the city of Columbia, occupy the city, and "destroy the public buildings, railroad property, manufacturing and machine shops," while sparing "libraries, asylums, and private dwellings." Howard's men were then to head out toward Winnsboro, leaving no usable railroads in their wake.[81] If the best-laid schemes of mice and men often go awry, so too did Sherman's for Columbia, leaving nothing but decades of angry recriminations and controversy in their wake.

Much of what happened in Columbia on February 16–17 is disputed; perhaps more accurately, the questions swirl around the who and the why.[82] We know that Union artillery was set up across the river, after the Saluda River Textile Factory had been burned. From there Sherman ordered that the guns aim at the newly built (so newly built that it was not yet in use) South Carolina statehouse, leaving chips and dents in the walls that persist today. On the morning of February 17, Mayor Thomas L. Goodwyn rode out of the city and surrendered it to Sherman, making it the third state capital he had taken (Jackson, Mississippi, in 1863, and Milledgeville, Georgia, a few months before). Despite promises that no one would be harmed, many civilians either fled or locked their doors.[83]

They were wise to do so. Union soldiers found caches of liquor and guzzled it down. By nightfall, thousands of them were roaming the streets, along with prisoners from the state penitentiary, former slaves, and newly released Union prisoners of war. "This gobbling of things so, disgusts me much," complained Charles Wills, who was appalled by his drunken division. "I think the city should be burned," he confided to his diary, "but would like to see it done decently."[84] Fire broke out, possibly from embers left smoldering after the Confederates had retreated the day before, possibly from Sherman's men. At any rate, most of the city became an inferno, and by the morning, three fourths of the city had been consumed, more than fourteen hundred structures. For South Carolinians in particular, and white Southerners in general, it became an indisputable article of faith that Sherman's men had burned Columbia. Indeed, it often seemed as though Sherman himself had lit the first match.[85] There are at least nine historical markers in Columbia describing how Sherman burned the town, and the fire is often used to explain many of the economic hardships that followed in Columbia, sometimes being conflated with Reconstruction.[86]

Thomas Osborn, like many Union soldiers, spent the day of February 17 around the city, watching the looting, helping to put out smaller fires, and

A depiction of Columbia in flames, published in Harper's Weekly, *vividly captures the chaos and confusion of February 17, 1865. It was sketched by the well-known illustrator William Waud. (*Harper's Weekly, *April 8, 1865)*

protecting the family with whom he lodged. He was both awed and saddened by the chaos:

> The flames rolled and heaved like the waves of the ocean; the road was like a cataract. The whole air was filled with burning cinders, and fragments of fire as thick as the flakes of snow in a storm. The scene was splendid—magnificently grand. The scene of pillaging, the suffering and terror of the citizens, the arresting of and shooting negroes, and our frantic and drunken soldiers, is the other side of the picture.

While Osborn did not like to see Southern civilians suffer, he shed no tears, seeing Columbia's destruction as both helpful to the Union cause and "a just retribution to the state of South Carolina."[87]

Of course, the view from the other side was much different. Just as Osborn can stand in for Union soldiers, so can teenager Emma LeConte voice the panic, fears, and ultimately depression and anger that so many white Columbians felt. On February 14–15, LeConte described the "panic-stricken crowds," and in her own home on the university campus, "the back parlor strewed with clothing, etc. open trunks standing about, while a general feeling of misery pervaded the atmosphere." Whatever the family had time to send away was sent; Emma debated whether to burn all of her letters, not wanting them to "share the fate of Aunt Jane's and Cousin Ada's in Liberty County [Georgia], which were read and scattered along the roads."[88] That night and the following day, Emma recorded the sounds of shells and alarm bells.

In the chaos of February 17, the LeContes sent their slaves out to procure what provisions they could. Emma was horrified by the sight of the U.S. flag flying above the State House, calling it a "degradation" and "the hateful symbol of despotism," and she scoffed at Sherman's promises of safety for civilians. She called the Union troops rampaging through the streets "drunken devils" and believed that the guards only helped in the mayhem. The LeContes survived the night of the fires, which Emma vividly described: "Imagine night turned into noonday, only with a blazing, scorching glare that was horrible—a copper colored sky across which swept columns of black, rolling smoke glittering with sparks and flying embers." Like Osborn she compared the scene to a "quivering molten ocean," describing her experience as "nearer realizing the material ideal of hell than anything I ever expect to see again."[89] Still, the LeContes were lucky: their home remained intact and, aside from a few stragglers, unvisited; no raid by Union soldiers occurred.

In the days and weeks that followed, stories flew around the South, detailing the hardships faced by families less fortunate than the LeContes. Mary Chesnut heard a rumor that Sherman's soldiers targeted all of the signers of the secession ordinance.[90] Members of the extended Smith clan gossiped about the unfortunate Mrs. Crafts, last seen with her children and black nursemaid riding off in one of Sherman's baggage wagons, choosing to take her chances traveling North to her family rather than starve in Columbia.[91] In the upcountry, Floride Clemson donated money, food, and clothing for the relief of Columbians, many of whom were homeless and sleeping outside.[92]

What is often forgotten in the stories of the burning of Columbia are the many kindnesses that Sherman's men also performed. Certainly, the thousands of African Americans who took advantage of the chaos to leave their places of enslavement saw little wrong with the fire or the troops who allegedly set it. General Howard worked with the mayor of Columbia to try to find housing for people, black and white, left homeless by the fire, and he supplied them with blankets and rations. When he and his men marched out of town, they did so without five hundred head of cattle, which they left behind grazing on the green of the University of South Carolina, for the people of the town to eat.[93]

North from Columbia

By February 20, the marchers were on the move again, heading north toward Winnsboro, where the army's right wing (which had done the damage in Columbia) rejoined the left. They split again, with the right wing moving east toward Cheraw and from there to Fayetteville, North Carolina (home to a Confederate Armory). Again, Sherman tried to deceive the Confederates, this time feinting toward Charlotte, when his ultimate destination was Raleigh, North Carolina's capital.[94]

If Sherman's men were ever out of control, it might have been on their movement north through South Carolina. There were stories of civilians being hanged if they did not reveal the locations of valuables, of women being raped.[95] As Sherman's men passed houses with white flags hanging out the windows, with whites and blacks hiding from them, they had to feel that their mission to sow terror was complete and successful. But they were not immune from Confederate retaliation. Wheeler's cavalry captured several different groups of Union foragers—7 one day, 21 another—and executed them. All together about 110 in South Carolina and 64 in Georgia died this way. Signs proclaiming "Death to All Foragers" often accompanied the bodies, which were left by the road so that the marching columns could easily find them.[96]

Sherman was livid. After learning that eighteen cavalrymen had been shot after surrendering to Confederates, he wrote to General Kilpatrick. Sherman conceded that some of the men had overstepped their bounds; he also believed that "we have a perfect war right to the products of the country we overrun, and may collect them by foragers or otherwise." Too, if Union soldiers needed to be punished, they should be punished by the Union army. "Never let an enemy judge between our men and the law," he warned. Finally, Sherman ordered Kilpatrick to respond man for man, message for message, telling him: "You will therefore, at once shoot, and leave by the roadside, an equal number of their prisoners, and append a label to their bodies stating that man for man shall be killed for every one of our men they kill."[97] This is reminiscent of Sherman's use of prisoners of war to test for mines in Savannah and is one of the few times that he seemed to be acting out of anger rather than strategic consideration.

Kilpatrick notified Wheeler of his orders, and Wheeler denied having anything to do with the killings. Similarly, Sherman wrote to Confederate general Wade Hampton expressing his anger at the killings, his plans for retaliation, and warning that he held more than one thousand Confederate prisoners and "can stand it as long as you." While Hampton threatened to kill even more Union men, officers first, should Sherman carry out his threat, the killings of foragers stopped.[98]

On March 3, 1865, Sherman arrived in Cheraw, South Carolina. Blair's XVII Corps was already there, seizing and redistributing warehouses full of ammunition and weapons, civilian and military supplies that had been sent up from Charleston earlier in the year. Some of the seized material was used in the army in the waning days of the war; some was shot off in celebration of Lincoln's second inauguration on March 4, 1865. Some of it was destroyed when a warehouse exploded. Sherman initially threatened to burn the town in retaliation for perceived sabotage, but once he learned that it resulted from a careless Union soldier, he relented. By the time the March moved on, there was little of Cheraw left to destroy—the men had foraged far and wide, taking whatever provisions remained after the winter.[99]

At the same time as Sherman and his men were moving across South Carolina, changes were also afoot within the Confederate command. In February, Jefferson Davis overcame his personal animosity toward Joseph Johnston and put him in charge of the Confederate Army of Tennessee. His job was to stop Sherman from what now seemed to be his ultimate destination: meeting up with Grant's army, still stuck in the trenches outside of Petersburg, Virginia. On the one hand, Johnston's army and orders meant that Sherman and his men would face a more organized opposition than they previously had along the March; on the other hand, one could also see the desperation that lay behind this abrupt shift in command. Sherman was not overly concerned, for he believed that he could beat Johnston in an open fight.

North Carolina

Union troops began entering North Carolina in early March, and Sherman himself crossed the Pee Dee River on March 6. By March 8, all of the wings of the army were in the state and heading toward Fayetteville. Just as Sherman had known that the men would deal harshly with South Carolina, so too did he want them to adopt a more measured approach in the Old North State. Thus, he urged General Slocum to remind his brigade commanders that they had left the Palmetto State behind and "a little moderation may be of political consequence to us in North Carolina."[100] Sherman's advice to

General Kilpatrick was even more direct and showed his awareness of the nuanced differences between the states:

> I want all to be easy on the citizens. . . . Deal as moderately and fairly by the North Carolinians as possible, and fan the flame of discord already subsisting between them and their proud cousins of South Carolina. There never was much love between them. Touch upon the chivalry running away, always leaving their families for us to feed and protect, and then on purpose accusing us of all sorts of rudeness.[101]

Essentially, if Sherman had allowed his men to take their metaphorical gloves off when crossing from Georgia to South Carolina, he was strongly advising that they be put back on. He was also assuming that he would find a large population of latent, supportive Unionists, who would welcome his arrival, and so he wanted to be sure not to do anything that would antagonize them.[102]

GENERALS BLAIR AND HOWARD were both disgusted by the destruction running rampant under the guise of foraging, and each issued specific and detailed orders designed to curtail the men's impulses and return to a more regularized and orderly system. These were not entirely successful. While the bummers might have restrained themselves from burning homes and farms, the vast pine forests of North Carolina seemed to go up in smoke almost spontaneously. The soldiers took a boyish delight in setting turpentine and rosin factories ablaze, then sitting back and watching the show that followed.[103] The marchers also continued to target the railroad, tearing up the tracks, making "Sherman's neckties," and burning the depots and railroad shops at Laurinburg, the bridges and boxcars at Lumberton.

On March 11, Union soldiers, and Sherman himself, marched into Fayetteville. After some skirmishing, and Confederate destruction of the bridge across the Cape Fear River, the city surrendered to Generals Howard and Slocum. Sherman used the former United States Arsenal (now Confederate) as his headquarters and happily received supplies and mail from steamboats out of Wilmington. Sherman also used the stop in Fayetteville to resupply, to switch out weary horses for fresh ones, and to encourage (strongly, even forcefully) the streams of African Americans following in his wake to travel to Wilmington in Federal care. As in Georgia, he resented the "dead weight" of thousands of "useless" mouths to feed.[104]

The process of making "Sherman's neckties" is depicted and explained on this stereograph. As noted on the back of the card, "The rails are first torn up, then the wooden ties are pried out and piled in heaps and burned; the iron rails are laid across the burning ties, and soon get hot enough in the middle that the weight of the ends bends the rail up here as shown." More creative men might twist the ties around trees or in loops. (Library of Congress, http://www.loc.gov/item/2011660475/)

Despite the orders to treat North Carolinians with care, in deference to their supposed Unionism, Fayetteville was hard hit. In large part this was because Sherman's men knew, or at least quickly realized, that Fayetteville was a Confederate stronghold—not just because of the presence of the armory, but because the townspeople believed deeply in the Confederate mission. Thus Sherman issued special instructions for Fayetteville, in the form of General Orders No. 28. Much like orders for other towns, his men were told to ruin railroad property, including trestles and bridges ranging up and down the river; burn and destroy all mills, including cotton mills, except for one gristmill; and to demolish the arsenal and destroy all of the powder and arms contained within it. The men also destroyed the three newspaper printing offices in town, perhaps in retaliation for their pro-Confederate stances.[105] The bummers also had a field day in Fayetteville. The expected army of Unionists had yet to materialize.

William Bluffton Miller was one of those angry bummers. A few days earlier, he had met a North Carolina woman who continued to defiantly predict a "Licking" for the Yankees. In Fayetteville a ball passed through his cartridge box "Searing" his side. For a brief sickening moment he feared that he had been "shot through." He regained his composure and was ordered to guard a warehouse. Despite being ordered not to take anything, he stole some meat and a barrel of flour, and some of his fellow soldiers "got gloriously drunk." But Miller was not without compassion, for he let some "poor women" take meat as well, explaining that he "thought it to[o] bad to deprive them when there was more than we could use."[106]

Mrs. Isabella Huske Williams was not so fortunate as the women who met Sergeant Miller, at least not according to Catherine Edmondston. Mrs. Williams was "robbed & treated with great personal indignity, her wedding ring torn from her fingers, & earrings from her ears, & a pistol placed at her head she was forced to show the wretches where she had concealed her silver." And then the Yankees burned her home.[107]

By March 15, all of the marchers were across the Cape Fear River, the left wing feinting toward Raleigh, the right destined for Goldsboro. The goal was to arrive there before the Confederates under Joe Johnston. For his part, Johnston's most immediate objective was to isolate and take out one of Sherman's four columns (each corps continued to march separately). But his forces were scattered, and he needed to bring them together and unify them before being able to take the offensive.[108] At the same time as Johnston sought to bring together the Army of Tennessee, Hoke's division, under the command of Braxton Bragg, Wade Hampton's cavalry, and Hardee's corps, word came that the latter was in trouble.

Hardee's men had retreated from Fayetteville and camped between the Cape Fear and Black Rivers, along the route of Sherman's left wing. On March 16, the two sides fought a small engagement, which came to be called the Battle of Averasboro. While the day's fighting slowed Sherman's March only a little, it did cost Slocum almost seven hundred men, a significant loss. Hardee's men took about five hundred casualties.[109] And every day that Sherman's men were held back from Goldsboro was another day for Johnston to bring his men together and get them into position to try to stop their inexorable enemy. He concentrated his men around Smithfield, North Carolina, midway between Goldsboro and Raleigh.

The last battle of the Georgia and Carolinas campaign took place between March 19 and 21, 1865. Howard's right wing essentially marched into Johnston's men, who had entrenched at Bentonville to meet them. The Confederates went on the offensive, attacking almost half a dozen times but always failing to push the Union soldiers back. On the second day, the heavily reinforced Union soldiers waited to see if Johnston would retreat, preferring that to more deadly fighting. On the third day, March 21, the Union advanced, and there were several skirmishes. That night Johnston learned that

General Schofield's right wing had reached Goldsboro. That, combined with his losses, led him to decide to retreat. Although the Union forces briefly pursued, it would be almost a month before they caught him. Bentonville's importance, like that of all the battles along the March, seems more symbolic than real. Certainly the battle did not change the course of the March. While Johnston did not succeed in overwhelming one of Sherman's wings, he did not allow his army to be captured.[110]

Sherman preferred to allow his men time to rest and recover after a battle, and he did lose more than fifteen hundred men (killed, wounded, captured, or missing). He and his men marched into Goldsboro, presenting a comically ragged sight. The soldiers' uniforms were dirty and tattered, with only a few men still in possession of socks. Their faces were grimy with pine soot and black powder, and they marched with the accompaniment of a variety of livestock and "pets"—squirrels, raccoons, and fighting cocks. African Americans cheered their arrival in town with the following song:

Brave Sherman, sent by God's decree
Has led the Yankees through the South
And set four million "niggers" free.[111]

Southern whites waited to see if the marchers would be as bad as they had anticipated. Sherman complained that his supply ships from Wilmington had yet to arrive, meaning that he had to send out more foragers. They were as effective as ever but seem to have behaved worse out in the countryside than in Goldsboro proper. Once the supplies arrived, around March 27, the men received an unaccustomed luxury—soap! The men were now expected to present a clean and tidy, shaved and shorn appearance. They also received more than five hundred bags of mail, the first in over two months.[112] While morale on the March had always been relatively good, a consequence of the loose discipline and lack of combat, it spiked even higher during the easy, contented days in Goldsboro.

While the men relaxed and recuperated in Goldsboro, Sherman took the train to City Point, Virginia, to meet with Ulysses S. Grant and plan the conclusion of the war. Sherman hoped to help Grant take Petersburg and then Richmond, sharing in the glory of final victory. Much to Sherman's surprise, when he arrived in City Point on March 27, Grant told him that Lincoln was also there. The two generals called on the president on the steamer *River Queen*, where they discussed not only military matters but, more importantly, the terms for peace. Lincoln appeared to want a relatively soft peace, with reuniting the nation as his primary concern and objective. This was certainly the impression that Sherman received, and would be the impression he acted upon.[113]

On April 10, the men broke camp and moved out toward Raleigh. On the same day, Joe Johnston's army, camped around Smithfield, North Carolina, did the same. That day saw some scattered skirmishing, but the important news came that night: Robert E. Lee had surrendered his Army of Northern Virginia at Appomattox Courthouse, Virginia. The excitement and joy spread throughout the Union camp, and Sherman immediately began to wonder if Johnston would encourage his men to form a guerrilla force—he felt sure that the Confederates knew they could not beat Sherman in the field.[114]

On April 13, the marchers strode into Raleigh. Citizens had been expecting them and had gone through the usual routine of hiding valuables. Governor Vance had been moving military supplies—blankets, cloth, shoe leather, bacon, corn—out of the city's warehouses for weeks. The mayor formally surrendered the city to General Kilpatrick, in hopes of avoiding Columbia's fate. Sherman arrived a few hours later and set up his headquarters in the recently evacuated governor's mansion. Union soldiers still went out on missions to capture what they could find, as they awaited Johnston's next move.[115]

Johnston's move was to write to Sherman on April 13, asking for "a temporary suspension of active operations, and to communicate to Lieutenant-General Grant, commanding the armies of the United States, the request that he will take like action in regard to other armies, the object being to permit the civil authorities to enter into the needful arrangements to terminate the existing war."[116] Johnston made this request with Davis's knowledge (the two had met in Greensboro, where Davis was on the run). Sherman replied quickly and also notified both Grant and Stanton, telling them that he would offer the same surrender terms as Grant had offered Lee. Consistent with his impressions after the meetings in City Point the previous month, he anticipated a "soft peace," without significant punishments for the white South after it rejoined the Union. While Sherman waited to hear back from Johnston, he heard the terrible news of Lincoln's assassination. Sherman wanted to keep the news from his men while he met with Johnston on April 17.

The two generals, longtime adversaries, met privately at the small farmhouse, really a log cabin, belonging to Daniel Bennett. Johnston suggested that they work out terms for a general Confederate surrender—a permanent peace, rather than the surrender of just his army. This notion, of bringing about a complete end to the war, appealed deeply to Sherman. Thus, in addition to the question of the armies at hand, the two men spent the afternoon

Sherman and Johnston met to settle issues related to the surrender.
This serene image belies the anger with which Sherman's original terms were
greeted in Washington, forcing him to modify them. (Picture Collection,
New York Public Library, Astor, Lenox and Tilden Foundations)

discussing broader political questions, including whether Jefferson Davis and his cabinet, would be included under a general amnesty clause. After several hours without resolution, they decided to meet again the following day.[117]

That night Sherman announced both the death of Lincoln and the temporary truce with Johnston. The latter did much to moderate the men's anger at the former. The notion that peace could be at hand helped blunt desires for revenge. Sherman and Johnston met again on the afternoon of April 18, and this time they were able to hammer out a series of terms, best summarized as follows:

> In general terms—the war to cease; a general amnesty, so far as the Executive of the United States can command, on condition of the disbandment of the Confederate armies, the distribution of the arms, and the resumption of peaceful pursuits by the officers and men hitherto composing said armies.[118]

These terms were quite generous to the defeated Confederates and indicative of Sherman's willingness to forgive Southern whites as soon as they admitted that they had been beaten. Sherman also maintained that these principles were in accordance with Lincoln's wishes. He could not imagine that his terms would be rejected.

But the terms were rejected, sharply. In Washington, they were seen as too generous in the angry atmosphere following Lincoln's assassination. Secretary of War Stanton was particularly upset with the terms, for they did nothing about slavery, and he hearkened back to their earlier dispute over African Americans and Ebenezer Creek. After President Johnson ordered that Sherman be told that the cabinet had rejected the terms, Stanton asked Grant to go down and tell him in person. Grant did that, but before he could even arrive, Stanton denounced Sherman and his treaty in the press. Jefferson Davis also disliked the terms, but Johnston ignored him.

Grant arrived in Raleigh on April 24, to Sherman's great surprise. He tried to smooth Sherman's ruffled feathers, urging him to offer only the terms that had been used in Appomattox. Sherman notified Johnston, and they met again in the Bennett house, on April 26. Eventually they came to an agreement, signed it, and Grant approved the revised terms. Sherman also offered 250,000 rations to Johnston's hungry men. All of this was accomplished without Sherman knowing of Stanton's denunciation and calls for his removal. In his honor, his soldiers set a cart of newspapers ablaze in Raleigh.[119]

But the March was not completely over. On April 30, the men left Raleigh, destined for Washington, D.C. Along the way they shared food and supplies with both African Americans, many of whom could hardly believe that they were freed, and former Confederate soldiers, who just wanted to get home.[120] They marched through Richmond on May 11; they visited the battlefields of Fredericksburg, Chancellorsville, and the Wilderness; and then they reached Washington. Their final March came in the Grand Review on May 24, when they strode down Pennsylvania Avenue and into their futures.

CHAPTER TWO

Southern Belles and Brother Masons

One can easily imagine Southern white children of a hundred years ago curling up on a rainy day with Howard Meriwether Lovett's poetically titled *Grandmother Stories from the Land of Used-to-Be* and losing themselves in tales of heroes and heroines from the nineteenth-century South. One of the most romantic and exciting was the tale of Zora Fair, the "girl spy of the Confederacy." Zora Fair was a teenager when the war began, and as it progressed she moved from her hometown of Charleston to live in sleepy Oxford, Georgia, with her uncle, Abram Crews, and his family. By the fall of 1864, she felt frustrated by the limitations of her place and gender. As Lovett floridly explained: "The blood of Carolina's patriots was in her veins; how her heart burned to do something for the Cause of the South!" She joined other girls in waving at the Confederate soldiers who passed on the trains, and listened with increasing anxiety to the booming Union guns at Atlanta, about forty miles away. Finally she decided to take action.[1]

Zora Fair decided to go to Atlanta, spy on Sherman, "and learn the worst." But an upper-class Southern girl could not travel alone, and surely would not be able to sneak through the Union lines unmolested. So she decided to disguise herself as "an old negress," complete with cast-off clothes, crimped hair, and skin dyed with walnut juice. Thus attired she was not just physically disguised but socially invisible, and she slowly made her way to Atlanta via foot and wagon. She talked her way through pickets by claiming to be looking for a husband who had run away to Union lines, and found her way to Sherman's headquarters where she was shunted aside, "dismissed as a simple creature, not worthy of notice." Before she was sent away, she heard Sherman's plans to divide his army and proceed, via Macon and Milledgeville, to Savannah. Her return trip back was more dangerous, and included being shot at by Union pickets, but she eventually arrived safely back in Oxford. She then wrote a letter describing the plans to Joe Johnston, but foolishly signed her own name. The letter was intercepted by Union soldiers, who came to Oxford to find her.[2]

Zora Fair hid out at various neighbors' homes and barns and slept in farm-houses while the Yankees searched for her. At one point she actually chatted with a Union soldier, who threatened to hang her (if she were found) and burn the home in which she hid. Then "the soldier passed on, never dreaming that this proud-looking young girl was the spy. He no doubt expected to find a buxom country lass, bold and daring enough for such an adventure." After searching unsuccessfully for Fair, the Union soldiers gave up and returned to Atlanta, only to pass through Oxford a few days later on the March to the Sea. Her efforts to stop Sherman had come to naught As Lovett reflected,

> Many were the tragedies and heartbreaks when Sherman "smashed things to the sea," but none more touching than the grief of Zora Fair over the desolation of our beautiful land. She had risked her life to turn Sherman back—and failed. It was like a butterfly against a hurricane. The girl seemed crushed. The fatigue and exposure of her experience as a spy seriously injured her health. She returned to Carolina to spend her last days, and there died a few months after leaving Oxford.[3]

A tragically brave Southern girl, hiding from Yankees, outwitting the enemy, even if only temporarily—the story of Zora Fair has all of the clichés that we have come to associate with Southern stories of resistance to Sherman's March. Indeed, the Zora Fair story seems too good to be true and does strain credulity at times. Could a girl really fool soldiers with walnut-juice stained skin and a cotton-stuffed mouth? Could she really have traveled so many miles on her own? The home in which she lived still stands on Asbury Street in Oxford, down the road from the original Emory University Campus, and her story is one of several inscribed on a bronze town marker.[4] It provides a powerful introduction to the ways that Southern civilians perceived, interacted with, and remembered Sherman's March.

SOUTHERN STORIES OF SHERMAN TEND to fall into one of two genres, emphasizing either victimization at the hands of evil Yankees or the cleverness of Southern whites in protecting themselves and their property from harm. Different stories seemed to serve different purposes. Cruel Union soldiers, who terrorized women and children for sport, served the Lost Cause well, allowing Southern whites to feel a sense of moral superiority toward their conquerors. When Union soldiers were shown to be thieves or killers of dogs and horses, they also seemed alien and gave credence to Southern myths of cultural difference. Their cruelty justified Southern white desires for separation. But at the same time, such stories painted white Southerners as helpless victims, inadvertently displaying weakness in a society that prized strength, appearance, and honor over all else. So another genre of story appeared, one that showed Southern civilians fighting back against Sherman's marchers. These tales featured narrow escapes, artfully hidden valuables, and sometimes outright defiance. These allowed Southern whites to recast the March from a story of domination and devastation to one of pride and superiority. Folklorist Elissa Henken has argued that these salvation stories bear a striking resemblance to older European tales, specifically the legendary Owain Glyndŵer who fought for Welsh independence in the fifteenth century.[5]

As we saw in chapter 1, when they lived through the March, Southern white women recorded a jumble of emotions: apprehension, fear, defiance, anger, depression. These powerful feelings persisted into the postwar years, in all of their emotional complexity. Their stories, whether written down in private or published memoirs or told and retold on porches and in parlors persisted for generations. Mayor Hartsfield of Atlanta, speaking at the fiftieth anniversary celebration of the Georgia United Daughters of the Confederacy (UDC), recalled his mother's telling of "seeing Sherman's troops strip her family of all their possessions, and that he heard the story of the Confederacy from her."[6] As late as the 1980s, the Jarrell family still told of the Union soldiers' visit to the family plantation, which resulted in the barn and two-story cotton gin being burned, along with three hundred bushels of wheat. Buckets and buckets of cane syrup were poured out, left to soak uselessly into the ground.[7] Butts County Georgians told of a mother, left home with four children sick with typhoid and measles, who was not spared and watched helplessly as the family silver was stolen and the family left to starve.[8]

In 1964 (presumably for the centennial), historian Katharine M. Jones compiled dozens of first-person accounts into *When Sherman Came: Southern Women and the "Great March,"* still a valuable compilation.[9] More recently, historians Jacqueline Glass Campbell, Lisa Tendrich Frank, and Jane E. Schultz have explored the interactions between Southern white women and Union soldiers. To varying degrees they argue that for Southern white women the March represented an upending of gender roles, where deference to men would no longer provide safety and protection. For these women, the majority of whom wrote in the immediate aftermath of their enemies' visits, the raids and violations were personal, as opposed to political or military in nature.[10] Schultz's largely wartime analysis argues that women had an almost "clerical zeal" with which they kept track of their stolen and destroyed possessions. They wrote often about their clothing, their fears of being caught while undressed, and their impressions of the soldiers with whom they interacted. Often their vivid descriptions of the raids contrasted with a sense of humiliation and demoralization that followed in their wake.[11] Others "seeth[ed] with passion about their ordeal as they extol[led] the virtues of the lost civilization."[12] Perhaps by cataloging their material losses they could keep the emotional ones at bay.

One other issue to keep in mind while analyzing these stories is how true they were. Schultz wrote that many memoirists claimed to have "underplayed" rather than exaggerated events.[13] White women's stories of Sherman were staples of postwar collections that paid homage to Confederate women, usually uncritically. The collection *General Sherman and the Georgia Belles*, published in 2006 is typical in its overwrought introduction, describing Sherman as a man who "some believed to be the devil himself," accompanied by his band of "sixty thousand fiends." It describes Georgia as full of frightened women alone on their farms, ultimately subjected to "an uncivil war."[14] Francis Butler Simkins and James Welch Patton's classic *Women of the Confederacy* acknowledged that "such stories . . . are without doubt exaggerated by their impassioned narrators" but further cautioned "that but the fact that they exist in such great numbers prevents their being ignored by the critical reader. They are likewise substantiated in many instances by contemporary chronicles and accounts from the pens of Federal officers and other observers who accompanied the Union army in the South."[15] For my purposes, the veracity of a story matters less than its deeper meaning or the patterns that can be revealed by repetition of certain patterns or tropes.

Similarly, it can be challenging to historicize many of these stories. The murkiness of memories, the vagaries of postwar publishing, mean that they do not proceed in a linear fashion. Many stories are simply told and retold, their initial origins (and a degree of verifiability) lost along the way. What this means is that there is no change over time, the historian's stock in trade. Rather, this is an argument based on coexistence or intersection. The stories do not move linearly from one genre to another but messily overlap and jostle against one another.[16]

Barbarities Inflicted

Most encounters between Sherman's men and Southern white civilians were tense and frightening but not necessarily violent. Florence Byrne, of

Waynesboro, Georgia, heard that the Yankees were coming and quickly put on all of her best dresses, in order to keep them from being stolen. While she held on to her finery, Union soldiers carried her piano out into the middle of the street and forced her to play for them. One version of the story does not mention the tunes; in another she claimed to have played "Dixie," "The Southern Girl," and other pro-Confederate songs. In this version, she was not punished for her boldness. Rather, the soldiers laughed, called her a "d—little rebel," and were driven off by Wheeler's cavalry.[17] Nellie Worth felt as though her "very soul had turned to stone" when Sherman's men invaded her North Carolina home. She must have been able to feel something, however, for when the men demanded she play the piano, she, like Florence Byrne, chose "Dixie" and "The Bonnie Blue Flag."[18]

Forcing women to play the piano or cook for soldiers might have been frightening but would not have resulted in permanent damage. Women also feared sexual assault, both for the physical trauma and the assault on their own and for their family's honor. A distinction must also be drawn between assaults on white and African American women. In the years after the war, white men and women railed against the much rarer attacks on white women, while only rarely remarking on assaults against black women. The numbers are not particularly reliable for either group. Anecdotally, there were very few, especially on white women, and similarly few instances of outright murder or assault on men.[19] There were about 250 Union soldiers court-martialed for rape, although we can assume that this number represents a serious undercount, as many sexual assaults would have gone unreported. As early as 1866, Cornelia Spencer claimed that many cases of sexual assault went unreported; historian Jane Schultz has found accounts of assaults on white and black women in soldier's diaries, particularly for Milledgeville and Columbia.[20]

I have found only one account with a name associated that appears in multiple sources. Certainly reports of sexual assaults would have been rare, which makes the presence of this one "in the diary of a young woman who later made an unsuccessful attempt to eradicate it" unusual. This was the attack on Kate Nichols, the wife of James H. Nichols, a member of the Horse Guards. She was bedridden at their home in Midway, a bit south of Milledgeville, when she was raped by two Union soldiers. Sadly, she later died in an asylum.[21] In addition to the known attack on Mrs. Nichols, another story of sexual violence came out of Milledgeville. In this one, probably more typical, a group of Union soldiers were assaulting about a dozen black and white women on the outskirts of town. Members of Wheeler's cavalry came upon them, and while some women ran away screaming, others were rescued by the Confederates. One can only imagine the trauma faced by one woman who was used as a shield by a Union soldier, who was then shot, "spattering blood and brains over this woman."[22] Other women, and some men, were so deeply traumatized that they went insane (in the parlance of the day). Historian Diane Miller Sommerville has discovered several people whose asylum records mentioned Sherman and the March specifically, attributing symptoms to that signal event.[23]

A similar story of assault and indignities perpetrated on Southern whites came from the pen of the Reverend Dr. John Bachman, pastor of Lutheran Church in Charleston. Bachman described a shocking scene of "barbarities inflicted" at Cash's Depot, near Cheraw, South Carolina. "Officers, high in command, were engaged tearing from the ladies their watches, their ear and wedding rings, the daguerreotypes of those they loved and cherished. A lady of delicacy and refinement, a personal friend, was compelled to strip before them, that they might find concealed watches and other valuables under her dress."[24] While these women were not raped per se, forcing them to remove their clothes in front of strange men was a close second in terms of trauma and dishonor.

Historian Crystal Feimster has argued that the very threat of sexual assault had real import for Southern white women, leading them to question the ability of Southern white men to protect them, and forcing them to protect themselves.[25] The latter is more true in case of Sherman's March than the former. Women knew they needed to protect themselves from the Yankees; but rather than turn their anger against their Confederate countrymen, they saved it for the invading force. One Southern historian conceded that "when the crime obtained, its victims were overwhelmingly black and its incidence was exaggerated by Southern writers."[26] The message of the sexual assault stories for the Lost Cause is clear: Union soldiers were vicious, dishonorable barbarians who could not be trusted around women of any color. And the violence need not extend all the way to rape.

To Leave No Stock Whatever

In addition to their assaults on people, Union troops attacked and stole livestock and dogs. In general, Union soldiers either butchered or took any edible livestock, including cows, pigs, and poultry. When they found horses and mules, they would often swap their worn out mounts for fresher Southern ones.[27] One postwar history noted that farming in 1865 and 1866 was done with "'Sherman horses'—the sore-backed, abused, and refused animals left upon the fields instead of the fat and sleek ones carried away by the enemy."[28] White Southerners might resent the loss of their animals for Union food or transport, but they could understand it. What seemed unduly cruel and barbaric to them was the wanton killing of horses, mules, and dogs. Union troops killed dogs on Southern plantations because they had been used to track runaway slaves, and thus could be used to track Union soldiers or escaped prisoners. Cornelius Cadle recalled seeing forty or fifty dogs killed at one time.[29]

What was most upsetting, though was the sheer wasteful destructiveness that many soldiers took part in. John Trowbridge traveled across the South in the months after the Civil War and commented with disgust on the "deliberate aim . . . *to leave no stock whatever in the line of the march.*" He mentioned used-up horses being shot, along with "inferior herds [of cattle] slaughtered in the fields and left." Trowbridge described soldiers who "would shoot down a drove of hogs, cut out the hind-quarters, and abandon what remained." He told of a pile of sixty-five dead horses and mules left to rot beside the Congaree River for six weeks. They could not be buried, "all of the shovels, spades, and other farming implements of the kind having been carried off or destroyed."[30]

There are several stories of similar mass killings of horses. J. A. McMichael, a resident of Butts County, Georgia, claimed that the Yankees, after burning buildings and stealing valuables, "killed about one thousand horses on one of the seven islands in the Ocmulgee river." He described the horses has having been taken from citizens, but then deemed unfit for military use, and chillingly recalled that "the island was covered with bones for years after."[31] A similar story details dozens of horses being shot on the banks of the Oconee River, whose bodies then fell into the water. The following spring "many catfish were caught in the Oconee and it was a common saying 'They are fat on Sherman's horses.'"[32] These killings seemed to have no distinct perpetrators, just the nameless, faceless Yankee horde. Another rumor placed the blame squarely on Sherman. According to this story, as he moved through Georgia, Sherman had been collecting five hundred "snow white" horses to present to President Lincoln as a gift. But, as he approached Savannah, he realized that "the horses were more trouble than they were worth and that the city itself would be a far finer present." He then, allegedly ordered the horses shot were they were, and residents of Oliver, Georgia, remembered digging bullets out of the headstones at the Little Ogeechee Baptist Church.[33] This story presents many angles on the idea of violation: the stolen horses, probably so meaningful to their owners, but simply cast aside by Sherman, the offhanded cruelty, and finally the casual desecration of the local churchyard.

It seems unlikely that Sherman had collected five hundred snow-white mounts, only to kill them, but that does not mean that soldiers never participated in mass killings of horses. Smith Atkins, who served in the Union cavalry under Kilpatrick, described leaving the bodies of five hundred horses around a house briefly used as a headquarters. He does not express any sadness or remorse but instead notes that "the owner of the mansion appeared on the porch at daylight, and taking in the situation at a glance, he raised both hands, exclaiming, 'My God, I will have to move away!'. . . as that was easier than removing the dead horses."[34] In this story, Atkins seems to be rendering judgment on the plantation owner, laughing at his discomfiture, but noting that he was unwilling to do the hard work of clearing the destruction.

Brother Masons

In 1964, *Macon Telegraph News* columnist Spencer B. King reflected on the persistence of certain legends about Sherman's March:

> In spite of the efforts of the historians, both Northern and Southern,
> to get at the truth of history, many good people here in the Deep
> South cannot free themselves from the attitude that Sherman's bite
> was as bad as his bark. The wide swath that he cut through Georgia,
> in their way of thinking, was one long path of blackened chimneys
> and smoking ruins. They think he never left a private dwelling
> standing unless it happened to be the home of a Mason; and in that
> case, of course, he always ordered it to be saved![35]

A large kernel of truth lay at the heart of King's sarcasm. Of course, many homes survived Sherman's March, many more than were destroyed. But as Southern whites promulgated tales of the March's horrors and devastation, they needed a way to explain why so many homes were still standing. Tales of narrow escapes or clever manipulation filled the bill.

Almost every county in Sherman's path can boast a home saved through the intervention of Masons. The Weems house in Henry County, Georgia, was spared, although the gin and cotton bales across the road were burned. Later the family repapered their dining room with Confederate money.[36] In Jasper County, Georgia, a fourteen-year-old boy stopped Union soldiers from destroying Smith's mill by telling them that his father was a Mason who had opposed secession. Other homes in the county had Masonic emblems posted outside, signaling that they should be left alone.[37] Sometimes the protection came almost too late. Union soldiers were in the midst of looting Farmingdale Plantation (in Jasper) and building a bonfire of dining room furniture and family portraits, while the family daughter was going into labor from the fear and stress. As a soldier opened a desk, searching for money, he found Masonic papers, and "a Mason himself, the officer ordered the troops away," saving the home from the torch.[38]

Women in particular seem to have availed themselves of the Masonic protection, ironic perhaps in light of the fact that they could not be members themselves. Smith Atkins remembered that as he passed through Jonesboro, Georgia, on November 17, 1864, "while many houses were burning, one large mansion was left undisturbed, on the porch of which sat several ladies; a Freemason's apron was pinned up against the side of the house, and that talismanic emblem gave them and their property complete protections."[39] Southern white women were well aware of the apron's talismanic properties. These stories bring to mind the biblical story of the ten plagues, where Jews marked their homes to prevent the slaying of the firstborn in Egypt. Mrs. Joshua (Patsy) Ammons of Walton County, Georgia, has come down in history as "plucky," for her interactions with Sherman's men. While the Federals cut up her best quilts to make saddle blankets for their horses, she freely admitted that she had sons serving in the Confederate army, "adding with pride that she only wished she had more." While one might have expected this to provoke Union troops to angry mayhem, Ammons had cleverly wrapped her family silver in a Masonic apron, and thus it (and she) were spared.[40] Mrs. Caroline Palmer Johnson used her late husband's Masonic membership to similar advantage at her home outside Stark, Georgia. Her family had enough time to hide the silver and horses before "the marauders" arrived. She showed her husband's apron and insignia to the approaching soldiers, and one of the officers "gave her a signed order to present to any who might threaten to burn her dwelling." Mrs. Johnson had to brandish it three times, and while it saved her home, she still lost her smokehouse, barn (filled with feed for the winter), and gristmill to the flames.[41]

Women were threatened not only in their homes but also at their places of business, and in those spaces they relied on hand signals or secret handshakes as opposed to Masonic artifacts. Sarah Brinson was working as the postmistress in Canoochee, Georgia, when Sherman's men came through, "loading pigs, hogs, taking everything they could find including butter out of a butter dish." Sarah gave a "Masonic distress signal" that her father had taught her, and the lieutenant in charge ordered his men to return her possessions and posted a guard to protect her.[42] A similar story comes from McIntyre, Georgia, where a Mrs. Hyman was the depot agent for the Central Georgia Railroad. Even though the railroad's property was all destroyed, Hyman saved her home by flashing the Masonic symbol. A sympathetic captain stopped and placed a guard around the building.[43] These stories all emphasize the more traditionally chivalrous gender relationships that had been turned upside down by the war and the March. It seems that while sectionalism and secession could shatter social convention, the bonds of Masonic brotherhood could not be so easily sundered.

Union soldiers did not just post guards or issue orders that houses be left unmolested. Sometimes they found themselves embroiled in human dramas of birth and death. A story from Duplin, North Carolina, was entitled "The Strength of Brotherhood," but the teller knew that it was as much about underlying "genuine respect for Masonry." In this case, Bathsheba Mallard Carr was about to give birth and was trying to stop Yankees from foraging around her farm. First she sent her sixteen-year-old stepdaughter to appeal to their consciences, but they still wouldn't stop. Finally, she remembered that her husband told her "in case of *real* distress she should hang his Masonic apron where it could be seen." She did just that, the ransacking stopped immediately, and an officer placed a guard around the house and visited with the new baby. The guards were left in place and protected the Carr women until the army and stragglers passed by.[44]

Occasionally the Masonic deliverer was Sherman himself. There is no evidence, however, that Sherman was a Mason himself, which puts these stories into the realm of legend.[45] Why include Sherman in a story? Perhaps it elevates the tale, makes one person's or one family's salvation special or extraordinary. It certainly makes the tales more memorable and romantic. The Pope family told the story of its matriarch, Mary Pope, who watched soldiers snatching food out of her starving children's hands. In response, "Miss Mary stepped right up to the General hisself, and *that* fixed things." Rumors around the county had her giving the Masonic distress signal, and in return, Sherman himself threatened to shoot anyone who took the children's food and stationed an officer in the family kitchen to keep watch.[46] Essentially, this is the same story that other women told—flash the signal, hang the apron, receive protection—just with the added Sherman twist. In a similar vein, D. J. Thaxton of Jackson, Georgia, was told that the reason that the Masonic Hall survived the March was that it had been "left standing by order of General Sherman himself." Thaxton may have weakened his own story, however, by noting first that Price's Mill south of town was left standing (in order to provide food for the Union soldiers if needed), and that supposedly Sherman had passed down Third Street, "and saw the courthouse as it was tumbling to the ground."[47] One story out of Screven County, Georgia, hits many of the legendary high points by having a faithful slave approach Sherman on behalf of a house full of young ladies.[48]

An even more dramatic version comes out of Sandersville, Georgia, where someone had opened fire on the marchers. In angry retaliation, Sherman ordered the town razed. Brother Anthony, the Methodist minister, begged Sherman to change his orders, arguing that the shooters were not from Sandersville and indeed, were not even from Georgia. No response from Sherman. Then Brother Anthony tried appealing to Sherman's heartstrings pleading in the name of Christ, "but General Sherman was not a Christian. He did not care if delicate women and little children perished in the cold." Finally, in desperation, the minister flashed a Masonic sign, and Sherman responded by amending his orders, saving the town from the flames, though not from the foragers, for "everything of value and comfort had been destroyed."[49] What is interesting about this story is the way it paints a merciful Sherman with the brush of cruelty. He spares the town, but only just barely.

While Price's Mill may have survived because it was useful to Sherman's marchers, another gristmill was rumored to have fallen under Masonic protections. Mrs. Beall's Gristmill, which still stands today in Putnam County, Georgia, was visited by Sherman's troops relatively early in the March. Mrs. Caroline Davis Beall had run the mill on her own since her husband's death in 1861, and in late November "the upper floors bulged with grain stored by the farmers of Pea Ridge." The soldiers took over the mill on November 22, and spent the day grinding corn that they had stolen from surrounding farms. Once they finished loading all of the grain, they planned to torch the mill. They were unable to do so because of rain, and the mill survived. As for the Beall's home, it was spared because the late Mr. Beall had been a Mason. Soldiers initially took the family's prized Steinway piano outside and were in the process of tearing off the lid to use the instrument as a horse trough. But the children and their mother wept and pleaded (and apparently used the magical Masonic words), and an officer ordered the men not only to stop but to repair the damage. Perhaps in return, perhaps out of simple humanity, when a sick Union soldier came to the house after the war, the family cared for him. He died before giving his name and was buried in the "Yankee Grave."[50]

The Masonic connection saved not only property but also, in at least one case, a man's life. J. D. Miller told the story of his father's encounters with

Sherman's March. His father, W. W. Miller, had been working for the railroad east of Macon. Although Miller's uncle was taken prisoner by the Yankees, his father was "allowed to pass on, after being warned by a brother Mason to steer clear of the Yankees." A few days later, Miller's father ran into a second group of troops and was almost shot, but "his relationship as a Mason was again recognized by an officer," who saved him and shared his brandy. The officer advised the elder Miller to hide back in the swamps, which he did. Even then, the Miller family was not entirely safe. While Miller's father was back at work, rebuilding the railroad, troops came to the family farm near Toombsboro, "and were boisterous, rude, and unmanly until my mother handed an officer . . . a book telling him it was her husband's." The book was a Masonic manual, and it had the desired effect: the officer immediately posted guards around the house for three days and nights. That's not to say that the protection was complete or absolute. While the house remained unmolested, the rest of the farm was ransacked and destroyed.[51]

The Masonic stories also follow a pattern in that the saviors are always officers. The Southern stories of Yankee depredations highlight class differences, whether real or perceived, within the army with the lower-class enlisted men rampaging out of control, only occasionally checked by their well-bred officers. Perhaps, too, stories that highlighted the gentility of the enemy implicitly highlighted the gentility of the tellers. After all, they were saved, deemed worthy of protection, without ever having to renounce their Confederate allegiances. At least one Union officer lived up to these professions of honesty. D. Hare of Ashley, Ohio, had passed through Sandersville, Georgia, along the line of the March. The story has Hare, a Mason, taking the jewels from the Masonic Lodge and leaving them with some ladies in the town for safekeeping. This arrangement, though, does not make a lot of sense: presumably, valuables would have been safer *in* the temple than in a private home, so perhaps this part of the story is backward. The second half, however has Hare buying a stolen worshipful master's apron from a fellow soldier for five dollars. Years later, he returned it to the Sandersville Masonic Lodge, explaining that he had tried immediately after the war, but had never received a response.[52]

Ultimately, however, the Masonic stories are more symbolic than real. Perhaps they are all true. Perhaps none of them are. The Solomon Goodwin House in Brookhaven is supposed to be the oldest house in northern Georgia, but the reason that it survived the March is unclear. One story has faithful family slaves left in charge of the property, who managed to tearfully convince Sherman's men "not to burn the house, although evidences of vandalism still remain." The other one was told by Merle Arnold, who managed an antique store in the home in 1980. She had always been told that the home was being ransacked by Union soldiers, who, upon finding a Masonic apron, were ordered to stop and put the house back in order. She heard that a local man had the actual apron but then concluded: "I just tell tourists who come here from out of town to pick which story sounds best to them to tell when they get back home."[53]

Hiding Places

One way to protect property was to throw oneself on the mercy of the Union; another was to hide or conceal valuables and hope for the best. Many Southern civilians took pride in their ability to outwit Sherman's bummers with clever hiding places. In general, when Southerners had advance warning they would send their livestock to swamps and thickets, and bury trunks and boxes of valuables. One county history remarked that "to this day many can point with pride to some old trunk and tell how it was buried full of articles when Sherman came."[54] Although many of these hiding places were discovered, a few succeeded in this game of hide and seek.

The Carroll family of Gwinnett County, Georgia, used hollow spaces within their walls for something that would prove to be even more valuable than jewelry and silver: their supply of wheat, which they accessed from holes drilled in the baseboards and hidden behind various pieces of furniture.[55] The mistress of Glen Mary Plantation in Hancock County, Georgia, had to endure soldiers riding their horses through her home's large open windows and stealing her locket (though it was later returned). However, she safely hid her silver under the dining room floor, a spot later rediscovered during a twentieth-century home renovation.[56] The Williams family of Bryan County, Georgia, lost a gun and some food to bummers but managed to drive the hogs into the woods, hide five hundred bushels of corn, and conceal a five-hundred-pound bale of cotton in the swamp. That cotton sold for a dollar a pound after the war, which presumably allowed the family to rebuild and prosper.[57]

No matter how good the physical hiding place, an element of luck came into play in keeping valuables hidden. Perhaps the soldiers did not care to dig up the floors, or chose not to follow tracks into the swamp. In other cases, Southern white civilians used actual deception and subterfuge to preserve their possessions. One commonly used ruse was to feign illness in the house. A mother in Emanuel County, Georgia, put her eleven-year-old son to bed

Distressed white women watch as foragers tear up their yards.
The enslaved man in the foreground appears to be directing the troops to
hidden valuables. (Nichols, The Story of the Great March, *113)*

with all of the family treasures and then told the soldiers that he had scarlet fever. The troops, afraid of getting sick themselves, left him (and the valuables) alone.[58] In Screven County, a mistress yelled "Smallpox" whenever soldiers approached, which kept them away.[59] In a slightly different vein, a plantation in Herndon was set on fire, but when the mistress refused to leave her sickbed, the soldiers put it out rather than let her burn to death. Another version of the story has her dramatically clinging to her bedpost, with the same results.[60] In Thomasville, Georgia, white mothers feared their boys would be taken by the Union soldiers and disguised them as girls. But when the "girls" were spotted climbing trees, the disguises were rendered moot.[61]

On occasion, the valuables saved were government property: courthouse documents, deeds, and record books. Records from before the Civil War are often difficult to find in the South, sometimes because of Sherman's March, other times from other fires. The farmers of Butts County, Georgia, brought their tithes of produce to the courthouse in Jackson for safekeeping during the war, and these bales and bushels remained when the March came through on November 17, 1864. The soldiers burned the courthouse and Mc-Cord's store (though they appear to have left most houses standing), and the corn and cotton went up in smoke as well. But Wiley Goodman, the county ordinary, took the record books and hid them in the swamps north of the

Ocmulgee River. All that was lost was one deed book and some Superior Court records and treasurer's vouchers (the latter may have been stolen). The community took great pride in this thwarting of the forces of destruction.[62]

A much more significant and better-known story of preservation and salvation comes from Milledgeville, Georgia's capital during the war. The town had a few days of warning before the arrival of the marchers, enough time to do some preparations, and for the governor to flee. State officials managed to hide most of the state's archives and many of the books by sending them off on trains and in wagons both to local homes and, in some cases, as far as Columbia, South Carolina.[63] But the state seal, whose imprint was needed to make documents official, and some incomplete legislative books (including some unsigned acts) were left behind. Georgia secretary of state Nathan Barnett and his wife Mary Ann (sometimes called the Dolley Madison of Georgia) took charge of them. The Barnetts knew that as long as the seal was hidden, the Yankees would not be able to pass any new state laws. Under cover of darkness, Barnett turned away as Mary Ann and their son buried the seal under one of the brick pillars of their home. He did this so he could truthfully say that he did not know where the seal lay hidden. Then Mary Ann took the legislative minute book, wrapped it in oilcloth, and buried it in the pigpen, counting on the warmth of her "four fine porkers" to keep the papers safe. Accounts differ as to whether Barnett fled before Sherman arrived or faced the general himself and went to prison. Some stories claim that Mary Ann threatened to poison Union soldiers if they made her cook for them. Another story has her making a false seal. Either way, the seal and minutes remained hidden until the Georgia legislature met again in February 1865. Given that some of Sherman's men held a mock legislative session, during which they rescinded Georgia's secession, one can perhaps understand the Barnetts' anxiety.[64]

Most stories of white Southerners resisting Sherman's March have been passed down from person to person or are written in dusty county histories and Civil War compendiums. Comparatively few can be seen on the landscape itself. But the Milledgeville story has not one but two commemorative markers on the grounds of the Old Baldwin County Courthouse. The first, more of a monument, was erected on April 26, 1939 (Confederate Memorial Day) by the state of Georgia after a campaign by the United Daughters of the Confederacy. The granite slab is inscribed as follows:

In commemoration of the safeguarding of the Great Seal of Georgia and the Unfinished Acts of the Legislature 1864. Within five hundred feet east of here lived Georgia's wartime secretary of State, Nathan C. Barnett. At midnight November 18, 1864, just before the arrival of the Federal Army, he and his wife Mary buried the Great Seal under their home. His wife hid the unfinished acts of the Legislature under the pig pen. These with the Great Seal were returned unharmed to the State Legislature at Macon in February, 1865.

The second marker, just a few feet behind the first, was erected in 1960, as part of Georgia's state roadside marker campaign. It reads:

When Federal troops entered Milledgeville in November, 1864, Georgia Secretary of State Nathan C. Barnett hid the Great Seal under a house and the legislative minutes in a pig pen 30 yards east of this point. Later they were returned to the Statehouse.

Again in 1868 Governor Charles J. Jenkins (Governor, 1865–1868) removed the Great Seal to thwart state fund payments which had been ordered by the United States military authority which inaugurated Georgia's carpetbag regime. Federal General George Meade replaced Governor Jenkins with United States General Thomas H. Ruger of Wisconsin (who served only part of the year 1868), the last of the Milledgeville governors. With the return of home rule in 1872 the Great Seal was returned to the new capitol in Atlanta.

This second paragraph, I would argue, shows the degree to which the memory of Sherman's March has been conflated with memories of Reconstruction and the perceived horrors of one combined with the other. How both markers, and indeed all versions of the story, highlight the pigpen, arguably the least dignified part of the tale, is also interesting.

Women not only took part in hiding objects of value within (or under) their homes; they also concealed valuables on their persons. For example, Mrs. Murrell of Dell Delight, near Oxford, stood stock still as Union soldiers ransacked her house (whether while searching for Zora Fair or on the March). She did so, not out of fear, but because "she had around her waist a quantity of family silver, spoons, knives and forks, it being concealed under her crinoline skirt; and she was *so* afraid it would jingle."[65] Of course, this was a rather risky strategy, as there was always the possibility of discovery, and discovery through intimate physical contact. It was this very possibility, what one historian described as "the sexual drama enacted in the ruse— the risk of search and exposure and the implied possibility of rape"—that made these stories of bodily (or sartorial) concealment so compelling.[66] In this context, the story of Mary Amarinthia (Yates) Snowden takes on a larger cultural meaning. Snowden was one of the founders of the Ladies Calhoun Memorial Association (LCMA) and had played an instrumental role in raising money for a monument to Calhoun in Charleston. Once the war began, the ladies turned their attentions toward the Confederate cause, founding the Soldier's Relief Association of Charleston and holding a variety of charity bazaars to raise funds. By 1865 Snowden had left Charleston for Columbia and took charge of one last relief effort: the Great Bazaar in January and early February 1865.[67]

As Sherman approached South Carolina's capital, Snowden faced a dilemma. She had not only the money from the bazaar but, more importantly, the assets of the LCMA in the form of bonds, stock certificates, and Confederate money. How would she keep them hidden from the Yankees? In some tellings of the story, a faithful slave helped hide them; in another, Sherman himself helped her spirit them away (she had supposedly met him before the war at a wedding).[68] The most common version, and the one that seems to capture all the tropes and commonalities of concealment, has Snowden and her sister Isabella sewing the securities into her skirt. A history of the Calhoun monument describes the women "quilting the bonds . . . at the dead of night . . . with trembling and flying fingers," all the while under the watchful eye of their mother's (enslaved) maid, who gladly kept their secret. Supposedly she did this even at the expense of her own wealth and personal property.[69] Thus carefully attired, she saved the funds, which were later used not just for the monument but to help fund a home for Confederate widows and orphans.

Occasionally stolen items made their way back to Georgia and the Carolinas. In 1868 the *Atlanta Constitution* reported a stolen gold watch was returned to its owner, via a Catholic priest. A repentant veteran had given it to a priest who sent it on. In 1880, both the *New York Times* and the *Washington Post* reported on the case of Milo A. Boynton, a Michigan lawyer who was arrested for possessing several thousand dollars worth of bonds that had been stolen from Camden South, Carolina, during the March. Boynton claimed to have received the bonds from a widow, who had gotten them from her late husband. There was no statute of limitations on the crimes of the war.[70]

Women Are the Toughest Set

Women defied Union soldiers even more directly at times. Perhaps they believed that, despite all of the demonization of Yankees as heartless beasts, their gender still afforded them some protection; maybe in the heat of the moment they simply reacted with blind emotion. Regardless of the rationale, stories of women rebuking the marchers are staples of the literature. In part they play into the stereotype of the defiant Southern belle, angry and unconquerable. The 1896 "Eulogy on Confederate Women," a tribute delivered to benefit the Confederate Monument in Cuthbert, Georgia, claimed that a high-ranking Union officer "said to a Carolina lady: 'You women keep up this war. We are fighting you.'" In a similar vein, Sherman was supposed to have told the wives of Confederate officers and soldiers who were being expelled from Savannah that "you women are the toughest set I ever knew. The men would have given up long ago but for you. I believe you would keep this war up for thirty years."[71]

Examples of this toughness abound and provide an alternative to images of terrified, sobbing, and cowering civilians. In an example reminiscent of Florence Byrne (the young woman who retaliated, when forced to play piano in the street, by playing *Dixie*), Anna Maria Green wrote of singing "We Live and Die with Davis," while Union troops were in her hometown of Milledgeville.[72] In Savannah, Miss Fanny Cohen allegedly received Sherman when he came to call but refused to offer him a seat.[73] A cavalry squad rode up to a Georgia plantation and "were pretty crabbedly received by the girls of the house who desired to known 'Why in thunder you'uns can't let we'uns be?' and hoped the devil would get the Yanks." In retaliation, the lieutenant in charge decided to make off with the family beehive and hoisted it up on his shoulder. The joke, however, was on the Union man: the bees came out the wrong way, and swarmed the lieutenant and his horse, "compelling the former to drop the hive *sans ceremony*, while the taunting Georgian girls on the porch clapped their dainty, tiny hands, stamped their little feet, and screamed 'goody! goody!! goody!!!' until they cried for joy."[74] These were all pretty innocuous insults, wounding only the Union soldier' pride but not putting anyone in real danger (unless perhaps they were allergic to bees).

In Jenkinsburg, Georgia, a group of women led by Mrs. Harriet Jenkins Barron was in "desperate" straits during the March, presumably from hunger and hardship. According to a history of Butts County, a "the women armed themselves, held up a supply wagon, and took supplies food, and wool for making clothing for their families." It seems hard to believe that this would not provoke a retaliation from the Union forces, but none seems to have followed.[75] The same could not be said for an old woman in Lamar County, Georgia. According to one of her neighbors, "a soldier entered the house on a search for valuables. She locked him in a closet and sitting nearby, began singing a good old hymn. When released the soldier was so furious he caused the burning of the gin house, within which was stored many bales of cotton." The old woman's experiences stood in marked contrast to her neighbor, who took the advice of others and hung a white cloth out of the window (albeit resentfully), and watched the army pass by without stopping.[76]

Yankee Protectors

While most stories of interactions between Sherman's men and Southern white civilians are fraught with tension and animosity, a subset of more upbeat tales exists. After all, both sides were human, and human emotions like kindness and generosity were sure to break through the rhetoric of hatred and resentment. Too, these stories may have been emphasized because of their obvious connection to sectional reunion. How better to bring North and South together than by showing that the worst episodes of the war were tempered by good feelings? Madison, Georgia, provides a good example of this on a large scale, and much has been made over the years of its salvation.[77] But these incidents also happened on a personal level.

Just as every town along the route seems to boast a home saved by a Masonic apron or handshake, so too do they often show off one spared because one of Sherman's sweethearts lived there. If that were the case, observed James Reston tartly, Sherman would have been one of the great ladies men of history. (Truthfully, he did have a wandering eye, but not enough of one to account for every spared home.)[78] There is one documented example of Sherman saving a home for an old friend, although it took place on the Atlanta campaign rather than the March to the Sea. As a young man at West Point, Sherman had fallen in love with Cecilia Stovall, the sister of a classmate. Joseph Hooker was also reputedly quite taken with her. According to the oft-repeated story, she once told Sherman, "Your eyes are so cold and cruel. How you would crush an enemy. I pity the man who ever becomes your foe." For his part, Sherman supposedly replied that he would "ever shield and protect" his erstwhile sweetheart. By 1861, Cecilia Stovall had married Captain Charles Shellman and lived on a plantation known as Shellman Heights on the banks of the Etowah River, near Cartersville. On their way to New Hope Church, Sherman and Hooker stopped at the home, and a distraught slave mentioned "Miss Cecilia." When Sherman discovered her full name, he realized that he had known her and wrote a brief note:

A drawing by Thomas Nast, originally published in the London Illustrated
News, *portrays an idealized version of interactions between Union soldiers and Southern
civilians. The soldiers are politely greeting the women of the house, while
curious African Americans are regaled with stories. This image minimized the fear and
violence that often accompanied such meetings. (Picture Collection, New
York Public Library, Astor, Lenox, and Tilden Foundations)*

My Dear Madam—You once said that you pitied the man who would ever become my foe. My answer is that I would ever protect and shield you. That I have done. Forgive all else. I am but a soldier. W. T. Sherman.

With that he ordered guards posted, and any stolen property returned. A related rumor has Cecilia meeting or corresponding with Sherman and begging him to spare her hometown of Augusta. While the idea of him altering the plans for the March for the sake of a decades-past sweetheart is romantic, it is also implausible and belied by his strategic reasons for the path of the March.[79]

More frequently, Union men—sometimes flirtatiously, sometimes through genuine kindly impulses, would offer household help to Southern white women. Memoirist Myrta Lockett Avery told of "one of the loveliest of Atlanta's gray-haired dames," who described herself as "unreconstructed . . . Southern to the backbone." Yet, to Avery's surprise, she "speaks of Sherman's godless cohorts as gentle as if she were mother of them all." The woman had lived next door to a Union encampment and suffered only some pilfering of food. More importantly, as she struggled to do her own wash for the first time (presumably her slaves had run away to freedom), "a big-hearted Irishman" came over and did the wash, as well as cut wood for her to use in ironing. "I'm your Bridget every wash-day that comes roun'" he proudly proclaimed, and then joined the woman in complaining that the government was providing rations to slaves without forcing them to continue working.[80] Perhaps this was a case of the two being joined by a common distaste for African Americans, but regardless of motive, the Union soldier's help was surely both unnecessary and appreciated.

Often these stories of kindly Yankees centered around children.[81] Fanny Thompson Latham was a child in Goldsboro, North Carolina, when Union forces used her home as a headquarters. She recalled the soldiers giving the family rations and being "very kind to us." One captain jokingly offered her mother five thousand dollars to take Fanny home but settled for buying her "a pretty pair of new shoes" instead.[82] Shoes also featured in Ellen Nelson's memories: she had a new pair, made by the best shoemaker in Butts County, Georgia. She hid them in the family corncrib, but they were found and taken by Union soldiers as they "plundered" the house. The next day an officer asked if the family had been bothered, and hearing their complaints brought Ellen and her older sister to meet with General Kilpatrick. Despite his tough reputation, Kilpatrick promised the girl that he would try to find her shoes. The following day a soldier appeared the Nelson home, "stating that General Kilpatrick could not find her shoes but sent a pair of army shoes instead." Young Ellen was disappointed, but took them, and then exchanged them for a new pair.[83]

As in the stories of Masonic deliverance, General Sherman himself is also given a starring role. Lavinia Lane was also a young girl when Sherman's March came past her home. Her father had taken the family's slaves, livestock, and valuables and hidden them in the nearby swamps, leaving his wife (Lavinia's mother) and daughters behind. Lavinia first chatted with a soldier on horseback, whom she later believed was Sherman himself. Whether that was true or not, she also took it upon herself to make a deal with one of Sherman's subordinates, General Osterhaus. She asked him to spare her family's home and cotton in exchange for assistance. The general agreed, "and in return Lavinia guided him to a safe location to build a pontoon bridge across the nearby Ogeechee River." Interestingly, young Lavinia does not appear to have suffered for aiding the Yankees—her story appears in a celebratory history of Emanuel County, Georgia.[84]

Jack and Asbury Smith, twelve and eleven years old, respectively, appear to have had a similarly surprising encounter with Sherman. The boys came out and watched the Yankees march down the road near their house, to see if they really "had long tails with a fork on the end and if they wore their tails inside their britches." According to family lore, Sherman rode up to the boys, stopped his horse, and held out his hand. Jack refused to shake it, saying "a Yankee will never touch me." Rather than be insulted, Sherman seemed impressed by the boy's moxie, and asked his aides to lift the boy onto his horse. Jack agreed, "and rode down the road sitting in front of Sherman on his horse, leading the army." Sherman asked Jack who his father had voted for in the election, and Jack supposedly replied Lincoln, because his father had opposed slavery and had in fact freed the family's slaves. Jack and Sherman rode into the yard, to be greeted by a throng of ex-slaves and children, and his mother shouting "Here come the Yankees and bless God, Jack is leading the Northern Army!" In exchange for these few moments of levity, or a respite from the stresses of command, Sherman ordered that "no matches are to be struck," thus preserving the family's home and cotton. They were not so lucky when it came to their chickens, cows, hogs, and horses, which were taken away (the horses, in keeping with the usual practice, were shot a few miles away).[85] What is interesting about this story is its mix of plausibility (stolen animals, but a protected home and kind treatment of children) and too good to be true (Sherman himself leading a column, the idea that the senior Smith would have voted for Lincoln). Perhaps it happened exactly this way; or perhaps it was a mix of memory and self-aggrandizement. After all, a good story is made even better with the inclusion of the greatest Yankee devil of them all.

One episode bringing Union troops and Southern white children together seems as though it must be fictional but is in fact real, a testament to gentle feelings. Sherman famously presented Savannah as a Christmas gift to Lincoln, but some of his soldiers got together to bring Christmas to the children of the city. The idea came from a Union sergeant, but Sherman approved it. Many of Sherman's men were missing their own children at the holiday, and so decided to make toys and parcel out their rations. They took a wagon and decorated it like Santa's sleigh, and put improvised reindeer antlers on the mules in charge of pulling the cargo. They then had a sergeant dress up like Santa to deliver toys and food all over town.[86]

Interactions between Southern white civilians and Union troops were of course neither uniformly hostile nor uniformly pleasant. Rather they fell into gray areas, often depending on the individuals involved. One soldier might be kind, but the ones who followed might not. One group could plunder, and the next help rebuild a kitchen. The "Ten Day Ordeal" of Mary Butrill Wilson well illustrates these complexities. When Mary was a girl in Georgia, she and her Aunt Emma and a few "maids" (presumably enslaved women) were left behind while the men in the family headed to Macon with wagons of valuables, in order to keep them out of the grasp of Sherman's men. Soldiers detained the women in Jasper County, and Mary boldly asked if any of them was a "gentleman." One soldier spoke up, saying that the Butrill women reminded him of his own mother and sister, and volunteered to protect them. The soldier brought them to a house where Mary's father, Asa, had also been captured. But at the same time as he brought the women under Union protection, he also broke open the family trunks and distributed their contents to the nearby "factory" people.[87]

The Butrills were then placed under General George Spencer's protection. The general noticed that the women's clothes had been torn and made sure to find replacement for them. But this small kindness was contradicted by the soldier bringing the Butrills to a small cabin, inhabited by Mrs. Fears and her two children, where "he told Mrs. Fears to take them in or he would burn her cabin." Then the Union men posted guards around the cabin and its livestock and arranged for meals to be brought to all of the women. Were they protected or prisoners? It seems to have been a fine line.[88]

The women spent ten days in the cabin, where they "witnessed soldiers with patterns of 15 yards of silk from their trunks wound around horses galloping up and down the red muddy hills of Jasper County. One had his horse covered with Mrs. Butrill's handsome white crepe shawl." They eventually made their way back to their plantation, where they were reunited with Butrill's mother and "her loyal negro woman." Despite having been used as headquarters for General Blair, the outbuildings and fences had been burned and most of the furniture destroyed. Hundreds of soldiers had camped on the grounds. Mary felt pity for herself and her family, though none for the Fears with whom they had been forced to live. Too, looking back from the 1930s, she included the somewhat stereotypical recollection that the family would have starved had not their "faithful servants" picked up scraps from the Yankee camps until family could send food."[89]

Mary Butrill injected a bit of levity into her recollection of what was, probably, the most frightening time of her life. Perhaps General Spencer's kindness was motivated by his interest in her aunt: for the next two years he tried to court Emma Manley, sending her letters, books, and flowers, "but was never able to win her."[90] Other Union soldiers were luckier in their attempts at romance, and these stories were staples of what historian Nina Silber has called "The Romance of Reunion."[91] Some had particular connections to Sherman's March, although not all of them began during the 1860s. Under the title "A Pretty War Story," the *New York Times* reprinted the tale of Kansan Davis Rogers and Miss Goodman of Forsyth, Georgia. Rogers had kept a diary during his military service but had lost it somewhere in Georgia. A child found it and kept it. Years later, he showed it to his younger sister, who wrote to Rogers, and offered to return it. She continued to correspond with the veteran and his wife, until his wife died. Rogers decided to visit Miss Goodman, and "it was love at first sight." He stayed until the couple could be married, thus "[forming] a union from which there is no secession."[92]

These stories of kindness and correspondence turning to friendship combine in the story of Mrs. Jesse Hunt (née Mary Elizabeth Carver). During Stoneman's Raid, Mrs. Hunt cared for several wounded Union soldiers. In return, they left a letter addressed to Sherman asking that the family property be left unmolested. As Sherman's troops approached Jones County, the family fled, and thus there was no one to display the letter. The furniture was stolen, though the house was not burned. But twenty-four years later, one of the soldiers, B. F. Morris wrote to Mrs. Hunt, and the two struck up a correspondence. Morris came to visit the Hunts and then invited them to visit him at home in Ohio. Mrs. Hunt could not go, but her husband did, and was the guest of honor at a Sherman Brigade Reunion. He sat next to John Sherman, the general's brother, and "it is said when Jesse Hunt got to speak he picked up a silver fork, looked it over carefully, and said, 'I was just seeing if this was my wife's silver the Yankees carried off.'"[93] By all accounts he was warmly received, and we can imagine that his joke brought down the house. With the passage of time, the anger waned, and the sentimentality rose, with bad feelings suppressed and reunion paramount.

CHAPTER THREE

Freedpeople and Forty Acres

By the early 1930s, eighty-seven-year-old Henry Jenkins had long transcended his origins as a slave on a plantation in Sumter County, South Carolina. He owned 480 acres of land, and was described as a respectable "church member, citizen, and tax payer." While he owed his emancipation to Sherman's marchers, he recalled them more with anger than gratitude. "When de Yankees come, what they do?" he asked rhetorically, and then answered "They did them things they ought not to have done and they left undone de things they ought to have done." Jenkins complained that jewelry and silver "was took and carried 'way by a army dat seemed more concerned 'bout stealin', than they was 'bout de Holy war for de liberation of de poor African slave people. They took off all de hosses, sheeps, cows, chickens, and geese, took de seine and de fishes they caught, corn in crib, meat in smoke-house, and everything." Jenkins knew all too well that in taking food from plantation owners, Union soldiers took food from African Americans as well. He also understood that for most Union soldiers, the March had very little to do with black liberation, and he waited patiently for judgment to come. "Marse General Sherman said war was hell," Jenkins told his interviewer. "It sho' was. Mebbe it was hell for some of them Yankees when they come to die and give account of de deeds they done in Sumter and Richland Counties."[1]

For African Americans, Sherman's March was the epitome of a double-edged sword. While many enslaved people were liberated by Union soldiers as they moved across the plantation landscape, that emancipation was often accompanied by hunger, destruction, and mistreatment. If African Americans stayed put while the army moved on, they would have had to live amid ruined farms and looted storehouses, side by side with angry masters, who might not see themselves as "former" slaveholders.[2] Those who chose to follow Sherman's army found themselves largely unwelcomed, left to fend for themselves, often trapped by Confederates in their wake.

The stories told by and about African Americans reflect this ambiguity. African Americans sometimes recalled Sherman as a liberator, even as they resented his soldiers' casual demolition of the food that they, not Southern whites, had grown. Southern whites, for their part, saw African Americans as filling one of two stock roles: either as faithful retainers, helping to hide valuables and livestock from the Yankees, or (less frequently) as ungrateful turncoats who betrayed the family's trust. Union soldiers, starting with Sherman himself, presented a similar spectrum of attitudes.[3] Although the importance of the March for African Americans seemed to wane over the twentieth century, it reappeared in the 1960s, as its 100th anniversary coincided with the burgeoning civil rights movement.

Like a Blue Cloud Coming Through

The Works Progress Administration (WPA) slave narratives are both tremendously valuable and deeply problematic as a source of information about African Americans' lives before and during the Civil War. Briefly, the flaws include biased interviewers, faulty memories, and an inherent bias toward people who lived into the 1930s (and were consequently young during the years before emancipation).[4] Approximately seventy African Americans mentioned Sherman and his March in their narratives, with the majority of them coming from Georgia and South Carolina. Their stories tended to be brief, perhaps a reflection of the limited number of questions being asked about the war specifically.[5] Despite their myriad limitations, the narratives are still worth using, because they are the largest single cache of African American memories of Sherman that I have been able to find. Other sources used in this chapter, observations by travelers, soldiers, or white Southerners, are also biased and problematic. What the narratives can reveal are patterns and similarities across the range of the March, and they form the basis of this section.

A number of African Americans mentioned Sherman in the broader context of Union leaders like Lincoln and Grant and, more strikingly, included a personal encounter with one of these men. For example, Frank A. Patterson, of Raleigh, North Carolina, remembered "during that campaign, Lincoln came to North Carolina and ate breakfast with my master." He described the meal in great detail, from ham with gravy to biscuits, poached eggs, waffles, and grits. Lincoln supposedly chastised Patterson's "old boss" for "[con] 'ceivin' children by slaves and buyin' and sellin' our own blood and it will have to be stopped."[6] Sam Rawls described Lincoln as "a good man," who demanded that whites free their slaves. "He come did his two men, Grant and Sherman, and captured de slave bosses."[7] An obituary for a woman who had been enslaved in Georgia told of her churning butter all day, only to be visited by a "grim-visaged general," who drank her buttermilk and made off with her butter.[8]

Dilly Yelladay was actually born after the war, but she remembered "what my mammy tole me 'bout Abraham Lincoln, Grant, an' a lot of dem Yankees comin' down ere 'fore de surrender." Yelladay claimed correctly that Sherman "knowed de South like a book 'fore he come thro' last time" and asserted that "Yankees come thro' dressed like tramps an' dey wus always lookin' fur some of dere people."[9] The idea that Lincoln, Grant, and Sherman might have wandered the South in disguise also appeared in Charity Austin's reminiscences. Austin was born in 1852 and lived in Georgia during the war. She told of local whites holding "big dinners and speakin'" as the war began: "Dey tole what dey were goin' to do to Sherman and Grant. A lot of such men as Grant and Sherman and Lincoln came through de South in rags and were at some o' dese meetings an' et de dinners. When de white folks foun' out, dere was some sick folks." Austin claimed to have even seen the disguised Lincoln, explaining that "he wus just the raggedest man you ever saw. . . . He said he was huntin' his people; and dat he had lost all he had. Dey give him somethin' to eat and tobacco to chew, and he went on." Only after Lincoln was elected president did Austin and her fellow slaves realize who the ragged man was.[10]

It hardly seems necessary to point out that Lincoln, Grant, and Sherman were not in fact traveling throughout the wartime South disguised as beggars, dining and breakfasting with planters. But the stories that place them there have something to say about the individualized nature of wartime emancipation and of the need to personalize the grand currents of war. In this they echo white stories of encounters with Sherman. Emancipation, as innumerable historians have shown proceeded in fits and starts, town by town, plantation by plantation, farm by farm.[11] Nowhere was this more true than during Sherman's March, where the armies brought freedom with their arrival and then moved on the same day or the next. This signal moment in an individual's life was not always accompanied by fanfare and trumpets. Perhaps claiming a personal connection or personal relationship with the seeming agents of emancipation gave greater weight or meaning to the moment. The tales of Lincoln wandering in rags seem to paint him as a messianic figure, which evokes postwar imagery of religious martyrdom.

African Americans also shared more specific stories of Sherman, attributing all sorts of actions to him, echoing the stories white families told of Sherman personally sparing them or their property. Tina Johnson had just moved to Augusta when the March began, and she asserted that Sherman's sister lived there as well. "Dat's the reason dat Sherman missed us, case he ain't wantin' to 'sturb his sister none."[12] This is a clear echo of the stories that had Sherman bypassing Augusta out of respect for a former girlfriend, or his own affection for the place. Jesse Rice recalled Sherman coming through Yorkville, South Carolina, "wid dem awful mens he had," though he also believed they were going through Charlotte to then come down to Columbia. Regardless of their route, Rice also shared stories "'bout Sherman shooting folks. Some say dat he shot a big rock off'n de State House in Columbia."[13] Phil Towns painted a different picture of Sherman: not a murderer but a gentleman, who had found conditions on the plantation of "Gov." Towns near Macon "so ideal" that he left them unmolested and "went gaily on his way."[14]

The likelihood of individual African Americans encountering Sherman himself was not great. Jesse Rice, in fact, hid with his parents explaining "Lawd God no, us never wanted to see him."[15] African Americans did, however, both observe and engage with Sherman's soldiers. In Atlanta, a frightened Susan McIntosh saw Union troops marching down Peachtree Street, marching alongside homes riddled with holes from shelling. Later her father saw them in Athens, "like a blue cloud coming through."[16] Just like white observers, African Americans were struck by the amount of time it took the army to pass. Elijah Henry Hopkins thought that it took "more than a day," for Sherman's men to march into Atlanta. He went on to describe civilians scrambling in response: "I recollect when all the people came up to swear allegiance, and when they were hurrying out to get away from Sherman's army."[17] Months later, near Fayetteville, John Bectom was "nearly scared . . . to death" by the passing troops, who "began passing, so the white folks said, at 9 o'clock in the mornin'. At 9 o'clock at night they were passin our door on foot. They said there were two hundred and fifty thousan' o' them passed."[18]

Bectom did not say if he actually hid from the Yankees, but he would not have been alone had he done so. A woman, known only as "Aunt Josephine," lived on the Rogers Plantation near Atlanta and, with her mistress and mistress's baby, hid for three days in the swamps. Her little brother spent three days in a dry well on the property, usually used to keep stored food cool. Her master was in Virginia and came back to find everything destroyed.[19] William Ward had been owned by Georgia governor Joe Brown but in 1864 had been hired out and was living in a mansion on Peachtree Street in Atlanta. Despite being 105 when interviewed, Ward "vividly" remembered Sherman's March, first describing the bombardment of Atlanta and whites frantically trying to hide their valuables "under stumps of trees and in sides of hills."

Not that these hurried caches were especially effective, as "Sherman's army found quite a bit of the hidden wealth." Ward went on to describe leaving Atlanta with Sherman's men, eventually following them to Virginia.[20] Willis Williams also followed along with Sherman's men, going from South Carolina to Richmond. He recalled seeing Sherman in Petersburg, saying that "he had a big name, but he warn't such a big man; he was a little spare made man . . . what clothes he had on. He was dressed down in finest uniform."[21] Both Williams and Ward seem to illustrate that Sherman's marchers had no problem with young men following along, men who could presumably be put to work in some capacity. It was the older people and families with young children who were the problem.

Lorenza Ezell, who had been enslaved near Spartanburg, South Carolina, also followed in the wake of Union soldiers, leaving home to work as a Union mail boy. He told of his master running off and hiding in the woods "a whole week," when the March came near, but "he didn't need to worry 'cause us took care of everythin'." Judging by the song that Ezell and his uncle made up, his definition of taking care of everything might not have been what his master had in mind:

White folks, have you seed old massa
Up de road, with he mustache on?
He pick up he hat and he leave real sudden
And I 'lieve he's up and gone

Chorus: Old massa run away
And us darkies stay at home.
It mus' be now dat Kingdom's comin'
And de year of Jubilee

He look up de river and he seed dat smoke
Where de Lincoln gunboats lay
He big 'nuff and he old 'nuff and he orter know better,
But he gone and run away

Now dat overseer want to give trouble
And trot us 'round a spell
But we lock him up in de smokehouse cellar
with de key done throwed in de well.[22]

There's a powerful inversion of the traditional master-slave relationship in this song, the epitome of the bottom rail being on the top. Instead of slaves running away from their masters, the master runs away from his slaves. Instead of slaves being imprisoned, it is the overseers. And for Ezell, who was a teenager during the war, it was Sherman and his men who were the agents of this upheaval, the catalysts. But the complicating factor is that there is no evidence that Sherman's March came through Spartanburg. What may be happening here is the conflation, after the fact, of Union soldiers in general with Sherman's men in particular. In the same way that people claimed to have met Lincoln, it seems there was more drama in being freed by Sherman's men than unnamed soldiers.

As marchers poured onto plantations, we can imagine the mixed emotions with which they were greeted by African Americans: joy at the implications of emancipation and the misery of white owners, but also perhaps fear and concern. Lorenza Ezell did not seem to mind that when Sherman's men found a neighborhood stash of cotton, "as big as a little courthouse"; they set it afire, "and it took two months 'burnin'."[23] Alice Lewis proclaimed that she saw Sherman in North Carolina, along with his soldiers "gathering up all the hogs and all the hosses and all the cows and all the little culled chillen." She recalled those times not as ones of liberation, but instead as "dreful days!"[24]

Claiborne Moss had a similar sense of resentment toward Sherman's men, perhaps because he knew one personally. Moss lived on the Duggins' plantation, about fifteen miles from Sandersville, Georgia. When the March came through, Moss recognized Cooper Cuck, a former peddler who had joined the Union army. Cuck hung back at first, afraid of being recognized, but when the majority of soldiers had passed, Cuck and a friend "came back and stole everything that they could lay their hands on—all the gold and silver that was in the house, and everything they could carry." Moss recalled having to feed Union officers for a night, angry that "they didn't pay nothing for what they was fed," and then "took every horse and mule we had."[25] When they marchers moved on, they also "took" Moss's uncle with them. Moss said "took"; we have no way of knowing whether he went of his own accord or not. We do know that:

> They got in a fight. They gave Uncle Ben five horses, five sacks of silverware, and five saddles. The goods was taken in the fight. Uncle Ben brought it back with him. The boss took all that silver away from him. Uncle Ben didn't know what to do with it. The Yankees had taken all my master's and he took Ben's. Ben give it to him. He come back 'cause he wanted to.

Lorenza Ezell claimed to have been freed by Sherman's men, although that may not have been the case. He was eighty-seven years old when this photograph was taken during the mid-1930s. (Library of Congress: ppmsc 01099)

What might Uncle Ben have thought of all this—Yankees steal from planters, give their ill-gotten gains to Ben (presumably for safekeeping), and then Ben's master steals them from Ben. But Ben also seems to have fallen into that population of African Americans who chose to remain with the devil they knew, their former masters, rather than take their chances on the March.[26]

Claiborne Moss appears to have resented having to feed Union officers; Lewis Ogletree described a similar situation with a combination of excitement and fear. Ogletree and other enslaved children waited inside the fence of their plantation in Spalding County, Georgia, although when they could finally hear the troops approaching "they hid in the bushes or under the house." As the troops "poured into the yard and into the house," they forced an enslaved woman to open the smokehouse, give them the best whiskey, and "oftentimes they made her cook them a meal of ham and eggs."[27]

While thefts of food and forced work could certainly have been frightening, they were not deadly. Fire, and the soldiers' often indiscriminate use of it, was. Amie Lumpkin was sixteen when the March came through Fairfield County, South Carolina. She told of soldiers "ridin' by for hours, some of them laughin' and many of them has big balls in their hands, which they throw against de house and it explode and burn de house." Lumpkin's owners were fortunate, for she explained that "as de army pass by we all stand by de side of de road and cry and ask them not to burn our white folk's house and they didn't." Lumpkin suspected that these balls of incendiary material were used in the burning of Columbia.[28] While Sarah Poindexter did not personally witness the burning of Columbia, she knew it was happening "'cause we smell it and de whole east look lak some extra light is shinin'." In her estimation after a visit, "there wasn't fifty houses standin'. Chimneys standin' 'round, is about all there was where most of de city was standin' befo'."[29] John Franklin had an even closer vantage point, from a hill just outside the city. He could not sleep, "for it was 'most light as day, and the smell of smoke was terrible. . . . Next mornin' we look over the city from the bluff and only a few houses was standin' and hundreds of tumble-down chimneys and the whole town was still smokin'." He confessed to having "dreams yet 'bout that awful time," but took comfort in seeing the city rebuilt, all the way out to where he watched it burn.[30] George Briggs, of Union County, South Carolina, also saw Columbia burn, but in a different way than most others did. He had been enlisted in the "16th Regiment," but never made it "North." As he and his fellow enlistees reached Charleston, they were turned around and sent back to Union, via Columbia: "Us heard dat Sherman was coming, fetching fire along 'hind him." It is unclear why they went back; Briggs attributes the decision to "de bosses," perhaps indicating a sort of peacekeeping role. It is also possible that Briggs and his companions wanted to go back to keep their families safe.[31]

Most African American stories about fire involved setting it or watching towns burn. Emmaline Kilpatrick told a different version, but one that clearly echoed those of whites as well. Asked by the granddaughter of her former master about the burning of Jewell, Georgia, Kilpatrick explained that the cotton mill survived because "de boss uv dem sojers" saw a Masonic sign in the upstairs window.[32] A Mason himself, he forbade them to burn down the mill (although some of the works were torn out).[33] While gauging tone from a narrative like this is hard, it does seem that Kilpatrick approved of this small act of mercy.

To Keep Him in Slavery or Free Him

Not all interactions between Sherman's soldiers and African Americans involved fear and flames. Many African Americans described the soldiers within the context of emancipation. While enslaved in Newberry County, South Carolina, Alfred Sligh heard rumors of emancipation in 1863, but they had no effect on his daily life. "We work on," he told an interviewer, "'til Sherman come and burn and slash his way though de state in de spring of 1865."[34] Reverend James H. Johnson might have spoken more formally than Sligh, but the story he told of meeting Sherman's soldiers in Camden, South Carolina, was much the same. Regardless of the Emancipation Proclamation, "the status quo of slavery kept right on as it had been until Sherman's army came through."[35] Henry Wright's memories supported the notion that Sherman's men tailored their destructiveness to individual situations. As troops moved through his master's Georgia plantation, they asked if the master had been mean to his slaves. "As the answer was 'no,'" Wright explained, "the soldiers moved on after taking all the livestock that they could find. At the neighboring plantation, where the master was mean, all property was burned."[36]

John Bectom, who recalled watching soldiers march by for more than twelve hours, eventually got to know some of the soldiers personally as they camped for the night in his master's field. Bectom seemed to enjoy time by the soldiers' campfires: "The Yankees called us Johnnie, Dinah, Bill and other funny names. They beat their drums and sang songs. One of the Yankees sang 'Rock a Bye Baby.'" It wasn't all songs and jokes, however. One soldier stole Bectom's (presumably better) shoes, replacing them with his own shoddy pair. On a brighter note, a different soldier killed a shoat and gave some of the meat to the boy to take home to his mother.[37]

The image of soldiers arriving on the plantations and being greeted as liberators was a tenacious one. One turn-of-the-century children's book featured foraging parties being "surrounded by crowds of negroes, who everywhere left their masters to follow the Union army; men, women, and children, all knew they were emancipated. They swarmed around the column, clinging to the horses, kissing the hands and feet of the officers, frantic with joy at the arrival of those whom they looked upon as their deliverers." During the 1990s, Jerry Ellis punctuated his account of marching across Georgia with weirdly paternalistic reveries about jubilant African Americans dancing around campfires and flirting with soldiers. His visions have no downsides.[38]

Sherman and his soldiers are often portrayed as unwilling Pied Pipers, leading an ever-growing trail of former slaves in their wake. The aptly named William Sherman of Black Swamp ran away when he learned that Sherman's troops were nearby in Robertsville, South Carolina. He joined the soldiers on the far side of the Savannah River, claiming that the soldier who let them approach the camp was court-martialed for his kindness. Nevertheless, once the former slaves were in camp, the Federal officers gave them a choice of continuing along with them or heading back to Savannah. Will Sherman chose to go to Savannah, a decision that very well may have saved his life. Several hundred freedpeople elected to go with Sherman's men, but while en route to Barnwell, South Carolina, "most of these hunfortunes slaves were slain by 'bush whackers' (Confederate snipers who fired upon them from ambush). After being killed they were decapitated and their heads placed upon posts that lined the fields so that they could be seen by other slaves to warn them of what would befall them if they attempted to escape."[39] This grisly warning did not appear to have much of a deterrent effect.

The inconsistencies of Union policy toward runways are exemplified in Will Sherman's story and reflected in the memories of other former slaves as well. Shang Harris cast doubt on the portrait of unwilling liberators, claiming: "Dey try to git de niggers to back North wid 'em and dey had a big crowd o' colored goin', but I wouldn't go."[40] William Ward seemed to explain why the soldiers would have been willing to bring at least some African American civilians along, explaining that "Sherman took him and his fellow slaves as far as Virginia to carry Powder and shot to the soldiers." But Ward also injected a note of poignancy, demonstrating the confusion that surely reigned over every individual encounter: "He states that he himself did not know whether Sherman intended to keep him in slavery or free him."[41] Ward came through his experiences unscathed, but the same might not be said for Phil Towns. Towns lived on a plantation near Macon and was "so impressed with Sherman" that he joined the March, camping alongside the soldiers. We can imagine him awed by all of the hustle and bustle, impressed by the uniforms and commands. "He thought that anything a Yankee said was true. When one of them gave him a knife and told him to go and cut the first man he met, he followed instructions even though he knew the man." Only then did Towns come to his senses and apologize, leaving us to wonder at the casual cruelty of the Union soldiers.[42]

Many African Americans giving their life histories were openly critical of Sherman and his marchers.[43] Often their anger centered around the lack of food left in Sherman's wake. Jesse Rice, who hid when the March came through Yorkville, South Carolina, claimed that times were harder after Sherman than during the Great Depression. He recalled surviving on nothing more than "ash cake and 'simmon beer."[44] Some seventy years later, Ferebe Rogers still seemed upset by soldiers coming onto her master's plantation near Milledgeville, Georgia, complaining that "they done eve'thing dat was bad." This included the usual burning and thefts, including taking over a thousand bushels of shucked corn. "I jes' can't tell you all dey done," Rogers concluded sadly.[45] Her neighbor, Snovey Jackson, told a similar story, complaining that the Yankees "ruin[ed] eve'thing!" leaving Milledgeville as "nuttin mo'n a cow pasture."[46] This was not literally true, as many buildings still stood in the town, but seventy years later the perception outweighed the reality.

Devastation often led to starvation and desperation. Frank Magwood's neighborhood had been devastated by both Union and Confederate troops, with little remaining to eat. Thus, "where Sherman's army stopped and ate and fed their horses the Negroes went and picked up the grains of corn they strowed there and parched and ate them."[47] George King remembered that after Sherman "there wasn't no cornbread, no bacon—just trash eating trash. . . . Darkies search 'round the barns, maybe find grains of corn in the manure, and they'd parch the grains."[48]

Many of these stories of starvation and survival are echoed in white memories of the March. Hardship proved to be color-blind. In Liberty County, Georgia, home of Mary Jones and Cornelia Jones Pond, the African American "settlements" were repeatedly ransacked. Soldiers took provisions, including several months worth of stored corn, drove off livestock, and took household goods including "blankets and clothes, the women's pails, piggins, spoons, buckets, pots, kettles." African Americans who had little to begin with were left with even less.[49]

A black barber in Fayetteville, North Carolina, laughed as he told newspaperman John Dennett that local African Americans "prayed about as hard for Sherman to go as they had prayed for him to come." Every black home in town had been ransacked, black men with good clothes and boots were stopped on the street and forced to give them up to soldiers on the spot. Even the barber's own razors were taken. But at least Dennett found a silver lining in this cloud of ill-treatment, for blacks in Fayetteville "no longer believed that every man of Northern birth must necessarily be their friend, and they more clearly saw the need of looking to themselves for their own elevation."[50] One wonders if that lesson really needed to be taught, and how Dennett would have felt to be on the receiving end.

Rather than trying to fit Sherman's marchers into a binary of either liberators or pillagers in terms of their relationship to blacks, it might be better to see them as catalysts. The relationship between masters and slaves in parts of Georgia and the Carolinas had already been tested and was fraying around the edges.[51] The arrival of marchers fundamentally undermined white control, allowing African Americans to seize the moment, if they so chose.[52]

One old slave made his calculations about the ambiguity of freedom in wartime explicit when he purportedly told Sherman that "you'se'll go way to-morrow, and anudder white man'll come."[53] Waiting could be the more prudent strategy. Certainly many who followed in the army's wake wound up broken down and malnourished.[54] Abe Glass was fifteen when he found himself following a wagon "plumb full of Yankees" all the way to Savannah and ultimately Washington, D.C. He then moved to Illinois in the care of a Union captain and did not make his way home to Covington, Georgia, for more than a year. He never left Georgia again.[55]

Nor did all African Americans who followed Sherman do so willingly, as was the apparent case with Claiborne Moss's Uncle Ben. Working for the army was a sort of impressment and, coupled with military discipline, could arguably be seen as bondage by another name. Freedmen who wound up in Virginia with the army might wonder if they would ever return home.[56] And many who left with Sherman did eventually come back to families and familiarity, where they might not be welcomed with open arms. In Scotland, North Carolina, one planter reported that thirteen of his slaves had left with Sherman's men and three returned. Whether from this or other sources, he believed that as many as three-fourths of Sherman's followers died. This seems high, particularly for the latter stages of the March. Records of Scotland's Laurel Hill Church mentioned African Americans returning from the

March being prohibited from taking communion "except those who could give a satisfactory account of their conduct."[57]

"Faithful Slaves"

For all this discussion of the interplay between African Americans and Sherman's marchers, we cannot forget that there was always a third party to the conversation—whether explicit or implicit. Southern whites, particularly slaveholders, had their own ideas about what their slaves should do when confronted with Yankees, and their own explanations for black actions. When former slaves looked back on their leaving, as we have seen, they hardly reflected on their masters and mistresses. The calculations that they made seemed influenced by opportunity and safety rather than past treatment. Freedom and the future mattered more than the relative kindness or cruelty of their masters. But masters found this hard to comprehend. White stories of this moment of decision rarely saw African Americans as actors in their own right. African Americans had a choice, in white stories. They could openly betray their white masters, giving away hiding places and actively casting their lot with the invaders. But these were not the usual tales. Far more often whites wrote about blacks being enticed away, or somehow bamboozled, as Gertrude Thomas believed about Henry in chapter 1. "Aunt Silvey," the cook on Dell Delight plantation, near Oxford, Georgia, was thought to have been lured away from home in an army wagon "because she was promised a silk dress."[58]

One Georgia planter, Captain Truwhitt, complained bitterly about his former bondsmen a few years after the March. He heaped scorn upon them for singing Sherman's praises and for thinking "he was comin' in a chariot of fire." In Truwhitt's telling, his slaves had behaved foolishly, "a group of life-long bondmen, sleepless with the vague and ineffable transports of that coming something, sitting and singing at midnight, and watching that great glare in the heavens, where Sherman, by the light of a burning State, was gathering his red sheaves." Truwhitt seemed to paint Sherman as satanic figure, bringing fire and flames, yet worshiped by African Americans. When the bummers couldn't get any valuables from Truwhitt, they turned to the slaves, "and told 'em a long cock-and-bull story about Uncle Abe and his dear children, and how they'd never want anything more in this life, and wouldn't have to work, and then they made the niggers give 'em all their silver—and many a nigger in the old time had more ready cash hid in old rags than his master—all their silver, and rings, and things, and they rode off with 'em."

What really upset Truwhitt, however, was that even after he had treated his slaves well, cared for them while they were sick and so on, and even after they were so ill-used by Yankees, "every last skunk of 'em run away," when Sherman came.[59]

Whites wanted to believe that their slaves had loved them, and so they became invested in tales of faithful bondsmen and women. Firm numbers are hard to come by. Sherman passed through thirty-one counties in Georgia, with an 1860 aggregate slave population of 152,884. His men went through eighteen counties in South Carolina, with an 1860 aggregate slave population of 161,802. Finally, he moved through fourteen North Carolina counties, which were home to an 1860 aggregate slave population of 66,318.[60] Obviously Sherman's marchers did not come into contact with every single one of these enslaved people, but at least this gives us a rough sense. Estimates from historians and the *Official Records* of the numbers of African Americans who followed Sherman ranged from 17,000 to 25,000 for Georgia, probably about the same for the other states.[61] Some African Americans participated in looting and devastation alongside the soldiers, but outright attacks on masters were quite rare.[62]

What this means is that the vast majority of African Americans stayed put, but for their own reasons. Fear and self-preservation played prominent roles. But what this also means was that whites fundamentally misunderstood African Americans motives and intentions. But it is these misunderstood motives that came down as the dominant white story. As historian James Loewen explains:

> From Tennessee through Georgia to the Carolinas, not one historical marker tells about the jubilation Sherman's arrival occasioned among most of the people who witnessed it—black people. The few markers that do mention African Americans honor those individuals who behaved heroically on the Confederate side. No marker notes that Sherman's men freed many of the people they encountered. Sherman himself didn't always want to, and his officers tried to convince slaves that the army could not feed them and the war would soon free them anyway.[63]

What happens is a divergence of types of stories. White-authored narratives, whether memoirs or county histories, tended to emphasize faithfulness, perhaps in self-justification.

Blacks were praised for preserving white property, using the same masks and professions of innocent simplicity against Union soldiers that had served them under slavery. In Sandersville, Georgia, a "faithful slave" begged soldiers to spare his mistress's piano (they torched the rest of the house). As soon as the Yankees moved on, "he, with the help of other negroes who loved their white folks, hid it in the swamp and covered it with blankets and quilts." It stayed safely hidden for months until the white family returned.[64] Jacob Walker, who had been enslaved by the Whitehead family near Waynesboro, Georgia, first held on to his own set of wolf's head shaped gold shirt studs (a gift from the family). He told the Union soldier who wanted them that they were merely polished brass, "and the officer 'not desiring to go off the gold standard,' left the old man in undisturbed possession of his treasure." This story had the added benefit of mocking Yankee greed. Walker and his wife also hid away the family silver, and then Walker told the soldiers that it had all been taken away to Augusta. When the family cook heard a Union officer praising the quality of the family's spoons (the only utensils that had been left behind, she slipped them away and saved them as well.[65]

Female slaves sometimes interceded to protect their female mistresses. Martha Allen of Jasper County, Georgia, "had beautiful long, curly hair which attracted the attention of some Union soldiers who told her they were going to cut it off. An old slave of the family intervened, begging them not to cut her hair, and the soldiers left it unharmed."[66] This raises some interesting aspects of gender roles: the Union soldiers were striking at Martha Allen's femininity. Perhaps the Union soldiers listened to the family slave in a strange inversion of roles, respecting the African American woman at the expense of the white one. A similar situation arose in South Carolina, where a young woman had hidden a gold watch in her bosom. As Union soldiers were about to grab her and take it, her "Delia, her faithful servant" took action warning that they would have to "knock Delia down fust" before they could lay a hand on her young mistress. Again, the soldiers backed down.[67]

A woman in Orangeburg, South Carolina, told John Trowbridge first of a neighbor's slave moving around the district for three days with a wagonload of goods, eluding the Yankees at every turn. For her own part, her "old cook" first told her mistress to send all the other slaves away while the cook and her son hid the flour and valuables. The white mistress complied, but then the cook had a dream that the Yankees found everything. She dug up the valuables and hid them elsewhere. "Sure enough," the mistress told the reporter, the Yankees found the flour, "but her dream saved the rest."[68]

Perhaps inspired by the bicentennial, a Butts County, Georgia, paper published an article about long-standing harmony among blacks and whites, featuring a roster of "slaves fondly remembered." What made them worthy of being remembered: faithful service rendered. Thomas Hardwick was taken by Union soldiers but snuck away at night to return to his master. Uncle Ned tried to hide horses and mules. Arta Johnson hid the carriage and the family silver. Abraham Foster made the greatest of all the sacrifices. He had been able to earn enough money on his own to buy a gold-headed cane, a gold watch, and a violin, all of which a bummer tried to steal. Foster begged for them back and then managed to get the Yankee's gun away from him. He planned to kill the soldier and bury him beneath the floorboards, but thought better of it, ostensibly because he did not want to get his beloved mistress in trouble. So he lost his hard-earned possessions. The paternalism running through these stories is palpable, if not always explicit. The items that mattered and were worth saving in these white-told tales were those of white families. Black possessions were expendable.[69]

African Americans also saved whites' homes. Uncle Caesar, who belonged to General Gustavus Hedrick of Butts County, watched Union soldiers camp overnight on the plantation; steal the horses; butcher hogs, chickens, and geese; and burn the brick mill, cotton press, and slave cabins. But he acted only when the main house was threatened. As retold in 1976, "When Uncle Caesar saw that his master was much agitated over his house to which the Yankees had set fire, he fell down on his knees and despite the threats of the enemy, prayed loud and fervently that the house be spared. The fire was put out and the mansion saved." Like Abraham Foster, Uncle Caesar lost something of his own, while saving something of his master's.[70]

African Americans, at least those singled out in stories of faithful slaves, seemed to have no qualms about lying to Sherman's men in the service of their white masters and mistresses. One story, retold under the title "A Woman's Ingenuity," featured an enslaved woman who saved Confederate soldiers by running up the road in the opposite direction shouting, "Come back Marse Taylor and give up, those Yankees will kill you." The Yankees, as one would expect from this kind of anecdote, fell for the ruse, and the Confederates escaped.[71] One canny and trustworthy slave was entrusted with family valuables and kept them safe by joining up with Sherman's men for several days to avert suspicion. He then returned home with the white family's valuables intact.[72] In Wilkinson County, Georgia, Ben was caught by the Yankees but pretended to be someone else, so that he would not be forced to tell where his master had hidden valuables. Even more dramatically, Injun Jack Deese was taken by Union troops who wanted to know where his master, Joel Deese, was. The soldiers hung him by a rope over a tree limb, almost strangling him. Deese was finally saved when an officer forced the men to cut him down, but he never gave up his master.[73] One is left to wonder if the masters would have risked so much for their slaves.

Even after the March moved on, praise was heaped upon those (now former) slaves who helped whites survive the hardships and hunger that followed in its wake. "The loyal slaves helped to salvage enough to keep women and children from starving," proclaimed one history of Butts County, Georgia, which then went on: "Their attachment to their 'white folks' was so great that they preferred servitude to freedom."[74] Paternalistic ideas ran deeply through these narratives. The idea that blacks might have been acting in their own self-interest does not occur to these writers. A history of Jefferson County, Georgia, makes this point even more explicitly:

> The slaves, in turn, gave love and service to their white folks. This was demonstrated after Sherman's march to the sea, when but for these faithful servitors, many a child and the older ones, at the "big house," would have suffered more; for negroes have an uncanny way of finding things to eat, and they shared it all liberally with their mistress and her children, leaving their own family to get what was left.[75]

The idea that African Americans would have fed whites at the expense of their own families strains credulity. The image of white helplessness and inability to function in disaster is a sort of backhanded compliment, emphasizing the wealth and privilege of a population that never had to shift for itself before.

Only rarely would whites grant blacks independent agency in choosing to stay and help. The story of "Old York," who helped to run Walton's Mill in Georgia, is one of the few. York ran the mill independently, selling corn and meal. He saved it "by pleading with the soldiers, telling them that not only the white people but the negroes would have nothing to eat if the mill were burned." Not only did this credit York, but it implicitly credited the soldiers as well. They might not have been moved by the plight of starving whites, but helping former slaves was an action they could get behind.[76]

Ambivalent Liberators

For all that Sherman's March served as an agent of emancipation in Georgia, North Carolina, and South Carolina, for all that at least some of the soldiers thought of themselves as emancipators, their record is mixed at best.[77] One story that circulated after the war featured Sherman himself encountering an archetypal "old Negro woman . . . bending under the burden of a huge bundle which contained nearly all her earthly possessions." Sherman asked her where she was going, to which she replied "I's gwine whar you all's gwine," came the reply. The anecdote ends there, with the implication that Sherman was delighted by the reply.[78] That hardly seems likely, given what we know of his attitudes.

And the ambivalence started right at the top, with General William T. Sherman himself. From his earliest commands Sherman was unwilling to allow fugitive slaves into his lines, largely because he did not want to have to worry about feeding them or having them distract his men or slow his columns. As one biographer, Michael Fellman explained, "Sherman was at war with the master classes, but not for the benefit of their bondsmen and bondswomen." Or did he favor emancipation in the abstract, although he did accept its utility as a war measure and, perhaps more importantly, as a means to punish Confederates?[79] Not surprisingly, he was also resistant to including black soldiers in his army. As Sherman embarked on the Atlanta campaign he made his unwillingness explicit, in the form of Special Field Orders No. 16, in which he forbade the recruitment and enlistment of black freedmen. When pushed, he expressed willingness to use contrabands as laborers and teamsters, but he remained adamant about keeping black men out of his ranks, edging toward, if not over, the line of insubordination.[80] And if he did not want black soldiers in his army, and accepted black laborers only grudgingly, it only stands to reason that he would not want newly freed slaves—not just young able-bodied men, but older people, women, and children, to follow in his wake. Despite their hopes, Sherman was no friend to African Americans.[81]

Yet others reported that Sherman took "'especial pleasure' in informing escaped slaves that they were free."[82] One story has Sherman standing on a second floor balcony in Milledgeville, Georgia, addressing a crowd of newly freed African Americans, pleading with them to stay on their plantations rather than follow his army. That seems to follow with what we know of Sherman. But according to one version of the tale, "He told them: 'Stay on the plantations . . . for they will soon be yours!" That seems less like him, since he showed no special interest in upending the economic status quo of the South.[83] James Reston also used Sherman's memoirs to show him as a sort of benevolent paternalist, very much a creature of his own racist times. Even in the retrospective lens of his memoirs, Sherman saw blacks as, in Reston's phrase, "an amusing, poignant subrace. . . . He chortled at the Negro's 'simple' character and was amused by how they flocked to him shouting praises of 'de Lawd and Abrum Lincom.'"[84] But Reston's contemporary, traveler Jerry Ellis, tells a tale of a Sherman as less tolerant of free blacks. In this telling, Sherman slips out of Covington, Georgia, via a different route from his army's, in order to avoid freed slaves, because "he was tired of them grabbing and kissing his feet as they sang praises to the 'massah' for releasing them from bondage."[85] Whether willing or unwilling, Sherman became fundamentally identified with liberation, for the black neighborhood that sprang up in Atlanta on the land that had once been occupied by Union soldiers became known as "Shermantown."[86]

Major Henry O. Marcy displayed mixed emotions toward African Americans in his memoir of the Carolinas campaign. He seemed to relish being greeted as a liberator, describing African Americans as variously delighted and respectful when soldiers marched past. In Columbia he asked the African Americans crowding the streets if they feared Yankees and quoted them as replying "'Lors, no massa, we knowed yous coming. We's prayed de good Lord dis long time for yous, and we t'anks him dat Mister Sherman an' his company is here sure enuff.'"[87] Marcy's somewhat patronizing use of dialect obscures his larger point: whatever ills Sherman's marchers might bring, they were better than the alternative (he believed). In some places the arrival of Sherman's men took on the air of a religious revival, with prayers of thanks and jubilation.[88] Elsewhere in his account, Marcy noted the willingness of African Americans to pick up "at a moment's notice" and follow the Union soldiers. But to him it made sense. Home, Marcy reflected, was not a place of comfort and love but rather "a synonym of task, compulsion, tyranny and fear." Little wonder that they were willing to take their chances on the road. Marcy was open about the inability to allow women and children to "encumber and delay the trains," allowed that those left behind "were sadly disappointed, but showed their confidence and hope by being easily satisfied with the promise that *next* time we would take them too." As for the men, Marcy was happy to have them. He used African American men as guides and foragers, found them ever ready to tell where 'Massa' had hidden his horses, mules or provisions, and not infrequently suggested to the inquisitive soldiers which part of the yard was best to experiment upon with ramrod or sabre." He cited only one instance of a slave remaining true to his masters and claimed that he was still waiting for recompense from his devious owners.[89]

While Marcy seemed respectful of, if somewhat amused by, freed slaves, other Union men were not necessarily so kind. Black women were surely subjected to sexual assaults. African Americans were subjected to abuse at the hands of frustrated, out of control bummers. Prince Clark had been enslaved on the Jarrell Plantation in Jones County, Georgia, and was asked by soldiers where the meat was hidden. He told them it had been buried beneath mashings of sugarcane. The Yankees "became frustrated at the job when the first layer uncovered no prize and concluded that Prince was lying. So they strung him up by his thumbs, with his toes just reaching a nail, and left him to be cut down by his master."[90] This kind of cruelty was not unusual. A generally lighthearted reminiscence of a foraging trip undertaken by Wisconsin troops in South Carolina turned ugly when soldiers could not find any food or valuables. "About noon," one participant recalled laconically, "we saw a negro going across the land, and, in order to bring him in, shot at him." The terrified man initially claimed not to know where the hiding place was, "but we did not believe him and made him agree to show us." Eventually the man complied, though one is left to wonder how his agreement was secured.[91]

In a similar vein, an Iowa veteran related a "laughable incident" that took place at the very tail end of the March that well conveyed the casual meanness of many marchers. As the troops marched past a large plantation, African Americans lined up to watch, and celebrate. Then it turned ugly:

> One great stalwart darkey standing near the marching troops drew
> the attention of comrade Hague of our company, who slipped his
> bayonet on his gun, and when opposite the darkey made a lunge
> towards the Negro, and told him to howl. The darkey let out an
> unearthly yell and the troops in our rear as they came up, and seeing
> what the matter was would repeat the order to the darkey, and after
> marching a quarter of a mile we could still hear the darkey yelling,
> and I sometimes think he is yelling yet.[92]

More striking than the bayonet lunge is the humorous tone, the delight the soldiers took in terrorizing someone they were ostensibly fighting to free.

Even when not being sadistically cruel, Northern men were products of their time and place, and thus would have had no qualms about greeting blacks with racial epithets and airs of white supremacy. Slave cabins were easy to pillage: what little food and property (tobacco, money, personal items) African Americans had was out in the open and accessible to unscrupulous thieves. And African Americans resented Union soldiers for it.[93] Charles Hopkins exemplified some of this Union ambivalence. He expressed a sort of grudging admiration for the freedmen's "intense longing for freedom," and wondered how they were able to survive: "Their privations must have been very great, yet, patient and uncomplaining, they plodded on, one great hope, the hope of their race for two centuries, animating their hearts and lending strength to their weary limbs."[94]

Ebenezer Creek and Special Orders No. 15

On December 9 the XIV Corps, under the command Brigadier General Jefferson C. Davis (no relation to the Confederate president), was approaching Savannah and needed to cross Ebenezer Creek's deep, wide, and icy waters. The Union troops swiftly set up pontoon bridges and crossed, mindful that Confederate raiders were close behind. Several hundred former slaves, who were afraid of being captured by the Confederate troops, were told to wait to cross until all the soldiers and wagons were over. But, after the soldiers had crossed, they pulled up and dismantled the bridges, leaving the African Americans stranded, trapped between the frigid water and Confederates firing upon them. Colonel Charles D. Kerr of the 126th Illinois Cavalry witnessed the event, and wrote of the horror that ensued as, "with cries of anguish and despair, men, women, and children rushed by the hundreds into the turbid stream, and many were drowned before our eyes. From what we learned afterwards of those who remained upon the land, their fate at the hands of Wheeler's troopers was scarcely to be preferred."[95] Even as a soldier loyal to the Union, Kerr was unwilling to excuse what he witnessed: "It is claimed that this was done because rations were becoming scarce; in short, that it was a military necessity. There was no necessity about it. Not only the dictates of humanity, but the call of duty as well, demanded that we should afford these helpless creatures the protection within our power. . . . It was unjustifiable and perfidious."[96] Kerr's anger was not matched by Sherman, however. While men throughout the ranks expressed outrage, Sherman defended Davis's actions as unavoidable and militarily necessary.

The evidence indicates that Brigadier General Davis planned to rid himself of his African American followers several days before the event. In no way could the deaths be excused as the product of a quick decision. How many African Americans were left behind is unknown, but estimates are about five thousand, made up primarily of old men, women, and children (able-bodied men were working for the Union army and would have already crossed).

Sherman was not present at Ebenezer Creek, and no one has claimed that he explicitly ordered Davis to take such cruel measures. In fact, at the time he was engaged in his own skirting of the laws of war, forcing Confederate prisoners to clear a minefield. How responsible was Sherman? He never

This peaceful scene of Union soldiers helping African American refugees across a stream belied the awful reality of the incident at Ebenezer Creek. (Picture Collection, New York Public Library, Astor, Lenox, and Tilden Foundations)

condemned, and indeed defended Davis. He seems to have regarded this as a necessary cruelty of war.[97]

Its not even possible to know how many people drowned at Ebenezer Creek, how many were captured by Wheeler's Confederate troops, and how many escaped. Modern stories clam that the bodies filled the creek, creating a "macabre dam" and that on cold, dark nights you can still hear the ghostly cries.[98]

Some good did come indirectly out of the atrocity at Ebenezer Creek. The outrage it engendered brought Stanton to Savannah, and Stanton in turn forced Sherman to meet with twenty freedmen in Savannah. These men were all ministers, some freeborn, some recently emancipated, and they told Sherman that they wanted opportunities for landownership and self-employment.[99] From that meeting came Special Field Orders No. 15, which most famously set aside 400,000 acres of abandoned lands in coastal South Carolina and Georgia for the settlement of newly freed blacks. Each family, headed by a "respectable" negro was entitled to a plot of up to forty acres. The order, which also included provisions for men to work for the army, applied to more than forty thousand former slaves.[100] It was, in the words of one Sherman biographer "beyond emancipation itself, the single most revolutionary act in race relations during the Civil War."[101]

Did Sherman suddenly have a change of heart and become the great liberator that he was imagined to be? No. It was a purely utilitarian exercise, one that in fact solved several of Sherman's problems. First, it got Stanton off his back.[102] Second, it solved the problem of the trailing freedmen. Now Sherman could leave them behind. Third, the presence of all of these freedmen served as a coastal buffer. The special area extended thirty miles inland, and thus Sherman would not need to worry about leaving many troops behind (some did remain under General Saxton's control). Certainly, Sherman did not care enough about the order to protect it or fight for it once Andrew Johnson repealed it in 1866. Indeed, given his rather generous feelings toward white Southerners after the war, it seems likely that land redistribution was quite far down on his priorities list.[103]

African Americans remembered though, and they resented losing the land that had been promised to them. When Union veteran Russell Conwell visited Beaufort in 1869, he found blacks angry.[104] Ultimately the importance of Special Field Orders No. 15 was more symbolic than real. The promise of land, wrote one historian "probably did much to stem, for a while, the growing disillusionment among these blacks, and eventually it became incorporated into their folklore although in actuality it remained but a promise and a dream."[105]

For the remainder of the nineteenth and into the early twentieth century, African Americans tried to hold on to a narrative of the Civil War that emphasized emancipation. The process of recapturing and retelling the stories of Sherman's March was less important to leaders like Frederick Douglass than attempting to stem the rising tide of Lost Cause sentiments.[106] African Americans continued to celebrate Emancipation Day, and to celebrate those men who served in the United States Colored Troops and other black regiments (none of whom participated in the March).[107] The rise of the Negro Education Movement during the early twentieth century, which emphasized the study and teaching of African American history, deemphasized the military aspects of the Civil War in favor of scholarship on slavery and Reconstruction.[108] Not until the 1950s and 1960s, when the civil rights movement intensified at the same time as the Civil War Centennial began, did African Americans focus their attention on the commemoration of the war itself.

To Burn Jim Crow to the Ground

Congress and President Dwight D. Eisenhower set up the National Civil War Centennial Commission in 1957. From the start it was dominated by traditional interpretations of the war, often with a Lost Cause bent, and African Americans felt shut out from official commemorations, festivals, and re-enactments. Even after President John F. Kennedy accepted the resignation of the original chairman, businessman Karl Betts, and appointed well-known historian Allan Nevins in his stead, the official observances still emphasized unity and sectional harmony. In 1962, the Reverend Martin Luther King Jr. (acting in his capacity as leader of the Southern Christian Leadership Conference) appealed to President Kennedy to commemorate the Preliminary Emancipation Proclamation with an executive order prohibiting segregation. Kennedy, loathe to alienate Southern white Democrats, did not. In fact, he did not attend the commemoration at the Lincoln memorial at all, sending a filmed message while he attended America's Cup yacht races.[109]

Against this backdrop, during the summer of 1963, John Lewis, the recently elected chairman of the Student Non-Violent Coordinating Committee (SNCC), found himself writing the most important speech of his life. He would be speaking, along with a handful of other civil rights leaders, from the steps of the Lincoln Memorial as part of the March on Washington for Jobs and Freedom. Lewis wanted his speech to show the students' frustration at the slow pace of change, to show anger, even militancy. As he recalled in his autobiography, "I wanted this march to have some sting, and if the only place for that sting would be in my speech, then I needed to make sure my words were especially strong." The speech needed to show that the civil rights movement represented a revolution in the South, and Lewis hoped to find a powerful analogy to convey that meaning. Eventually someone came up with the idea of Sherman's March, of portraying the students as an army—albeit a nonviolent one—bringing the destruction of segregation in its wake.[110]

Lewis saved Sherman for the final paragraph of his speech, adding to an already searing indictment of white racism and dilatory tactics. He warned his listeners:

> The time will come when we will not confine our marching to Washington. We will march through the South, through the heart of Dixie, the way Sherman did. We shall pursue our own "scorched earth" policy and burn Jim Crow to the ground-nonviolently. We shall fragment the South into a thousand pieces and put them back together in the image of democracy. We will make the action of the past few months look petty. And I say to you, WAKE UP AMERICA!

Initial requests for Lewis to change his speech made by Bayard Rustin and Washington, D.C.'s Archbishop Patrick O'Boyle dealt with other sections and language. Lewis reluctantly and unhappily, even angrily made changes. On August 27 as the program began, the Sherman section was still in the speech, but a small group gathered literally in the shadow of the Lincoln statue asked for further changes. Dr. Martin Luther King Jr. was "surprised" by the Sherman section, gently telling Lewis that it didn't sound like him. But Lewis maintained that it sounded like SNCC.[111]

As the program continued, the battle over the speech continued along with it. At last A. Philip Randolph, the driving force behind the March on Washington, appealed to Lewis to tone down the language, and Lewis felt he couldn't say no. James Forman quickly typed out the changes on a portable typewriter in the security office within the Memorial. Among the changes was the removal of the Sherman language. Ninety-nine years after the March, the analogy was still too raw, too incendiary.[112]

CHAPTER FOUR

Brave Bummers of the West

The 1868 children's story "'Bummers' in Sherman's Army" is a typical tale of Sherman's March. Written in the second person, the story takes readers along an expedition with a "motley" band of foragers. The soldiers were "rough and ragged from their long campaign; some in blue uniforms, some in rebel gray, and others in ministerial black broadcloth, with, perchance, a woman's hat, in place of Uncle Sam's somber 'tar bucket.'" Their mounts were equally disheveled—a mixture of young colts and broken-down nags, with few proper saddles or reins. The narrator then, under the guise of warning Southerners, lays out an indictment of the bummers' behavior that seems straight from the land of Lost Cause stereotypes:

> You must look well to your jewelry and watches, for bummers are
> none too scrupulous when gold is visible. Ostensibly, they seek
> eatables; but every thing that suits the eye is just as likely to be taken,
> whether of any possible use to a soldier or not. They will take—just as
> a spoiled child would with its playthings—every thing, and perchance
> they will, by strange caprice, take nothing. I have seen a bummer
> carry for two miles a huge eight-day clock, because it had a cuckoo
> in it which he wanted to show his 'partner' or chum, and then throw
> it away. At the very next house he will work for an hour helping the
> inmates save their property, which again he will regret, so far as to
> steal a silk dress at the next house.[1]

Stolen jewelry, ruined heirlooms, destruction for its own sake, unpredictability—all of these are elements of the bummer story. So too were their assaults on Southern larders:

> As for eatables, they may be considered as doomed, if the bummers
> get into the premises, for you can not say what, or how much will be
> taken—from the cattle running at grass in the pasture, to the meal in
> the sack, in the corner of the store-room. Your chickens and turkeys

had best be at once entered on the debit side of the profit and loss account, for their innocent bones will be picked by many a hungry Yankee, this night, if the bummers come. A few choice hens you may save, by hiding them in a barrel with a false lid, covered with seed-corn. A few pieces of select meat from the smoke-house may also be saved, perhaps by hiding them between the mattresses of your bed. But, with this, as well as other moveable property, you can say that nothing is certainly your own.[2]

The story's perspective then shifts, as the narrator describes a Union visit through the eyes of a Southern woman. Her sense of violation seems clear, as her home is ransacked, with trunks and drawers emptied, and beds tossed in the search for food and valuables. Ribbons are torn, hats are taken. Chicken and pigs are slaughtered, the dog is shot (on suspicion of being a slave-tracking dog), the hidden horses are found and stolen. The men are portrayed as filthy and smelly, though not entirely heartless: one "tries to re-assure you by protesting that 'Yankees never hurt anybody—you need not be afraid—they only want chickens and sweet potatoes to keep them alive' (you wish the potatoes would stick in their throats), and he closes by asking you to sing some rebel songs." The reader, in the persona of the Southern woman is astounded by "the cool impudence of this thieving before your eyes, as if it were done every day."[3] And the bummers seem to be having a wonderful time. The illustrations, though relatively crude, show the wild-haired Union men smiling and singing, taking great pleasure in their destructive impulses. They have no apparent qualms about their rampage and instead are the picture of contented savagery.

Were this a story published in the *Southern Illustrated News* or the *Atlanta Constitution*, we would hardly be surprised. This would be a standard story of white Southern victimization at the hands of rapacious Yankees, perhaps used to spur on resistance to Radical Reconstruction. But it was not. Rather, "'Bummers' in Sherman's Army" was the first story to appear in the first issue of *The Soldiers' and Sailors' Half-Dime Tales of the Late Rebellion*. Children who received copies would have been delighted by its lurid cover (featuring a soldier on crutches shaking hands with a one-armed sailor) and its vivid tales of heroism and adventure. The magazine was designed to raise funds for Union soldiers' widows and children and, as such, painted a picture of Federal troops as brave and honorable, worthy of emulation. While at first the Bummer story might seem an aberration, it took a more serious turn in its later pages.

Raucous carousing by Sherman's troops was illustrated in the story "Bummers in Sherman's Army." The grizzled, hard-drinking men are enjoying themselves at the expense of a Southern white woman, and appear unabashed. (Soldiers' and Sailors' Half-Dime Tales of the Late Rebellion *1, no. 1 [1868]: 8*)

The jaunty foragers come across a deserted farmhouse and find two dead Union soldiers, shot only hours before. Now the burnings are based in grim vengeance, not wanton pleasure. Indeed, the unnamed bummers place the blame for this squarely at the feet of the Confederates, explaining that while in South Carolina "Wade Hampton, the cavalryman, took it into his head that it was not proper for us to eat our daily bread at the expense of the people who were fighting against us. Accordingly he issued his fiat that all United States soldiers found foraging should die. After this, we used to find daily, dead bodies of our soldiers, labeled, 'Death to foragers!' These were buried by our army, their only epitaph being, 'Murdered.'"[4] Only "prompt and rigid retaliation, man for man," stopped the killings. Essentially, the bummers are justifying their actions in two ways: first, that it was within their rights to seize food (and presumably property) from enemies and, second, that violence could be met only with violence. The story closes with the bummers relaxing around a campfire, unapologetically enjoying the fruits of their foraging.[5]

This openness about what would in other circumstances be considered crimes is quite characteristic of postwar writings by Sherman's soldiers. While we might expect them to have been embarrassed or chagrined by their wartime excesses, they were not. Nor did they use memoirs or fiction to pour out their hearts and souls, expressing shock or trauma at what they saw or did. Today we are accustomed to stock war stories with their mix of crusty old generals, fresh-faced young recruits, and eventually the traumatized veteran, forever haunted by the things he saw and did. Think, for example of Philip Caputo wracked with guilt over his actions as a young Marine lieutenant in Vietnam, or the World War II soldiers described by Paul Fussell in his influential book *Wartime*.[6] Recently, we've seen the twenty-first-century version, with a host of new memoirs of Gulf War service. In April 2008, a Rand Corporation study announced that one in five service members who served in Iraq or Afghanistan reports symptoms of post-traumatic stress disorder or major depression.[7] We think that soldiers are forever scarred by their service, especially when they are asked to make war on civilians.

But what of their nineteenth-century counterparts? Analogies have often been made, albeit imperfectly, between the Vietnam War and Sherman's March. James Reston's 1986 work, *Sherman's March and Vietnam* makes the connection most explicitly, arguing that Sherman was the metaphorical father of destructiveness and that connections can be drawn between the soldiers of the 1860s and 1960s. In Reston's words, "the wanton violence of Sherman's bummer and Westmoreland's grunt differs as looting differs from killing, but neither time nor morals are static. Stealing the jewels from a peasant's hooch in Vietnam would be precious little crime today. The patterns of behavior in both armies were encouraged by the official policy and extended the rules of permissible conflict in the same degree."[8] So, if Vietnam (and now Gulf and Afghanistan) veterans have been troubled by their service, and indeed, the vast majority of their writings seems to indicate that they were, one might be able to assume that Sherman's veterans felt a similar sort of, if not remorse, at least discomfort.[9]

Except they were not. Overwhelmingly, those veterans who reflected on their time marching through Georgia and the Carolinas did so in a light or celebratory fashion, more like the bummers story than *Jarhead* or *Platoon*.[10] They recalled the March as a picnic, a lark, a time of good food and short marches, not searing flames and frightened women. Rather than facing bullets and artillery, they collected jewelry and silver. And, to top it off, they firmly believed that they had won the war. In this, their writings echoed observations made in letters and diaries during the March itself. As they reminisced about their time in Georgia and the Carolinas, they took the term "bummer," once vaguely pejorative as a badge of honor and service. This chapter explores veterans' memories of the March, showing the ways that they expressed pride and suggesting that this pride perhaps complicates our understanding of the place of Sherman's March in American cultural memory.

Throughout the nineteenth century, as the Lost Cause took root and came to define most Americans' memories of the war, Sherman's veterans actively pushed back, crafting their own story of the March. They did this in a variety of public forums—newspapers, magazines, and especially through speeches and papers given before organizations like the Military Order of the Loyal Legion of the United States (MOLLUS) and the Society of the Army of the Tennessee. They were active participants in the broader culture of nineteenth-century veterans. Even speeches given privately were often republished and distributed as pamphlets. They were engaged in a self-conscious work of memory creation. And they did this, not in the interests of securing political power (à la the Grand Army of the Republic) or crafting a purely sentimental reunion tale. Instead they sought to secure their place in history and to make sure that their version of the March dominated. We shall see if they succeeded in their efforts.[11]

That Kindly, Cordial, and Social Feeling

The Society of the Army of the Tennessee predated its much better-known sibling, the Grand Army of the Republic (GAR). In fact, it predated the end of the Civil War itself. The society was founded on April 14, 1865, while Sherman and his men were still on the march in Raleigh, North Carolina (almost two weeks before Joe Johnston's surrender), by a group of officers, in order to "perpetuate the history of the army and to 'keep alive that kindly, cordial and social feeling which was one of its characteristics during the war, and which gave it such harmony as contributed in no small degree to its glorious achievements in the country's cause.'"[12] Its membership remained limited to former officers, although men of any rank could and did attend the reunions, and at the same time most of the society's members were also members of their local GAR posts. They gravitated toward the society because of its vision of their army as close-knit and free from infighting, a sort of divisional chauvinism. As planned, the society held its first meeting in 1866, under the direction of General John A. Rawlins, who was president until his death in 1869. After Rawlins died, Sherman was chosen as president, a position he held until his death in 1891. Much of the society's efforts were devoted to raising money for two statues in Washington, D.C., one of General James B. McPherson and the other of Sherman.[13]

The society's annual reunions, held for at least forty years, tended to follow set scripts and patterns. They were usually held in Midwestern cities: Cincinnati, Cleveland, Chicago, and St. Louis were particular favorites. They included various orations and committee meetings, parades and excursions, and always featured an elaborate banquet, followed by speeches, songs, and a dozen or more toasts long into the night. Sherman often gave the keynote speech, but sometimes other generals were given the honor. Taken together, the reunions served to celebrate and glorify the men's wartime experiences especially, although not exclusively, their time on the March.

The 1868 Reunion, held in Chicago, Illinois, can stand in for many others. It took place in a lavishly decorated hall, the highlight of which was a larger than life painting of "the Bummer . . . including his mule, and engaged in his favorite profession."[14] Fifteen years later, the décor included "a festooning of flags and wreaths, encircling a painted scene representing a squad of foragers returning to camp from one of their expeditions."[15] It is hard to imagine a similar scene glorifying foraging and destruction in the twentieth century, and it exemplifies the degree to which the veterans felt comfortable with their past.

The festooned halls would ring with music and laughter as well. As the members dined on oysters and sweetbreads, tenderloin and quail, all washed down with wine, sherry, and champagne, they were entertained by a range of speakers and singers. Various banquets featured songs like "Marching through Georgia," "Tramp, Tramp, Tramp," "Sherman's March to the Sea," and "We Are Coming, Father Abraham," often keyed to the program of toasts (which were essentially short speeches). The toasts ranged in topic from praise for the current president, to the army, and navy, the patriotic women of the Union, and of course, the war dead and the volunteers themselves.[16] Sometimes the toasts were even more specific. In 1875 the hall filled with cheers for "The March to the Sea! Happy in its conception; fortunate in its leader; glorious in its results." In 1871 the banquet featured a round of toasts from the floor, which included both "the Bummers of the Army of the Tennessee" and "Sherman's Bummers." These prompted laughing reminiscences of the bummers' skill at seizing supplies, concluding with the old chestnut that "the only thing they couldn't carry off was a branch railroad that wasn't down on the chart."[17]

The speeches and responses were often lighthearted, filled with jokes and anecdotes and a sort of gentle romance. In 1869, General Noyes recalled that

> in this rollicking picnic expedition there was just enough of fighting for variety, enough of hardship to give zest to the repose which followed it, and enough of ludicrous adventure to make its memory a constant source of gratification. I have no doubt that "Sherman's bummers" will be an important figure in fourth of July celebrations for a hundred years to come; that boys will shout and old men cheer as the counterfeit soldiery come to the ground laden with chickens and honey, molasses and hams, flour and potatoes, pigs and confectionary, and an occasional flagon of wine, carefully concealed from the commanding officer.[18]

Other speeches echoed this sort of nostalgia, which seems to hearken back to a simpler time. In an 1883 response to the toast "the Memories of the War," General John W. Fuller waxed poetic for several pages about the "most charming [days] of our soldier life." His idealized days were sunny and beautiful, with the men first zestily twisting railroad tracks into corkscrews and serpents, then freeing slaves along their path. (Just as an aside, Fuller was one of the few speakers to discuss African Americans at all, though he did so in rather patronizing ways.)[19] Fuller's days on the March ended idyllically as well, with the men singing around campfires and strolling around with pipes.[20] It sounds wonderful. There is not an iota of remorse or regret contained within these speeches. Of course, this is one of the functions of these reunions, to create a space where these men could safely tell their stories, to perhaps express feelings they could not in "polite society" at home.

One could easily continue on with other examples in this vein, jokes about hogs and sweet potatoes, further tales of "ludicrous adventure." But to do so would be to miss out on the other theme running through these reunion speeches: a deep-seated sense of moral righteousness and purpose. The flip side to the fun and frolic was a serious defense of the March and a window into veterans' attempts to define the meaning of the war and their participation in it. In particular they were keenly aware of the emerging Lost Cause and actively sought to counter it. Once again, Sherman set the tone. In his 1867 speech, he turned from past to present and wondered

> how any Southern gentleman, with these facts plain and palpable everywhere staring him in the face, and recorded forever in the book of history, can still boast of his "lost cause" or speak of it in language other than that of shame and sorrow, passes my understanding;
> and instead of being revived, I know that their lost cause will sink deeper and deeper into infamy as time more keenly probes its hidden mysteries, and reveals them to the light of day.

His remarks were greeted with loud applause, showing that the contest over the memory of the war was well underway.[21]

Nor was Sherman just preaching to the choir with this assertion. His speech was reprinted in its entirety (three full columns) in the *New York Times*, and one could easily assume in other newspapers as well.[22] Indeed, the *Times* regularly covered the activities of the society, announcing the reunions and printing excerpts from speeches and toasts. So the speakers were surely aware that they had multiple audiences, and while the jokes might be for the live one, the defenses of the March were for the broader nation.

What sometimes resulted from this was a strange hybrid of celebration and justification. Thus, in 1868 General Cogswell unabashedly recalled his (and his men's) "delightful and unmolested trip" across Georgia and went so far as to list the amounts of food and supplies taken by one of the thirty-five brigades in the army. Proudly he proclaimed that Sherman's men took more than twice what they needed and concluded that he "thank[ed] God [he] was permitted to take part in such great events." Yet after this jovial litany of destruction, Cogswell abruptly shifted gears and maintained that he had "no feelings of exultation or boasting." With the utmost seriousness, he outlined his solemn belief that "all the acts done, by orders, on those two marches were just and necessary, and that by reason of them, full as much as by anything, the war was ended, the shedding of fraternal blood was stopped, and the deluded people of the South made readier to accept the issue of the contest." Essentially, Cogswell was making the argument that the March was right, proper, and ended the war.[23]

Other speakers over the years made similar claims. In 1888, General M. D. Leggett praised that Army of the Tennessee's foragers, recalling that he never needed to break into his wagonloads of rations. He joked about catching hogs and reminded his listeners that Sherman's men made a practice of shooting mules that could no longer be used (so that Southerners could not nurse them back to health). But he felt no shame or remorse about leaving "not enough . . . to keep a rat alive" in his wake. Rather, he explained, "I have often thought that was the correct mode of warfare. It was a mode of warfare that would be felt in the future. General Sherman . . . said there was no mercy in war. He was correct in that. The more terrible war can be made, the sooner it is brought to an end. We all understand that."[24]

Sherman's Bummers

According to the *Oxford English Dictionary*, the word "bummer" first appeared in print in an 1855 edition of the *Portland Oregonian*, meaning an idler, loafer, or lounger, and appears to have derived from the German word *bummler*.[25] This meaning held for the early years of the war, with "bummer" being an epithet hurled at thieving stragglers, and a distinction was often drawn between bummers and legitimate, organized foragers. Historian Joseph Glatthaar has argued that eastern and western troops had different definitions of the term, with the easterners emphasizing the unauthorized or "self-appointed." Bummers were generally cast as somewhat lazy and undisciplined but gifted in their foraging skills, and certainly willing to work when properly motivated.[26] In a regular campaign, only a small proportion of the men would have been designated as foragers, and that was the basic idea in Sherman's March as well. What complicates this was the expansiveness of Sherman's orders, directing the army to "forage liberally on the country during the march," and empowering commanders to destroy buildings and take livestock. While the foraging was supposed to be done by "regular foraging-parties," encamped soldiers were also "permitted to gather turnips, potatoes, and other vegetables, and to drive in stock in sight of their camp." The result was an army of foragers, and a shift in the meaning of "bummer."[27]

Essentially, Sherman's men took the title "bummer" on as a point of personal pride. Many postwar reminiscences took pains to legitimate the foragers, minimizing their excesses with a sort of "boys will be boys" tone. One example of this came in General Horace Porter's eulogy for Sherman, published in *Harper's*. Porter described the bummers as "a novel feature of Sherman's command . . . organized for a very useful purpose from the adventurous spirits which are always found in the ranks." In Porter's definition, the bummers served more like scouts and were "a regular institution."[28] One member of the 116th Illinois, who fondly recalled his days along the March, quoted extensively from Sherman's orders in order to claim that the bummers were a "necessity." While he concedes that these "devil-may-care fellows" might have overstepped their bounds at times, they were isolated instances of disobedience, followed by punishment. Most foraging operations, he assured his readers, "were marked by a rigid adherence to the restrictions laid down in orders."[29]

One of the greatest defenders of the bummers was Charles Belknap, who had initially enlisted in the 21st Michigan as a sixteen year old. In his "Recollections of a Bummer," Belknap (who as a young captain led a ninety-man foraging detail) first claims that he had never heard the term until they were outside of Savannah, "and then as a 'Boomer,' from the almost constant booming" of the guns attacking the city.[30] This explanation strains credulity, if for no other reason than Belknap was contradicting himself. In his "What a Bummer Knows of Bentonville," delivered five years earlier, Belknap carefully, though humorously, defined his terms. He acknowledged that many people (almost thirty years after the war) recalled the bummers as disgraceful tramps. But to Belknap:

> Bummer was a title born to Sherman's army on the march to the sea.
> In the scramble for corn and bacon its pedigree was lost, and he who
> seeks to claim it now is liable to receive a bad title. However, the
> Bummer in his degree of rank commandeered all the corn-cribs and
> fodder-stacks in Georgia and the Carolinas. He made of his profession
> high art, and high art is always morality.

We can imagine Belknap's audience of fellow veterans at the Washington, D.C., MOLLUS commandery meeting breaking into gales of laughter at this. But Belknap did have a more serious defense to follow, explaining that "the variety of work and duties called the best men from the ranks—men of known endurance and courage. Strict discipline was maintained and there were no stragglers."[31]

Although the March was largely unopposed by Confederate soldiers, the Union men still needed basic structures and protections. Thus, the officially detailed foragers (as opposed to the more rough-and-tumble Bummers) also served as military scouts, often a day or two out ahead of the main column. This was the most dangerous position, for they did sometimes skirmish with Home Guards or Wheeler's cavalry, and risked occasional capture.[32] Charles Belknap told of eleven Union men being captured, "and all shot, their bodies being placed in a row by the roadside, that all passing that way might see them and take warning."[33] One might conclude it was rather effective, but the display might also have backfired, leading to greater anger and vengeance on the part of the Yankees. Nevertheless, the foragers did manage to insulate the main columns with, as one veteran put it "a wide-spread cloud of skirmishers, which the enemy could not push through." No less an opponent than Joe Johnston supposedly praised the foragers after the war, calling them "the most efficient cavalry ever known." More significantly, Johnston also praised the men for their discipline, given that they spent so much time away from their commanders, yet always returned.[34] Too, at least the official foraging details, like the one of ninety men led by Charles Belknap, provided some valuable local intelligence, for Belknap recalled collecting "letters from the few post-offices in the country, maps hanging on the walls of village and country homes, newspapers old and new" and forwarding them all on to headquarters.[35]

Belknap and his fellow bummers constantly sought to strike a balance in their stories of the March. The overarching story that they told was of the March as, in Lt. Marcus Bates's words, "a delightful memory to every one privileged to have had a part in it." Bates nostalgically recalled living on "the fat of the land, the milk and honey of the confederacy," with little thought for the original producers of that milk and honey.[36] But at the same time, as they tried to paint the March as a party or a harmless lark, they realized that it was more than that, that when viewed from the perspective of Southern civilians, the March was no fun at all, and in fact was horrifying and destructive. One way to reconcile those two views was to claim that foraging was justifiable, and legitimate. General Adam Badeau did just this in his children's story "The March to the Sea." He began by reminding his young readers "that soldiers must eat" and that they needed to eat before they could fight. Once that was out of the way, Badeau explained that men were ordered to "forage liberally" and that they were able to load themselves down so bounteously because this part of the country had been untouched by war. Even Badeau must have realized how feeble his argument was when it came to household goods like furniture and clothing, for he ultimately threw up his hands and conceded that "war is often only organized robbery." In the end, though, Badeau could not condemn the March and marchers, finally concluding that "the romantic character of the march is unsurpassed."[37]

Not surprisingly soldiers minimized the thefts of personal property. Occasionally items were returned in the years after the war, sometimes with great fanfare, sometimes quietly and anonymously. Stories circulated of Southerners recognizing family heirlooms on Northern wrists and fingers, and of soldiers showing off "vases and trinkets which they 'picked up when they were in the army.'"[38]

When veterans remembered the March, they too emphasized its romantic character, easy pace, and lighthearted tenor. These men were hardened

A bummer returns to camp, laden with stolen food and property.
(Soldiers' and Sailors' Half-Dime Tales of the Late Rebellion *1, no. 1 [1868]: 16*)

fighters who had marched long and fought hard for up to three years, and they quickly realized that this expedition would be different. Colonel Charles D. Kerr recalled that "the brilliancy of the move lay alone in its conception. Its execution was simple and easy as a pleasure trip." He described the men's unshakeable faith and confidence in Sherman and their belief that they were embarking on a grand adventure. His delight leaps off the page as he remembered that, marching out of Atlanta, "the men were cheering and singing patriotic songs, and fairly reveling in the excitement and novelty of the situation."[39] In an 1890 speech, General Henry Slocum, who commanded the left wing of the army, called the March "one great picnic from beginning to end" and regaled his listeners with stories of marching bands and dancing by firelight, with "just enough fighting and danger of fighting to give zest to the experience."[40] Charles Hopkins, of the 13th New Jersey, thought that the combination of high spirits, good weather, and abundant food turned the March into "one continual pleasure trip."[41] William Duncan described the combination of "good roads, pleasant weather, and practically no enemy," along with plenty to eat, as "a picnic every day" as they marched toward Savannah.[42]

Part of pride in the March came in the form of pride in one's foraging skills, and as veterans reminisced, they often provided primers. In his MOLLUS lecture, "Marching across Carolina," Manning Force, a brevet and brigadier general who commanded the 3rd Division of the XVII Corps, described the foragers as performing "a service without which the army could not have advanced." On the fifty-four-day march from Pocotaligo, South Carolina, to Goldsboro, North Carolina, Force's men were given ten days' rations before setting out, which translated into only three days of "hard bread" (hardtack) and some coffee and sugar. If they wanted more to eat, they were expected to procure it themselves. Indeed, those were the only supplies available, for Force's supply wagons contained only twenty-five days' worth of hard bread and thirty days' of coffee. He carried no meat, and had only a few head of cattle, for Force preferred "trusting to the country for meat."[43] Charles Kerr echoed Force when he explained that there was no centralized system for the distribution of supplies. Rather, "so far as supplies were concerned, each regiment was a law unto itself." Each regiment had its own wagon onto which its supplies would be loaded and taken to camp.[44]

Most veterans' reminiscences dealt largely with the army's movements or its occasional skirmishes with Confederates. These men might describe foraging, or they might not. But a few veterans took bumming or foraging as their main topic. Major Samuel Mahon was one of those who did, describing the process (at least as it functioned in the Carolinas) to the Iowa MOLLUS commandery in 1896. He stressed that there was some organization to the system, if for no other reason than to make sure that there was no interference or overlap among the foragers. Before finding food, the foragers had to find their own transportation, and thus they wound up on a motley assortment of animals, "from the humble donkey to the thoroughbred pet of the plantation and perhaps a zebra or two occasionally." Their tack varied similarly, from "rope halter and corn sack saddle" to gilt mounted bridles and family carriages, even the occasional lady's sidesaddle. A forager, Mahon declared, faced danger and excitement and needed to excel at "woodcraft," finding his way without roads, outriding enemies, and simply enduring long hours in the saddle.[45]

Once the men found a farm or plantation, according to Mahon, the real work would begin. Cattle were the preferred livestock, for they could be managed and driven back to the main column, whereas swine were far less compliant. The men would be pleased to find mules, but often had to repair the harnesses before they could be led away. "Flour, bacon, potatoes, corn meal, sorghum, poultry, rice etc. had to be loaded into vehicles, carts, plantation wagons, and even carriages before being impressed. . . . Often the concealed supplies of the plantation had to be discovered before being taken, but the negroes were our allies here, as well as on every other occasion, and the supplies were soon found and exhumed from the pits where they had been consigned and carefully covered up from sight."[46]

The best foragers were like First Lieutenant Richard Kennedy of the 13th Iowa, praised by his fellow soldiers for his audacity. In addition to having an eye for sweet potatoes and horses, he claimed to have the best mules around. Kennedy and his teamster, Julius T. Chaffee, "could take a southern mule from a canebrake, and with a pair of sheep-shears transpose him to a government mule with the U.S. branded in five minutes so that his owner would not know him."[47] Charles Hopkins also proved a deft hand with livestock, skillfully butchering a flock of sheep, though he claimed that as a regular forager he was outclassed by the less-regimented bummers, who "would probably have hunted up the owner of them . . . and have served a requisition on him for a wagon or two. If he had no farm wagon, a family coach, gig, or buggy would do." Indeed, Hopkins pointed out that even though Southerners might hide their horses and mules, if they left the wagons behind, the foragers would know to search for the stock.[48]

Just as Sherman's veterans painted portraits of the March as a picnic or a lark, so too did they use humor and exaggeration when describing their fellow soldiers. Henry Marcy stated it most simply: "There is a comic side to many of the stories of these adventurers."[49] By describing the soldiers as "adventurers," Marcy and his fellow veterans created an image of the bummer fully at odds with his Southern portrayal. Rather than a terrorizer or a thief, these bummers were rogues with raffish charms. In his piece "The Army Bummer and Good Night," Captain Joseph G. Waters paid laughing homage to the bummer's "boundless per capita of utility and gall," while declaring that "he was a larger book of strategy than De Jomini ever wrote, and beyond doubt he was the only personage of whom William Tecumseh Sherman ever had cause to be envious or afraid." While there is little evidence of Sherman fearing any of his men, Waters continued in his hyperbolic vein, declaring that the Bummers could have taken Jerusalem with the Crusaders (while sporting "the hen lyant or the razor back rampant") or helped King Arthur against the French. These "American Knights" lifted the spirits of the despairing North as they made their way across Georgia and the Carolinas.[50]

Joseph Waters and many of those who lauded the bummers singled out their appetites, for both food and liquor. Waters called his bummer "an Octopus of Abdomen, whose tentacles reached every hen roost and pig sty," and one who jousted with swine and mutton, while Charles Belknap recalled "many a gallant fight . . . made for hogs and hominy."[51] Henry Marcy characterized the bummers' "gastronomic propensities" as "simply enormous; chickens, turkeys and pigs, honey, butter and eggs, sweetmeats, preserves and wines all found their way to stomachs as ignorant of dyspepsia as the consciences of their owners to confession." That is, the men felt no shame about their enormous appetites, no remorse for devouring Southern foodstuffs.[52]

These conquests of comestibles were often accompanied by all sorts of other pilfering, most of which was described with winks and nods, and a sort of boys-will-be-boys attitude. That is, time and again, Sherman's bummers were praised for what would under other circumstances be regarded as simple theft. Thus, Charles Hopkins provided listeners with a tongue-in-cheek discussion of the "professors of foraging," who returned with "contributions" from a "kind and generous planter." The veterans' accounts seem to contain a sort of progression of taking: first food, which was clearly justifiable; then wagons and carriages to carry the food; and, finally, in Hopkins's words, "anything that would contribute to the general frolic."[53] Stories abound of men riding into camp with carriages full of bacon, or feather beds thrown across the backs of mules.[54] One 1866 account of the March condemned the bummers for plundering and destroying personal property but ultimately undermined its argument by conceding that "some of the foraging stories are, however, full of humor, and could hardly be otherwise regarded than as excellent jokes, even by the sufferers themselves."[55]

The degree to which white Southerners might laugh at these stories is debatable, but we can certainly envision veterans' audiences chuckling at some of the images with which they were presented. In particular, the bummers were often described as having put together outlandish costumes, adding to the frolicsome spirit. One observer described the bummers and their mounts as having been "bedecked in the most independent, unmilitary, Don Quixote style imaginable." These mixtures of old-fashioned coats and enormous hats, the author assured, reflected not "distaste for the uniform he wore, but a strange longing for citizen's dress."[56] It seems unlikely that the soldiers really longed for civilian clothes, given the crazy ensembles they put together. Rather, they seem more like boys playing dress-up, adding further insult to Southern whites by disrespecting even their attire. The stories call to mind the tradition of *charivari*,[57] of graphically demonstrating the world turned upside down. Charles Kerr's evocative list can stand in for many others:

> a score of men dressed beyond the possibility of recognition, with head-gear from the skull-cap to the bell-crowned stove-pipe, with white pants, swallow-tail coats, and satin vests, all mounted, one on a blooded stallion, one on an unbroken filly, and the rest on mules and horses of every color and condition; in the midst of the troop an old fashioned family carriage with a gorgeously-attired darky mounted on the steps behind as a footman, the vehicle loaded to the guards with butter and eggs, and sweet-potatoes and honey, and flour and meal, and vegetables of every grade, from the pumpkin to the gruber-pea, and drawn by a jackass about the size of a sheep, and a horse as big as a small elephant on the pole, and mayhap a cow in he lead, or a rawboned plantation mule flapping his patient ears as he munched his stripped corn fodder.[58]

This tale has all of the elements: the men in costume, the loads of food, and a variety of livestock, including what one could presume was a prized mount. The black man dressed in finery and used as a footman is a mocking reminder of perceived pretensions, an elevation of common soldiers into elite men.

Veterans' stories also expressed pride in the bummers' ability to find hidden Southern valuables. Marcy's "good natured vagabonds" kept a sharp eye out for freshly turned earth, into which they would poke their bayonets and sabers, "and when some lucky digger found a vein" of money, jewelry, or silver, "the spade was brought into speedy requisition and hopeless and irretrievable confiscation followed."[59] Manning Force and Charles Belknap both describe lines of men crossing yards and gardens stabbing their ramrods and bayonets into the ground in search of buried treasures.[60]

Veterans also used humor to mock themselves and their superiors. One tale repeated in an obituary for General Sherman took aim at the bummer's tendency toward wanton destructiveness. According to General Horace Porter, a bummer in North Carolina was found cutting the Union telegraph lines which led out of Wilmington. When asked what on earth he was doing, "The man cast an indignant look at the questioner, and said, as he continued his work, "I'm one o' Sherman's bummers, and the last thing he said to us was, 'Be sure and cut all the telegraph wires you come across, and don't go to foolin' away time askin' who they belong to.'"[61] While this clearly mocks the lower-level soldiers, other tales turned the tables. One that appeared in a compilation of wartime stories came from the family of an Ohio soldier. A group of soldiers caught, butchered, cooked, and ate a pig, burying the skin so they would not be caught. When a Southern woman came by the camp in search of her pig, "the Captain, who had a private tent the boys seldom entered, said, 'Oh, I'm sure you are mistaken. I haven't a boy in my company that would do such a thing. I'll order all tents searched.'" While he was occupied, "the boys" slipped around and hid the meat in the Captain's tent, which he ordered searched along with the others: "And there they found the meat. The embarrassed captain found it hard to explain."[62]

Many of the funny stories are directed against white Southerners. Just as Southern whites took pride in their ability to outsmart Sherman's bummers, so too did Union troops enjoy taking advantage of their enemies. Manning Force retold one typical tale, where a sergeant arrived at a plantation and asked if anyone had recently died. While the family initially denied it, they finally admitted that they had buried a slave boy the previous day. The sergeant then adopted a solemn tone and went on "'I only wanted to let you know that I have opened that grave and taken out the corpse.' There were loud expostulations then, for this corpse, so called, was the plantation supply of ham."[63] Score one for the Union in this instance.

Perfect and Complete Destruction

One might be able to find some humor in stealing food, finding hidden hams, even taking clothes and valuables. But we know that the bummers went further, torching barns and cotton gins, destroying mansions and cabins. How did they feel about that level of destruction?

One area that veterans seemed to recall with unabashed pride was their skill at destroying railroads. Certainly, this was an easy activity to laud: railroads were clear military targets, and their destruction could save Union lives. The usual way was to heat the rails and twist them once or twice into what came to be known as a Sherman's necklace or Sherman's necktie. Sometimes, though, the men went further. William Duncan recalled seeing the ties "twisted into a monogram U.S." in South Carolina, making "a perfect and complete . . . job of destruction." Henry Marcy saw the same thing in South Carolina, noting first that the men would often cut images of their various corps badges into tree trunks. Then, "with the aid of neighboring trees the ponderous iron rails were shaped into huge letters of U and S. With bolts and spikes these were fixed and firmly nailed upon the crossings, and left for the consideration of those who should come after." Marcy explains that this was not simple vandalism, but rather was designed to send a message, reminding "this misguided state, of union more enduring than the iron of which they were made." One expects that the meaning came through.[64]

That both Duncan and Marcy note this extra step being taken in South Carolina is striking, for many veterans felt that the Palmetto State, more so than Georgia or North Carolina, deserved whatever it got. South Carolina was seen as the seat of the Confederate rebellion, the cause of all of the war's death and devastation. Frank Putney, who served as a second lieutenant in the 12th Wisconsin during the March, made this difference explicit in his "Incidents of Sherman's March through the Carolinas." Putney addressed the March's destruction and devastation more directly and less humorously than most of his fellow veterans. In doing so, he also unconsciously endorsed the Southern claims that the Union men were not simply running amok but instead could be controlled and reined in or let out. He first claimed that the devastation in Georgia was "not through any hatred of the section through which the army passed" but rather proceeded on orders from commanders, "according to the measure of local hostility manifested by the inhabitants." In South Carolina, however, despite the fact that the orders to respect private property were ostensibly still in place, "the soldiers knew that the state was the originator of secession and had led all her sister states into rebellion, and a revengeful feeling against her filled their hearts, or rather a joyful feeling over being able to pay an installment of a debt long overdue."[65]

Like many of his fellows, Putney described the process of "confiscation," complete with the requisite image of men plunging their ramrods into newly turned ground and seizing food and valuables as "fair spoils of war." Unlike them, however, Putney also addressed the question of fire, noting tongue-in-cheek that the plantation homes of middle South Carolina "all seemed to have in them a tendency to ignition." He recalled seeing smoke rolling from the windows of homes and black columns rising from further outbuildings and neighbors. While widespread burning of private property was against orders, Putney explained, "no watchfulness could protect it." Even when guards were posted on one side of a home, "spontaneous combustion would take place on the other," though the culprits could never be found. More strikingly, even after the passage of decades, Putney could not remember "that any of us felt any sadness at seeing the destruction of venerable or even historic homes that had sheltered Greene or Cornwallis or Tarleton, or that we were moved to any active measures to stay the waste." His one twinge of conscience came at the home of William Gilmore Simms, whose poetry he had long admired. Putney claimed that he personally tried to protect Simms's home and especially his library, but to no avail.[66]

William Royal Oake, a member of the 26th Iowa, was another marcher who was willing to indict himself for participating in less than savory activities. His posthumously published memoir details several such activities, with varying degrees of introspection. Oake wrote of marching into Columbia and joining other Union soldiers in looting stores and trampling merchandise "under foot as so much worthless rage." Oake himself broke into a music shop, and "it looked like a sacrilegious act to see the fine instruments that were ruthlessly destroyed, broken into pieces. Large French mirrors that would cost hundreds of dollars would have the butt of a musket or hilt of a sword thrust through them, breaking them into fragments." One wonders if he used the passive voice to unconsciously remove himself from direct participation in the devastation.[67]

While Oake may have wanted to distance himself from participation in wanton vandalism, he was much more open about the petty thefts he engaged in. A few days out of Columbia he came across a sleeping old man, and stole his shoes, an act that he justified on the grounds of need. Oake also rationalized that surely the shoes he took were the man's everyday pair, and that his victim would still have a Sunday pair someplace.[68] In Fayetteville, Oake came to possess "a very fine velvet bound pocket bible," which was given to him by a comrade. Writing many years later he still had the little cards and locks of hair that had been tucked inside, and patted himself on the back for maintaining it in "good condition."[69] Outside Raleigh, Oake supplemented his new shoes, explaining,

> I at last secured a pair of very fine white pants and a fine velvet vest together with a fine plug hat. Putting on the pants, which I found about six inches too long I then donned the vest, and to put a finishing touch to it put the plug hat over my army cap, and with Webster's unabridged Dictionary under my army and with the chickens and other plunder started for camp. It was amusing to see the boys look as I approached camp clad as I was in that scandalous manner.

This is an excellent example of the reasons that Sherman's bummers took planters' clothes—as much for fun as for physical coverage. They stole because they could.[70]

For all of their infusions of humor, or gentle sentimentality, those veterans who wrote and spoke about their experiences along the March had to address the fact that unsavory things did occur. Men stole, and not to survive, but because they wanted to. They burned down property, they terrorized women and children, assaulted people, and left former slaves as destitute as their masters. And how veterans chose to address this fundamental paradox perhaps tells us something about how they saw themselves and their past.

One way veterans excused the very real violence and devastation of the March was to blame the majority of the excesses (as they would have termed them) on a few bad apples. The author of an obituary for General Slocum took an unusual tack in explaining that "the respectable soldiers shirked the duty of foraging, and thus it fell into the hands of the rude and mischievous men of Sherman's army." He also asserted that these "bad men" were largely residents of border states, out to exact their own special vengeance.[71] Only morally suspect men, apparently, could be persuaded to participate in morally suspect activities. Charles Belknap, the great celebrator of bummers in his speeches, also lamented that some (though not all) of them were "physically and morally unfit for foraging." For Belknap, the fact that foragers were occasionally captured "had the effect of weeding out of the commands the less courageous men, and the filling of their places with a more determined lot."[72] Determined, one might assume, to take whatever they could.

This "bad apples" argument also comes into play in the instances when veterans drew sharp distinctions between the official foraging details (as one might find in any war zone), and the bummer (at least as traditionally denoted). Major Samuel Mahon sought to vindicate official foragers from "imputations" of theft and plunder. Instead, he blamed stragglers and skulkers, who hid from the enemy and the regular columns, appearing only before helpless women and children. Mahon further absolved the regular foragers of any wrongdoing by asserting that he "never knew of any instance where people were left destitute of food, no matter how pressing the needs of the army; enough was left to keep the people from hunger, and I verily believe that the system, harsh at best, was carried out in as humane a manner as ever has been done in civilized warfare."[73] While this certainly strains credulity today, even other veterans seemed to have thought this went too far. Charles Kerr was not responding directly to Mahon when he scoffed at stories that claimed everything taken was done so legitimately. Rather, he appealed to his fellow veterans' knowledge of the difficulties in command when he acknowledged how hard it was to "check the inclination of soldiers to plunder. Here were thousands of men sent forth each morning with absolutely no restraint but their own will, with no chance of discovery and no fear of punishment." One could hardly expect them, Kerr seemed to be saying, to behave with absolute restraint.[74] Major Henry Marcy also seemed to offer a degree of absolution for those soldiers who "had to learn to consider the danger just enough to give zest to personal adventure, and prompted by its spirit . . . temporarily deserted the ranks."[75]

Not only did Mahon minimize the wrongs inflicted by Sherman's marchers, but he also emphasized the struggles they faced. In contrast to those who described the March as a nonstop party of easy marching and full stomachs, Mahon refused to minimize the hardships along the way. He recalled that as the army neared Savannah and began to move much more slowly, it also began to run out of food. For several days the men had to subsist almost entirely on rice, which was issued in sheaves, meaning that the men had to spend hours threshing it.[76] William Oake also lamented the low rations outside Savannah and the work needed to thresh and hull the rice, noting that "if any of my readers ever undertook to hull oats with the end of an iron rod they can form some idea of the task we had in hulling rice with the end of our bayonets. We would manage to get about half the hull off, and then getting tired of the job we would cook, and eat it, hull and all."[77] These Georgia hardships paled, however, compared to the rigors of the Carolinas. That part of the March lasted about seven weeks, Mahon explained, "and for each week the man who served continuously on forage duty, lived . . . one year of his life." For Mahon, "the strain of physical fatigue and mental anxiety [had] no parallel . . . in the severest active service."[78]

Another hardship came in the form of Wheeler's cavalry, although the veterans often minimized this. They tended to be described in one of two ways, neither necessarily the expected one. That is, the Confederate cavalry was rarely described as a real threat to Union men's safety but more as a kind of Keystone Kops that would come along and break up the fun of foraging. A Captain Reed once asked his listeners if he had ever told the story of grinding corn for Wheeler's cavalry. He described his foraging party bringing corn from several barns to a mill, grinding it through the night, and then using women's clothes tied up in knots as sacks, which were then loaded onto mules. But when Wheeler's men appeared, "our little party had scattered, and our mules were flying in all directions. Some of them strewed meal over the fields for miles, and the way feminine apparel was distributed was ludicrous to behold."[79] Charles Belknap painted a similar funny picture of encounters with Wheeler's "Critterbacks": the bummers would take off and "in their wild flight chickens were left orphans by the wayside. Hams, pickles, preserves and honey were cast aside with reckless prodigality."[80]

A few pages later, Belknap again used humor in conjunction with Wheeler's name. While the first anecdote is at the bummers' expense, in the next one he targets the Confederates. Union soldiers are foraging on a plantation when the approach of Wheeler's men drives them into the woods. The Confederate lady asks if she can help her fellow Southerners and is told to try to draw out the Union soldiers. So she shouted: "'Oh you miserable Yankees. You have taken every chicken on the place.' 'What's that,' said the Confederate, 'taken all the chickens? Then there's nothing left here worth fighting for.'" And off they went, allowing the bummers to reemerge, come back, and finish the job.[81] This idea, that Southern civilians had as much to fear from their own men as they did from the Union, was one way to absolve Sherman's men from responsibility for terror and theft. Charles Hopkins made the same point, much more seriously when he explained that, as destructive and wasteful as Union foraging was, "the damages done by our troops were not so great, according to the statements of their own newspapers, as those inflicted by Wheeler's cavalry."[82] Manning Force echoed this when he asserted that "even in South Carolina . . . the people said that both armies, the national and the Confederate, were alike in taking their property; that the difference was we also burned their houses, while their own soldiers abused and insulted them."[83]

Force was not the only one to claim that Union bummers attacked only property, not people. In 1891, General Andrew Hickenlooper proclaimed unequivocally that "to the credit of Union soldiers and honor to their loyal mothers," there was "not one single recorded act of hostility toward unarmed men or insult to unprotected women" to stain the marchers' reputations.[84] This is, of course, a profound overstatement. Plenty of civilians were battered and bruised after their encounters with Sherman's men, and while there were few recorded sexual assaults against white women, scores of black women were not so fortunate.[85] Henry Marcy had a slightly more measured approach, conceding that "no doubt our soldiers were guilty of unjustifiable acts," specifically the burning of private homes. But those homes that were burned—and indeed, Marcy insisted, even most of those that were plundered—were empty, left in the wake of fleeing owners, and, he added, he had "yet to learn of a single instance where injury or outrage was committed upon women or children."[86] Frank Putney tried to split hairs even further, noting that he had "never heard of a case of criminal assault or any injury of the person of a civilian in South Carolina." Of course, many attacks might not have risen to the level of criminality but would have been no less traumatizing. Putney went on to say that the only exception he had to this tale of general kindliness came when he discovered a woman standing screaming in a barrel. Apparently, she had tried to pour boiling water on a group of Union foragers, so they stuck her in a molasses barrel to "sweeten her temper." Putney thought she seemed fine and unhurt, so he simply left her in place and went on his way. One can only imagine that her version of the story would be quite different.[87]

Some bummers went further than claims of doing no harm and retold stories of kindnesses doled out to Southern civilians. In a commemorative address, General Slocum claimed that when the Confederates withdrew from Savannah, the "rabble which collects in all large cities" began to riot and break into private stores and homes. Sherman's men stopped the mob, "and the people eagerly welcomed the protection of our army from these plunderers among their own people."[88] Oftentimes individual soldiers would choose to spare one home or grant some small privileges to its residents. Cornelius Cadle, adjutant general of the Iowa Brigade was hardly an ordinary bummer when he and General (then Colonel) Hickenlooper entered one Southern home, inhabited only by a woman and three attractive young ladies. Ruefully, Cadle concluded that he "had stood before the bullets of the enemy, but tears from young, blue eyes were more fatal." The degree to which he was moved is debatable, however: he allowed the women to move their supplies of meat and corn into the house before burning all of the outbuildings. Nevertheless, Cadle and Hickenlooper found themselves subjected to a rueful tongue-lashing (a tongue-in-cheek lashing?) from General Blair, who complained, "I knew . . . that if there were any good-looking girls there you would not carry it out. I think that for such duty hereafter I shall send older men."[89]

Some Union soldiers went further in the amount of protection they offered to Southern civilians, with pleasant results. William H. Duncan found himself living with the women of the Meikle family in Columbia, South Carolina. Duncan convinced the family to stay put during the fire so that he could protect them and their property. While Duncan saved the family home, he could not stop a detachment of a Union provost guard from digging up valuables hidden in a yard. Nevertheless, Mr. Meikle was so grateful that he wrote to Duncan after the war, inviting him and his wife to come visit, although they never did.[90] Duncan protected the Meikle home while knowing that Mr. Meikle was off in the Confederate army. Although Duncan never explains exactly why he protected them, one could imagine that he was motivated by an impulse similar to that of Fred Reitz, a member of the 21st Wisconsin. Reitz and his fellow men came across a young Southern couple in a small home in South Carolina; the husband was home on furlough after having been wounded at Petersburg. "To show you that even Sherman's bummers respected the soldier who was manfully fighting us in front," Reitz recalled with evident satisfaction, "I will say that nothing had been disturbed around his little home; even his chickens were left untouched." The soldiers brought some food to supplement what the couple had (though Reitz does not indicate the source of *those* supplies), the "pretty wife" cooked a large meal at Union request, "we had a very enjoyable dinner together, and when we left in the afternoon the young couple had a much better idea of Sherman's Yankees."[91] One is left to wonder if the Southerners recalled the afternoon so warmly.

While bummers might feel resentment toward white Southern men and women for their possible roles in bringing on the war or the assistance they offered the Confederacy, the soldiers' hearts often softened when children were involved. One veteran recalled an army surgeon who brought food and other supplies for a sick Southern child, even though his father was serving in the Confederate army.[92] Charles Belknap told two self-congratulatory stories that centered on soldiers and their kindness. In the first, he and his men came across two dirty, starving, abandoned little girls, about three and five years old, as they moved through Georgia. The soldiers fed and bathed the girls "and well washed they were as pretty a capture as ever made by the 'Bummers Bold.'" The soldiers then tried to convince neighbors to take in the girls, but no one would (though they did give clothing). The girls therefore joined the March, riding a mule by day, camping with the soldiers by night, until they reached Savannah. They were finally taken home by a furloughed lieutenant and adopted.[93] Whether or not the story is true, it provides an interesting corollary to stories of the romance of reunion—in this case the sections are reunited by parents and children, rather than husbands and wives.

Belknap also related a somewhat less heartwarming story. Later in the March, he and his men came across a woman about to give birth. The Yankees fetched a neighbor and helped care for the woman throughout the night until her son was born. The next morning found a grizzled old veteran softly crooning a lullaby. But then, "We christened that one with a canteen of applejack, and named him Billy Sherman, and took for our reward the family carriage loaded with dead pigs, some corn and chickens, and other things necessary to the conduct of the army." While one might assume the child was renamed by his mother, it is fundamentally confusing that Belknap and his men would take the time to make sure the baby was born safely, and then leave his mother destitute and starving. Yet this seems not to have occurred to him.[94]

When Sherman's veterans did pause to think about the March from the perspective of Southern civilians, they often did so with a mocking or laughable tone. Part of painting the March as a lark and a party involved minimizing any real harm it might have caused. One way to do this was to highlight some of the absurd rumors that flew around Georgia and the Carolinas. Thus one author could joke about a woman who dramatically proclaimed that "you Yankees have been *recommended* to us to be a very bad and murdersome people."[95] A soldier who rode up to a house in Screven County Georgia found several women screaming for help: a boy had been hidden in the gin house, which was on fire. The boy was rescued, and one of them explained that "'we uns heered that you uns killed all the little boys to keep them out from growing up to fight ye and we hid 'em.'" The soldier reflected that this was a common belief and "in consequence of this, there were found many infant Moseses and Jeffs hid away in cellars and corncribs—though none in bulrushes."[96]

One question that was perennially raised was the degree to which the bummers were following orders or were entirely out of control. E. J. Hale, writing in an homage to Confederate women, argued that while Yankees would have people believe that the only bummers were stragglers and shirkers, intercepted letters from officers showed otherwise. According to Hale, the letters described an organized and authorized system of plunder: "that one fifth of the proceeds fell to General Sherman, another fifth to the other general officers; another fifth to the line officers, and the remaining two fifths to the enlisted men." Nor were the bummers generalists in their thieving, for Hale asserted that "there were pure silver bummers, plated-ware bummers, jewelry bummers, women's clothing bummers, provision bummers, and in fine, a bummer or bummers for every kind of stealable thing. No bummer of one specialty interfering with the stealables of another."[97] To believe Hale is to see Sherman's men as a literal machine, with thousands of individual cogs, an immoral juggernaut that could not be slowed or defeated.

A different view of discipline came from Pascal Raines, an acquaintance of Albion Tourgée, who lived at the forks of the Ogeechee River. Years after the war Raines praised the March as "a brilliant movement, conducted with a laxity of discipline that would have been impossible to an army drawn from any other people." What Raines meant was that the democratic and republican character of Sherman's army allowed for an essential modicum of discipline and control. "There were, it is true, many acts of pillage and some needless destruction of property, . . . but it should always be remembered to the credit of republican institutions that this army of invasion marched from Atlanta to the sea, subsisting itself mainly off the country through the agency of loosely organized bands of pillagers, without any non-combatant's life or woman's virtue being placed in peril." He's perhaps damning with faint praise, but it is praise nonetheless.[98]

Many of Sherman's veterans preferred to recall the March as an orderly one, without the damage and destruction wrought by the bummers. (Browne, Bugle-Echoes, *242.)*

WILLIAM T. SHERMAN DIED ON FEBRUARY 14, 1891, but the meetings of the Society of the Army of the Tennessee continued on without him. As one might imagine, the October 1891 meeting was dominated by tributes and eulogies, none more effusive than General Andrew Hickenlooper's. His speech, which was later published in pamphlet form as well as included in the regular society report, laid out Sherman's life and military career. Hickenlooper's March was a heroic one: "Happy in its conception, wonderful in its execution, glorious in its results, but above all, fortunate in its leadership, Sherman's March to the sea will ever be regarded as one of the grandest accomplishments of modern warfare." Nor would he brook any criticism of the March and its results, explaining that "the unavoidable suffering which ensued through the appropriation of subsistence was only that which naturally and inevitably followed in the wake of an invading army." So far this seems like the standard hagiographic justifications that one would expect to hear in this venue and at this time. But then Hickenlooper went on to make the case that the March and Sherman did not only end the war but also saved the South. Indeed, Hickenlooper claimed, "even those who suffered most are now rejoicing in the birth of a 'new south,'" which gladly shares "the universal prosperity of a country saved by Sherman's military genius from disunion, slavery, and national death." While this did not address the Lost Cause explicitly, it certainly provides an implicit refutation. Far from being a Lost Cause, Hickenlooper seemed to be arguing, Sherman's March represented the hand of providence, bringing the nation to its rightful place and lifting the South along with it.[99]

The 1892 banquet at the Lindell Hotel in St. Louis proceeded according to the usual patterns, with toasts to "Lincoln and Grant," "The Army of the Tennessee," and "Lessons of the War" (to which P. Tecumseh Sherman offered the response). But the greatest applause and the loudest cheers were reserved for "Our Quondam Enemy," and the response offered by General Charles E. Hooker, of Mississippi and the Confederacy. According to the report in the *New York Times*, "there was much humor, but more pathos and more patriotism in the stirring words of Gen. Hooker as he delicately complimented the valor of the Army of the Tennessee and referred to the "Lost Cause" of the Confederacy as a matter which had been adjusted by the stern logic of war and had now passed into history beyond appeal and beyond regret."[100] Would that it were true. Little did these old soldiers realize that the Lost Cause would reign supreme for more than one generation, and that their own attempts to rehabilitate their reputations would be forgotten.

CHAPTER FIVE

Uncle Billy, the Merchant of Terror

Disentangling images of William Tecumseh Sherman from images of the March itself is almost impossible. One seems to define the other, and as the March came to stand in for all of the atrocities of war, so too did Sherman come to be the ultimate personification of those evils. If the marchers were "Huns" or "Vandals," then Sherman was Attila; if the March was one long arson spree, then Sherman was Nero incarnate. But Sherman was not only defined by others; he was also a master at self-creation and self-definition. In his long post-March life, Sherman became a professional veteran, writing and speaking about his motives and expectations and using his *Memoirs* to settle scores and make his version known. His death in 1891 prompted a national outpouring of grief and memorialization. The wars of the twentieth century prompted a burst of interest in Sherman and the March, this time reaching backward for the origins of total war and attacks on civilians. These constant reassessments have kept the March and Sherman alive for successive generations.

Sherman's Memories

There was no more canny shaper of William Tecumseh Sherman's image than the man himself.[1] And his efforts began with the end of the war. One could argue that this process began with the Grand Review.[2] Ever sensitive to the popular notion that the western armies were less polished, less disciplined, and implicitly, less skilled, than their eastern counterparts, Sherman ordered his men to march with eyes front and in tight order. Men in fresh uniforms and polished shoes, rifles shining and bayonets glinting could never have run amok, never have committed all of the atrocities of which they were accused. The impression to be given was that these men were soldiers, not bummers. As he explained, "Many good people up to that time, had looked upon our Western army as a sort of mob; but the world then saw, and recognized the fact, that it was an army in the proper sense, well organized, well commanded and disciplined; and there was no wonder that it had swept through the South like a tornado."[3] Their neat rows and precise strides might have been negated by the inclusion of the spoils of the March among the columns: cows, sheep, and goats, along with mules laden down with supplies. Similarly, the corps of black "pioneers," muscular, hard-working black laborers carrying their axes and spades, gave way to entire families of freedpeople, including children. Sherman wore his dress uniform, buttoned tightly, a contrast from his more slapdash style in the field. He initially rode at the head of the column, leading them down Pennsylvania Avenue. Walt Whitman watched him ride by, quickly jotting down a description and noting:

> the perfect deafness &
> immobility of the great
> soldier—with I think
> a shade of scornfulness & haughty ~~ines~~
> ~~& scornful p~~ passion
> on his nervous face.

Sherman then sat in the reviewing stand (coolly rebuffing Secretary of State Stanton's proffered handshake) and watched his men march by for hours. It took six hours for them all to pass, a march that transformed them from battle-scarred warriors into heroic veterans.[4]

Four days later, on May 30, 1865, Sherman issued his Special Field Orders No. 76, in which he officially disbanded his army. In so doing, he also built the initial scaffolding for his interpretation of the March and its meaning. He began by reminding his men of the challenges of the Atlanta campaign and the importance of taking Atlanta itself. He quickly dispensed with the March across Georgia, invoking instead the swamps of South Carolina and the battles in North Carolina—Averasboro and Bentonville. He made no mention of foraging expeditions or fires, choosing to stress the cold and hunger that the men faced, the difficulties of the marches, and then the magnanimity of the surrender terms. He closed by urging his men, whether they returned home or stayed in the army, to work hard and with discipline, "with the full belief that as in war you have been good soldiers, so in peace you will be good citizens."[5]

Interestingly, Sherman's original version of the address had less to do with the responsibilities of individual citizens and more about the obligations of their leaders. In this, historian William M. Ferraro argues, Sherman was attacking Stanton and Halleck for the controversy over the surrender terms. Ultimately, however, Sherman decided that civil peace was more important than settling political scores, and so he urged his men to effectively lay down their swords. He wanted to set an example of public rectitude for his men, to present a united national front as the work of Reconstruction began.[6] Furthermore, Sherman's elision of the actual events of the March and his privileging of the few battles are equally significant. He seems to be beginning the process of sanitizing and regularizing the March, emphasizing it as a military action directed against military targets—cities and armies—rather than Southern civilians.

Sherman's greatest act of self-creation and self-definition—both personally and regarding the March—came in the writing of his memoirs. Published in 1875, they presented a man who rarely regretted or apologized. The publisher's note to a 1957 edition describes them as "brusque and candid," intended as personal recollections for his men, rather than a general history of the war.[7] While today we look at the March through the lens of destruction, Sherman's recollections seemed designed to settle scores with Stanton and the War Department, particularly over the freedmen and the disputed surrender terms. This focus is not terribly surprising; he had a decade to absorb criticisms of the March and must have written with them in mind. He minimized the damage done by his soldiers, calling it "exceptional and incidental," and described stopping men who foraged without explicit orders. Sherman was struck by the wide variety of provisions that could be found in Georgia, a function of the state being largely untouched by war up until that point. "As a rule," he recalled disingenuously, "we destroyed none, but kept our wagons full, and fed our teams bountifully." At times he contradicts himself: he admitted ordering that nothing be spared at Howell Cobb's plantation, but then expresses pride that "little or no damage was done to private property" in Milledgeville.[8]

Sometimes Sherman seemed almost nostalgic for the days on the March, sounding like one of his veterans, recalling with pleasure "the sight of our camps by night, lit up by the fires of fragrant pine knots," and the easy pace of his marching men. Indeed, the fires that Sherman does mention when writing about Georgia were those set by Confederate cavalry, who burned fields and foodstuffs, prompting threats of retaliation. Sherman repeatedly veers between acknowledging the destruction that he ordered and that his men wrought and minimizing its impact.[9]

As he did in Special Field Orders No. 76, Sherman emphasized that the March from Atlanta to Savannah was chiefly a military maneuver, in his words "a shift of base . . . a means to an end and not as an essential act of war." Disingenuously, he argued that he was just moving the army from point A to point B, albeit in a rather dramatic fashion. In that vein, he was matter-of-fact about one of his most controversial orders: using the prisoners of war to clear mines near Sandersville. Similarly, he argued that if he and his men were as wantonly cruel as they were rumored to have been, Confederate generals Hardee and Smith would never have told their wives to go to Sherman for protection. He reminded his readers that he ordered his men to feed civilians from their supplies while in Savannah from December 1864 to January 1865. No mere butcher would have done that, seems to be his implication.[10]

Sherman was eager to leave the comforts of life in Savannah; it had "become dull and tame," and he wanted to free himself from both Confederate women begging for protection and profiteers coming down from the North. This march through the Carolinas was the section of the March that Sherman deemed the most important, though ironically the section that the public seemed less interested in. Here, too, Sherman seemed more open about the psychological warfare in which the March was designed to engage. As he set off for South Carolina, he reflected that "it was to me manifest that the soldiers and people of the South entertained an undue fear of our Western men and, like children, they had invented such ghostlike stories of our prowess in Georgia, that they were scared by their own inventions. Still, this was a power and I intended to use it." He knew that his men blamed South Carolina for starting the war, knew that they were eager to metaphorically "take the gloves off," and he was loathe to restrain them.[11]

When his narrative arrived at Columbia, Sherman waded right into the controversy over the city's conflagration. Sherman, as he had done consistently for a decade, denied ordering that the fires be set. He described meeting with various Columbia women, offering them food and protection, using this as evidence that he personally bore no malice toward Columbia and that he was not the one who torched it.[12] Later he argues that the fire was an unfortunate accident, ignited by the cotton that Wade Hampton ordered set ablaze. But perhaps he tips his hand a bit, explaining that in his official report on the fire, "I distinctly charged it to General Wade Hampton, and confess I did so pointedly, to shake the faith of his people in him, for he was in my opinion boastful, and professed to be the special champion of South Carolina."[13] Sherman's original report judged Hampton harshly, but it would be a mistake to see the statement in his memoirs as an admission of lying. Sherman never backs away from blaming Hampton; he simply tells his readers that he used the situation to his advantage. It was another in his attempts at psychological warfare against Southern whites. It also backfired because there is little evidence that Southern whites turned away from their affection for Hampton; rather, this became exhibit A in arguments about Sherman's perfidy.

Columbia was one issue that Sherman hoped to settle with his memoirs; the other was the controversy over his initial surrender terms. Sherman believed that they had been sanctioned, implicitly if not explicitly, by Lincoln, and he wrote extensively about them. Sherman recalled meeting with Grant and Lincoln at City Point in Virginia, described Lincoln's curiosity about the March, and noted that the president "seemed to enjoy very much the more ludicrous parts—about the 'bummers' and their devices to collect food and forage when the outside world supposed us to be starving." He argued that Lincoln was in a magnanimous mood and quoted from Porter's notes on the meeting, which indicated that the general "yielded his views to those of the President, and the terms of capitulation between himself and Johnston were exactly in accordance with Mr. Lincoln's wishes. He could not have done anything which would have pleased the President better." Sherman blamed Stanton for countermanding his surrender offer, embarrassing him, and adding to their existing feud.[14]

Sherman and Stanton had already struggled with each other during the March, on the issue of African Americans, and here, too, Sherman used his memoirs to enhance his image. First, Sherman portrayed himself as a benevolent father figure to African Americans along the route of the March. He recalls them greeting him eagerly, painting them as almost childlike in their delight, and himself as a sort of bountiful master, dispensing freedom in his wake. At the same time, however, he also ordered them to stay put, to not slow down his army by following along behind the marchers.[15] Sherman told of showing Stanton around Savannah, presenting their conversation as an amiable one: "He [Stanton] talked to me a great deal about the negroes, the former slaves, and I told him of many interesting incidents, illustrating their simple character and faith in our arms and progress." In this passage Sherman reveals, perhaps unintentionally, his deep-seated paternalism. More controversially, Sherman also maintained his defense of General Jefferson C. Davis for allowing African Americans to drown or face Confederate capture at Ebenezer Creek. For Sherman, the decision was less dramatic, as he argued that the crossing happened while the freedpeople were back from the banks and asleep (as opposed to right there trying to cross). Too, he argued that Davis was acting as a soldier, who wanted to move quickly without the "encumbrances" of "the poor negroes." Finally, Sherman tried to argue that he and his commanders were not unfeeling or uncaring. Rather, they all felt sympathy for the former slaves "but a sympathy of a different sort from that of Mr. Stanton, which was not of pure humanity, but of *politics*." Essentially, Sherman tried to turn the tables, arguing that he cared for African Americans as people, whereas Stanton saw them only for their latent political utility.[16]

Sherman was also angry that Stanton dared to challenge him on racial issues, claiming that "because I had not loaded down my army by other hundreds of thousands of poor negroes, I was construed by others as hostile to the black race." There was an element of the self-serving in Sherman's rhetoric, as he repeatedly invoked a kind of paternalistic protectiveness towards blacks. He charged that there was corruption in the recruitment of black soldiers, using that to explain his reluctance to have any black units on the March. He went on to explain that he didn't want help from African Americans because he didn't want Southern whites to claim that the Union needed their help to win, hardly an expression of support for any future racial equality. Sherman defended himself first by insisting that Lincoln never doubted him—though arguably that might have been regarding Sherman's commitment to the Union rather than to black freedom. He then returned to his benevolent paternalism, reminding readers that "as regards kindness to the race, encouraging them to patience and forbearance, procuring them food and clothing, and providing them with land whereon to labor, I assert that no army ever did more for that race than the one I commanded in Savannah."[17] Sherman was referring to his Special Field Orders No. 15, which he thought so significant that he included the full text in his memoirs. That brief experiment in land redistribution was his ironic legacy.

Although readers praised Sherman's memoirs as detailed and accurate, and Edwin Stanton, the target of much of Sherman's criticism had died several years before, not everyone found the memoirs to their liking. Henry Van Ness Boynton, a former *Cincinnati Gazette* writer and brevet brigadier general, attacked the memoirs, and Sherman himself, charging him with not just exaggeration and self-aggrandizement but also outright fabrications. Boynton called Sherman "erratic" and accused him of malicious or vicious attacks on the reputations of any number of generals, including Grant, Thomas, Buell, Schofield, McPherson, Rosecrans, Hooker, and of course Secretary Stanton.[18] Boynton claimed to have compared Sherman's recollections to the actual records, and he argued that the March to the Sea was more Grant's idea than Sherman's, claimed that Sherman was so careless at Bentonville that the battle was almost lost, and challenged his account of the surrender negotiations. Boynton may or may not have been hired by Secretary of War

William Babcock and Grant's personal secretary Orville Babcock (both of whom resigned on corruption charges), but he was not entirely wrong in his calling Sherman out for errors and misstatements.[19]

Although Boynton's work angered Sherman, many of his friends and comrades leapt to his defense, writing to newspapers and publishing pamphlets, like C. W. Moulton's rather inelegantly titled "The Review of General Sherman's Memoirs Examined, Chiefly in the Light of Its Own Evidence." Moulton, who had been engaged by Sherman, went back to the same sources used by Boynton to argue that they had been misread through the lens of Boynton's own biases. This kind of back and forth could go on *ad infinitum*, but the ultimate effect was to limit the impact of Boynton.[20]

Much more damaging criticism came at the hands of Jefferson Davis, who excoriated Sherman in his *Rise and Fall of the Confederate Government*, published in 1881. He described Sherman's treatment of civilians as "barbarous cruelty" and an "infamous disregard of the established rules of war, but of the common dictates of humanity."[21] His greatest anger regarded Columbia, and Sherman's supposed besmirching of Wade Hampton's name by blaming him for the fire. Davis defended Hampton's personal honor and pointed out that Sherman's claims that he did not order Columbia put to the torch would have been more convincing had he not ordered so much other destruction. For all the venom that dripped from Davis's pen and lips, he did agree with Sherman on one point: that Sherman's initial surrender terms were endorsed by Lincoln, and it was only after Lincoln's death that he was forced to change them.[22]

Ulysses S. Grant's 1885 memoirs also made this point, defending Sherman's peace, as well as the marchers themselves. He minimized the level of devastation and destruction, emphasizing instead the romance and the gaiety of the March.[23] He addressed Boynton directly (though not by name), by assuring readers that Sherman was the architect of the March. According to Grant, Sherman ordered the flames in Columbia extinguished, rather than setting them. Most importantly, Grant took Sherman's side in the debate over the surrender terms. Sherman, Grant proclaimed, was loyal to the Union, the president, his army and his men.[24] And this largely positive view of Sherman, and by extent of the campaigns themselves, held sway, at least in the North, in the historiography for generations.

Sherman spent the years after the war as president of the Society of the Army of the Tennessee, making speeches all over the country at reunions, graduations, and funerals. He generally enjoyed his fame. And as befitted a man who always felt a deep affection for the Southern (white) people,

William T. Sherman with a group of unidentified Union veterans.
He met with hundreds, if not thousands of veterans every year before his death in 1891
and delighted in chatting with them. This photograph was taken in the early to mid-1880s.
(Library of Congress, http://www.loc.gov/pictures/item/2001695616/)

and no great inclination toward African American civil rights, Sherman's speeches focused on praise for Union soldiers but an ultimate message of reunion. The destruction was a necessary cleansing in order to enable the reunification of the Union.[25] An early example came in an 1866 speech from Salem, Illinois. "Now, my friends," Sherman said, "I know there are parties who denounce me as inhuman. I appeal to you if I have not always been kind and considerate to you." This was met with cheers. "I care not what they say." Now he was interrupted with "Bully for you and cheers." He explained that he worried about leaving his men behind to guard cities, which would have been more dangerous for them, and "Therefore we destroyed Atlanta, and if we had destroyed all the cities of the South in order to bring about the result in view it would have been right." The glee club sang "Sherman's March to the Sea" after his speech.[26] This early on, it's not surprising that he emphasized victory over reunion, but that would change.

One of Sherman's best-known speeches is famous not for what he said but for who followed him on the dais. On December 22, 1886, Henry W. Grady, the editor of the *Atlanta Constitution*, and William T. Sherman shared the honor of addressing the New-England Society of New York's annual dinner. (Sherman had actually addressed the members of the New-England Society of Brooklyn the night before).[27] This was the occasion of Grady's "New South Speech," which greatly overshadowed Sherman's more prosaic remarks. The men dined at Delmonico's, and then the toasts commenced. Sherman told a story of his days on the March, where he discussed the vastness of the free states (and their correspondingly large population) with a Milledgeville planter. Ultimately, the planter concluded that the Confederates had been "——fools" to have ever left the Union. "I saw one reconstructed man before I left Georgia," Sherman noted wryly, before concluding on his typical note of reconciliation:

> We did not wish to strike the blow. I grieved as much as any man when I saw houses burning and other signs of desolation, the sufferers from which were in many cases innocent. The question was forced upon us by politicians, and you and your fathers took up arms and settled it forever. I hope you will stand by the flag and will ever honor those forefathers in memory of whom you are gathered this evening.[28]

It's interesting that Sherman spoke of his sadness at the March's destruction to a distinctly Northern audience; perhaps he did it out of deference to his dining companion, perhaps a softening in the decade since his memoirs were published.

And then came Henry Grady, who began by declaring the Old South of slavery and secession to be dead. Grady's most famous comment about Sherman was that he was "considered an able man in our parts, though some people think he is a kind of careless man about fire." We can imagine the dining room in Delmonico's erupting into laughter at that crack, but let's not lose sight of the first part: Sherman was "considered an able man," and Grady goes on to describe the "brave and beautiful city" that arose from the ashes. He also describes the end of the war, including Sherman's defeat of Johnston, as the moment that the South became loyal again to the Union, and accepted the results of the war. While this may be an overstatement on Grady's part, what he seems to be saying is that its time to let bygones be bygones, to let the New South flourish.[29]

The General as Tourist

In 1879 Sherman decided to take a trip around the South. It was partially official, one of his duties as general-in-chief of the army. But he also wanted to see the South again, in the words of one historian, "less as a soldier and more as a tourist." This seems to have been tied to his general tone of reunion. Interestingly, while he had told an acquaintance in 1874 that it was too soon to return to Atlanta, he felt no such qualms this time, for his itinerary retraced both the Atlanta campaign and the March to the Sea. Perhaps it was the conclusion of Reconstruction and the removal of troops from the South in 1877 that enabled the trip. At any rate, Sherman and his party left Washington on January 25, 1879, and arrived in Chattanooga on January 27, greeted by cheering crowds and local dignitaries. Then they set out for Lookout Mountain, and arrived in Atlanta on January 29.[30]

According to the *Atlanta Constitution*, "a sort of light good humor pervaded the crowd, spiced up with curiosity to see the man who burned Atlanta. There was no perceptible indignation or feeling of prejudice." The predominantly white crowd was full of pranksters cracking jokes about having the train met by a parade of widows with bunches of kindling, or starting to ring the fire-bells as the trains rolled in.[31] One diarist noted brightly that "Gen. Sherman has just honored our city by a visit to see how nicely we have builded it up after his burning it."[32] Sherman, by all accounts enjoyed his visit, eagerly driving around the city and pointing out landmarks from the war. He and his party, which included his daughters Ellie and Lizzie, were feted with a ball and tour of McPherson barracks. The general joined eagerly in the dancing. The Shermans also dined with local leaders and attended several receptions.[33]

Overall the tone of the articles in the *Constitution* reporting on the visit is cheerful and respectful, though they did dispute Sherman's claim that he had never burned any homes in Atlanta, only storehouses, commenting that "according to this, the city was composed mainly of store-houses when he first visited it." Sherman was praised for his "cordiality," and his obvious pleasure in the rebuilt Atlanta. The *Constitution* fairly glowed with happiness when Sherman "also spoke in terms of high praise of the evident industry and thrift of the Southern people generally, and said several things concerning them that were very complimentary indeed."[34]

On this happy note Sherman and his party headed to Savannah on February 1, and from there on to Florida and New Orleans. While in Florida, Sherman received a letter from Evan P. Howell, editor of the *Constitution*. Clearly pleased by Sherman's kind words, Howell was soliciting a letter from Sherman that might be used to encourage Northern investment in Atlanta, and the South as a whole. Sherman replied with a mixture of praise for the region's potential, but also some criticism, specifically of the ways that the South was not welcoming enough to outsiders, his recent kind treatment notwithstanding. The letter was reprinted in several newspapers, garnering praise not only from the *Constitution* but from the *Charleston News and Courier* and the *Savannah Morning News* as well.[35] It seemed that Sherman and the South had reconciled.

It was in this spirit that Sherman took part in Atlanta's 1881 International Cotton Exposition. Atlantans, led by Henry W. Grady, saw the fair as a way to both show off the achievements of the New South and attract investment to turn their city into the "Manchester of America." The exposition was to be funded through a joint-stock corporation, and none other than William T. Sherman offered to head the Northern subscription drive; he bought twenty shares himself.[36] Although the exposition lost money, it certainly succeeded in advancing the image of vibrant, entrepreneurial, commercial Atlanta. It also advanced the cause of sectional reconciliation, showing that Northerners (and their money) were welcome. Sherman's presence at the fair was essential in underscoring that point, for if the great villain of the war could be forgiven, anything was possible.

Sherman attended the exposition on November 15, 1881, exactly seventeen years after he left Atlanta on the March to the Sea (though several newspapers erroneously reported that this was the anniversary of Atlanta's burning).[37] This was a pure coincidence, as he was there to take part in Mexican War Veteran's Day. Sherman initially refused to join the scheduled speakers on the platform, but eventually relented in response to the crowd's chanting "Sherman! Sherman!" He spoke briefly of his pride in having served as a soldier in the Mexican War, and of his pride in being an American. He struck a note of unity and reconciliation, noting that "to-day we are the same nation, the same soldiers, the same Government, the same flag, and, so far as I am concerned, I am just as friendly to Georgia as I am to my own native state of Ohio." This proclamation was greeted with "immense applause," and one newspaper report described him as "enthusiastically received."[38]

Perhaps too enthusiastically. On November 19 the *Atlanta Constitution* published "A Justification of Whatever Courteous Treatment Was Accorded General Sherman in Atlanta." Apparently, other papers had been criticizing Sherman's appearance and trying to stir up trouble through references to "Sherman's Day" at the exposition. Sherman, the *Constitution* (and one can infer Henry Grady) explained, attended the exposition as a private citizen, and while "there are special reasons why Gen. Sherman would not expect the citizens of Atlanta to meet him with any expressions of joy," one could also expect "good breeding" to result in him being treated politely. The article takes pains to paint Sherman in an inoffensive light, noting that he attended in civilian clothes, and resisted speaking publicly at all. The piece closed with as good an explanation for the rapprochement between Sherman and Atlanta as one could imagine: it claimed that the general "doubtless appreciated the manly and frank manner of his reception, and respects our people more than if the most elaborate formalities had been tendered him." At the same time, the author continued, "it is but just to say that he won the respect of many of our people by the unaffected and straightforward way in which he took things, and his sensible understanding of the situation." So the two sides seem to have settled into a quiet detente, letting the past be the past and looking toward the future.[39]

Some historians have picked up on a slight change of tone between 1879 and 1881: after all, Sherman was tendered elaborate formalities—balls, and drives, and receptions—when he toured Atlanta the first time. They have attributed this new coolness to the publication of Jefferson Davis's *Rise and Fall of the Confederate Government*.[40] Certainly there was no love lost between Davis and Sherman. In a speech promoting his memoirs, Davis damned Sherman with faint praise, describing him as having "waged war with more ferocity than any soldier since Attila," and he called the March "absurd." Then Davis stopped mincing words:

> The truth is . . . that Sherman is a vain man, who has been possessed of a chronic hallucination that he is a great General. He is really a man of very mediocre talents, either civil or military, and owed his success entirely to superior numbers and the lack of enterprise on the part of his antagonist, who either could or would do nothing but retreat. . . . Had Stonewall Jackson confronted Sherman in 1864, instead of Joe Johnston, a different tale would be told in my book.[41]

(Notice, by the way, how Davis settles scores not only with Sherman but with his longtime Confederate antagonist, Joe Johnston.) For his part, Sherman called Davis everything from a "monomaniac" to "the impersonation of all that was wicked." Their feud went on until Davis's death in 1889.[42]

Part of the reason Davis's attack on Sherman resonated in the 1880s, after some fifteen years of relatively good press, may have had to do with generational changes. Perhaps the devastation wrought by Sherman was being conflated with the economic challenges of Reconstruction, and a sense of nostalgia for an imagined golden age. Thus Sherman became the symbolic repository for white Southerners frustrations.[43]

"The General Was Not without His Good Points"

Sherman's visits to the South and his reception show that a subset of white Southerners—some transplanted Yankees, some native-born, some who lived through the March, others untouched by it—felt warmly toward him.

Many of them recognized the March for what it was, a sort of interregnum in Sherman's affection for the South and its people. Rather than focus on the devastation and destruction of his war, they concentrated on the softness of his peace. Thus, an undated entry into a United Daughters of the Confederacy (UDC) essay contest, entitled "Reconstruction in Georgia," stated simply: "Surrender left the state in military hands. General Sherman, who was as gentle in peace as he was relentless in war, considered the State restored to its original status when arms were laid down." The problems that followed were the fault of the radicals, argued this young author.[44]

Why were Southern whites (none of whom identified themselves as Unionists or transplanted Northerners) willing to praise Sherman? Some looked to Sherman's well-documented past in the antebellum South, as well as his self-professed affection for the region.[45] In 1910 the *Confederate Veteran* published a surprising article, entitled "Gen. W. T. Sherman: His Early Life in the South and His Relations with Southern Men." The article was written by Major David Boyd, a Virginian who had worked with Sherman at the Louisiana Military Academy from 1859 to 1861. According to Boyd, "in association he was rather a Southern man than a Northern man," so influenced by his southern friends that he shared their "free and easy manners, warmth of heart, social and hospitable disposition." Boyd tried to stack the deck by arguing that Sherman was bothered more by secession than anyone, with the possible exception of Robert E. Lee, claiming that their views "about the relations of the States were identical."[46] Just as Lee felt he needed to support his state, so too did Sherman. Boyd also claimed that whenever any of Sherman's Southern friends were captured, they "soon felt his sympathy and his helping hand." Boyd also praised Sherman for his generous postwar support of the Military Academy (which became Louisiana State University).[47] This homage seems to have fallen on deaf ears, however. The same issue featured an editorial condemning Boyd's piece, and complaints about it followed for several months.[48] Nevertheless, those who were well disposed toward Sherman would point to his Southern sympathies when they sought to explain his postwar behavior.

In that vein, one author of a history of Georgia took a stab at it, explaining that "some Southerners even among the survivors of Sherman's historic raid conceded later that the general was not without his good points. When he was not fighting he was a reasonable sort of fellow. He lacked the petty vindictiveness of the long-haired men and short-haired women who as Abolitionists dominated the federal government's post-war policy."[49] So in this case, what mattered most was not the war, but Reconstruction. And since Sherman was a far cry from a Radical Republican, or a friend of African

Americans, he seemed to be on Southern whites' side. This same history claimed that Sherman (unlike Lee) "approved of slavery," and disapproved of African American troops.[50] While this first premise is debatable, the second is accurate. Too, white Southerners recognized the generosity of the surrender terms that Sherman offered Joseph Johnston in April 1865.

Those white Southerners who would praise Sherman frequently drew this distinction between "Sherman at war" and "Sherman at peace." Reconstruction, along with its attendant granting of civil and political rights to African Americans, was a frequent source of white anger and fed into both racial violence and Jim Crow. Because Sherman himself was no great believer in racial equality or Radical Reconstruction, he became a strange sort of ally.[51] If even Sherman, the great enemy and despoiler of the South, could oppose Reconstruction, white Southerners reasoned, than surely this would be seen as a legitimate position in Northern eyes as well. One contributor to the *Confederate Veteran* used quotations from Sherman's own reports (as recorded in the *Official Records*) to make the case that his career could be divided into before and after Johnston's surrender. The 1863–65 quotes show a man pleased with his army's harsh treatment of Southern whites, unashamed of its destructive power. But the selections from "After the Surrender" are much less inflammatory. This Sherman denies that Jefferson Davis could have had anything to do with Lincoln's assassination, pledges kind treatment toward his erstwhile enemies, and opposes black equality. One can imagine this being the favorite quote of Southern whites: "I prefer to give votes to the rebel whites, now humbled, subdued, and obedient, rather than to the ignorant blacks that are not yet capable of self-government."[52] Sherman seemed to have put the war behind him, forgiven former Confederates, and moved on; white Southerners could now count him as a friend.

A Peace Monument for All Our Peoples

Sherman's death on February 14, 1891, sparked a national paroxysm of grief. The affection, even love, that Sherman's men felt for him was well documented and poured out after his passing. They defended him as "free and easy" with his men, clear-eyed, and with "a depth of meaning in his semi-playful words that we did not then comprehend."[53] Others took pains to repudiate the notion that Sherman was a butcher, a man who had no respect for human life (whether those of his men or his enemies). General Slocum drew a pointed distinction, writing that Sherman "handled his army as a fencer would handle a rapier," while "Grant went at the enemy as with a meat axe" and called his commander "sensitive and poetic."[54] That might have been overly romantic. Other men claimed that behind the harshness of the March lay an essential humanitarianism. After all, the harshness of the March brought the war to a close and prevented further loss of life. Sherman was forced into war, proclaimed another eulogist, always wanting peace, fighting "with the sword in one hand, and the olive branch in the other."[55]

Sherman's family sought to keep his memory alive, in part by retelling his stories, and keeping his version of events at the forefront. In 1908 his son P. T. Sherman, who was born after the war, gave a speech at the Society of the Army of the Tennessee's Reunion. In it he reminded the veterans that his father had always considered the March to the Sea as "a soft interlude" between the harder campaigns for Atlanta and through the Carolinas, one that was "overrated . . . its audacity exaggerated." He quoted from the *London Times*, which variously described his father as Napoleon, Hannibal, Xerxes, and Xenophon. Ultimately, P. T. Sherman concluded with a critique of the bitterness of Reconstruction, deeming it "altogether contrary to the terms of the original convention" between his father and Joe Johnston, and claiming that Sherman was positively Lincolnian in his essential moderation.[56]

The first memorial to Sherman marked his gravesite. On February 21, 1891, a procession of twelve thousand, including veterans, dignitaries, and current military members, marched through St. Louis streets lined with mourners, bringing Sherman's body to its final resting place in Calvary Cemetery. Although Sherman was living in New York at the time of his death, he was to be buried next to his wife Ellen (who had passed away in 1888), in St. Louis. The graveside prayers were led by Sherman's son, the Reverend Thomas Sherman, who had become a Jesuit over his father's objections. The grave marker describes him simply as "General U.S. A." and "Faithful and Honorable."[57] Later memorials would be constructed on a much grander scale.

In 1888 members of the New York City Chamber of Commerce, many of whom were friends of Sherman, had commissioned a large equestrian statue of the general from Augustus Saint-Gaudens (best known for his Shaw Memorial). Saint-Gaudens did not start on the statue for several years, until after the general's death, and when he did, he worked from a bust of Sherman he had made in 1888. The statue, cast in bronze and covered in gold leaf, has an allegorical figure, representing the Angel of Victory, leading Sherman on horseback, his cape billowing behind. Finally completed between 1897 and 1903 and set on a granite base designed by the architect Charles McKim, it was the sculptor's last major work.

The St. Gaudens statue of Sherman in New York City's Grand Army Plaza.
The Angel of Victory leads him, carrying a palm frond symbolizing peace. (Library
of Congress, http://www.loc.gov/pictures/item/det1994005600/PP/)

Sherman had posed for more than thirty-five hours for the bust, and Saint-Gaudens's deep familiarity with his subject is evident in the intimacy of the portrait of the aging general. Supposedly, Saint-Gaudens asked the oft-disheveled Sherman to straighten his tie and button his collars, to which Sherman grumpily replied: "The General of the Army of the United States will wear his coat any damn way he pleases."[58] Saint-Gaudens wanted to portray Sherman's grim determination to end the war through the harsh cruelties of the March, but at the same time to temper it with a sense of human costs. Elihu Root made a similar point in his speech at the monument's dedication: "We can tell those who came after us that not only was Sherman great but his people loved him. This stern and relentless master of horrid war had a heart as gentle and tender as a woman's."[59]

A bough of long-leafed pine at Sherman's feet symbolized the March through Georgia.[60] Interestingly, especially given Sherman's complex attitudes toward the freedpeople, the choice of model for the Angel of Victory was Harriette (Hettie) Anderson, an African American woman. Anderson was from Columbia, South Carolina, a coincidental link to the March itself.

She carries a palm frond, as she faces south, symbolizing peace as well as victory.[61]

Both the statue itself and its location engendered controversy: Saint-Gaudens wanted to place it at the entrance to Grant's Tomb. Relatives of both of the generals objected, and ultimately the statue was unveiled at the corner of 59th Street and Fifth Avenue, the southeast entrance to Central Park, on Memorial Day in 1903. A few years later the statue was moved to the central area of Grand Army Plaza, near the Pulitzer Fountain, where it still remains.[62] As for the subject, Henry James "deplored 'all attempts, however glittering and golden, to confound destroyers with benefactors'—in this case, a man 'symbolizing the very breath of the Destroyer' with 'embodied grace, in the form of a beautiful American girl, attending his business.'" Some Southerners have quipped that it symbolized Yankee rudeness, to have the man riding while the woman walked.[63] Poet Henry Van Dyke summed up the meaning and the power of the monument in four brief lines:

> This is the soldier brave enough to tell
> The glory-dazzled world that "war is hell":
> Lover of peace, he looks beyond the strife
> And rides through hell to save his country's life.[64]

Sherman's fellow soldiers were not to be outdone. The Society of the Army of the Tennessee's October 1891 meeting happened as scheduled in Chicago, and one of the highlights of the meeting, indeed the reason for its timing, was the unveiling of the equestrian statue of General Grant in Lincoln Park on October 7.[65] During the meeting, the society resolved to begin fundraising for a monument to Sherman, and began with a contribution of $500.[66] The following year Congress approved the Sherman Statue Commission, and apportioned $50,000, with the understanding that the society would raise the same amount. The society approached the other Union veterans' societies, including the Grand Army of the Republic and the Military Order of the Loyal Legion, urging them to contribute "so that when the statue is erected in Washington every soldier who sees it will feel that it is part of his efforts." Despite these lofty goals, the veterans raised only $14,469.91, and Congress was forced to double the size of its appropriation. A formal invitation to sculptors went out in March 1895, and the ultimate winner of the competition was Carl Rohl-Smith of Chicago. Even this was not without controversy, as some of the losers in the completion complained to Congress and the press.[67]

The contract between the commission and Rohl-Smith detailed what the statue and its pedestal should look like, including the following features:

- A main equestrian figure of Sherman, plus secondary groups representing both "War" and "Peace"
- Bas Reliefs on the base entitled "Marching through Georgia," "Battle of Atlanta," "General Sherman Planning while the Army Sleeps," and "Missionary Ridge"
- The badge of the Society of the Army of the Tennessee, and the Coat of Arms of the United States
- Statues representing the Corps of Engineers, Cavalry, Artillery, and Infantry
- Eight portrait medallions, to be decided by the Society of the Army of the Tennessee

The statue would be located just behind the White House and the Treasury Department, the spot where Sherman had watched the Grand Review pass by in 1865—a prominent location. Work on the statue began in the spring of 1898, but Rohl-Smith passed away in August 1900. His widow was determined to complete the statue. She also provided insight into her husband's artistic choices, which themselves helped to fix the Northern, triumphalist narrative of the March in bronze.[68]

Certainly it is striking that the statue showed only Sherman's 1864–65 achievements: the Atlanta campaign and the March, regardless of the rest of his long career. Rohl-Smith chose to portray the general himself on what he supposed to be "the happiest day of his life," as he rode up Pennsylvania Avenue during the Grand Review to the "plaudits of the people." Rohl-Smith sought to reveal Sherman's pride in and love for his men. Among the reliefs, Mrs. Rohl-Smith explained, the one depicting the March "was found not to be so dangerous as feared in the North. The men are singing and somebody is calling out to 'Uncle Billy,' . . . while the colored folks, hearing the clatter of the hoofs, have stepped outside their huts and with awe look at the spectacle, not exactly understanding the 'cause.'" This was a portrait of the March as lighthearted fun, with the real political meaning of emancipation subsumed under the spectacle. And because it was cast in bronze and carved in marble, it conferred a permanence and legitimacy on this story, at the expense of others.[69]

The statue was finally finished and unveiled to great fanfare on October 15, 1903. The reviewing stand was decorated with red, white, and blue bunting, elaborate flower arrangements, festoons of laurel and galox leaves, and

Flags being pulled away to unveil the statue of Sherman in Washington, D.C., in 1903. President Theodore Roosevelt and General Daniel Sickles were among the speakers at the ceremony. (Print Collection, Miriam and Ira D. Wallach Division of Art, Prints and Photographs, New York Public Library, Astor, Lenox and Tilden Foundations)

shields representing the different Civil War armies. The statue itself was hidden by a large arrangement of flags. The festivities began with a military review, featuring members of the army, navy, Marine Corps, and the D.C. National Guard, passing in front of President Theodore Roosevelt himself. At the conclusion of the review, the Marine Band played the "always applauded 'Sherman's March through Georgia.'" Then came the dedication, and the unveiling of the statue by Sherman's young grandson, William Tecumseh Sherman Thorndike. And then the speeches, by a variety of Sherman's fellow generals, including David B. Henderson and Daniel E. Sickles, and finally, by President Roosevelt himself.[70]

The Sherman they came to praise was the general as he would have wanted to be remembered. General David Henderson and Brigadier General Charles H. Grosvenor of Ohio both remarked that the March through the Carolinas was even more significant—"the greatest work of Sherman's life"—in Henderson's word, than the dramatic March to the Sea. The speakers also tried to walk the line between celebrating Sherman's skills as a warrior and remaining mindful of the fragility of reunion sentiment. Thus, Henderson praised the statue because "It does not represent Sherman in battle. It is Sherman amid the well-won glories of peace. It is Sherman the peacemaker, receiving the thrilling, rapturous applause of the bronzed peacemakers of a saved republic." Henderson wanted the statue (and, by extension, Sherman himself) to be an icon of reunion:

> May this statue ever stand in our capital as a monument to American courage; as a monument to military education; as a monument to Americanism, combining the citizen and the soldier; as an inspiration to the ambitious young American; as a proof that the heroes of the Revolution and their deeds will never be forgotten or neglected by their descendants. Let it ever stand as a peace monument for all of our people, and therefore it must stand as the monument of William Tecumseh Sherman.[71]

Roosevelt invoked Sherman less as a reunion figure than as a savior of the Union, less a universal man than an exemplar of the Union veterans who thronged the city for the ceremonies. Too, Roosevelt took the opportunity to call for ethical behavior in public service, holding Sherman up as a model of American citizenship, celebrating "his courage, his kindliness, his clean and simple living, his sturdy good sense, his manliness and tenderness in the intimate relations of life, and finally, in his flexible rectitude of soul and his loyalty to all that in this free Republic is hallowed and symbolized by the national flag."[72] A memorial is not the place for a critical assessment, and particularly not at the dedication. Still, it is striking how much of Sherman's varied life and career was boiled down into the events of a year.

The Laws of Civilized Nations and the Customs of War

One of the thorniest questions regarding the impact of Sherman's March has to do with its legality, arguably as distinct from its morality. Questions like "Was Sherman a war criminal?" or "Did Sherman invent terrorism?" proliferate on Civil War blogs and message boards, along with accusations that he was the originator of "total war." A history of Henry County, Georgia, explained simply that "Sherman's March to the Sea was the first hint of the concept of 'Total War,' which was to come to full fruition during the Second World War, in which civilian infrastructure is considered a legitimate military target."[73] Later writers, notably James Reston Jr., tried to connect the March to atrocities in Vietnam, arguing that "when a rash Confederate ventured a shot on his trains from a courthouse, the courthouse was burned. When a lady burned her corncrib, she lost her house. The 'proportionality' of the retaliation is roughly the same, if geometrically less, as hostile fire from a jungle rifle being greeted by a B-52 strike."[74] Not that most writers even define what they mean by "total war" or "laws of war." Often Sherman seems to be judged by the standards of today, rather than his own time. Often "total war" seemed to refer to the degree of national mobilization, as opposed to the range of targets.[75]

In 1864 there were no Hague or Geneva conventions to govern the actions of belligerents. That is not to say there were no guides for military behavior and conduct. By the time the March began in 1864, the Union army was governed by Abraham Lincoln's General Orders No. 100, better known as the Lieber Code.[76] Named for its author, the Prussian-born Francis Lieber, the code was designed to codify the laws of war, especially as they pertained to interactions between civilians and soldiers. One of the most significant sections of the Code was Articles 14–16, which defined "military necessity."[77] Lieber's relatively broad definition, while deploring "cruelty" and acts of vengeance, did allow the making of war on civilians, as in the following:

- Article 17: War is not carried on by arms alone. It is lawful to starve the hostile belligerent, armed or unarmed, so that it leads to the speedier subjection of the enemy.
- Article 20: Public war is a state of armed hostility between sovereign nations or governments. It is a law and requisite of

civilized existence that men live in political, continuous societies, forming organized units, called states or nations, whose constituents bear, enjoy, suffer, advance and retrograde together, in peace and in war.

- Article 21: The citizen or native of a hostile country is thus an enemy, as one of the constituents of the hostile state or nation, and as such is subjected to the hardships of the war.[78]

Among the code's prohibitions, however, was the theft or destruction of artworks and the like (Article 35); and, under the punishment of death, "all wanton violence committed against persons in the invaded country, all destruction of property not commanded by the authorized officer, all robbery, all pillage or sacking, even after taking a place by main force, all rape, wounding, maiming, or killing of such inhabitants."[79]

Historian Daniel Sutherland argues that the emergence of total war began even before Grant and Sherman came east, with John Pope in 1862. Pope issued a series of orders that allowed the Army of Virginia to subsist on the produce of the local countryside (among other things), and a desperately frustrated Lincoln approved them. Pope's soldiers went on a tear of destruction and violence, reminiscent of the stories that would come out of Georgia and the Carolinas two years later. So great were the abuses perpetrated on civilians that Pope was forced to condemn his men; these misdeeds were what prompted Lincoln to ask Lieber to draft the code.[80]

Confederates claimed that the code was so broad as to license "mischief" under the grounds of military necessity; certainly, by 1864 Lincoln and the Union had become comfortable with a high degree of destruction of private property (cotton and the contents of homes, if not homes themselves), in areas like Missouri and the Shenandoah Valley.[81] Thus one could argue that the Lieber Code, at least as it pertained to the treatment of civilians, was honored more in the breach than closely followed.[82]

Francis J. Lippitt's *Field Service in War*, a manual on military logistics published just after the war, leans on military necessity to justify foraging, arguing that it was a "well-established right of war." But at the same time, Lippitt did concede that it was incumbent on commanders and soldiers to restrain themselves. To do otherwise would be to bring dishonor upon the country.[83] Lippitt's own work demonstrates the complexity of the moral issues surrounding foraging. By its very nature the act of seizing supplies inflicts hardships on the civilian population. In order to inflict the least amount of harm (and thus to operate within the moral, if not the legal boundaries of so-called civilized warfare), tight control must be maintained. Without defined foraging parties and a centralized distribution system—that is, when a commander allowed troops to supply themselves—chaos would ensue. Specifically, Lippitt warned, it would lead:

(1). To an entire relaxation of discipline without which a military force is only an armed mob
(2). To universal pillage, and to murders and other outrages by the troops upon the inhabitants, which always follow in its train
(3). To the consequent massacre of straggling parties, in retaliation, by the inhabitants, who are thus made bitter enemies
(4). To an enormous waste and destruction of the supplies themselves over and above what is actually consumed[84]

One might have expected Lippitt to use the recent example of Sherman's March, but he did not, hearkening instead to Napoleon's Russian campaign. He did not just ignore the March; Lippitt instead defended it, first claiming that when seizing household goods the men carefully "discriminat[ed] between the rich, who were generally hostile to us, and the poor and industrious, who were usually friendly or at least neutral." Too, he described an organized and controlled system, complete with detailed rules and receipts. Any deviations from them were the fault of a few bad apples, stragglers and the like, not the main force of marchers.[85]

White Southerners frequently drew comparisons between Sherman's March and Robert E. Lee's invasions of Maryland in 1862 and Pennsylvania in 1863. They often quoted Lee's General Orders No. 72 to his soldiers on the Pennsylvania campaign, in which he reminded them that "the duties expected of us by civilization and Christianity are not less obligatory in the country of the enemy than in our own," and "that we make war only upon armed men, and that we cannot take vengeance for the wrongs our people have suffered without lowering ourselves in the eyes of all whose abhorrence has been excited by the atrocities of our enemies." Those who praised Lee, like the UDC member who penned a detailed comparison of the two campaigns, did so selectively, however, ignoring the many wrongs perpetrated by Lee's men on African Americans.[86]

Despite innumerable allegations to the contrary, Sherman himself was well aware that war was governed by rules. Many have used his September 12, 1864, letter to the mayor of Atlanta in which Sherman asserted "War is cruelty and you cannot refine it" to make the argument that he was willing to do whatever worked, to wreak all kinds of havoc on civilians in order to end the war. But in other letters written at the same time, Sherman is quite explicit about following the laws of war. In fact, he was quite angry when Confederate general John Bell Hood challenged the legitimacy of evicting civilians from Atlanta. "I think I understand the Laws of Civilized nations and 'the Customs of War,' he snapped in one letter, before suggesting that the Confederates ought to take better care of Union prisoners at Andersonville. In his final letter to Hood, he proclaimed that he "was not bound by the laws of war to give notice of the shelling of Atlanta," because the city was fortified and used for military purposes. "See the books," he testily concluded.[87]

Sherman believed he was operating within the laws of war and parameters of so-called civilized behavior, but that did not mean that he was unwilling to push up against the boundaries of those rules. Frightening people, stealing their supplies, even burning their barns was one thing; wholesale killing or raping, as happened in areas riven by guerrilla violence, was beyond the pale. Sherman biographer Michael Fellman has argued that while the March "stopped well short of a 'total war' in the twentieth-century Nazi sense," Sherman's rhetoric of destruction implied that he could make war on whomever he chose, and that Southern whites would be powerless to stop him.[88]

Did that make Sherman a terrorist? He certainly used calculated brutality to terrorize the Southern population. Fellman describes Sherman as having "terrorist capacities."[89] And what responsibility, for both destroying and reigning themselves in, accrues to the soldiers on the March? Part of the reason that the March was not "total" in the twentieth-century sense was because the veterans limited themselves, held back by their own internal, cultural sense of morality.[90]

Sherman himself may have overstepped the bounds of legality a few times, each time in retaliation for Confederate actions, each time regarding his use of prisoners of war. In the first instance, when Sherman learned of torpedoes or mines buried outside of Savannah, he called for prisoners to be brought up to clear them. In the second, when Union foragers were being captured and killed by Wade Hampton's men in South Carolina, Sherman ordered prisoners to draw lots, and chose one to be killed, thus setting an example.[91]

But what keeps Sherman from being a terrorist, in the modern sense of the word, is that he was operating during wartime, with the full sanction and support of his government. When the war ended, so too did his hostilities and destruction. A better analogy to terrorism in the wake of the Civil War would be the waves of violence that confronted African Americans during Reconstruction as they sought to exercise their new economic, social, and political freedoms. The notion that Sherman brought forth a different kind of war with the March makes sense only retrospectively. As the nineteenth century became the twentieth, and as wars of increasing deadliness and destructive power broke out around the globe, the March seemed to reappear again and again. Often, the analogy was strained, but it revealed much about the common understanding of the March, or of a simplified version of it.

Thus in 1902, a humor column in the *New York Times* reproached the Democrats for criticizing soldiers' activities in the Philippines. Written by Robert Welch in the colloquial voice of Silas Larrabee of Ogunquit, Maine, the column called for loyalty to the soldiers (rather than criticism). He minimized the cruelties perpetuated on the Filipinos, comparing them first to American activities against Indians in the West, and then moved on to the more distant past:

> And how about Sherman's march through Georgy? That was deverstation, wasn't it? And didn't the people of the North say it was a good job? Ever know a band up North that couldn't play 'Marchin' Through Georgy? Why they sing it to babies—make it a cradle song. Somehow I rayther think when we come to know the hull story we'll pootty much all of us agree that Smith's operations was jest about on a level with Sherman's accordin' to.[92]

Welch is highlighting an essential hypocrisy: if Americans were comfortable with swaths of destruction at home, why should they have a problem with them further afield? If excuses could be made for Sherman's bummers, why not for Smith's soldiers?

Over a decade later, Sherman's March reappeared in the national and international discourse, as Germany marched through Belgium, and the world erupted into war. A piece in the *New York Times* in September 1914 attempted to calculate the collective cost of all wars in human history, concluding that the human toll was some 15 billion lives. As for the costs of destroyed property, the authors threw up their metaphorical hands, determining it to be both "enormous" and incalculable. This is where Sherman's March came in: they used it as an example, citing Sherman's own estimate of $300 million property destroyed. But the value of the property lost in the Civil War would pale in comparison to the amount currently at risk in Europe, particularly Belgium and France. In this instance, the devastation of Sherman's March is being minimized, rather than connected to the wars of the twentieth century.[93]

More commonly, the devastation of Sherman's March was used to remind Americans of the costs of war, however justifiable. Professor William

M. Sloane of Columbia University, prophetically called the war "a world disaster of unparalleled significance," and warned against American intervention overseas. He cautioned Americans against becoming too outraged by atrocities perpetrated against civilians, lest that lead them to intervene. Patronizingly, Sloane opined that "the sense of outrage which Americans feel over the horrors of war, while most creditable to them, is very often based upon an ignorance of the rules and regulations of so-called civilized warfare, and upon a sentimentality which, though also very creditable, is unfortunately not one of the factors in the world's work." He called upon his readers to put their sentimentality aside, and to recall both Sherman's March and Hunter's 1864 Valley campaign, noting that "at that time, in what we considered the supreme danger to our country, the conduct of those men was approved and they themselves were almost deified for their actions."[94] Sloane seems to be saying to readers that if Sherman could be not only forgiven but celebrated, then Americans should remember the Monroe doctrine and give the Germans a pass in the interests of their own security.

These early references to the Civil War and Sherman continued to pop up during the years of World War I. In May 1915 Professor Yandell Henderson (of Yale University) wrote a pro-German column in the *New York Times*, again encouraging American neutrality. Henderson minimized Germany's invasion of Belgium, pointing out that, "as for atrocities, Belgium, Serbia, East Prussia, and Poland have probably been no more thoroughly desolated than Georgia after Sherman's march to the Sea. Away from ordinary social restraints, men always do such things. It is rare for a militia company here to have a field day, or a college class to hold a reunion without a certain percentage making beasts of themselves." Like earlier writers, Henderson is downplaying the March in order to make his broader political point: that atrocities overseas should not warrant intervention, and that Americans should not go to war with Germany.[95]

Henderson's letter prompted a series of angry responses. Historian G. M. Trevelyan listed the atrocities being perpetrated in Europe and challenged Henderson's "boys will be boys" attitude. The attacks on civilians in Europe did not constitute normal behavior by soldiers or young men; and Trevelyan wrote in to "deny that Sherman's troops either burned women and children alive or gouged people's eyes out or murdered civilians wholesale, as the Austro-Hungarian troops did in Serbia." The following day's paper contained a letter from Mary Cadwalader Jones, who had lived in the South during the waning days of the Civil War. She remembered seeing "grim" evidence of devastation, starving civilians, "but here were no 'atrocities' and no 'frightfulness.'" She deplored the damage, for which she blamed bummers and faithless slaves, "but it was not accompanied by beastliness or cruelty, nor was the desolation to be even compared with that of Belgium and Serbia now."[96] This flies in the face of the conventional wisdom that to Southern whites Sherman's March was the ultimate destruction, the worst of the worst.

George Haven Putnam, whose Civil War career included service in New Orleans in 1862, the Shenandoah Valley in 1864, and North Carolina and Savannah in 1865, joined the attack against Yandell Henderson. Henderson drew a distinction between Germany's officially ordered and sanctioned shootings of civilians, sinkings of ships, and generally making war on noncombatants and the destruction of property in the Civil War South. Putnam perceived Henderson's essay as an attack on the honor and reputation of American (read Union) soldiers, and one that he felt was not befitting a professor at Yale.[97]

Thus far the responses to Henderson's initial article took issue with his equating Sherman's March and German attacks on civilians. But at least one reader, a military historian named John A. Bigelow, thought that the quest to minimize Civil War antecedents went too far. Bigelow rightly pointed out that just because Sherman's men were not as brutal as German troops does not mean that they should be absolved of all guilt. Bigelow noted that the men of 1864 and 1865 went well beyond their written orders and seemed to be unstoppable. Is "an army which waits to act frightfully, until it is ordered to do so . . . more to be criticized than one which resorts to such action without orders and persists in it when ordered to desist," wondered Bigelow. That is, where do the moral bearings of the men themselves come in? Is terrorizing civilians not terrorizing civilians, whether under orders or not? Similarly, Putnam wondered, "If Sherman was not wanton in his harshness because he had a military object in it, may not the Germans be similarly justified?" Bigelow is raising one of the central moral questions of the March and its legacy: do we retrospectively excuse the excesses of Sherman's men because we agree with their cause? Do we excuse them because they won?[98]

In an editorial on June 15, the editors of the *New York Times* weighed in on the controversy, proclaiming that "Georgia Was Not Belgium." They reminded their readers that the "atrocities" in Belgium shocking the world included using civilians as shields, misuse of white flags, taking and murdering hostages—all crimes of which Sherman's men were not even accused, much less guilty.[99] The next column featured a reply to Bigelow, this one advocating intervention precisely because of the level of German cruelty against civilians, which was so much greater than that of the Union army.[100]

Bigelow responded in turn on June 19, arguing that the differences in execution between the Germans and Sherman's men did not account for similarities in impulse. That is, both sides were animated by the same intentions: "Each officer placed efficiency before humanity, except so far as efficiency meant humanity to him. If one may take Sherman at his word, he would not have stopped at a massacre had it seemed to him necessary to the attainment of his military object." Bigelow went on to clarify his earlier point about the differences between 1864–65 and 1914–15, explaining that "things do not have to be parallel to be properly comparable." Bigelow continued to insist on the utility of the American past for the global present.[101]

Once the United States became involved in World War I, the usable past of Sherman's March ceased to be a significant point of discussion.[102] The analogy reappeared briefly after the war, during testimony before the Senate Committee on Propaganda in 1919. Grant Squires, a New York lawyer who visited Belgium, testified to the cruelties he saw perpetrated by the Germans: men and women beaten with rifle butts, children and babies murdered, and families starving without shelter. Squires was then asked to counter earlier testimony by German sympathizer, Dr. Edmund von Mach to the effect that Sherman's March had "also been a very cruel expedition." This enraged Senator Knute Nelson (a Civil War veteran), who angrily proclaimed that American soldiers had never "killed women and children. Whatever they did, they did not do that." Nelson specifically asked Squires to address von Mach's charges that the Germans were no worse than Sherman's men; Squires confirmed that the Germans were different from any predecessors.[103] Essentially, what this exchange shows is that a new standard was being set for violations of civilians. Where once Sherman's men's thefts and fires were the worst that could be imagined, the Great War issued horrors of an entirely different order of magnitude.

Not everyone got the memo that Sherman was no longer the epitome of evil. The English novelist, critic, and travel writer Ford Madox Ford reflected on Sherman during his travels in the United States during the 1930s. Unlike other writers who began their musings by visiting the sites of the March (whether in Georgia or the Carolinas), Ford's reverie began far away, at the home where a woman was killed during the battle of Gettysburg. Why was such a fuss made over this one unfortunate woman, he wondered, as "there were plenty women killed and worse by Sherman's licensed plunderers, and one does not much bother about them."[104] Ford then went on to condemn

Sherman for burning "Columbus" (clearly he meant Columbia), blaming Wade Hampton, and admitting that his soldiers were drunk when they did it. He compared the burning of Columbia to the burning of Liège, Belgium, but noted approvingly that "the Great German Staff had at least the decency to deny fiercely that their troops were drunk," regardless of whether they were inebriated or not. Ford praised Confederate generals like Robert E. Lee and Stonewall Jackson, while condemning Grant, Sherman, and Sheridan as "murderers," who disobeyed "the dictates of humanity." His ultimate point, clearly influenced as much by his World War I experiences as his travels in America is that

> it is silly to say that the butchering of civilians shortens wars and is therefore more humane. . . . Or burning their houses or crops or furniture or clothing. I suppose that if you completely wiped out a whole nation, civilians plus armed forces, you might stop a war. But, horrible as they are, modern methods of war are not as efficient as all that—and not quite stamped out peoples develop a philoprogenitive-ness, a tenacity of purpose, a vindictiveness.[105]

The "war to end all wars" reanimated debates over attacks on civilians. Ford was certainly right about the vindictiveness that would continue to burn through the survivors of scorched-earth tactics.

A 1937 article in the *Milledgeville Times* noted that a new three-cent stamp, featuring a portrait of Sherman, "caused a considerable stir" in Georgia's erstwhile capital. According to one report, the paper interviewed the town's last surviving veteran, who "pronounced Sherman not only an unfit subject for such a stamp but for history books as well." The ire of Milledgevillians was quelled only by the realization that there was in fact a Robert E. Lee stamp, and that cost *four* cents, indicative of Lee's exalted position.[106] In fact, both the Georgia and the South Carolina state legislatures protested Sherman's appearance on the stamp, which boosted sales considerably, according to one postal official.[107]

On the surface this seems like a typical story of unreconstructed rebels and quaint holdovers of anger. What is interesting, however, is that this was not the first stamp to feature Sherman, and in fact he was not even alone on the stamp—he shared it with Grant and Sheridan. In 1893 and 1895 the Postal Service issued eight-cent Sherman stamps, without apparent controversy. These were issued in the wake of Sherman's death, at the height of sectional reunion. In 1911, the citizens of Huntsville, Texas, petitioned the postmaster general, asking him to refrain from selling any stamps or postal cards featuring Sherman. Their angry insistence did not seem to be prompted by any particular issue; rather this was a preemptive measure, and one that did not seem to be common practice. In contrast, the 1930s were a period of greater strife and nascent sectional and political tensions.[108]

The Vietnam War, perhaps because it coincided with the centennial of the Civil War, raised more analogies to Sherman's March. Historian Theodore Rosengarten recalled being astonished in the 1960s and 1970s when he heard a variety of cultural critics and opponents of the war in Vietnam (including Mary McCarthy, Howard Levine, and Michael Hess) "compare Sherman's operations in Georgia and the Carolinas to crimes committed by Americans in Vietnam. They called Sherman our first merchant of terror, the spiritual father of such hated doctrines as search and destroy, pacification, strategic hamlets, free-fire zones. You had to wonder whether without Sherman the atom bomb might not have been dropped."[109] Perhaps the connection had to do with loss and defeat, as C. Vann Woodward described in *The Burden of Southern History*. Perhaps it had to do with the intimacy of the fighting and the hand-to-hand targeting of civilians, different from the massive battles of World War II. Perhaps it had to do with the need to knit a divided nation back together.

The most detailed and culturally significant exploration of this relationship came in James Reston Jr.'s 1984 book *Sherman's March and Vietnam*. Reston retraced the March through Georgia, looking to the past to explain the more turbulent present. He seemed at times to draw a straight line of connection between nineteenth- and twentieth-century violence:

> Gen. William Tecumseh Sherman is considered by many to be the author of "total war," the first general of modern human history to carry the logic of war to its ultimate extreme, the first to scorch the earth, the first to wreck an economy in order to starve its soldiers. He was our first "merchant of terror," and the spiritual father, some contend, of our Vietnam concepts of "search and destroy," "pacification," "strategic hamlets," "free fire zones." As such he remains a cardboard figure of our history: a monstrous arch-villain to unreconstructed Southerners, an embarrassment to Northerners who wonder if "civilized war" died with him, whether without Sherman the atom bomb might not have been dropped or Vietnam entered.[110]

Reston did concede that the connection was more metaphorical than real, but at the same time it raised real questions about limits during wartime, and how those limits could shift. What was the conceptual or theoretical difference between destroying property and killing people? While conceding that much of what Americans thought about Sherman (and, by extension, his men) was informed by mythology rather than facts, those myths mattered. Reston wanted to shape the inevitable mythologizing of the Vietnam experience as well. Thus he concluded that "Sherman's soldiers and Westmoreland's soldiers have important things in common."[111] What they had in common, Reston argued, was being animated by a desire for vengeance and reprisals. Where they differed was in questions of scale, which was as much a function of technology as of desire.[112] Men in the twentieth century had weapons of mass destruction; Union soldiers did not.

One of the signal differences between the March and Vietnam, however, came with the environment to which the soldiers returned. Vietnam divided the nation profoundly, with the result that soldiers were demoralized, both in the field and upon their return. But Sherman's men were greeted as heroes, at least at home in the Union.[113] Even more importantly, Sherman's men won their war.

What of more contemporary times? In 1995 the United States Postal Service issued another set of Civil War stamps. Again they included Sherman, pictured alone, holding binoculars, seemingly about to set out on the March. The back of the stamp included these explanatory remarks:

Union Major General
William Tecumseh Sherman
1820–1891
Blunt, grizzled strategist distinguished himself at Shiloh and Vicksburg. Captured Atlanta. Introduced total warfare in the March across GA and through the Carolinas. Negotiated lenient peace.

This moderate portrait befits a sheet of stamps that advertised itself as "Once Divided, Now Perforated." His introduction of total war could be countered by his lenient peace.

CHAPTER SIX

On Sherman's Track

In 1869, Union veteran and journalist Russell H. Conwell set off to see the South, sending letters back for the edification of the readers of the *Boston Evening Traveler*. Like so many other visitors, he boarded a train in Savannah and headed toward Macon to see "the traces of Sherman's great march which are still to be seen on every side." The countryside through which he passed was "a hideous ruin." Chimneys stood everywhere, "surrounded by weeds and wild shrubs. Old posts and here and there a broken rail are all that is left of the fences." The pine and oak forests still bore the scars of fire "and the Negroes plant cotton between the dead and leafless trees, where before the war was a wild and impassable thicket." Conwell retold stories of devastation and theft and skies glowing red with fire, all the while admitting to skepticism. "But, alas!" he concluded, "the proofs show us some acts of heinous barbarity, preclude a denial, and show the worst side of war. We must say that the ruin and ashes we saw and the tales with which the people filled our head destroyed all the poetry we used to see in . . . 'While we were marching through Georgia'"[1]

Sherman's men had scarcely completed their march through Georgia and the Carolinas before travelers started flooding into the South. Visitors came by the dozens to see the devastation firsthand and later to trace the scars on the landscape. From Reconstruction-era newspaper reporters to novelists, from riders of freight trains to hikers on foot, they retraced Sherman's path through Georgia and the Carolinas. The places they visited illuminated struggles over history and interpretation. As these travelers recorded their impressions, they revealed much about themselves and their attitudes toward the Civil War.[2]

This chapter draws on several dozen accounts written by either Britons or Americans (all men but one) published between 1866 and 1998. I have divided them into three chronological groups: the Reconstruction writers; the 1980s and 1990s writers; and the one that I call "the middle," which includes writers active roughly from 1880 to 1960. For reasons that are not entirely clear to me, I have no travel accounts from the 1960s-1970s. The Reconstruction writers, not surprisingly, focused on stories of destruction and rebuilding, with a side interest (especially during the 1860s) in the plight of the freedmen. The middle group is the hardest to characterize: some novelists, some more attuned to sociological studies, and a very few more interested (particularly in the 1930s and 1940s) in the "race problem" in America. Finally, the members of the more contemporary group seem to be on more explicit journeys of self-discovery, with Sherman's path serving as the medium.

Reconstruction Writers

Northern writers like Whitelaw Reid, Sidney Andrews, John Trowbridge, and John Dennett came to see the impact of the war on the region, to gauge the degree to which former Confederates were cowed and defeated, and to see firsthand the freedmen's struggles in their new lives. While their routes often varied, their impressions rarely did. As historian Megan Kate Nelson has pointed out, some of what they explicitly came to assess were the ruins of the war, seeing them as physical symbols of cultural change. This was especially true in places traversed by the March.[3]

Like many a nineteenth-century traveler, visitors to Georgia and the Carolinas complained about their traveling conditions, especially the "execrable" conditions of the roads.[4] Of course, such complaints had been a staple of prewar writings, and four years of wartime and neglect in general could not have helped. Almost without fail, Reconstruction-era writers remarked on the condition of the railroads, noting the prevalence of "Sherman's necklaces"— hairpins, bars, corkscrews, twists—but often with an amused tone, as though marveling at the Yankee ingenuity involved. In Blackville, South Carolina, Sidney Andrews noted his "profound admiration for the genius displayed by his troops in destroying railroads. Literally their work must be seen to be appreciated. To wind a bar of iron twice around a telegraph pole or a small tree seems to have been but mere pastime, and to fuse a dozen bars together at the center by an immense fire of ties appears to have been thought a happy joke."[5] On New Year's Eve 1865–66, John Dennett took the train from Augusta, Georgia, to Atlanta, thus moving from an area that had been spared into the zone of devastation. As he drew closer to Atlanta, he "saw burned buildings at the way stations, rails fantastically twisted and bent, and ruined locomotives— remembrances of Sherman and Johnston."[6]

John Trowbridge praised the "conscientious thoroughness" of the devastation and deemed the range of twisted shapes in Georgia "amusing," noting: "Hair-pins predominated. Corkscrews were also abundant. Sometimes we found four or five rails wound around the trunk of a tree, which would have to be cut before they could be got off again." While in South Carolina, Trowbridge again noted the variety, this time struck by the differences in technique between one group of soldiers and the next:

> For a mile or two you would see nothing but hairpins and bars
> wrapped around telegraph posts and trees. Then you would have
> corkscrews and twists for about the same distance. Then came a party
> that gave each heated rail one sharp wrench in the middle, and left
> it perhaps nearly straight, but facing both ways. Here was a plain
> business method, and there a fantastic style, which showed that its
> authors took a wild delight in their work.[7]

Within a few years, however, visitors saw little evidence of these happy jokes, remarking instead on the rapidity with which at least the Georgia Central Railroad was reconstructed. The exception was one woman who professed to prefer walking to allowing freedmen on the railroads, a presaging perhaps of postwar railroad segregation.[8]

John Trowbridge paid particular attention to the differences in relative destruction between Georgia, North Carolina, and South Carolina. Rumor had it that Sherman remarked in Georgia "that he had his gloves on as yet, but that he should take them off in South Carolina." In North Carolina, Trowbridge heard the continuation of the anecdote that featured Sherman telling his soldiers "Boys . . . remember we are in the old North State now," meaning it was time to put the gloves back on. Not surprisingly, residents of Georgia and North Carolina resented the implication that they had not borne the brunt of the destruction. A Confederate brigadier general put it somewhat differently, telling Trowbridge that Sherman "did a sort of retail business in North Carolina, but it was a wholesale business, and no mistake, in Georgia, though perhaps not quite so smashing as his Carolina operations." Trowbridge sought to further parse the ruination, arguing that devastation was worse in eastern Georgia than the middle of the state "the General having . . . slipped one glove off."[9]

Wherever the postwar travelers went, they remarked on destruction and retold tales of atrocities: homes and businesses plundered, livestock stolen, hunting dogs killed, pianos smashed.[10] The specifics offer few surprises and tend to blur together. They are not significantly different from the stories told by Southern civilians or African Americans. This is what the travelers were coming to find: empty fields, unplanted or ungrazed; struggling farms; a "ghastly ruin and silence of death."[11] Sometimes the stories seemed unbelievable, "too sickening and disgusting to be repeated or too hideous to be thought of without chills of horror."[12] But often they were true.

If ruin and wrath were all that travelers found in the immediate postwar years, this would be a brief and repetitive chapter. But they wrote not purely to describe but also to persuade and influence. Thus, they also sought to minimize the destruction and havoc that had been wreaked, as a way to perhaps absolve Union soldiers of their guilt or make the March seem more justifiable and less abjectly cruel. Few did it as openly as John Kennaway, who defended the destruction, even the excesses, on the grounds that "possibly Sherman believed that so severe a punishment would in the end prove the truest kindness to the South, if it should be the means of perceptibly shortening the war."[13] This was more akin to the argument that the veterans themselves made. Robert Ferguson made related assertions when confronted with the ruined home of South Carolina poet William Gilmore Simms. Ferguson didn't quite say that Simms deserved it, but he did describe it as having been "one of the show places of slavery." Now Woodlands was reduced to "wild disorder": blackened walls, trampled rose beds, and overgrown grass. While languidly condemning such "vandalism," Ferguson does two things to deflect blame. First he quoted Sherman's famous assertion: "War is cruelty and you cannot refine it." Then he went on to blame much of the devastation on the ill-mannered bummers, rather than the supposedly more disciplined regular troops. But in the final analysis, Ferguson decided that few Northern soldiers would have held back, instead seeing the destruction of the property of one of the leaders of the secession movement as nothing more "than a righteous judgment."[14]

Rather than argue that destruction was excused by the greater good (a sort of ends-justifying-the-means argument), other visitors claimed there was much less destruction than they had been led to believe. Less than a year after the March, John Dennett was surprised at how few houses were missing between Columbia and Augusta; he made similar comments about the countryside northwest of Columbia and in the Alston, Fairfield, and Richland districts. According to his calculations, only about one-fourth of the homes near the roads had been burned and "no Negro cabin seems to have been destroyed." Even when he complained about the roads in South Carolina, he attributed their poor condition to years of prewar and wartime neglect, not the depredations of Sherman's marchers.[15] The notion that not one slave cabin had been destroyed strains credulity, but the relatively low number of ruined plantation homes was echoed by Sidney Andrews, who visited around the same time as Dennett. Andrews also claimed that some burned homes were fired by Confederates or disgruntled locals, using the cover of Yankees to settle old scores. While this comports with the facts that Sherman's men spared homes while burning outbuildings and barns, it also demonstrates a desire, presumably on Andrews's part, to minimize Union violence in public eyes.[16]

Three years later, Stephen Powers walked across the South and was struck not by what had been destroyed but rather by what had been rebuilt. The split rail fences looked pristine, the hogs were back, the stacks of fresh-cut shingles flanked the roads again. Occasionally, he came across "a pair of spectral chimneys, whose great eyes of fireplaces aglow and aloft glower wrathfully at each other across the intervening heap of ashes, flickering at each other as the cause of the disaster."[17] But these were the exception rather than the rule according to Powers.

Travelers were deeply interested in the plight of the South's freedmen, and all of the accounts include some discussion of their status and conditions after the war. Mentions of African Americans seemed to fall into three categories: stories of faithful slaves, white Southern complaints about unfaithful slaves and impudent freedmen, and more editorial expressions of concern that the freedmen were not getting all they had been promised or needed. Faithful slaves hid valuables or led plunderers astray; unfaithful ones who abandoned their masters led Union troops straight to the silver. Angry white Southerners portrayed the freedmen as foolish dupes of the Yankees, taken in by promises and "cock-and-bull" stories about Union concern.[18]

If travelers often used their published accounts to minimize or excuse the devastation of the March, their discussion of the freedmen's postwar struggles seem designed to galvanize Northerners and perhaps the government into taking action on the freedmen's behalf. This is not surprising, given that many of these writers had abolitionist sympathies before the war and supported emancipation.[19] Thus, Trowbridge ruefully described the great "destitution" among free blacks, particularly "the negroes that were run off by their masters in advance of Sherman's army [who] had returned to a desolate place with nothing but the rags on their backs." He was concerned about the failure to get crops in the ground in parts of Georgia. He thought their best hope would be the Freedmen's Bureau, which could organize labor to benefit both laborers and employers. Trowbridge believed that "the better class of planters" recognized the bureau's efforts and would support it. In this he was rather naïve.[20]

Trowbridge's optimism was shared by Russell Conwell, who saw the war's fire and blood as a small price to pay in order to root out slavery. As he saw Southerners, black and white, engaged in the business of rebuilding, and the corn and cotton growing again, Conwell confidently believe that under free labor the land would "blossom as the rose," slowly eradicating memories of conflict. After all, he mused, "Some must die that others may live. Some must suffer that others may be happy."[21]

This really was wishful thinking, and one wonders how much Trowbridge and Conwell believed their rosy proclamations. Most Southern whites were angry and resentful, more along the lines of the woman on the border between North Carolina and South Carolina who complained to John Dennett that "the niggers is jest gone to ruin, and I wish old Sherman had taken 'em every one when he freed 'em."[22] One might expect that the former Confederates with whom travelers chatted and reminisced would have nothing good to say about Sherman and his marchers, and this was often the case. On the train from Augusta to Atlanta, John Kennaway laughed at the degree to which "the natives . . . execrat[ed] Sherman!"[23] John Trowbridge's traveling companions cursed Sherman, hoping the devil would get him.[24]

Surprisingly, however, not all white Southerners had bad things to say about the March. One erstwhile Confederate officer even went so far as to argue that the Union soldiers had "generally behaved very well" in Georgia. He didn't expect any better behavior from any other army, not even the supposedly more honorable and restrained Confederates, and he thought that the strategic destruction of railroads, mills, and cotton gins was "perfectly justifiable." He reserved judgment and blame for the foreign-born stragglers, scapegoating them, rather than the native-born Yankees.[25]

Other Southern whites went further, blaming either Confederate troops (particularly Wheeler's cavalry) or even neighbors for some of the ruin and destruction left behind by the war. Robert Ferguson, traveling just after the war's end, came across several examples of this. The *Savannah Republican*, he reported, claimed that Southerners dreaded the arrival of Hood's men more than Sherman's; the mayor of Cheraw, South Carolina, believed that at least some of the fires in his town were set by locals, because as Federal troops tried to put out one blaze, another would start across the street. In fact, Ferguson noted, both Sherman and Sheridan (who sowed destruction in the Shenandoah Valley) were arguably the two most popular Northern leaders in the postwar South.[26] An Atlanta man echoed the words of the mayor of Cheraw opining that it was his neighbors who set fire to his home, though not before stealing some of his furniture—which he found in their postwar houses.[27] After describing a litany of mistreatment, an Orangeburg woman finally conceded that "some of our own soldiers, especially Wheeler's men, were about as bad."[28]

Shifting even a little of the blame away from Sherman and onto Confederates seemed a way to balance the scales and bring the sections back together. Before embarking on his tour of the immediate postwar South, Sidney Andrews reflected on the men he found in Charleston who were economically devastated and unable to pay their debts:

> It would seem that it is not clearly understood how thoroughly Sherman's army destroyed everything in its line of march,—destroyed it without questioning who suffered the action. That this wholesale destruction was often without orders, and often against most positive orders, does not change the fact of destruction. The Rebel leaders were too, in their way, even more wanton, and just as thorough as our army in destroying property. They did not burn houses and barns and fences as we did; but during the last three months of the war, they burned immense quantities of cotton and rosin.[29]

Andrews hits all of the themes here: the worst destruction was done against orders, by a few bad apples, and the Confederates were just as bad. No, they were worse, because they burned commodities, not just houses, barns, and fences. Though not a strong argument, it was probably well-received in the North.

Occasionally travelers reminded their readers about the presence of Southern Unionists. Trowbridge told the story of one Union man, a Georgia "cracker" named Jesse Wade. Wade claimed to have worked as a scout for Sherman on the Atlanta campaign and complained that the "Rebs" destroyed his home, stole his hogs, mule, and horse, and burned his four bales of cotton. They "treated us a heap wus'n than Sherman did," he remarked, going on to tell Trowbridge that he had two new horses and a wagon that he wouldn't have had "if Sherman hadn't gin 'em to me."[30] From this, one could deduce, that the Yankees were not all bad.

Sergeant Bates and Father Sherman

On March 5, 1868, the *New York Times* wondered why so little attention had been paid to the man who had been walking across the South for almost six weeks: Sergeant Gilbert Bates.[31] On that same day, Bates arrived in Milledgeville, Georgia. Several months earlier, while at home in Wisconsin, Bates had defended the honor and loyalty of Southerners, asserting that they were loyally back in the Union and not the enemies of the federal government, Radical Reconstruction notwithstanding. Unimpressed, a Republican friend believed Southern whites to be largely unreconstructed and challenged Bates to prove that he could walk unarmed from Vicksburg to Washington D.C., carrying the Stars and Stripes the whole way, without being attacked or otherwise molested. He set out in January, 24, 1868, with much fanfare and goodwill.[32]

Bates's efforts initially met with great skepticism. Mark Twain mocked him in a newspaper column, calling him an "ass," and predicting that

> this fellow will get more black eyes, down there among those
> unconstructed rebels than he can ever carry along with him without
> breaking his back. I expect to see him coming into Washington some
> day on one leg and with one eye out and an arm gone. He won't
> amount to more than an interesting relic by the time he gets here and
> then he will have to hire out for a sign for the Anatomical Museum.
> Those fellows down there have no sentiment in them. They won't buy
> his picture. They will be more likely to take his scalp.[33]

But by early March, Twain seemed to be wrong. He crossed Mississippi and Alabama without incident, and while not explicitly retracing Sherman's March, headed into Georgia along much of the same route. The human residents of Milledgeville welcomed Bates graciously, with the local newspaper deeming him "open, frank, and agreeable," and warning that any harm he came to on his journey would be at the hands of Radicals, not Southern whites. The canine residents were less friendly, as he was surrounded by a pack of dogs, which Bates fought off with his flagstaff. While he laughed at the unreconstructed curs, who had yet to take the test oath, Bates also used this as a moment to mock black suffrage.[34] In Augusta, Bates received word of a potential threat on his life, ironically to be at the hands of a black man. (Bates sloughed this off as the work of unscrupulous and manipulative whites.)[35] Indeed, Bates did not mention African Americans often, and when he did it was to complain about their lack of industry.[36] He was much more interested in white unity than in civil rights, like most white Northerners during this period.

Bates continued to be warmly received as he moved into South Carolina, even in the Columbia, where he was struck by the fact that three years later the city remained "a forest of blackened chimneys surrounded by ashes and desolation." Ever the optimist, however, Bates predicted the city would be a phoenix and rise again.[37] He spent much of his time in South and North Carolina in the company of former Confederate soldiers, individually and in groups, a living embodiment of the spirit of sectional reunion and reconciliation. In this he contrasted significantly with other travelers who sought to illuminate the plight of African Americans.

A generation later, another traveler would stir up controversy. Thomas Ewing Sherman was the fourth of William T. Sherman's eight children and the first son to survive to adulthood. In 1878, to his father's dismay, Tom abandoned his budding legal career to become a Jesuit priest and, in fact, would preside over his father's 1891 funeral. After the ceremonies that marked the unveiling of the Sherman statue in Washington, President Theodore Roosevelt invited Father Sherman to accompany a cavalry detail that would be retracing Sherman's route as part of its program of study. The plans were set for the spring of 1906, and all seemed in order as Father Sherman boarded the train from Illinois, headed for Fort Oglethorpe in North Georgia. But then the press got wind of the expedition, and all hell broke loose.[38]

The primary complaint had to do with the militarized nature of his trip, which sprang from a misunderstanding. Essentially, the opponents believed that Father Sherman had asked for a military escort, implying that he felt somehow unsafe on his journey. Confederate veterans and sympathizers across the region weighed in, charging that the planned "march" impugned Southern honor and, indeed, besmirched the memory of Sherman himself, who had traveled the region unmolested twenty-five years prior. Newspapers, particularly the *Chattanooga Times*, the *Atlanta Journal*, and the *Atlanta Georgian*, also kept the controversy and outrage going.[39] The kerfuffle reached Washington and finally President Roosevelt. He professed to have never issued any sort of invitation to Father Sherman and called a halt to the troop movement, ordering that the unit turn back at Resaca, well short of Atlanta, to say nothing of the Sea. Father Sherman was, however, welcome to continue on alone and unescorted.[40]

All of this had gone on while Father Sherman and the eleven soldiers were already on their way, camping out and enjoying themselves. They toured Dalton and Resaca and were not stopped until Cartersville. By all accounts he was bitterly disappointed that the expedition had caused such a fuss and was frustrated about how it had all turned out. By the time the group returned to Fort Oglethorpe, he was exhausted and returned to California as quickly as possible. Stopping in Chicago on his way home, he blamed "politicians" rather than the ordinary people of the South for "stirring up any unkindly feeling between the North and the South." His intentions were entirely good, he continued, and remarked that "the people along the march were glad to see me. We shook hands and swapped stories."[41]

Northerners by and large deemed the entire affair a pathetic comedy of errors. *Harper's*, despite its long Yankee lineage, was largely sympathetic to the Southern view, characterizing the combination of Sherman's son and a cavalry squad as "an indiscretion, the ineptitude of which might easily have been forseen."[42] While Father Sherman might have had the best of intentions, Southern whites seemed to take some pleasure in stopping at least one Sherman, even if he was a fifty-year-old priest.[43]

Atlanta and Columbia: Rebuilding Ruins

Regardless of their routes, travelers came to see Atlanta rise from its ashes, struck by the speed with which piles of rubble turned into buildings of brick.[44] John Kennaway couldn't decide whether to be shocked by the range of the ruins or the speed of restoration when he arrived in 1865.[45] Robert Ferguson explained to his readers that as a railroad center, Atlanta was much too important to leave in ruins.[46] Sidney Andrews took pains to dispel the illusion that the city had been entirely destroyed. Rather, only about half of it had burned, and while "the marks of the conflict are everywhere strikingly apparent," he also thought that "the ruin is not so massive and impressive as that of Columbia and Charleston; but as far as it extends it is more complete and of less value." Everywhere he went Andrews found piles of charred wood and tons of building debris, as well as pieces of cannon balls and shot. Rather than dwell on the devastation, however, Andrews chose to emphasize the speed of rebuilding, the general air of hustle and bustle, and the high rents, all of which combined to remind him of Chicago.[47] Whitelaw Reid also thought of Chicago when he watched "pure Southerners" rebuilding and re-establishing stores with "Yankee" speed and ingenuity.[48]

All was not rosy to Reid, however. With Chicago-type buildings came Chicago-type urban problems, and he struck a rare sour note as well. He lamented the "bad passions and disregard of moral obligations," as well as the rising crime that accompanied the boomtown. John Trowbridge also looked behind the optimism and sound of hammers to find a struggling population. Trowbridge found "ruins and rubbish, mud and mortar and misery." Rather than serving as an urban booster, he worried about the people, white and black, forced to live in "wretched hovels."[49]

A decade after the war, Edward King praised Atlanta for being "eminently modern and unromantic," a city more like northern and western ones, the "antithesis of Savannah." This was largely a good thing, it seemed. It had risen from its ashes bigger and better than before, with the only cost a loss of Southern languor.[50] Implicit in this was the notion that maybe Sherman had done the city a favor, a literal interpretation of the Vietnam-era burning the village in order to save it.

If that were really true, if Sherman deserved to be praised rather than buried for burning Atlanta, wouldn't the same hold true for other cities, like Columbia? But that did not seem to be the case for Columbia, which was often portrayed as the sort of designated victim of the war. Sidney Andrews was not often given to rhetorical flights of fancy, but he let fly when discussing South Carolina's capital: "Columbia is in the heart of Destruction. Being outside of it, you can only get in through one of the roads built by Ruin. Being in it, you can only get out over one of the roads walled by Desolation." In a similar vein, John Dennett called the city a "melancholy sight," one much worse than Richmond or Charleston.[51] Only enough of the city's former beauty remained, he reflected, as to make the devastation all the more poignant. Andrews too compared Columbia to Charleston, describing the ruins as "neither half so eloquent nor touching" as those in the latter. He found the city a "wilderness of ruins," with a blackened heart and crumbling exterior.[52] This ruined world could be re-created now that it had been cleansed by fire.

The corollary to the physical destruction of the city was the destruction of personal relationships. Andrews used his visit to Columbia to describe the visceral anger Southern whites felt toward Northern soldiers. Everywhere he went in Columbia he found people bursting to complain about Sherman, deeming him "infernal," "atrocious," "cowardly," and "devilish." "Whatever else the South Carolina mothers forget," he quipped, they do not seem likely in this generation to forget to teach their children to hate Sherman."[53] John Dennett also found that residents of Columbia were more bitter than those anywhere else in the former Confederacy. They seemed more open, more visceral as well, as evidenced by one "gentleman," who flatly stated that he would like to pay a call on Sherman and "blow his brains out."[54]

The source of this vehement hatred was the conflagration that enveloped the city, which Southerners were convinced had been set on Sherman's orders. For their part, Sherman's men and many Northerners placed the blame squarely on Wade Hampton and his retreating soldiers. It was an intractable debate, and travelers seemed eager to weigh in. As in other aspects of their reports, their political proclivities tended to dictate where they came down on the controversy. Thus, John Trowbridge began his discussion of Columbia's destruction by claiming that in the panic that overtook the city as Sherman approached, "numbers of the poorer classes," along with members of Wheeler's cavalry and other "citizen marauders," took advantage of the confusion to loot and plunder. Trowbridge evaluates Sherman's claim that he neither ordered nor turned a blind eye to the torching of the city, and finds it credible. He cites an unnamed member of Sherman's staff who blamed the entire fire on the bales of cotton the Confederates torched before leaving town.[55]

Trowbridge interviewed Mayor Gibbes of Columbia, and even he seemed to damn Sherman's troops with (extremely) faint praise, rather than condemn them outright as barbarians, arsonists, and vandals:

> Not much drunkenness was observed among the soldiers until after the sacking of the city had been some time in progress. Then the stores of liquors consumed exhibited their natural effect; and it is stated that many perished in fires of their own kindling. Yet the army of Sherman did not, in its wildest orgies, forget its splendid discipline. "When will these horrors cease?" asked a lady of an officer at her house. "You will hear the bugles at sunrise," he replied; "then they will cease, and not till then." He prophesied truly. "At daybreak, on Saturday morning," said Mayor Gibbes, "I saw two men galloping through the streets, blowing horns. Not a dwelling was fired after that; immediately the town became quiet."[56]

This implication of control, the idea that the soldiers were not simply running riot, dovetails with the idea that the soldiers took their gloves off in South Carolina, only to put them back on as they moved further north. It effectively negates any sort of defense that damage was done by a few bad apples, or without explicit coordination from the top. While this might seem to contradict Trowbridge's earlier argument regarding who set the fires, I think it does not, because he is presenting the Southern view.

In 1873, *New York Tribune* correspondent James Shepherd Pike came to see South Carolina for himself. His letters back became classics of the anti-Reconstruction genre, describing the biracial South Carolina legislature as a carnival of corruption, and South Carolina whites as victims. Despite these biases, he argued that the controversy over the burning of Columbia was "quite superfluous," since the clear facts pointed to Wade Hampton ordering that all of the cotton in town be burned, and the railroad bridge destroyed. But, he also did not absolve the Yankees, who were "exasperated" and set additional blazes to exact revenge. Essentially, Pike blamed both sides: Sherman's marchers for making war according to their own sets of rules, and

Confederates for doing the same, burning as much as they could when they evacuated. Ultimately, he concluded "the war burned Columbia."[57]

Little Removed from the Pillage of the Past

If the first generation of travelers seemed to want to minimize aspects of the March by accentuating the positive, later visitors seemed more interested in finding the traces, however faint, that remained. On some level this should not be surprising. After all, what would be the point of retracing the March if there was nothing to see. Thus travelers during the late nineteenth and early twentieth centuries tended to remark on the enduring poverty of the region and were quick to attribute that to Sherman. A typical example came from Walter Rollo, who rode the rails across the United States in 1939. As soon as his train crossed into Georgia, Rollo noticed "the gaunt telltale chimneys" standing "everywhere."[58] He counted over two dozen in two hours, imbuing his recollections with sepia-toned romance. What seems not to have occurred to him was that the homes surrounding the chimneys might have burned sometime in the decades following the Civil War.

Visitors during the Gilded Age and early twentieth century often remarked on the endurance of agricultural poverty in middle Georgia. During the 1930s Englishwoman Ursula Branston visited the South, traveling by bus from Baltimore to Texas. As she left Augusta, "retreating along the line of Sherman's March," she described entering the realm of the Georgia "crackers," which she described as

> shacks rather than farms. Peeling, unpainted wooden walls, broken
> porches, roofs with holes and hanging tiles, yards which were rubbish
> dumps, rusting iron, bedding spread out on splintered rails. Here
> and there the spectre of a mansion; skeleton lines of an avenue;
> shadows of tall columns, broken glass in Georgian windows. . . .
> The devastation of the present seemed very little removed from the
> pillage of the past. I was looking at fields of battle; these farms were
> ruins in the path of an army, and these people were the defeated.[59]

Branston evoked a land out of time, echoing James Agee's *Let Us Now Praise Famous Men* as much as Sidney Andrews or John Dennett. Her image of ruined mansions and decaying shacks could have been painted in 1870 or 1900 or 1930. But it is significant that she ties the poverty of her present to the traumas of the past, as though Sherman's March happened just a few days, rather than seven decades, prior.

Branson's countryman Morgan Phillips Price also visited the United States during the 1930s (in his case to retrace his parents' nineteenth-century journeys) and also linked rural poverty and Sherman's March. In Price's case, as he took the train from Atlanta to Savannah he reflected on the cotton plantations, once worked by slaves and then by sharecroppers, or day laborers. Surprisingly, for him the sight of the "dismal little villages of negroes" did not evoke destruction and devastation as it did for so many others; rather, it reminded him of the stories of liberation, of "dashing Yankee boys" emancipating slaves.[60]

Hal Steed called Depression-era Georgia an "unfinished" state, and remarked upon the "general air of abandonment" along the erstwhile route of the March. While he claimed that the property that Sherman destroyed had never been replaced, Steed was a bit more realistic than others, for he went on to reference the boll weevil and the Great Migration as further adding to the region's woes.[61] In this he echoed an earlier assessment of Georgia that had appeared in *National Geographic* during the 1920s. That author lamented the passing of Georgia's glory days as the "Empire State of the South in wealth and culture." Finally, something worse than Sherman: "the devastating and irresistible boll weevil army, marching eastward from Texas," bringing even more devastation and financial disaster than the army that had preceded it.[62]

Stephen Graham retraced the March through Georgia in 1919 and described his experiences in two articles for *Harper's Magazine*. He chatted with some survivors of the March, black and white. While walking, he would accept rides from whoever offered them, dumfounding drivers when he explained he was retracing the March. He found "a surprising absence of bitterness" about the war, and even about Sherman himself. Graham found that poor or working-class people felt less resentment toward Sherman than did the wealthy, perhaps because the poor had less to lose. He too noted the relative poverty of Georgia: its farmers needed to purchase meat, and the only produce in abundance was sweet potatoes.[63]

Graham ruminated on the ways that African Americans had helped the marchers find food and valuables and belied the racial harmony he had found along the way: "One reason why Georgia burns and hangs more negroes than any other state to-day is probably because of the bitterness caused by the unstinted foraging and the 'setting of the niggers against us,' as they say." It hardly seems plausible that the problem of lynching could be attributed to this alone. He linked the drownings at Ebenezer Creek, at least metaphorically, to the "twilight of ruin and disillusion" under which African Americans lived.[64]

Of course, all had not been flattened along the path of the March, and twentieth-century travelers remarked on what remained. Hal Steed visited Sherman's headquarters in Savannah; Morgan Price saw the former slave quarters and outbuildings of the Hermitage plantation, along with a spot where Sherman's men supposedly shot deserters and Confederate spies.[65] Medora Field Pekerson opened her *White Columns in Georgia*, a guide to historic homes, on a surprisingly breezy note, cracking puns about blazing a trail across Georgia in search of antebellum survivors. Briskly, she cut through the mists of memory when visiting the Green House in Eatonton, Georgia, which was supposedly saved because Sherman thought it was a girls' boarding school. First Pekerson noted that the neighboring homes had also survived, but then continued:

> In view of all this, it is not strange if people along the line of march were sometimes inclined to think their property had been spared by special dispensation. Sherman was teaching in the Louisiana Military Academy when the war broke out. To think that he remembered this when he gesticulated toward the children in the garden of an impressive Greek Revival house in Eatonton is, after all, a pretty bit of sentiment and a rare-enough local compliment for the general.[66]

Such clear-eyed understanding was rather unusual among travelers, who seemed to prefer to print the legends rather than the realities.

By the 1930s, travelers also felt free to make jokes to Southern whites about Sherman's March in ways that they might not have a generation or two earlier. Morgan Price was dining in a Georgia home when he "unwisely" mentioned that his father had known and respected Sherman. Fortunately for Price, "every Southerner has the manners of an aristocrat, and knows how to get out of an awkward situation," and his *faux pas* was quickly swept under the metaphorical rug.[67] Henry Rollo was chatting with a fellow rider on the train to Atlanta when he let slip that he had been born not far from Sherman's Ohio birthplace. His companion quickly warned Rollo to keep that fact to himself, "at least till we get past Atlanta."[68] Lighthearted tales to be sure, but ones that betray just an edge of residual hostility and grievance, in a kind of clichéd manner.

David J. de Laubenfels, a geographer at the University of Georgia during the 1950s, was a very different sort of traveler from the others. A member of his family had a journal that had been kept by Captain John Rziha, chief topographical engineer of Sherman's XIV Corps. The maps in the journal covered a sixty-mile section of the March in Georgia, from just east of Covington to Louisville, which is southeast of Milledgeville (with a six-mile gap around Eatonton). In the summer of 1955, de Laubenfels retraced the path in Rziha's journal and then published two scholarly articles about his findings.[69] Rziha's maps were notable for their level of detail—he included information about topography, homes, barns, and other outbuildings, fields and forests and roads. De Laubenfels found the maps to be "exceedingly accurate, it being possible to find the hills, roads, streams, and even houses exactly where he mapped them for most of the route." He did not, however fall into the trap of believing that the landscape had remained static for ninety-one years, noting that the composition of fields and forests had changed considerably, and that many new roads had sprung up.[70]

De Laubenfels was struck by how many of the houses that Rziha had marked in 1864 were still standing in 1955, and he realized that his findings had implications for the myth that Sherman's men burned everything in their path. He was able to find seventy-two houses between Covington and Milledgeville, including three that Rziha had marked as "ruined" or "on fire" on his map. At least twenty-two were still standing when de Laubenfels came looking, and he received confirmation that at least nine others had been destroyed since the end of the Civil War. He also found another twenty-seven sites that had new buildings on them; he could not pinpoint with certainty what happened to the original buildings, but assumed that at least some of them had survived Sherman.[71] While the landscape and the patchwork of fields and farms had changed considerably over the intervening decades, he attributed those changes to broader structural shifts in Southern agricultural, rather than the ephemeral impact of the March.

The Chicago of the South

Just as Reconstruction-era visitors were eager to see Atlanta rise from the ashes of war, so too were later tourists. They bought into Atlanta's resurgent narrative, praising it for slipping the shackles and "slipshod air" of the antebellum period. The natural metaphor for the city's new hustle and bustle was that of the phoenix rising from the ashes, and Atlanta finally made it official in 1887 by adding the phoenix to the city seal.[72] Travelers often compared Atlanta to Chicago (favorably), describing the city as busy and bustling, substantial, proud, and energetic. All that was good about the New South was concentrated in its crowded streets.[73]

Alexander McClure believed that Atlanta represented the combination of the "best vigor" of both North and South, praising the city as the "Queen of

Beauty among Southern cities." He drew a distinction between not just the places of the past (Old Atlanta vs. New Atlanta) but the people as well: the "old regulation Southerners" were being replaced by the young go-getters of the 1880s.[74] McClure also contrasted Atlanta's growth and sprit with that of Columbia. While Atlanta had gotten right to the work of rebuilding, Columbia had not. In that city McClure remarked on "blackened and crumbing piles of what once were attractive homes or public edifices" that still remained. Interestingly, he did not place all of the blame for Columbia's devastation on Sherman's "destructive" march: rather it was the carpetbaggers who followed. McClure never explains why these venal Yankees did not wreak the same long-term havoc on Atlanta.[75] Stephen Graham, who visited in 1919, was so impressed with the hustle and bustle he saw, as well as the ways that blacks had risen from slavery, that he was prompted to muse "that Perhaps Atlanta did not burn in vain."[76]

A few travelers looked beneath Atlanta's gloss and glamour. An obsession with looking forward can often impede reflection on the past. In the 1930s Ursula Branston tartly noted that "mourning becomes not Atlanta," quipping that "the mere expression of gloom . . . was likely to be punishable under some city ordinance." Indeed, she astutely realized that when Atlanta looked to the past, it did it in a commercialized way, using the battle for and burning of the city as "no more than a historical tailpiece to the brochure of attractions offered the convention bound or the speculator in real estate." She even went so far as to warn readers of *Gone with the Wind* off visiting, for the reality would never live up to the novel.[77]

Despite the shiny newness everywhere, Henry Field still found memories that haunted him. Not only did the collision of old and new, or "Dead Past" and "Living Present," bring his mind back to the war, but, unusually for travelers in this period, he also thought of "the terrible problem that it has left behind."[78] That terrible problem was racial injustice, and by the time of Field's writing, the rise of segregation. Most visitors preferred not to think about that seemingly intractable issue. African Americans, when interviewed or mentioned, appeared as more illustrations of local color than as actors in their own rights.

Commemorating the Centennial

Civil War roundtables, professional historians, and the National Park Service began to lobby Congress during the 1950s to set up appropriate commemorations of the American Civil War. In 1957 the U.S. Civil War Centennial

Commission was charged with channeling the wide range of interest in commemorating the Civil War, but in very specific ways:

> The only questions were whether the many ceremonies in preparation could be organized without confusion; whether they could be carried out upon a dignified and elevated plane, free from stains of commercialism or vulgarity; and whether, above all, they could be planned in such fashion as not to reawaken memories of old sectional antagonisms and political rancors, but instead strengthen both the unity of the Nation and popular devotion to the highest purpose of the Republic.

Such lofty goals were quickly dashed against the shoals of Southern white racism and resistance to racial equality, as historian Robert Cook details in his history of the Centennial, *Troubled Commemoration*. Ultimately, the commission failed in its bid to unify the nation around a noncontroversial celebration.[79]

The national commission also worked with state commissions, and it was these organizations that grappled with the legacy of Sherman's March. In addition to forty-five state commissions, and one from the District of Columbia, there were also some regional associations, the best organized being the Confederate States Conference, founded in 1960 and comprising the eleven states of the Confederacy. In general, the states chose to commemorate the military side of the war, the battles and soldiers. As one might also expect, the Southern states did not want to commemorate emancipation or forge any kinds of connections between the Civil War and civil rights. Sherman's March, given its relative lack of open warfare, as well as the profoundly angry feelings it still engendered in corners of the South, would be hard to commemorate.[80]

Georgia's commission initially received only $25,000 from the state, but it made the most of its limited funds. Although it was one of the last commissions to be set up (in 1959), by the end of that year it also boasted two dozen county-level commissions. The title page of Georgia's guide for local committees made its objectives quite clear:

The Civil War Centennial
To Commemorate The War Between the States
To Honor Our Confederate Heroes
To Tell The True Story of Georgia's Role in the Conflict
To Dramatize the Great Ideals that are the Basis of Our Freedom
and Tradition

Peter Zack Geer, the politically connected chairman of the Georgia Commission had very specific reminders for the local groups. His manual listed five purposes for the centennial in Georgia, which centered on honoring Confederates, from both Georgia and the rest of the South, and, in language reminiscent of that of the United Daughters of the Confederacy's textbook controversies, to "educate the public . . . in the faith that the knowledge of truth will finally lead to understanding and not resentment." The guide emphasized lessons of character and honor that were to be taught, explicitly connecting the centennial to understandings of democracy and freedom (a preoccupation for the early leadership of the national commission).[81]

Most importantly, the manual wanted Georgians to remember that "FIRST OF ALL WE ARE DEALING WITH A SUCCESS STORY." That success was the endurance of the American nation, and for all its celebration of Georgia and the Confederacy, the centennial was supposed to instill pride, and make Americans feel good: "The War Between the States was a storybook war. It was a profound family experience, not only a divided nation fighting against itself, but brother against brother, and father against son. It contains the classic elements of the birth of modern warfare that a young nation endured and survived to become undivided under God."[82] How well did Georgia do with its self-proclaimed aims? And how might Georgians incorporate Sherman's March into its commemorations?

The commission's final report did include the March in its chronology of Georgia in the Civil War, and it argued for the significance of Georgia's fall to the eventual demise of the Confederacy. The commission did not, however, sponsor any events that focused on the March. Milledgeville hosted a three-day reenactment of secession in 1961 but nothing in 1964. It sponsored a special screening of *Gone with the Wind* complete with a gala costume ball. Several battles along the route of the Atlanta campaign were reenacted, and the commission worked with a local television station on a film about Sherman taking Atlanta. But that was it. For Georgia, the March was best left undiscussed.[83]

South Carolina did not totally avoid the March during its commemorative activities. The preamble to the legislation establishing the state centennial commission invoked the hardships borne by South Carolinians, how they were subjected to "a bestial ferocity unmatched by savagery, that laid waste our land and homes by death, destruction, fire, pillage, plunder, pestilence, famine, loot, poverty, and vandalism, invoking upon the defenseless women and little children of Columbia and of South Carolina a holocaust of horrors."[84] Oddly, despite this heated rhetoric, there does not appear to have been any kind of special centennial commemoration of Columbia's burning.

South Carolinians did commemorate the battle at Rivers Bridge, where South Carolina soldiers briefly stopped Sherman's advance. Every year on the anniversary, Southern (not just South Carolina) politicians would gather to memorialize this brief victory. In 1960, Mississippi Governor Ross Barnett delivered a "hard-hitting" speech on civil rights there, and it endured as a geographic symbol of resistance to Yankee invasion and tyranny.[85]

North Carolina, perhaps because the March ended there, perhaps because of some lingering sense of Unionism, held commemorations at both Bentonville and the Bennett Place. Vice President Hubert Humphrey spoke at the televised "Centennial of National Unity" at the Bennett Place, ending the commemorations on a positive note.[86]

The Search for Self

Late twentieth-century travelers veered between the cynical and the sincere. Both V. S. Naipaul and Tony Horowitz toured the South generally, stopping at some of the major Sherman spots. During his travels in the 1980s, Naipaul claimed that "not a day had passed" during his "turn" in the South where he did not hear or read about Sherman." In Columbia, Naipaul was struck by the immediacy with which South Carolinians discussed the events of the past, "as though it had happened quite recently," and wondered if Romans had not remembered Hannibal in much the same way.[87] He was struck by the unrepaired broken stones and statues at the State Capitol, especially the statue of George Washington bearing a plaque which described Sherman's soldiers "brickbatting" it.[88]

Strikingly, by the late twentieth century Columbia, like Atlanta, seemed to have moved away from a sense of itself as a pure victim of Sherman, to a realization that in tragedy lay tourist dollars. One ad placed by the Greater Columbia Convention and Visitors Bureau in the 1980s showed a photograph of the city's ruins with the caption "After Sherman's March we fired our booking agent!" One wonders how effective this tactic was, but at least its memorable.[89] In the 1980s, one could find Sherman-themed bumper stickers in Atlanta, calling him "the Original Urban Renewer"; rumor had it that a restaurant briefly offered "Shermanized toast" (burnt) alongside eggs and grits, but it went out of business. Perhaps that was a pun too far. Savannah, however, at least to James Reston, took more pride in its colonial past, perhaps a function of giving in so easily.[90]

During the 1980s James Reston visited Macon, a city that boasts dozens of antebellum homes and buildings. The pamphlet for the Hay House, arguably the best example of Italian Renaissance architecture in the South, boasted "Sherman Missed it—Don't You."[91] It seems that being either touched or spared by Sherman can be a claim to fame.

A decade later Tony Horowitz similarly described the grounds of the South Carolina Statehouse as "a memorial to Yankee depredations." Horowitz also toured Sherman- and *Gone with the Wind*–related sites in Atlanta and its environs (Naipaul focused his discussion of Atlanta on contemporary issues of race and religion). If nineteenth- and early twentieth-century visitors praised Atlanta for its modernity and hustle, Horowitz exemplified the late twentieth-century idea of the city as "a crass brash city . . . overrun by carpetbaggers, corporate climbers, and conventioneers." As one Southern observer quipped, Atlanta had become exactly what Confederates had sought to prevent.[92] Sherman's men burned about a quarter of the city; Franklin Garrett, the dean of Atlanta historians reminded Horowitz that "Atlantans leveled much more of Atlanta than Sherman did."[93] Horowitz came away surprised by the relative mildness of the March, particularly as compared to twentieth-century wars. He was particularly moved by a Sons of Confederate Veterans meeting, where members compared stories from 1990s Bosnia to 1864 Georgia and were unable to tell the difference.[94]

Neither Naipaul nor Horowitz focused exclusively on retracing Sherman's March, intersecting with its path only a couple of times. But two other men in the 1980s did retrace the March, each one on an explicit journey of self-discovery.[95] Journalist James Reston Jr. turned to the Civil War in general (and Sherman's March in particular) to understand the Vietnam War and how to rebuild and reconstruct the damaged lives of its participants. In searching for Sherman, Reston was really searching for the origins of barbarism and cruelty. "How does the process start? Once undertaken on a wide scale in one war, especially one that results in victory, does it not become accepted practice in the next war? And is the gulf between property and life so great?" Reston finds more complicated and nuanced views of Sherman on his trek across Georgia than he had expected to find. And while he ultimately blamed Sherman for making war on civilians, he also found his peacetime generosity toward his former foes to be praiseworthy and something to be emulated.[96]

Reston, who had both served in and written extensively about Vietnam, found a measure of peace and healing on his trip across Georgia. Jerry Ellis, a sort of professional walker-storyteller, used his 1993 retracing of the March (by foot, as opposed to road or rail), as a way of forging connections with his Southern past and his late father. Like Reston, Ellis saw the potential for cultural healing in the March. He explained that "the pain from old war wounds is still alive in Southern memory, and no wound is deeper than the one inflicted by Sherman's March to the Sea. . . . I also believe that as a result many of us Southerners have a great need to make something of ourselves." And the cure for that regional inferiority complex, thought Ellis, was to walk "if I could walk the path of the South's deepest wound, I could walk through the past and into the future. Then I could move on."[97]

As he camped at night, Ellis's imagination repeatedly conjures up the smells of burning flesh, or romanticized visions of soldiers and free blacks dancing and celebrating. Sometimes he dreamed of meeting Sherman and shooting him.[98] Like the generations of travelers before him, Ellis seized on images and fragments to try to find the traces of the March 130 years later. In one instance, the fragments are literal; coming upon some broken dishes in a cotton field near Covington, Georgia, sends him off into a reverie, day-dreaming about a Union soldier "smash[ing] the blue china on the ground just to see what kind of sound it would make."[99] Ellis's long march works. He walks and talks his way across Georgia and then returns home, "happy and at peace," at one with his past and looking forward to his future.[100]

Battle over Bentonville

Not as many people try to retrace Sherman's March through the Carolinas. Those who do and who stop at Bentonville Battlefield will see a peaceful landscape, the historic home of the Harper family, which is furnished as both a period house (upstairs) and a Civil War field hospital (downstairs). They will see five monuments of the type that typically dot Civil War battlefields, including one to mark the mass grave of over 360 Confederate soldiers who had died during the battle. Their bodies had been buried all over the battle-field, but their remains were disinterred and reburied under the monument with great ceremony in 1895.[101] What you will not find is a monument to the Union soldiers who also died there. In 1994 a group of Civil War reen-actors, the Cape Fear Living History Society, proposed such a monument, and reopened hostilities. Even though it proposed a monument that would have been smaller than the Confederate one, and had begun to raise money for it, the very idea of honoring Sherman's Marchers outraged many North Carolinians.

A letter in the *Raleigh News and Observer* implied that the monument would be a statue of Sherman (it was not). The local chapter of the Sons of Confederate Veterans also got involved and expressed horror at any kind of homage to Union soldiers. Chief among the outraged was Betty Ray McCain, the longtime secretary of the North Carolina Department of Cultural Resources. "Not on my watch," was her response to the proposal, and she claimed that her ancestors had fought off Sherman's men with brooms when they tried to burn down the family home. The only problem with McCain's family tale was that it took place in Wilmington, North Carolina, a place that was never visited by Sherman's men. But McCain held the power, and the monument was denied. The legends, even after more than a century, proved more powerful than the realities.[102]

CHAPTER SEVEN

Songs and Snapshots

"Tell about your family plantation burned by Sherman's raiders," advised the satirical book *Will Success Spoil Jeff Davis*'s list of qualifications to be "an amateur Confederate." "Grit your teeth when you say 'Sherman,'" it continued, "and challenge onlookers to sing 'Marching through Georgia.'" Elsewhere, the author joked that Sherman "lit a Georgia mansion every night to tell his wife he would be home for Yom Kippur."[1] If comedy equals tragedy plus time, a hundred years after the March, there was plenty to laugh about. Sherman's March, more than almost any other event in the Civil War, has reverberated through American popular culture. Poetry and photography, fiction and popular music, novels and films—all have engaged with the Georgia and Carolinas campaign in a variety of ways. Part of this fascination has to do with the natural narrative drama of the March, its relentless forward movement, its many conflicts between soldiers and civilians, its stories of freedom taken or taken away. The March can represent the war in microcosm. Its metaphorical meanings seem boundless. Yet the popular representations of the March are by definition incomplete, telling some stories while obscuring or ignoring others. While there is not one single cultural representation of the March, there are common themes of conflict and reconciliation, of life and loss, honor and vengeance, that thread through the retellings. This chapter explores shorter forms: music, poetry, and visual imagery and the ways that they help to preserve and transmit certain stories and images of the March.[2]

Then Sang We a Song for Our Chieftain

Sherman's March was being memorialized in song even as its men still slogged through the swamps of South Carolina. Samuel Hawkins Marshall Byers was the adjutant of the 5th Iowa Infantry in November, 1863, when he was captured during the battle of Missionary Ridge in Chattanooga, Tennessee. Byers was imprisoned all over the Confederacy: first at Libby Prison in Richmond, then later at prisons in Macon, Savannah, Charleston, and finally by late 1864, in Columbia. He and his fellow prisoners heard rumors about the March, saw the "exceedingly glum" looks on the faces of their Confederate captors, and eventually learned from smuggled newspapers that Sherman had taken Savannah. Upon hearing the happy news, he found himself "cogitating on the wonderful success of Sherman's campaign" and wondering what people would call it. "It was not a battle only," he reflected, "but a march as well—and a march to the sea." At that moment the song came to him, he recalled years later, much as the "Star-Spangled Banner" had come to Francis Scott Key, another prisoner of war.[3] He called it "Sherman's March to the Sea":

> Our camp fires shone bright on the mountains
> That frowned on the river below,
> While we stood by our guns in the morning
> And eagerly watched for the foe—
> When a rider came out from the darkness
> That hung over mountain and tree,
> And shouted, "Boys, up and be ready,
> For Sherman will march to the sea."
>
> Then cheer upon cheer for bold Sherman
> Went up from each valley and glen,
> And the bugles re-echoed the music
> That came from the lips of the men.
> For we knew that the stars in our banner
> More bright in their splendor would be,
> And that blessings from Northland would greet us
> When Sherman marched down to the sea.
>
> Then forward, boys, forward to battle,
> We marched on our dangerous way,
> And we stormed the wild hills of Resaca,—
> God bless those who fell on that day,—
> Then Kenesaw, dark in its glory,
> Frowned down on the flag of the free,
> But the East and the West bore our standards
> And Sherman marched on to the sea.
>
> Still onward we pressed, till our banners
> Swept out from Atlanta's grim walls,
> And the blood of the patriot dampened

The soil where the traitor flag falls;
But we paused not to weep for the fallen
Who slept by each river and tred,
Yet we twined them a wreath of the laurel
As Sherman marched down to the sea.

O, proud was our army that morning
That stood where the pine darkly towers,
When Sherman said: "Boys, you are weary,
This day fair Savannah is ours."
Then sang we a song for our chieftain
That echoed o'er river and lea,
And the stars in our banner shone brighter
When Sherman marched down to the sea.[4]

Byers gave his words to a Lieutenant Rockwell, a member of the prison's Glee Club. The Union men were allowed to sing for the prisoners and people of Columbia, as long as they included Confederate favorites like "Dixie" and "The Bonnie Blue Flag." Rockwell surprised Byers by writing the music for the song, which they performed for the prisoners, to great acclaim. Byers believed that it boosted the men's morale as well. The song was written down, and then smuggled out in the hollow wooden leg of a fellow prisoner who was sent North through the lines. Byers also tried several times to escape, finally succeeding in the confusion of the fires in Columbia on February 17, 1865. Sherman was so taken with the song that he sent for Byers and gave him a position on his staff. Byers eventually went on to serve as United States consul to Switzerland.[5]

Surprisingly, few of the song's verses deal with what we today consider the March to the Sea. That is, Byers seems to start his story while the army was still in Chattanooga, and he incorporates the battles of Resaca and Kennesaw Mountain, which are commonly considered part of the Atlanta campaign. Byers addressed this discrepancy in his story of the song, claiming that Sherman himself told him that the March commenced in Tennessee.[6] Byers's portrait of the March, even the Atlanta to Savannah section, is also entirely sanitized. No mention is made of foraging, sanctioned or otherwise, or of burning railroad depots or twisting ties. The mention of patriot's blood is striking on a march with so few casualties. The song is entirely about glorifying and, except for the specific places mentioned, rather generic.

Byers became relatively famous for writing "Sherman's March to the Sea," but he did not make much money off of it. Several different people and

"Sherman's March to the Sea," written by a Union prisoner of war before the March had even ended, became one of the most popular Civil War songs, selling over a million copies. (Library of Congress, http://www.loc.gov/pictures/item/89715613/)

companies published arrangements of the song, sometimes under the title "When Sherman Marched Down to the Sea." Later versions incorporated a brief chorus, and that was the version that Sherman used in his memoirs. Byers claimed to have sold the rights for a mere five dollars; he also claimed that more than a million copies of the sheet music sold in 1865–66.[7] The song is still being performed. In 2010, a group of interns at the Library of Congress discovered a manuscript version of the song and arranged it for an unusual assortment of instruments—horn, viola, and alto saxophone—"much like a prison camp musician would do." This performance can be viewed on You-Tube, introducing the song to a new generation.[8]

If "Sherman's March to the Sea" paints the marchers as uncomplicated, virtuous patriots, marching unstoppably, the better known "Marching through Georgia," takes a more light-hearted approach. Its creation story is not so dramatic, but the song itself had more propulsive motion. A different approach is perhaps to be expected in a song written not by a prisoner of war but by a professional songwriter from the safety of Chicago. Henry Clay Work wrote at least seventy-five songs for his publishers during the war, keeping up with the news to keep his work topical. Naturally, he followed the story of Sherman's March, and less than three weeks after Sherman took Savannah, "Marching through Georgia" was published, to immediate acclaim in the North.[9] Work's song seemed to capture the mood of the marchers themselves, allowing them to recall their triumphs, even though they were still on the move:

1. Bring the good old bugle, boys! we'll sing another song
Sing it with a spirit that will start the world along.
Sing it as we used to sing it, fifty thousand strong,
While we were marching through Georgia.
Chorus:
"Hurrah! Hurrah! we bring the Jubilee!
Hurrah! Hurrah! the flag that makes you free!"
So we sang the chorus from Atlanta to the sea,
While we were marching through Georgia.

2. How the darkeys shouted when they heard the joyful sound!
How the turkeys gobbled which our commissary found!
How the sweet potatoes even started from the ground,
While we were marching through Georgia.
Chorus:

3. Yes, and there were Union men who wept with joyful tears,
When they saw the honor'd flag they had not seen for years;
Hardly could they be restrained from breaking forth in cheers,
While we were marching through Georgia.
Chorus:

4. "Sherman's dashing Yankee boys will never reach the coast!"
So the saucy rebels said, and 'twas a handsome boast,
Had they not forgot, alas! to reckon with the host,
While we were marching through Georgia.
Chorus:

5. So we made a thoroughfare for Freedom and her train,
Sixty miles in latitude three hundred to the main;
Treason fled before us, for resistance was in vain,
While we were marching through Georgia.
Chorus:[10]

"Marching through Georgia" paints Sherman's soldiers as an army of liberation, "bringing the Jubilee," freeing both African Americans and white Unionists. They leave a trail of freedom in their wake, scattering frightened rebels before them. Work also did not shy away from gently referencing foraging, with the second verse's turkey and sweet potatoes.

"Marching through Georgia" has endured as a popular song, so much so that its original meaning seems obscured. According to one account, the Japanese marched into Port Arthur in 1905 to its strains, while British soldiers sang it in India. If true, a song ostensibly about bringing a nation back together after a civil war was being used to bolster colonialism.[11]

Sherman himself was said to loathe the song, no doubt because he had to listen to it over and over again for a quarter century. Every time he gave a speech, every time he attended a reunion, everywhere he went, bands played it, prompting him to (perhaps apocryphally) complain "I wish I had a dollar for every time I have had to listen to that blasted tune." In 1890 Sherman attended the national encampment of the Grand Army of the Republic (GAR) in Boston. The parade lasted seven hours, and featured 250 bands and 100 fife and drum corps. They all played "Marching through Georgia" when they caught sight of Sherman, prompting him to swear that he would never attend another encampment, unless "every band in the United States had signed an agreement *not* to play 'Marching through Georgia' in his presence."[12]

The Girl Who Wouldn't Sing

At least Sherman agreed with the sentiments behind "Marching through Georgia," no matter how much he might have tired of it. The song was not so well beloved south of the Mason-Dixon Line, as exemplified by thirteen-year-old Laura Talbott Galt, of Louisville, Kentucky. One day in June 1902, her eighth-grade class was singing "Marching through Georgia," and Galt refused to join in, even when ordered to by her teacher. She went even further, sticking her fingers in her ears so as not to hear the offensive tune. Laura's grandmother, Mrs. Laura Talbott Ross, a member of both the Daughters of the American Revolution and the United Daughters of the Confederacy (UDC), counseled her granddaughter to obey her teacher, but to do so under protest. Laura then complained that her teacher "refused to listen to her essays, in which she gave the Confederate soldiers credit for bravery on sea and land." She worried that she might be given so many demerits that she would not be allowed to proceed to high school. Thus, she chose to withdraw from school and complain to the superintendent.[13]

But the story did not stay local. Laura Galt became a celebrity, and her stance against "Marching through Georgia" was reported on throughout the country. The *Chicago Daily Tribune* emphasized her Confederate heritage, including a picture and describing her, not sympathetically, as being "of strong Southern sympathies and refuses to believe that the civil war is ended." Even more problematic from the *Tribune*'s perspective was that Galt's activism revived the long-standing debate over the teaching of Civil War in Kentucky.[14] According to the *Tribune*, the Civil War had not been taught for several years "on account of the partisanship of the parents of the pupils and the objections to the so-called standard war histories."[15]

Not surprisingly, the *Atlanta Constitution* saw the argument differently, blaming this new "'irrepressible conflict'" on Galt's teacher, "a school marm with Northern sensibilities," who unreasonably marked the girl down for impertinence. The *Constitution*'s editorial explicitly connected the incident to the battle over textbooks being waged by the UDC. Claiming that the fault lay with "northern made" histories of the war, it demanded "some adequate and honest history of that era which will not distort truth and miseducate southern youth." Its author expressed confidence that the Louisville School board would side with Galt.[16]

The July 1902 issue of the *Confederate Veteran* featured a letter from Laura Galt herself, thanking readers for their numerous letters of support. She also took the opportunity to explain herself more fully:

As for putting my fingers in my ears I did that because I would not listen to a song that declares such a tyrant and coward as Sherman and his disgraceful and horrible march through Georgia and the Carolinas to be glorious. I did not think, at the time, my teacher would think it very bad. I felt that forcing the Southern girls who were in the room to sing or listen to such a song was an insult that I could not stand.[17]

Laura Galt represented a new-generation figure around which anti-Sherman and pro-Confederate opinion could coalesce, and she became the belle of the Lost Cause ball. In August the Georgia Society of Montgomery, Alabama, presented her with a medal. In September the men of United Confederate Veterans Camp 435, in Augusta, Georgia, made her an honorary member and gave her a gold UCV badge. The only other women so honored before her had been Varina Davis and Mrs. Charles C. Jones Jr. (the daughter-in-law of Mary Jones, discussed in Chapter 1), putting her in rather august company.[18]

The accolades continued to pour in. The UCV camp in Los Angeles honored Galt with a series of resolutions, invoking her Confederate ancestors, and praising her virtues of "moral courage, filial love and reverence." The California veterans thanked young Laura for "her protests against that ignoble spirit which sometimes, even yet, delights to recall the devastation of the fair fields and homes of the South."[19] That this sense of sectional grievance persisted even during what historians have told us was the peak of reunionist sentiment, after the Spanish-American War, is telling. Beneath the placid surface of joint reunions and Southern whites fighting under the American flag again, lay a deep well of animosity.[20]

Over a year after the initial incident in school, Laura Galt was still being feted and celebrated in the former Confederacy. In November 1903, she was the guest of honor at an elegant luncheon in Augusta, where the room and tables were festooned with Confederate colors and flags.[21] The following February, the *Los Angeles Times* opined that she was likely to be chosen the new "Daughter of the Confederacy" at the 1904 UCV reunion.[22]

In the years that followed, Laura Galt continued to be held up as an ideal of white Southern girlhood. By 1906, "Marching through Georgia" was no longer being sung in the white schools of Louisville (whether it was banned from the black schools as well is unclear). As late as 1918, protests against "Marching through Georgia" continued to crop up, as when various UDC chapters in Virginia opposed the song's use as a "national march."[23] For President Jimmy Carter, it seemed equally inescapable. As a young plebe at the

Naval Academy, he was hazed and beaten for refusing to sing the song.[24] At a 1980 campaign rally in Phoenix, Arizona, a high school band began playing it to welcome him, leading Carter to exclaim in frustration: "Doesn't anybody realize that's not a Southern song?"[25]

Singing Contrabands and Bummers

One wonders what Carter would have made of other, lesser-known musical homages to Sherman's marchers. Sherman's March could sell songs that were seemingly unrelated, as in the 1864 galop for piano, "Sherman's Advance on Savannah." A 1931 article on Civil War music in the collections of the Library of Congress indicates that Georgians would not be apt to wish for a copy of this one.[26]

"Sherman's March," written by Michael Fee, describes the March from the perspective of a self-described contraband:

Now, listen to my song,
And I won't detain you long.
I just come from a Southern plantation;
I'm a contraband, you see,
And Sherman set me free..
For, he is the greatest General in the Nation!
When the Lincoln-Sogers come,
You ought to see Ole Massa run..
I thought sure that Babylon had fallen!
Then, I began to holler..
And after him did follow:
But, of course, he didn't seem to hear me call him.

Chorus: So, walk along, Beauregard,
And you'll have to go it mighty hard:
For, General Sherman's after you, like thunder!

Now, Ole Massa he has gone:
Since they've taken Charleston,
I saw him skedaddle on that occasion;
But, I guess, he'll leff us be;
For, he knows that we is free:
At least, so says Lincoln's Proclamation.
Now, the war is at an end,

To Beecher's church we'll all attend,
And hear Politics and Religion amalgamated.
Horace Greely, and Phillips, too:
They will tell us what they'll do
With those coler'd folks that am confiscated.
Chorus

The use of dialect makes it possible that this song was written to be sung in minstrel shows. Whether intentionally or not, the song captures some of the complexity of the relationship between Sherman and the freedmen. On the one hand, the singer praises Sherman as the "greatest General in the nation," but on the other hand, the General seems oblivious to African Americans ("he didn't seem to hear me call him"). Too, the singer is clearly pleased to be free, but at the same time, the final lines strike a distinctly antiabolitionist stance, mocking Henry Ward Beecher, Horace Greely, and Wendell Phillips, and implying that freedom won't be all that the naïve contrabands might have expected.[27]

"When Sherman's On De Track," by David Warden, seems more clearly to derive from minstrelsy, as it is written in very thick dialect. One could hardly imagine men marching to it, or respectable Northern girls playing it in their parlors.

1. Oh look a-way out yon-der,
For de dust am rising high,
Gen'-ral Sherman's comin' long
And Mas-sa's goin' to die,
He's got some nig-ger soldiers
Dat make de rebels run,
Just hold your breff a li-tle while,
And see de glorious fun,
Just hold your breff a li-tle while,
And see de glorious fun.

2. When Gen'ral Sherman ribes in town
We'll meet him wid a grin,
How is you Gen'-ral Sherman?
Glad to see you, pray walk in,
Old Mas-sa's in de par-lor
As sick as he can be,
Just tell him you're de doc-tor man

A-way from Ten-nes-see.
Just tell him you're de doc-tor man
A-way from Ten-nes-see.

3. The rail roads hab been torn to smash
De Lo-kies cannot run,
Old Hood has got his boi-ler bust
And dat hab stopt his fun,
Old Beaure-gard lies very sick,
Wid rup-ture and wid gout,
While Bob-by Lee begins to see
De game am most play'd out.
While Bob-by Lee begins to see
De game am most play'd out.

4. We'll take de Gen'ral wid his staff
And let dem take a peep,
Where Mas-sa's Cot-ton lays so snug
A-way down by a creek,
For con-fis-ca-tion berry good,
Al-do it's Con-tra-band,
'Twill make old mas-sa well a-gain
And turn him Union man.
'Twill make old mas-sa well a-gain
And turn him Union man.

Chorus:
Wake! Darkies wake!
Old Sherman's on de track,
He's knock'd de breff, from poor old Jeff
And laid him on his back.
Whack!

The proclamation that Sherman had black soldiers is hardly accurate, as is the mention of Bobby Lee. The contrabands described are not faithful slaves, as they lead soldiers to hidden cotton, but neither does the song portray Sherman's Field Orders No. 15 in a positive light. Would the master become a Union man in order to avoid having his land confiscated or to regain control over his former slaves? The specifics may be unclear, but the mocking of African American aspirations is not.[28]

Another subset of wartime songs is not exclusively about Sherman and the March but rather includes it in a litany of Union victories. Thus "A New Song for Sherman & Sheridan" begins by praising the latter's exploits in the Shenandoah Valley in 1864. Four of the seven verses sing Sherman's praises, for "routing" the Rebels on the way to Atlanta, taking Savannah, and (inaccurately) besieging Charleston. Unusually, this song also praises the softer side of Sherman, his relative kindness toward Savannah's civilians:

> He gave his good Union neighbors for to understand,
> That the Poor of Savannah wanted a hand,
> Like the Prodigal child they were taken in,
> And supplied with abundance by good Union men.

This version of the March emphasizes saving the Union rather than punishing the rebels.[29]

These songs were all written during the war, designed to motivate and inspire. But as the war ended and faded into the past, the songs continued. In 1881, as veterans were becoming a social and political force, Thomas Fanning published "The Sherman Bummers," dedicated to the Soldiers' and Sailors' Memorial Association:

> 1. Oh, with cheers the air was rent, when the boys "due South" were
>   sent,
> From Atlanta's captured outposts scarce a span;
> Where our foe-men of the South failed to feed the cannon's mouth,
> There the ever-glorious Sherman march began.
>
> CHORUS:
> Cheer! cheer! cheer! the Sherman Bummers,
> Boys in blue—the tried and true, as beneath the banner free
> Then we sang of victory,
> So we now our bond of brotherhood renew.
>
> 2. Thro' the marsh, by river side, over leaf strewn paths they glide,
> With a will and eye un-swerving as they move;
> Where the whistling bullets rang these gay Bummers march'd and sang
> As an answer their pulses thrill to prove. —*Chorus*
>
> 3. Not a weary pilgrim's strays, travel-stained in ancient days,
> Has more placidly with burden moved serene
> Than these Bummers of the West, facing foes the bravest, best,
> That dame Nature furnished Dixie near the scene. —*Chorus*

4. Then hurrah! ye Bummers brave, 'twas no useless help ye gave,
By your skirmishing and scouting in the van;
It was moving with a dash—ending discord with a crash,
Till, through Sherman's noble leading, Peace began. —*Chorus*

5. No great contested field has this warlike earth revealed
In upholding deeds heroic in this land,
Where Columbia reigns supreme, and her sons their wrath redeem,
By the victor and the vanquished clasping hands. —*Chorus*[30]

Fanning's homage to Sherman's bummers shows us a couple of things: first, that "bummer" had been successfully transformed from an epithet to a badge of honor. Second, it represents a complete sanitization of the March. The verses are generically celebratory, mentioning only Atlanta as a point of reference. They emphasize the belief among Sherman's veterans that their march, their efforts, brought about the end of the war. Too, this is both an explicit and an implicit call to reunion: explicitly, by describing "the victor and the vanquished clasping hands"; and implicitly, by making no mention of the destruction and theft that made the bummers famous, or perhaps, infamous, throughout Georgia and the Carolinas. This is a song designed to knit a nation together, not polarize it.

These impulses toward reunion were not always well received by Southern whites, as exemplified by one of the few openly anti-Sherman songs to be published. Mrs. Sadie Colbert Burke, of Bainbridge, Georgia, received a letter from a friend in New York, who had watched Ulysses S. Grant's funeral procession. Among the marchers was Confederate general John B. Gordon, who was insulted by a group of children serenading him with "Marching through Georgia." In angry response, "with trembling hands and throbbing pulse," Mrs. Burke wrote her own response, entitled "Sherman's Raid through Georgia." She then sent it to Mrs. Pickett, General Pickett's widow, who tried to get it published "but there was an enemy in every music house," and it languished, until Mrs. Burke sent it in to *Confederate Veteran*. Her reply to "Marching through Georgia" is angry and pointed:

The pride of every nation is her brave and gallant men.
Their praise is rung from mountain top and echoed in the glen;
Then here's to Sherman's "dashing boys," who won glory on the day
They desolated Georgia homes when the owners were away.

Chorus: Hurrah! Hurrah! We heard your "jubilee!"
'Twas sung in dear old Georgia from Atlanta to the sea.

Hurrah! Hurrah! It made old Cuffee shout.
For Marster an' de boys were gone and none to turn you out.

When you marched through dear old Georgia, leaving sorrow in your
  train.
The cry of hungry children and mothers all in vain,
Your cruel song was chorused by the darky's lusty shout,
For "Ole Marse an' de boys" were gone and none to turn you out.

The boasted "Union men" were deserters from our ranks
That gave such lordly welcome to fifty thousand Yanks;
And the spirit of our fathers would murmur in the grave
If o'er such wily traitors the dear old flag should wave.

The stars and stripes, the honored flag, our fathers' sacred trust,
Once proudly borne by Valor's hand, you trailed it in the dust
The day you quit the battlefield and raised the private latch
To raid upon the "goobers and the sweet potato patch."

We bravely met you in the field our pluck you can't deny,
And though your numbers trebled our, we often made you fly.
A lesson true we taught to you at the battle of Bull Run
That a little war with Southern boys was anything but fun!

No treason moved the Southern heart, so noble, true, and brave;
The sacred cause we loved, though dread, sleeps in an honored grave;
And glory wreathes our heroes' names on Fame's bright page to-day.
God bless the men that fought and lost, our men that wore the gray![31]

Burke strips away the romantic blurring that occurs in the Northern-writ-
ten songs, by emphasizing Union foraging and destruction. She argues that
Sherman's men lost their moral superiority when they turned from fighting
man-to-man on the field of battle to making war on civilians. Even as she denies heroism to Union soldiers, she employs the standard Lost Cause tropes
of fierce fighting (hearkening all the way back to the beginning of the war)
and stressing Confederate heroism. She also injects race into her arguments,
with the disparaging mention of "Cuffee" shouting. Needless to say, it never
became as popular as "Marching through Georgia."[32]

We now skip ahead by a century to 1978. Musician Paul Kennerley, inspired
by both the American bicentennial and the election of a Georgian to the White
House, wrote *White Mansions*, a Civil War–themed "concept album" which
tried to tell the story of the Confederate people through country music. It

featured four main characters: Matthew J. Fuller, the twenty-three-year-old son of a Georgia planter and a captain in the Confederate infantry; his sweetheart, Polly Ann Stafford; Caleb Stone, a poor white man who works as an overseer and resents the white aristocracy; and the Drifter, a sort of omniscient figure, supposedly a veteran of the Mexican War. The slaves are largely silent, because they were seen as silenced during the war. The songs take the listener from the beginning of the war through Matthew's and Caleb's enlistments in different regiments, their battlefield experiences, and the Drifter's realization that there was no way for the Confederates to win the war. There's a definite Lost Cause inflection to this work, which comes through in its celebration of futile military actions and the "Confederate Dead."[33]

Toward the end of the album, Caleb, Matthew, and the Drifter return to Georgia to view the devastation wrought by Sherman and his men, described as "a move designed to knock the wind out of the South and was enforced with unnecessary relish." Together they sing "They Laid Waste to Our Land":

they laid waste to our land, they took it from our hand
from Atlanta to Savannah, they scorched our earth
they stole our corn and wheat, they left no food to eat
they slaughtered all the cattle, took the things of worth
well, we got women and children too
just the same as you
ain't it enough just to know that you got us beat

the hatred will never cease, even now that there's peace
the feelings will run as deep as the scars we bear
this ain't cloth we wear it's a rag, we're at the mercy of the carpetbag
what you call justice is plain unfair
how the hell can you ever claim
it's bin worth all of the pain
just to have us live together under one flag
they laid waste to our land, they took it from our hand

(the following is spoken by The Drifter during the rest of the verse):
On November 15, 1864, Gen. Sherman cut out the back of Atlanta with 68,000 hard worn Yankees, he drove 'em down through Georgia to the sea. With hate in their hearts, they moved in a line, cutting a scar through God's Blessed country 50 miles wide. Burning, looting and gutting our land like vultures. They tore up the railroad tracks, they burnt the cotton and the gins, Lord, they made everybody suffer.

These lyrics are the polar opposite of "Marching through Georgia" and well encapsulate the white Southern sense of grievance. The mentions of deep scars, unending resentment, and the conflation of Sherman's March and Reconstruction (with the references to carpetbags) show the depth of anger. Nor is this balanced by the voices of the newly freed African Americans, who only sing a brief spiritual, praising Lincoln for their freedom.[34]

White Mansions was well-known in the 1970s, in large part because of the musicians who played on the album.[35] Country star Waylon Jennings played the central role of the Drifter, and Eric Clapton was a guest musician on one of the tracks. The album was reissued in 1999, and continues to be sold as of this writing. It was performed live in the United Kingdom in 2010, thus coloring another nation's understanding of the war and Sherman's March.[36]

Photographic Views of Sherman's Campaign

That the Civil War was the first American war to be photographed is so oft-repeated as to have become a cliché. Photographs seem more realistic, more immediate, than the other kinds of illustrations—engravings, drawings, even paintings—that tell the story of the war. Yet we can too easily forget that these photographs are subjective and do not provide a full or "objective" telling of the war. They are the result of choices made by photographers—of where to be, of when to be there, of what to photograph and what to leave out. These inclusions and omissions are especially significant in the case of the few photographic representations of Sherman's March, the most significant of which is George Barnard's 1866 collection, *Photographic Views of Sherman's Campaign.*

George Barnard was already a well-known photographer when Sherman summoned him to Atlanta in September 1864. In fact, he had worked as a daguerreotypist and photographer for more than twenty years by then, first in Oswego, New York, then in New York City, and ultimately in Washington, D.C. In both New York and Washington he worked alongside well-known colleagues like Edward Anthony and Matthew Brady. He took portraits and field photographs during the early years of the war, including at Yorktown and Second Bull Run. He became the Army of the Cumberland's director of photographic operations in 1863, and was in Tennessee during the Atlanta campaign (although his photographs were used in creating topographical maps).[37]

Barnard took photographs around Chattanooga and along the route of the Atlanta campaign, including Resaca and Kennesaw Mountain. In Atlanta, he made images of fortifications, the spot where General McPherson fell, and several buildings before they were destroyed. He managed to get a few stereographs of soldiers tearing up railroad tracks, although they were not included in *Photographic Views*.[38] Although Barnard accompanied Sherman on the March to Savannah, he did not take any photographs along the way. Barnard explained that the men were moving too fast, and that the technical requirements of processing, especially the need for both time and fresh water, as well as a place to set up and work, could not be met. But one could also argue that the March did not lend itself to Barnard's usual style and subject matter. There were few battles, so no battlefields to memorialize. He could not, or perhaps would not, memorialize the burning buildings, frightened people, and casual destruction that marked so much of the March. After all, he would have spent a couple of days in Milledgeville, so presumably he could have made photographs had he chosen. He claimed to have been bothered by the destruction of buildings in Atlanta, but became less so after he saw Camp Lawton, the prison camp outside of Millen.[39]

Barnard took advantage of the weeks spent in Savannah to both take photographs and print copies. When Sherman moved on, he and Barnard parted company. Barnard then visited and photographed Charleston in March 1865, Columbia in April, and was ultimately discharged from the Army in June 1865. Once Barnard decided to publish his album of photographs, capitalizing on public interest in wartime reminiscences, he realized that he needed to return to the South and take more photographs, which he did in 1866.[40] Although *Photographic Views of Sherman's Campaign* was published in a limited edition, at the high price of $100 per set, it exerted an influence disproportionate to its circulation, because there were so few photographs of the campaigns at all. Barnard also included maps by Orlando Poe and commissioned accompanying text from Theo Davis, the *Harper's* illustrator. He carefully organized the photographs in sequence from Chattanooga to Charleston, allowing the readers to feel as though they themselves were retracing the March.[41]

The result of this is a work of both literal and metaphorical weight.[42] Barnard's visual version of the March became the authoritative one, enshrining a particular view, rather than an all-encompassing one. For example, Barnard not only included Charleston, which was not even part of the March, but also the ruins of the Pinckney Mansion, which had burned in 1861. He included Fort Sumter, not in the interests of representing Sherman's campaign (because it wasn't part of it), but because he wanted to represent the war's conclusion as having gone full circle.[43] Similarly, Barnard chose to

Columbia's destruction. The photograph, a plate from Photographic Views of Sherman's Campaign, *was taken in 1866, a year after Sherman's men came through. (Wisconsin Historical Society, image number: 78918)*

photograph landscapes and ruins, presenting a picturesque and pastoral view of the South. Sherman's March, in Barnard's view, is both a literal and a metaphorical scourging and cleansing of the region, the destruction needed before the restoration. There are no photographs of soldiers (only the opening portrait of Sherman and his generals), no images of the dead to shock Northern sensibilities, no groups of newly freed slaves taking to the roads. The landscapes are still and empty. Ironically, the dramatic cloudscapes for which Barnard was known were not part of the landscapes either—Barnard added them in with a special double negative technique, a nineteenth-century version of Photoshop.[44]

As for other contemporary images of the March, some of the illustrated weeklies sent artists down to observe. Theo Davis, an illustrator for *Harper's* traveled with the March from Atlanta to Savannah; he sent back sketches of troops pillaging and looting, but they were never published. *Harper's* did at least acknowledge some of what went on during the weeks on the move, including engravings of Madison Station, Millen, and Winnsborough aflame and Savannah being bombarded. As for the bummers, they were represented only by two decorous images of "Foragers 'Starting Out' in the Morning" and

"Foragers Returning at Night." The vast majority of illustrations portrayed the March as any other military operation, showing soldiers on the move, pontoon bridges, and views of the towns through which they passed.[45] *Frank Leslie's Illustrated Weekly* similarly used illustrations to show the progress of Sherman's marchers across the landscape. These images, however, did not shy away from showing the soldiers at work burning and tearing up tracks, in places like Atlanta and South Carolina. Too, *Leslie's* even showed bummers shooting livestock at one point, bringing the grimmer realities of war home to Northern readers.[46]

These images were created in the moments of the March. But in the years that followed a variety of other representations appeared, often in the pages of reminiscences, dime novels, and memoirs. The imagery tends to fall into a few categories: illustrations of specific places, sometimes in ruins following destruction; African American and white refugees fleeing either to the March or from it; and images of Sherman's soldiers themselves. This last category further subdivides the men into two contrary portraits: either as an orderly, disciplined, fighting force or as foragers and bummers, mischievously wreaking havoc all around them.

One of the finest examples of the marcher as a respectable figure is Thomas Nast's 1864 painting *The Soldier's Halt*, also known as *The Halt—A Scene in the Georgia Campaign* and *The Halt (Drink of Water)*, which also appeared in *Harper's* in 1866. The painting shows a pair of Union soldiers (identified as New York troops by their uniform details) outside a simple home. One soldier is playing with a dog, the other is reaching out to tickle a baby held in his mother's arms. Two small children stand by, their posture indicating interest, rather than fear. There are no flames, no broken furniture, no stolen hams to be found. The woman holds a pitcher, and it appears she has just poured the thirsty soldiers a drink. The image is one of quiet, sun-dappled, domesticity. The soldiers are respectful, respectable professionals, a far cry from the stereotype of the undisciplined bummers. The absence of African Americans is also significant. The home is modest, as opposed to a plantation manse, and the implication is that this white woman is the wife of a yeoman farmer. The image, which was reprinted and exhibited numerous times, is designed to encourage white Northerners and Southerners to move beyond the battlefield, into peace. At one point, Chicago merchants tried to raise money to purchase the painting and present it as a gift to General Sherman. In 2007 it sold at auction for $252,000, a record for a painting by Nast.[47]

Popular artistic representations of the Civil War today are dominated by three men: Don Troiani, Dale Gallon, and Mort Künstler. All three pride

This engraving allowed Thomas Nast's pastoral scene to reach a broad audience, making an argument that Sherman's March was gentle and benign. (Library of Congress, http://www.loc.gov/pictures/item/89715613/)

themselves on their meticulous attention to historical detail and accuracy. Their paintings and prints are dominated by military, and particularly Lost Cause, themes. Historian Gary Gallagher analyzed nearly three thousand advertisements that ran in national Civil War magazines between 1962 and 2006 and found that subject matter was strongly dominated by Confederate themes. In addition, portrayals of the eastern theater, and Robert E. Lee and Gettysburg in particular, far overshadow those about the war in the West. Gallagher attributes much of this imbalance to a similar imbalance in recent films about the War, particularly the importance of 1994's *Gettysburg*.[48]

Searching for representations of Sherman and the March in these artists' oeuvres can be frustrating. Don Troiani, who calls himself "America's Most Respected Historical Artist" offers an online gallery of his work, divided into several subjects and series. Currently the only available image out of several hundred that deals with the March is *Signaling the Assault on Fort McAllister*, December 13, 1864. This rather formal image shows Generals Sherman and Howard preparing their final assault. There are no bummers, no civilians, and no African Americans. No houses or barns burn in the background, which is instead dominated by signal flags. The March itself is not referenced directly. Clearly, this is a painting designed not to offend, while showing Sherman in a positive, commanding, light.[49] Dale Gallon does not have any images of the March available, though he did include the burning of Chambersburg, Pennsylvania, so it can't be because of a distaste for destruction.[50]

Mort Künstler, who bills himself as America's Artist, has both a standard portrait of Sherman, alone against an American flag background, and a portrait of him on horseback, surrounded by cheering soldiers. The latter is entitled *Sherman Marches to the Sea* but seems to show him having already arrived at Savannah. Like Troiani, Küntsler's Sherman seems the sanitized military man, with no images of devastation to chip away at his achievements or heroism. His most famous image of Sherman is ironically the one that was never released as a print, only a poster. Entitled *War Is Hell*, he painted it for a special event at the Booth Western Art Museum near Atlanta. It depicts the general on horseback, accompanied by a few soldiers, almost silhouetted against the backdrop of burning buildings in Atlanta, ostensibly on November 15 as the men moved out. While clearly not a real scene, since Sherman observed the flames from a distance, this best captures the popular understanding of Sherman as the bringer of flames and despoiler of the landscape. This, it appears, is what the people want to see.[51]

Poetic License

The epic qualities of the March naturally lent themselves to poetry. Most of the poems about the March written during and in the years immediately following the war tended toward the celebratory, along the lines of Byers's "Sherman's March to the Sea" (which began life as a poem). Most were written from a Union, pro-Sherman perspective, most focused on the soldiers in some way or another. By the late twentieth and early twenty-first centuries, poems that referenced the March were more oblique, often more personal, and sometimes written by Southerners.

Two of the best-known poems about the March were also two of the first to be written and published: Herman Melville's "The March to the Sea" and "The Frenzy in the Wake." Both appeared in his 1866 collection *Battle-Pieces and Aspects of the War*, which Melville dedicated to the memory of the Union dead. He claimed to have written the majority of the poems following the fall of Richmond, and reflected that "yielding instinctively, one after another, to feelings not inspired from any one source exclusively, and unmindful, without purposing to be, of consistency, I seem, in most of these verses, to have but placed a harp in a window, and noted the contrasted airs which wayward wilds have played upon the strings."[52] This is certainly the case in "The March to the Sea" and "The Frenzy in the Wake."

"The March to the Sea" praises Sherman's soldiers as a powerful force spreading over the land, pushing even nature out of the way. Each stanza's penultimate line is "it was glorious glad marching," and most of the poem conveys that feeling: the men are powerfully moving forward, "the banners brightly blooming," collecting livestock, and frolicking, luxuriating in their freedom.

> The foragers through calm lands
>   Swept in tempest gay,
> And they breathed the air of balm-lands
>   Where rolled savannas lay,
> And they helped themselves from farm-lands—
>   As who should say them nay?
>   The regiments uproarious
>   Laughed in Plenty's glee;
>   And they marched till their broad laughter
>   Met the laughter of the sea:
>   It was glorious glad marching,
>   That marching to the sea.

Melville uses all sorts of natural metaphors to describe the March's inexorable force. The soldiers brush away their enemies as a bull does a gnat, "the columns streamed like rivers," they were a force of nature drawing the newly freed slaves to them. Only toward the end of the poem does a hint of darkness creep in. For in sweeping over the natural landscape of Georgia, they also devastate it:[53]

> The grain of endless acres
>   Was threshed (as in the East)
> By the trampling of the Takers,
>   Strong march of man and beast;
> The flails of those earth-shakers
>   Left a famine where they ceased.
>   The arsenals were yielded;
>   The sword (that was to be),
>   Arrested in the forging,
>   Rued that marching to the sea:
>   It was glorious glad marching,
>   But ah, the stern decree!

For behind they left a wailing,
    A terror and a ban,
And blazing cinders sailing,
    And houseless households wan,
Wide zones of counties paling,
    And towns where maniacs ran.
        Was it Treason's retribution—
            Necessity the plea?
        They will long remember Sherman
            And his streaming columns free—
        They will long remember Sherman
            Marching to the sea.

These final lines echo *Paradise Lost*, and with them Melville is making the argument, made by Sherman and his men, that the "blazing cinders" and trampled fields were the price of secession and war. Whether he fully agrees with it is debatable, and he seems to be encouraging Northerners to be magnanimous in their victory.[54]

If "The March to the Sea" illuminates the pro-Union, pro-soldier perspective, then "The Frenzy in the Wake" takes the opposite position. This poem was inspired by the Carolinas campaign, and it made no attempt to minimize or sugarcoat the impact of the March. "The Frenzy in the Wake" viscerally illuminates white Southern rage and resentment:

So strong to suffer, shall we be
    Weak to contend, and break
The sinews of the Oppressor's knee
    That grinds upon the neck?
O, the garments rolled in blood
    Scorch in cities wrapped in flame,
And the African—the imp!
    He gibbers, imputing shame.

The anger boils over: at the scorched cities, the newly freed African Americans, the soldiers from "frozen Maine" and "far Minnesota." The poem hints at white Southerners biding their time until they can rise up again, at the potential for distant revenge. It closes ominously:

With burning woods our skies are brass,
    The pillars of dust are seen;
The live-long day their cavalry pass—

No crossing the road between.
　　We were sore deceived—an awful host!

They move like a roaring wind.
　　Have we gamed and lost? but even despair
　　　Shall never our hate rescind.[55]

Melville invokes the specter of the March as an unstoppable juggernaut, one that smashes all in its path but never stops to rebuild.

In contrast to Melville's direct engagement, another great Civil War poet, Walt Whitman, wrote about Sherman's March only obliquely. In "Ethiopia Saluting the Colors," which first appeared in the 1871–72 edition of *The Leaves of Grass*, Whitman allows the reader to eavesdrop on the discomfiting interaction between one of Sherman's soldiers and an African American woman. Whitman did not write often about issues of race and emancipation, but this poem (whether by design or not) captures the casual condescension with which the marchers treated freedpeople. The woman is called, generically, "Ethiopia," twice described as "hardly human" and her interest in watching the marchers pass by is questioned, almost scoffed at. She has her own reasons:

Me, master, years a hundred, since from my parents sunder'd,
A little child, they caught me as the savage beast is caught;
Then hither me, across the sea, the cruel slaver brought.

No further does she say, but lingering all the day,
Her high-borne turban'd head she wags, and rolls her darkling eye,
And curtseys to the regiments, the guidons moving by

Whether the marchers wanted to be an army of liberation is immaterial to this woman, who stands in for all of the freedmen. She possesses her own inborn sense of dignity and respectability, one that cannot be shaken by the feckless young man who challenges her.[56]

Despite the somewhat insensitive portrayal of "Ethiopia," African American intellectuals embraced the poem. Harry T. Burleigh, the musical arranger of numerous spirituals like "Deep River," set it to music in 1915. The arrangement is a sort of military march and actually quotes from "Marching through Georgia." It was used as a marching song during World War I and continues to be performed today.[57]

Few other nineteenth-century poems about the March are as complexly evocative as those by Melville and Whitman. Many of them were written by and for veterans, and they tend toward the literal and the hagiographic. Oliver Wendell Holmes subtitled his verse "Sherman's in Savannah," as "a half-rhymed improtpu," and it's safe to say he proved a better jurist than poet. He praised Sherman and "his glorious band" for swooping in on "doomed Savannah," attributing their survival to divine grace. Holmes appears to have written this poem while the March was still ongoing, for he filled it with references to Confederate treason and closed with the following wish:

> Soon shall Richmond's tough old hide
> Find a tough old tanner!
> Soon from every rebel wall
> Shall the rag of treason fall,
> Till our banner flaps o'er all
> As it crowns Savannah![58]

Holmes was not a participant in the March, but he captured something of the experience of the men along it, with the excitement that it generated within the Union.

Similarly, J. Ward Childs was not a member of Sherman's XV Corps, but he adopted that persona in his poem "The Fifteenth Veteran Corps." This work, sort of a standard homage to the Union "veterans of the west," praises their bravery and determination, as well as their fearsome fighting. In an echo of "The Sherman Bummers," Childs explains:

> They call us Sherman's "bummers"
> And doubtless we are "some,"
> For marching down through Dixie,
> We went on many a "bum";
> We bummed it at Atlanta,
> And at Savannah, too,
> And all the way to Bentonville,
> Where we put the Johnnies through.

But Childs's poem does not end with this boast. Rather, his final stanza is a reminder that "now the war is over / the rebellion is no more." These later works seem to straddle the line between celebrating victory and at least paying lip service to some sort of reunionist sentiment.[59]

Charles G. Halpine is best known for the poems he wrote under the pseudonym Miles O'Reilly and for his work as a Democratic newspaper editor in New York City. His poem "Song of Sherman's Army" departs from the standard bland and general praise for the troops. He opens dramatically: "A pillar of fire by night, / A pillar of smoke by day." More than other poets (except perhaps Melville in "The Frenzy in the Wake") Halpine evokes the Union army's strategic use of fear and violence, explaining:

> There is terror wherever we come
> There is terror and wild dismay
> When they see the Old Flag and hear the drum
> Announce us on the way
> When they see the Old Flag and hear the drum
> Beating time to our onward Way

Halpine's soldiers know that they are relatively safe along the March, facing "just enough fighting to quicken our hearts." And as the poem progresses, it becomes more lighthearted, characterizing the March as a "gala," and "a picnic or a play." The fear invoked at the beginning seems justifiable and deserved, the price of saving the Union.[60]

Fred Emerson Brooks, a well-known turn-of-the-century poet and humorist, was moved to write his "Sherman's March" after meeting Sherman himself at a GAR reunion in San Francisco. Brooks called on the general and asked his permission to "put into verse" the story of the March; Sherman warned him that he had put off Thomas Buchanan Read, the author of "Sheridan's Ride," three times but then went on to tell Brooks several stories. From his notes on that conversation, Brooks created the persona of a blind Union veteran, groping at the lapel of a fellow GAR man. The old veteran is looking for comradeship and kinship, trying to find another veteran of the March with whom to reminisce. The descriptions of the March itself are rather conventional, with flying banners, "peerless" chieftains, and invocations of the men's love for "Uncle Billy." In this telling, the final objective was neither Savannah nor Columbia, but Richmond and the explicit end of the war. The poem's dramatic height comes at its conclusion, when the veteran realizes that he has been speaking to Sherman all along:

> What? You are General Sherman?
> Then you'll have to cheer for me!
> For I marched down behind you,
> From Atlanta to the sea.

Brooks first recited the poem at the GAR reunion, and he proudly recalled that he brought tears to General Sherman's eyes, and those of every other man in the room. This sentimental display was in part enabled by the poem's omission of anything controversial.[61]

Recitations of poems were staples of veterans reunions, with most of the offerings made by the veterans themselves. One standout was Brigadier General John Tilson's 1874 offering to the members of the Society of the Army of the Tennessee, "The March to the Sea." It's quite long—ten printed pages—and larded through with metaphors. The marchers are compared to night-flying birds, to Columbus and his mariners, to "a long blue serpent with shining scales." Unlike many of his fellow poets, Tilson reminds his listeners of the weeks when no one outside of Georgia knew where the March was and where it was headed. When he discusses the March itself, he lauds it as "wonderful" and "venturesome," his descriptive passages punctuated with the refrain "onward, still onward, on to the sea." Tilson sought to immortalize the March by comparing it to great victories of the past: Marathon, Waterloo, Hastings, and Bunker Hill. His bid for the March's immortality may have succeeded, but his poem appears to have faded into obscurity.[62]

The passing of the veterans' generation seemed to result in a lessening of writings about the Civil War. Perhaps too, the romance of the Civil War receded as the horrors of World War I and World War II took precedence. But, one hundred or so years after the passing of the veterans, modern poets have turned back to the Civil War in general, and the March in particular, as a potent source of inspiration. Unlike the poems of the past, which were dominated by Union sympathizers, many of the most evocative come out of the South.

Harold Lawrence wrote his 1994 collection of poetry, *Memory Hill*, about the people buried in Milledgeville, Georgia's Memory Hill Cemetery. "Resting Place" retells the story of Georgia secretary of state Nathan C. Barnett's hiding a legislative book in his pigpen and the Great Seal in his home. Lawrence's spare lines and imagery evoked the hurried whispers of a frightened family facing the loss of what it knew:

> There they laid down their hopes
> wrapped in sailcloth and linen
> and lowered the outward form
> of who they really were
> as gently as a child
> into the moist and secret dark
> to subsist on its finite charities
> until the day of its reclaiming

Eventually, the seal and book were returned, allowing the society they represented, in Lawrence's words,

to claim its rightful place
in all its might and power.

Lawrence's poem exemplifies the sense that even a century past the March, some sort of resentment lingered in the Southern white psyche, waiting to be reawakened.[63]

Ted Spivey included several poems about Sherman and the March in his Civil War–themed collection *To Die in Atlanta*. Two are about Sherman himself. In "Sherman," Spivey calls the general "war's genius" and "war itself," with "Wrath so great." Yet Spivey also sees him as fundamentally unknowable and inscrutable. Sherman haunts Spivey's 1980s Atlanta. He sees soldiers' ghosts everywhere and finds his thoughts turning to Sherman in places like MARTA transit stations or the Capitol. In "Worthies in Bronze" Sherman is "invisibly dominating the scene" on Capitol Hill, but is also a man of fundamental contradictions:

Sherman is magnanimous,
In Atlanta sparing a church.
Riding past burning columns,
Tears on desecrated graves,
He decides to rest
In tropic Savannah.
Once again the gentleman,
He personally carries her mail
To matriarchal Mrs. Gordon.

Spivey captures the essential duality of thinking about Sherman: it was not possible for white Southerners to fully hate him, because he treated individuals with small kindnesses.[64]

Spivey's poem "A Man of War" takes a similarly sympathetic look at Sherman, describing him not as a bringer of fear and terror but rather as the kindly, laughing "Uncle Billy," who "savored the small events" of march and campsite, rather "than all the grand designs about / Death for an upstart nation." This Sherman seems to fight for his own reasons, rather than ideological ones, and like the preceding one, bears no particular ill will toward Southerners. Sherman seems less detached as the unnamed narrator of "This Tropic City Savannah," in which he muses on the unassuageable wounds of "farm boys from Ohio." This Sherman takes pleasure in the humbling of a "feudal" place, lamenting that it remained "Haughty in defeat / Like fatal Cleopatra / Already dreaming / of another Antony."[65]

Spivey approaches Sherman and the March from a kaleidoscope of perspectives. "A Burning House," dated "Birdsville, 1864" describes a woman refusing to leave her bed, even as Union soldiers unearth her dead children while digging for treasure like "conquistadores / Come at last / to Georgia." The soldiers light her house on fire, but they are shamed by her strength and:

Suddenly remembering
Their own mothers,
They doused the fire
And walked away,
Conquistadores no more,
Now lonely men
In an alien land.

Spivey's retelling of the story of Mrs. William B. Jones of Birdsville Plantation, where soldiers dug up the fresh graves of her infant twins, treats the soldiers rather gently. He could have focused on the soldiers' traumatizing the newly bereaved mother, but instead he shows their essential humanity.[66]

Spivey writes also of Milledgeville, using the persona of Governor Joseph Brown's wife. He takes off from the legend of the Browns fleeing with all of the produce from the Governor's Mansion gardens, even the cabbages, by imagining Mrs. Brown "cooking turnips / To keep together, in flight, / Both body and soul." The Union soldiers in Milledgeville are scornful, mocking the "dead capital," but through it all, the Browns, and "the red earth" of Georgia endured.[67]

Taken together, music, visual imagery, and poetry all help to show the ways that stories of Sherman's March endured and were refracted through American culture. One can find dozens of versions of "Marching through Georgia" in iTunes, for example. Barnard's *Photographic Views* is more accessible than ever since it has been digitized. Poets recent and long past still dip into the rich well of the March for inspiration.

CHAPTER EIGHT

Fiction and Film

Tragically beautiful, spirited, Southern ladies. Handsome and gallant Union officers. Sneaky or comical bummers. Faithful, loyal slaves. Hidden valuables, secret messages, star-crossed lovers. All of these are staples of Civil War fiction in general and the Sherman saga in particular.[1] These tropes and clichés form the backbone of tales of the Lost Cause and reunion. The novels and films that focus on the March tend to emphasize certain themes and incidents—Sandersville, Ebenezer Creek, and Columbia are staples. They tend to focus on the dramatic clashes, and the melodrama, often at the expense of smaller moments. Many of the older novels have fallen out of favor, but they strongly influenced the popular cultural understanding of the March. Only in recent years have authors begun to capture the March's full complexity. Films, both fictional and documentary, have brought the March to a far larger audience than ever read the memoirs or poems, saw Barnard's photographs, or traveled through Georgia and the Carolinas.

Union Men and Southern Ladies

The first major novel about the March was published in 1867, when the physical scars of the March had barely healed, to say nothing of the emotional ones. The title page of *The M'Donalds; or, The Ashes of Southern Homes. A Tale of Sherman's March* is a masterpiece of signaling. Author William Henry Peck, already a prolific novelist, is identified as being "of Georgia," indicating Southern (and by implication pro-Confederate) bona fides. But the book itself is "Dedicated to the American People," indicating a desire to draw in a broader national audience. This might be seen as purely a marketing decision, but for the fact that Peck periodically addresses his Northern readers directly. The novel's first paragraph includes a call for enduring peace, invoking a "mental prayer that the great American people may never again be the sufferers or the perpetrators of similar atrocities."[2]

Peck never absolves Union soldiers and Sherman of blame for the March, but he does complicate the expected narrative. The story focuses on the widowed Mrs. Preston M'Donald and her beautiful daughter, Myrtis. They are stereotypical and idealized characters, brave and self-sacrificing, genteel and dignified. When the novel opens they are living in Atlanta in much reduced financial circumstances, along with their "aged and faithful" slave, Myra. Mrs. M'Donald has lost her husband and four sons to the war; her youngest son was serving with Wade Hampton. Myrtis has a beau, the handsome and brave (though prone to being wounded) Frank Bartow. The true villain of the novel is not Sherman (although his orders and actions drive much of the narrative) but the evil and ugly Seth Cashmore, a Northerner by birth who lived in Georgia, speculating and extorting, lusting after the lovely Myrtis, and generally making the M'Donalds miserable. Over the course of the novel he shoots Frank Bartow, throws the M'Donalds out of their home, spies on his Southern neighbors for the Union army, takes up with a group of thieving, rapacious bummers, sets fires to the homes he plunders in Columbia, and eventually dies from a combination of a gunshot wound and his own greed.[3]

In contrast to the venal Cashmore, we have the gallant Major Irving, a New Yorker attached to General Slocum's staff. Irving performs two functions in the novel: his overall nobility and helpfulness insulate Peck against any allegations of anti-Northern bias, and he serves as a mouthpiece for Peck to criticize Sherman and the bummers. One would expect Major Irving to fall in love with Myrtis, but he does not—he has his own lady friend back in New York, and thus his kindness toward the M'Donald women is entirely altruistic. And he is quite kind to them: he describes witnessing the death of one of the M'Donald sons, he arranges for them to get out of jail after being arrested on trumped up charges, and he protects them from bummers in multiple locations as they seek refuge during their travels from Atlanta to Oxford, Georgia, and finally Columbia.[4]

Ultimately, *The M'Donalds* is, as subtitled, about the ashes of Southern homes, and there are many. Peck describes bummers swaggering into family parlors across Georgia and South Carolina, stealing heirlooms and destroying everything they couldn't carry. Nor do they prey only on the wealthy; Peck includes an extended story of a frightening assault on a poor white family's cabin "an humble structure of logs," during which the bummers carry off all of the family's meager provisions and go so far as to pry the gold clasps off the family Bible. Peck's descriptions of foraging and the excesses— desecrated graves, torture, rapes, and murders—of the March are particularly effective because he quotes at length from Sherman's *Official Report,* using the general's own language of "relentless devastation" to make his case.[5]

The last section of the book takes place in Columbia, and here we can see the evolution of arguments about who burned the city. Peck explicitly does not take a position one way or the other, explaining that "it is not our place here to discuss by whose orders the capital was fired; that the question is still fiercely disputed." That said, however, the novel places the blame squarely on Sherman's men for literally fanning the flames and contributing to the conflagration. Ever mindful of his Northern readers, Peck was careful to praise Irving and the men like him who protected civilians, drawing a clear line between them and the bummers. He uses Irving to express outrage, having him reflect with horror that "if Columbia be destroyed, eternal infamy will rest upon our arms. An evacuated, surrendered, defenseless city laid in ashes by American soldiers!" Irving finds it impossible to believe that Sherman would have ordered the burning, yet is unable to be sure. Perhaps the fact that Irving rescued the M'Donalds and their kinsmen could absolve some of that guilt. And as early as 1867 we can see the elements of the standard plot beginning to harden into place.[6]

Just as Peck used Sherman's *Official Report* as evidence for his dramatization of the effects of the March, so too did Lieutenant Edward G. Bird draw on his own military experiences as a member of "Sherman's Command" while writing his dime novel *Sherman's March to the Sea; or, Fighting His Way through Georgia.*[7] Rather than beginning his tale of love and espionage on the first page, Bird instead opened with a long sketch of the Atlanta campaign, fall of Atlanta and its occupation, and then the March to Savannah, followed by a detailed biographical sketch of General Sherman himself. This gave a veneer of authenticity and accuracy to the story that followed. Finally, about a quarter of the way in, readers could dive into the story of the brave and handsome Lieutenant Harry Clinton, chosen by Sherman to track down a network of spies during and after the siege of Atlanta. The plot is full of narrow escapes and convoluted escapades, and includes a proper romantic interest for Harry Clinton: the Northern-born and staunchly Unionist Alice Field, who helps to bring down her evil and traitorous uncle. Despite the title, the actual March to the Sea does not appear until the last few pages of the book and is almost ancillary to the plot. Unlike Peck, who filled his book with stories of bummers, providing a graphic retelling of the worst of the March, Bird is more focused on his own plot, and the March is more background than foreground. Given the timing of the novel's publication, only months after Sherman's death in February

1891, it is entirely possible that Bird sought to capitalize on renewed interest in the man and the March.

Bird's is a rather conventional story of heroes and villains, coincidences and young love, one that could have been written against any dramatic backdrop. It is also clearly a work of fiction. *On the Plantation*, which was published in 1892 is a very different sort of book. Joel Chandler Harris, well known for both his Uncle Remus stories and his editorial work at the *Atlanta Constitution*, wrote this thinly fictionalized account of the wartime years he spent working for Joseph Addison Turner as a printer's apprentice. Turner published a newspaper called *The Countryman* on his plantation, Turnwold, just outside of Eatonton, Georgia (it appears to have been the only plantation newspaper in the United States). Harris worked on *The Countryman* between 1862 and 1866, from the ages of sixteen to twenty, cleaning up, setting type, and eventually writing several dozen pieces. Harris spent a lot of time in the slave quarters at Turnwold, and the African Americans he met became models for many of his fictional characters; their stories formed the basis of much of his later writing.[8]

The Harris figure in *On the Plantation* is named Joe Maxwell, and most of the book is a kindly yarn about Joe's various adventures and scrapes, suffused with nostalgia and local color. The war does not intrude directly until the final chapter, when Sherman takes Atlanta.[9] The news that Sherman's men will be passing through throws the plantation into a flurry of fearful activity. Joe helps to hide the horses and mules in the swamp, although they are quickly found and seized. The action then shifts to the plantation itself, which is "swarmed" by foragers, most of whom Joe found to be "good humored," even as they ransacked the house and outbuildings. The surprisingly gentle portrait of a foraging party coming through is far different from that presented in *The M'Donalds* and one that appears to be at odds with the actual events at Turnwold and in the surrounding county. It certainly differs from the stories that filled the pages of *The Countryman* after the March.[10]

The following day, Joe Maxwell sits on a fence by the road to Milledgeville and watches the men of the XX Corps march by. Though impressed by their numbers, he is surprised by their rundown, dirty appearance. The men crack jokes and sing, calling out and teasing Joe as they pass by, but the insults are good-natured, and there seems to be nothing to be afraid of. For his part, Joe took it all in as though "the outcome of some wild dream. That the Federal army should be plunging through that peaceful region, after all he had seen in the newspapers about Confederate victories, seemed to him to be an impossibility. The voices of the men and their laughter, sounded vague and insubstantial. It was surely a dream that had stripped war of its glittering trappings and its flying banners."[11] This air of unreality persisted in the unusual atmosphere that followed in the army's wake:

> Never before, since its settlement, had such peace and quiet reigned on the plantation. The horses and mules were gone, and many of the negro cabins were empty. Harbert was going about as busy as ever, and some of the older negroes were in their accustomed places, but the younger ones, especially those who, by reason of their field work, had not been on familiar terms with their master and mistress, had followed the Federal army. Those that remained had been informed by the editor that they were free; and so it happened in the twinkling of an eye, that the old things had passed away and all was new.[12]

Harris is unusual in the degree to which he deals with emancipation. There are few African American characters in nineteenth-century novels about the March, and they are primarily stock "faithful slave" figures like the erstwhile mammy Myra in *The M'Donalds*. *On the Plantation* includes the voices of African Americans, but only through the thick dialect that was Harris's signature. Thus young Joe Maxwell hears about Sherman taking Atlanta and the possibility of Yankees coming through the plantation from his enslaved friend Harbert, who assures Joe that he will "git up an' look at um, an' may be tip my hat ter some er de big-bugs 'mongst um, an' den I'm gwine on 'bout my business. I don't speck deyer gwine ter bodder folks what don't bodder dem, is dey?" This, of course, was exactly what white Southerners wanted to believe: that their slaves would stay with them, and that they could return to business as usual.[13]

They couldn't of, course, as Harris points out with the elegiac mention that "the old things had passed away and all was new." Would that the novel had ended there. But a few pages remain, and in them Harris turns to the darker side of emancipation. Joe finds a pitiful old couple who had been following "the army for many a weary mile on the road to freedom." The old man was already dead, and the woman's cries that "bless God, he died free!" seem to ring hollow, as does the news that the woman herself would die within days. The following day, Mink, a slave from the plantation who had run away to freedom returned and settled down as a tenant. It seemed that little would really change.[14] The gentleness of this tale of the March, particularly given that it was written by a native Georgian, is indicative of the degree to which reunionist sentiment seems to have permeated.[15]

Sarah Beaumont Kennedy's 1911 novel *Cicely: A Tale of the Georgia March* is a much more conventional example of both the "romance of reunion" and the literature of Southern female strength. Cicely is the stereotypically brave and beautiful Southern woman, newly engaged to a Confederate officer. She and her family flee Atlanta for the family plantation, Pinehurst, and prepare for the worst. She manages to hide most of the valuables, and just as a menacing group of foragers threatens to steal her necklace, she unfurls her father's Masonic apron, brandishing it as an icon of protection. In the nick of time, the handsome and gallant Captain Allyn Fairlee of the 6th Connecticut stops his marauding men and offers her his assistance, assuring her that the apron "will always serve as a flag of truce in the hands of defenceless women."[16] The invocation of Masonic protection echoes dozens of stories from all over Georgia, lending a veneer of authenticity to this romantic story.

Fairlee winds up wounded (from an altercation with his own men) and finds himself recuperating at Pinehurst. Like Major Irving in *The M'Donalds*, Fairlee serves as the counterpoint to the out-of-control bummers and allows Kennedy to criticize the March without alienating Northern readers. Thus, when Cicely details the fields stripped of produce, stolen heirlooms, and burned out homes in her neighborhood, "he made no attempt to justify or excuse such marauding tactics; only, he said, the leaders did not give such orders; it was the common soldiers who were to blame."[17] Kennedy returns to themes of destruction and devastation repeatedly, allowing her heroine opportunities to express her anger and resentment at the world the Yankees left behind. Cicely and other characters emphasize the degree to which women and children suffered, forced to leave their homes as refugees, sometimes multiple times, forced to "search the federal camp ground for grains of corn the army mules had left from the night's feed, for that is all they will have for the spring planting." It's surprising that Kennedy didn't invoke the oft-told tales of women and children forced to eat the scavenged corn.[18]

Unusually for one of these types of novels, Kennedy also mentions Ebenezer Creek, though obliquely (and incorrectly, blaming Kilpatrick rather than Davis for the debacle). It is mentioned in the context of slaves leaving the plantation and complaints about the "camp followers becoming a burden on Sherman." Kennedy has Cicely repeat the old chestnut that the only African Americans who ran away were the ones prone to misbehavior; the "faithful" stayed put and caused no trouble.[19]

Cicely's story extends long beyond the March, through the end of the war and into Reconstruction. Union officer Allyn Fairlee finds himself a changed man from his contact with Cicely and her family, newly sympathetic to the former Confederacy, daydreaming about the Lost Cause even as he rode in the Grand Review.[20] The last section of the book contains homages to the Ku Klux Klan and criticisms of Reconstruction, so much so that the United Daughters of the Confederacy endorsed the book, but all wrapped up romantically so as to be palatable all over the reunited white nation.[21]

Gone with the Wind

The best known of all novels that deal with Sherman's March is the best known of all Civil War novels: Margaret Mitchell's epic *Gone with the Wind*. Both the 1936 book and David O. Selznick's 1939 film have profoundly shaped American (and international) understanding of Sherman's March. And yet William Tecumseh Sherman, one of the great villains of Margaret Mitchell's *Gone with the Wind*, never appears on the page or screen. But his off-stage presence drives much of the action and provides the story's dramatic climax, as Rhett, Scarlett, Melanie, and Prissy flee the flames engulfing Atlanta. *Gone with the Wind* became so popular, and such an important cultural touchstone that it, in turn, has gone on to shape American's understandings of the Civil War and Reconstruction for over seventy years.

Part of the power of *Gone with the Wind* lies in its self-conscious presentation as accurate history. Margaret Mitchell was born in Atlanta in 1900, went North to attend Smith College, and then returned to her home city after her mother's death in 1919. She worked for the *Atlanta Journal* Sunday Magazine for a few years, but was forced to resign in 1926 because of ill health. In order to occupy her time she began writing—first short stories, which she was unable to sell, and eventually the novel that would become *Gone with the Wind*. The novel was published in 1936 and became an immediate and consistent best seller.[22]

Margaret Mitchell was deeply concerned about the accuracy of her story, and she drew on her own family history to ensure it. Her mother's parents had remained in Atlanta while it was under siege by the Union army in the summer of 1864; her father's family had lived south of the city in Jonesboro, Clayton County, the site of a July 1864 battle. Mitchell's grandmother's home in Atlanta had survived the war: both Confederate and Union forces had used it as a hospital, and the remains of Confederate entrenchments still ran through the backyard. As a child Mitchell would go to the family farm near Jonesboro and visit her great Aunts Miss Mary and Miss Sarah Fitzgerald (also known as Miss Mamie and Miss Sis). She recalled sitting on laps while hearing the stories of the war, imbibing the Lost Cause along with (we can

The home built by Margaret Mitchell's grandfather, Philip Fitzgerald, where Mitchell heard stories of the Civil War. It was known as the "Old Home Place" and was the original setting for Gone with the Wind. *(Georgia Archives, Vanishing Georgia Collection, clt011-82)*

imagine) endless glasses of sweet tea.[23] She also met several local Confederate veterans and would sometimes go riding around the countryside with them. According to her brother, the idea for Scarlett and Rhett's flight from Atlanta via the McDonough Road came from a Confederate veteran who had taken her on a search for his own escape route. Another veteran had supposedly told her that "the boys in Wheeler's [Confederate] Cavalry were worse chicken thieves than Sherman's men ever were." This detail seems not to have made it in to Mitchell's work.[24]

Mitchell also did considerable research in other sources. Several stories from her family's Clayton County neighbors, the Crawfords, seem to have made it into *Gone with the Wind*. Their home still had bullets from skirmishing in the early days of Sherman's March, and the Crawfords had supposedly filled the hollow columns on their porch with grain to hide it from the Yankees. More familiarly, the women in the family were supposed to have had their dresses stolen by the Yankees, and so they were forced to take down the parlor and dining room curtains to make new dresses. Ever since the war rumors have swirled that Mrs. Alice Crawford shot a Yankee deserter on the stairway of the family home. Her descendants denied it, but the story certainly found its way into Mitchell's work.[25]

In letters to readers after the book came out, Mitchell described her research methods and included citations to sources like Frances Mitchell's *Georgia: Land and People*, 1893; Avery's *The History of the State of Georgia*, 1881; and the *Official Records of the War of the Rebellion*. She writes of retracing the path of the Atlanta campaign herself, explaining in a letter to the *Chattanooga Times* that "however lousy the book may be as far as style, subject, plot, characters, it's as accurate historically as I can get it. I didn't want to get caught out on anything that any Confederate Vet could nail me, or any historian either." In another letter she explained that while her characters were all fictional, and Tara never really existed, "Practically all of the incidents in the book are true. Of course, they didn't all happen to the same person and a few of them didn't happen in Atlanta. The shooting of the Yankee bummer, for instance, did not take place on Sherman's March but on General Wilson's Raid, over in Alabama. But it could as easily have happened in Georgia and in Clayton County."[26]

Mitchell's use of Lost Cause sources is ironic in light of her own hopes for the book. As one of Mitchell's biographer pointed out, she "herself conceived of her history as radical, revisionary, and rebellious." Mitchell would poke fun at the "gentle Confederate novels," of authors like Thomas Nelson Page with their "moonlight on the magnolias," and their emphasis on honor and romance, and she saw her novel as more in line with the work of the Nashville Fugitives, Frank Owsley and Howard Odum. And to a great extent she did break free of that model—setting her story in Georgia rather than Virginia, including poor whites and yeoman farmers, and of course creating a heroine who was anything but sweet and gentle.[27] Yet at the same time, her novel is, as Malcolm Cowley wrote in a famous essay, "an encyclopedia of the plantation legend," full of faithful slaves, nasty Yankees, and evil carpetbaggers.[28]

The wind that swept through Georgia, which Mitchell refers to as a "screaming tornado" was Sherman, and the one hundred thousand soldiers who accompanied him on both the Atlanta campaign and then the March to the Sea. His inexorable progress toward Atlanta and then the month-long siege of the city dominates the middle section of the novel, and here we can see Mitchell's scrupulous concern for accuracy. Her descriptions of the campaign are precise and vivid, giving the narrative a sense of immediacy and a grounding in reality. Although Sherman and his men are a driving force in the novel, actual Union soldiers appear only infrequently. When Scarlett returns to Tara, she discovers that it had been used as a headquarters by Union troops during the battle of Jonesboro and that the soldiers had burned the fences, stolen the furniture, and eaten much of the livestock.[29]

The most dramatic confrontation comes when a Yankee cavalryman breaks into Tara. Scarlet is at first paralyzed with fear, recalling the "stories Aunt Pittypat had whispered of attacks on unprotected women, throat cuttings, houses burned over the heads of dying women, children bayoneted because they cried, all of the unspeakable horrors that lay bound up in the name of 'Yankee.'" But the only one to die that day will be the Yankee, shot by Scarlett in a fit of rage and vengeance. Mitchell is careful, however to make this act of murder a justifiable one—not only on the grounds of self-defense but also by showing the soldier to have been a thief. When Melanie and Scarlett go through his possessions they find not only money but also jewelry clearly taken from neighboring homes.[30] It's not entirely clear why this lone soldier was in the neighborhood. Mitchell indicates that it was about two weeks after Scarlett fled Atlanta, which would put it during the period in which Union soldiers were occupying Atlanta, but well before Sherman's March to the Sea.

Scarlett confronts Sherman's troops directly a few pages later, when the March began in earnest. The right wing passed through Jonesboro on November 16, pausing to destroy miles of railroad track. Upon learning of their approach, Scarlett springs into action, sending the dead Yankee's horse and Tara's meager livestock into the swamp, and then hiding the money and jewelry taken from the Yankee in the baby's diaper.[31] Mitchell describes the encounter in dramatic, hyperbolic language:

> Sherman was marching through Georgia, from Atlanta to the sea. Behind him lay the smoking ruins of Atlanta, to which the torch had been set as the blue army tramped out. Before him lay three hundred miles of territory virtually undefended save by a few state militia and the old men and young boys of the Home Guard.
>
> Here lay the fertile state, dotted with plantations, sheltering the women and children, the very old and the negroes. In a swath eighty miles wide the Yankees were looting and burning. There were hundreds of homes in flames, hundreds of homes resounding with their footsteps. But, to Scarlett, watching the bluecoats pour into the front hall, it was not a country-wide affair. It was entirely personal, a malicious action aimed directly at her and hers.[32]

With this passage Mitchell seems to place herself squarely in the camp that paints all of Sherman's men as rapacious bummers, hell-bent on destruction, devastation, and terror. And, indeed, the soldiers who come to Tara, a sergeant and a few privates, steal jewelry and trinkets, set fire to the cotton in the slave cabins and the kitchen, and take what little food remains.[33]

Yet Mitchell is a better writer than that, and a more careful one. For one of the strengths of *Gone with the Wind* is its attention to the subtleties of the human condition. Thus not all Union soldiers are evil. When Tara was being used as a Union headquarters, Gerald O'Hara told his daughter, the Yankee officer was "a gentleman," who fetched a "kind" surgeon and medicine for Scarlett's mother and sisters, ill with typhoid. Perhaps even more surprising, the sergeant who raids Tara allows Scarlett to keep her husband's Mexican War sword for her son, despite its solid gold hilt. These are small concessions, perhaps, and no one would argue that Mitchell portrayed Northerners in a sympathetic light, but for every story of evil Yankees, there is one of small kindnesses like these.[34]

Gone with the Wind was an immediate best seller and won the Pulitzer Prize in 1936. The story of the making of the film version is nearly as epic as the novel itself, but suffice it to say that it was an unprecedentedly ambitious undertaking. Just as Mitchell wanted her novel to be as accurate as possible (at least within the confines of her Lost Cause ideology), so too did David O. Selznick want the film to portray the fullness of the Civil War experience, and he became obsessive about accuracy, down to the smallest detail on the costumes. The screenplay went through multiple writers and drafts, and no less a writer than F. Scott Fitzgerald took a stab at adapting Mitchell's massive novel. While he reputedly excelled at condensing Mitchell's longer, flowery passages, he was let go after only two weeks. Not surprisingly, the film greatly simplified Mitchell's novel, cutting out secondary characters (and Scarlett's son Wade Hampton Hamilton) and reducing much of the plot by putting the love story between Rhett and Scarlett at the center.[35]

At Margaret Mitchell's suggestion, David O. Selznick hired Atlanta historian Wilbur G. Kurtz to serve as an historical consultant for the film, a task for which he was particularly well suited. Kurtz, along with his fellow founders of the Atlanta Civil War Round Table, Beverly M. DuBose and Franklin M Garrett, had been spending years traveling around Georgia looking all over for the traces of Sherman's campaigns, and he used many places that he found as models for the film (which was shot on studio lots and sets, rather than on location). Kurtz's responsibilities went far beyond the geographic. As he later recalled, "with the script writing, the historical references were mine to watch as to sequence and accuracy; the titles—unusual for their length and vigor in this picture—were scrutinized for accuracy of reference and statement."[36] Too bad Margaret Mitchell reportedly disliked them, complaining that they "lent a false note to her story. . . ."[37]

They certainly increased the melodrama: the enormous letters scroll across the screen, white against the vivid Technicolor, heightening the already intense emotions. "Panic hit the City with the first of Sherman's Shells. . . . Helpless and unarmed, the populace fled from the oncoming Juggernaut." Then, later in the film an even worse fate arrived. In the words of the titles, "And the Wind swept through Georgia . . . SHERMAN! To split the Confederacy, to leave it crippled and forever humbled, the Great Invader marched . . . leaving behind him a path of destruction sixty miles wide, from Atlanta to the Sea."[38]

Selznick's mania for authenticity was in part driven by economic concerns: Civil War movies (with the exception of *Birth of a Nation* and a couple of Shirley Temple pictures) had not been commercial successes (Louis B. Mayer had famously asserted, "You can never make a nickel from a Civil War Picture"), and Selznick believed that this was due to the perception of them as distinctly "Southern." So Selznick determined that much of the anti-Northern vitriol needed to be cut. Many of these cuts came in the latter half of the story, which had presented Reconstruction as a carnival of corruption straight out of the Dunning School, saved only by the presence of the Ku Klux Klan. Selznick also tried to tone down some of the most egregious examples of racism in the early scripts by cutting scenes of Prissy eating a watermelon and singing field hands, and consulted with the NAACP on aspects of the movie.[39]

Thus, the film has very few actual Union soldiers, and with the exception of the deserter whom Scarlett shoots, they are portrayed neutrally. The scene where Tara is raided along the March was cut entirely, though in so doing the Union soldier saving Charles Hamilton's sword was also omitted. The distinctions that Mitchell carefully drew between before Sherman's March and after were also largely erased. For example, one chronicler of the movie explains that the climactic fire scene (made by torching the remnants of other sets on the back lot at MGM) was "always referred to as the 'burning of Atlanta,' but was not the actual burning of the city by General Sherman in November 1864. What they filmed was the night two months earlier when the retreating Confederate army torched the ammunition dumps to keep the Union from capturing them."[40] This misnomer had the effect of placing the blame for the conflagration squarely on Sherman's shoulders, intensifying the perception of his villainy.

Some of Selznick's changes worked better than others. While the portrayal of Reconstruction and white Southern vigilantism might have been toned down to appeal to white Northern audiences, the image of Sherman as the architect of Scarlett's misery, and the lone despoiler of the South persisted. Some of it was tongue-in-cheek, as in a 1936 article about auditions for the film to be held in Georgia and neighboring states, entitled, "Another Yankee Invasion."[41] Others demonstrated a lingering bitterness. One reporter at the Atlanta premiere noted that "When Sherman's legion started their march to the sea, Loew's Grand Theater sounded like a pit of snakes," and that when Scarlett shot the Yankee straggler, "he believed applause lifted the roof several inches."[42]

Writers return to this scene, of Scarlett shooting the Yankee, again and again. It is not necessarily surprising—this is the most vivid moment of confrontation between North and South in the story, the moment when the battle lines seem most clearly drawn. Writing about the film's accuracy for the *Raleigh News and Observer*, Nell Battle Lewis remarked (in words that would surely have warmed David O. Selznick's heart):

> One thing that struck me about the picture was the fact that obviously effort had been made to keep it as much as possible from reviving sectional animosity. True, the Yankee Army was the villain—there couldn't be any other and have the story at all—but the Northern villainy was not underscored, and the Union soldiers themselves seldom appeared. The one whom Scarlett shot, though in the book one of Sherman's raiders, in the picture was a deserter—of course, a sop to Northern self-respect. But although Mr. Selznick plainly did everything he could to keep his picture from inflaming old enemies against each other, there is really no way in which to whitewash very effectively Sherman's march from Atlanta to the sea.[43]

No, there really is not. Nevertheless, the ways that *Gone with the Wind* discusses the March tend to highlight or privilege certain stories at the expense of others. Yes, Scarlett is victimized by Union troops, and Tara is raided. But she is far from a hapless victim. She outsmarts the Yankees by hiding the wallet in the baby's diaper, and she is protected by the kindly Union sergeant. But in deleting the story from the actual March and keeping the much more atypical, though also more dramatic, Scarlett shooting the deserter, Selznick's version flattened out the complexities of Sherman's March, and of the Southern white female experience. This portrayal highlights the worst of Union behavior and the best, or at least most assertive, of Southern actions. Of course, in reality, a woman could not have gotten away with shooting a Union soldier, which explains why it happened so rarely.

Why does all of this matter? In the end, isn't *Gone with the Wind* just a silly love story wrapped up in costumed pageantry and horrible racism? Well, yes, and of course no. For many Americans today, *Gone with the Wind*, especially the film, *is* the Civil War. And that means that the Civil War is Sherman's March, and the Lost Cause version of it: Yankees bad, Southern whites victimized, African Americans either loyally childlike or absent. And Sherman has no chance to defend himself in this version. He is the villain, not Lincoln, not Jefferson Davis, not Sheridan or Grant or Johnston or Hood. And as Sherman comes to be seen as the architect of total war, his catalog of sins grows throughout the twentieth century.

The Lost Cause Continues

One might be excused for thinking that *Gone with the Wind* so dominated the field of Civil War fiction that other authors chose to move on to greener pastures. However, novels (and occasional plays) about the Civil War in general, and Sherman's March in particular, have remained a constant and consistent presence on bookshelves. Few of them have broken through to become critically acclaimed or best sellers; some are self-published, or put out by small, regional or local presses. They tend to fall into a few categories: romances, much along the lines of *Cicely* or even *The M'Donalds*; soldier stories; and tales of the homefront.[44]

The first major novel about the March to follow *Gone with the Wind* is John Brick's 1956 novel *Jubilee*, which focuses on the experiences of men in the fictional 195th New York, and particularly their commander, Jeff Barnes. On the surface, the book seems as though it will be about Sherman's March in its entirety—the endpapers are a detailed map of the army's movements from Chattanooga to Goldsboro, with separate lines for each of the four corps and the cavalry. The epigram comes from "Marching through Georgia." Yet this seems to be an example of using Sherman's March as a hook for readers. Most of the novel takes place before the March, as we see Jeff Barnes, a recent West Point Graduate, come home to Highland County, New York, in 1862 to help raise and lead a regiment. We follow Barnes and a handful of men as they fight in Virginia, Pennsylvania, and Tennessee; Barnes rises from Lieutenant Colonel to General, always choosing his duty to the army over his love for his young wife, Kate.[45]

By the time the "apple-knockers" of the 195th reach Atlanta they are hardened and battle-scarred. Barnes lost his right arm at Lookout Mountain. They leave as members of the XX Corps, untroubled by what lay ahead:

"Young as they were they were hard and tough and battle-tempered. They worshipped Sherman. They didn't give a damn where they were going as long as Uncle Billy took them there. They had ripped up the railroad with enthusiasm, knowing that once it was gone, they'd be on their own."[46] These passages could easily have come from the reminiscences of veterans, spoken before their MOLLUS or GAR posts, written for their fellow soldiers. For much of the March the central characters do not engage in overt thievery or vandalism, just good-natured foraging for food. Sergeant Tuggle, for example, spends the first week of the March cautioning his men against looting and threatening to turn them in for violating orders. All of that changes, though, when he meets a few escapees from Andersonville prison and sees the horrible consequences of their imprisonment and starvation. From that point on, Tuggle dedicated himself to making Georgia howl.[47] But this sets up a moral equivalence, or at least a moral justification. Tuggle can burn houses, Brick seems to be arguing, because Union soldiers starved to death.

Brick slides over the details of the March, the obsessive cataloging of place to place that so many other novelists rely on. He spends no time at all in Savannah, moving quickly into detailing the challenges of marching through the swamps of South Carolina. He conveys the bitterness of the days in the Palmetto State, noting that "the bummers believed their spree was justified and condoned. . . . The army couldn't be stopped, because such an army had never existed before." Columbia's burning is dispensed with in a sentence, as the men keep marching, sweeping away everything in its path.[48] It all grinds to a stop at the battle of Bentonville, where Jeff Barnes is mortally wounded. The novel ends as the March did, with the pageantry of the Grand Review, the cheering crowds, and the implicit realization that the death of Jeff Barnes, and the soldiers like him, was the price to pay for saving the Union.

One reviewer described *Jubilee* as "manly."[49] The same could not be said of the majority of twentieth-century Sherman novels, many of which fall into the "romance" pile. *My Dearest Cecilia* is an unusual example of the romantic category because William T. Sherman is one of the main players. Rumors swirled all over Georgia and the Carolinas that houses, or even entire towns like Augusta, were spared because Sherman had courted one or another of the girls who had lived on the place while he was stationed in the south. In only one case was that actually true; that of Cecelia Stovall, of Cartersville, Georgia. Ironically, Cartersville was not even on the route of the March itself; rather Sherman and his army passed it by on the Atlanta campaign. No matter, though, because the story is so full of intrinsic melodrama. The facts are that Sherman met the lovely Miss Stovall in 1837, because she was the sister of his West Point roommate. They embarked on a whirlwind romance (to the dismay of Braxton Bragg, another of Cecilia's suitors), until her family sent her to Europe to break them up. There she met the man who would become her husband, Charles Shelman. Sherman eventually married his foster sister, Ellen Ewing.[50]

Author Diane Haeger creates a novel of star-crossed lovers, including a bevy of clichés: her father sleeps with Cecilia's childhood slave companion; her cruel older brother wants her to marry only for money; despite being born and bred into the slaveholding elite, Cecilia is secretly an abolitionist and enlists Sherman's help in spiriting her maid to safety. By the time the Atlanta campaign is underway in 1864, Cecilia is working as a spy for the Union, and she is sent to deliver a secret message to General Hooker. There she encounters Sherman again, gives him information that allows him to win the battle at Allatoona.

Back to reality: Sherman and his men came upon an abandoned plantation on the banks of the Etowah River. After talking to one of the African Americans on the place, he realized that it is Cecilia's home, and he left the following note, which was passed down through the family until at least the 1950s:

> You once said that I would crush an enemy and you pitied my foe. Do you recall my reply? Although many years have passed, my answer is the same. "I would ever shield and protect you." That I have done. Forgive all else. I am only a soldier.

He then ordered his men to leave the plantation alone and went on his way.[51] This story has endured for so long because it paints Sherman in a much more positive light than almost any other. While still crushing enemies and making Georgia howl (although in reality he hadn't started to do that yet), he still had human emotions. He could for a moment turn back into a lovestruck young man. It is an instance, perhaps, of beauty taming the beast. Too, from this grain of truth, a thousand legends grew.

Although Miriam Rawl Freeman's *From the Ashes of Ruin* was published in 1999, in many ways it could have been written a century earlier, for it falls squarely in the category of a romance of reunion. In this instance, sisters Ellen and Pamela Heyward were alone on their South Carolina plantation, except for a few faithful slaves, when they were accosted by some of Sherman's bummers. Pamela, the younger sister, was sexually assaulted and traumatized; her sister Ellen and some Confederate soldiers shoot the Yankees and hide their bodies. A Union officer, Major John Arledge, comes to investigate, and falls in love with Ellen, who although she is twenty-seven, is conveniently single. The novel is rife with stereotypes: the African Americans who stay with the family are loving and loyal and are invited to stay on for fair wages; those who left to take advantage of their emancipation were troublesome and are forced to come skulking back. Like with earlier Union men in *The M'Donalds* and *Cicely*, the Virginia-born Major Arledge is the character who can bridge the gap between North and South. Arledge disavows the bummers, by claiming (incorrectly) that they were conscripts who could not all speak English, who want to go home, and are out for revenge. This same claim is repeated throughout the novel, leading one to wonder if Rawl, from the distance of over a century, was trying to displace blame on outsiders rather than fellow Americans.[52]

The Heywards move to Columbia, in the mistaken belief that they would be safer there. The traumatized Pam is hidden away in the Ursuline convent, because they believe that Sherman would protect the sisters (his daughter attended a similar convent school). Major Arledge arranges for guards to protect Ellen and her aunt.[53] Rawl vividly describes the terror of the night of February 17, 1865, with the fires and soldiers running wild, slashing furniture and ruining property.[54] There's little question as to who is to blame for Columbia's predicament—if not Sherman himself, then certainly the subordinate officers who allowed their men to run rampant. Rawl does include mentions of Yankee kindnesses as well, such as officers bringing food to the Heywards, which they then distributed among their friends and neighbors. Sherman, after being chastised by the nuns, allows the sisters of the Ursuline convent to move their charges into an abandoned building.[55] The Heywards return to their plantation to begin the arduous work of rebuilding. The second half of the novel devolves into a rather conventional romance, ending with the marriage of Ellen and Arledge. *From the Ashes of Ruin* demonstrates the endurance of the Lost Cause in popular culture, and the degree to which anger still smoldered.

Louisa . . . A Southern Girl's Escape in 1864 exhibits a similarly retrograde sensibility. This children's book presents a fictionalized version of the true story of Louisa Varnedoe, who was twelve years old when the March came through Liberty County, Georgia. Louisa pluckily helps her family flee across Georgia. First, though, she faces down a group of bummers in her home, although they still steal some of the family's food and clothing. The book is full of stories of faithful slaves, and "good" slaveholders." Interestingly, the book includes a teacher's guide for students in the fourth through eighth grades and was endorsed by the Mississippi Writers' Association as "an excellent addition to Southern literature set during the War-Between-the-States." Clearly, the uncomplicated calculus of Sherman's Marchers as purely bad and white Southerners as purely victimized continues to be perpetuated.[56]

A more complicated account of the Georgia home front can be found in Thomas Babe's 1976 drama, *Rebel Women*.[57] The play describes one evening's fraught interactions between three elite Southern white women (along with their enslaved housekeeper) and General Sherman and members of his staff (including young Henry Hitchcock). Sherman wants to use the home of the fragile Mrs. Law as his headquarters but finds himself having to match wits with Mrs. Law's headstrong daughter Mrs. Robarts and her flighty friend Kate. The women are initially frightened, then frustrated with the intrusion of the soldiers into their lives, and the lack of control they feel over their situations. For his part, Sherman initially seems weary of the March and of being painted as wantonly cruel. He has a job to do, and he does it, but, he explains, "I lack the anger, the malice aforethought, and I am proud of this deficiency."[58] He is a sympathetic figure who takes no joy in the destruction he must do. Mrs. Robarts tries to convince Sherman to release her husband, a minister who has been arrested for spying. Their conversation quickly turns both personal and flirtatious, and they spend the night together, each trying to forget their personal circumstances.

The home in which the play takes place is spared from pillaging by virtue of being used as Sherman's headquarters, but foraging is taking place all around. In act 3, Sherman's fictional adjutant Major Robert Steele Strong, finally has had enough and explodes in frustration. He believes they are all in "a species of hell" and has "concluded that that we—this army—are irrevocably in the wrong, morally and God-foreknowingly in the wrong in how we have conducted this malignant rooting-out and rooting-up of this land and these people."[59] For his honesty, Strong is relieved of command, replaced with the laconic Hitchcock. Sherman will brook no opposition to his methods.

The drama concludes with the soldiers moving on. Sherman arranges for Mrs. Robarts's husband's release. But the two younger women, Mrs. Robarts and her friend Kate (who engaged in her own flirtation with a canny merchant) can no longer remain in their stifling lives of propriety and separately sneak out of the house. The African American housekeeper, Tussie, once enslaved and now free is given the last word, as she reflects on her freedom. *Rebel Women* opened in New York in 1976 to mixed reviews. Positive write-ups praised Babe for his portrayal of Sherman as intellectually complex, and its exploration of the impacts of war.[60] Other critics found the plot diffuse and meandering, and the characters somewhat unsympathetic. Memorably, a *New York Times* critic described the play as a "curious crossbreed of 'Birth of a Nation II' and any Chekov play you care to name."[61] Nevertheless, this post-Vietnam rendering of Sherman's March helped to keep the memory of the March alive and vivid.

African Americans in Fiction

Few books about the March engage with the experiences of African Americans. Most of them include one or two stock figures: usually faithful slaves, who stay loyally by the side of the kindly white protagonists, or perhaps a runaway or two who come into the army camp and start to work for white soldiers. Two books profess to focus on the stories of African Americans, but do so with only limited success. The first is Terry K. Howel's *Black Heritage*, the story of the slaves who lived on the Hennington plantation near fictional Melvin, Georgia.[62] Jim Hennington decides to free all of his slaves in advance of the March's arrival on his property, but only on the condition that they all leave immediately, even those who offer to stay on and work for wages. He keeps one man, Jeffery, on as a paid servant. Essentially, this is a faithful slave story from the African American perspective. As Union soldiers arrive on the plantation, the white family hides, leaving the loyal Jeffery to deal with them. He is shocked by the casual cruelties of the Yankees, finding it "baffling, nevertheless, that the attitude of these men who fought to free slaves was not too much different from the ones who made a slave of him."[63] This is the most perceptive and accurate aspect of the novel: the realization that not all Union soldiers were abolitionists, not all Union soldiers cared about African Americans.

The soldiers butcher hogs and cook an enormous breakfast, and then leave with horses but appear not to have stolen valuables from the house. They invade the small town of Melville, looting the store, and are about to burn the bank (and the Confederate money housed therein). But they are stopped, in the nick of time by Sherman himself![64] As in so many of these books, Sherman is held up as a "good guy"; the excesses and depredations of the March are always the fault of some bad apples who exceed their orders and authority.

Sherman stopping men from burning a bank has at least some basis in fact—he did periodically stop men from stealing and looting. Arguably, these tales of a kinder Sherman provide a welcome cultural corrective to Sherman the slavering devil. But poetic or fictional license can sometimes go too far. *Sherman's Fifth Corps*, an novel that began its life as a blog, weaves together actual and fictional letters, diary entries, and dispatches to tell the story of the African Americans who followed the March.[65] In some ways, this is very effective; entries from real people like Major Henry Hitchcock, Major George Ward Nichols, Daniel Conyngham, Theodore Upson, Dolly Lunt Burge, and Gertrude Thomas tell the story of the March day by day and well capture the conflicting emotions that whites, Northern and Southern, had surrounding emancipation. Were the novel composed entirely of these excerpts, it could have been quite powerful.

But instead the author creates a an eighteen-year-old newly freed African American woman, Jennie Lewis, and proceeds to have her fall in love with General Sherman, and he with her. The romance between them strains credulity, as does the creation of Sherman the emancipationist. He assures Jennie that she is free, installs her as his cook on the March (and eventually his mistress in Savannah), and goes so far as to suggest that she study at Oberlin College after the war! Sherman is described as "an angel sent by God" who "cares about the black people."[66] No attempt is made to reconcile the private, emancipationist, champion of black equality Sherman with the more hard-nosed Sherman of the dispatches, the Sherman who repeatedly complains about the African Americans slowing down his columns. The villain of the book is General Jefferson C. Davis, whose cruelty at Ebenezer Creek is central to the narrative. Jennie loses her sister and infant nephew to the icy waters and barely survives herself. She becomes a teacher in a freedmen's school in Savannah and stays behind when the army leaves, pregnant with Sherman's child. The melodrama detracts from what could have been a powerful story of enslaved people making their way to freedom. That story has yet to be written. Too, this intimate Sherman is utterly at odds with what we know of him from his own writings and actions. The pendulum has swung too far.

A somewhat more realistic take on Sherman in Savannah can be found in John Jakes's *Savannah; or, A Gift for Mr. Lincoln*. Jakes, the author of the *North and South* trilogy among many other works of historical fiction, takes a light-hearted tone in telling the story of twelve-year-old Hattie Lester and her adventures. She and her widowed mother are struggling to hold onto the family rice plantation: the family is vaguely Unionist, and all of their slaves have run away, which seems to be a way of making them more sympathetic to readers. They encounter a Dickensian array of characters: an evil brother-in-law, who is trying to steal their land, a young Confederate volunteer, a bummer with a heart of gold, reporters and bounty-hunters, and, of course, Sherman himself.[67]

Jakes uses Zip, an eighteen-year-old African American following Sherman's army to tell about Ebenezer Creek. His rescue by the bummer, Alpheus Winks, marks a moral turning point for the white man; there is less growth and change for poor Zip. The book's focus, however, is on Hattie and her adventures. She and her mother seek refuge in Savannah after Confederates flood their rice fields; there she watches the Union army march into town, calling Sherman "an evil St. Nicholas sent from the netherworld." She goes so far as to kick Sherman in the shins, but then discovers his softer side.[68] The book turns heartwarming at the end, as the characters (Sherman included) work together to bring Christmas to the struggling citizens of Savannah. In many ways this is a throwback to the romance of reunion stories: couples pair off in the end, and everyone is happy. Except, perhaps, for Sherman and his marchers, who have many more miles to go.

Modern Complexity

There are two recent novels about the March that stand out for their language and impact. They try to capture the fullness of the March experience from multiple perspectives and to reach some essential truths about it. The first is Cynthia Bass's 1995 *Sherman's March*. Bass divides her narration into thirds: Sherman himself, Nick Whiteman, a captain in the XIV Corps, and finally Annie Baker, a Confederate widow seeking refuge. Sherman opens the book, looking back on his past, with unapologetic bravado:

> What I do *not* accept is that we did wrong. I admit we were often harsh; I admit when we had a choice, we were not often merciful (although I might point out we did not often have a choice). I admit we stole. I admit we destroyed. I believe we didn't rape, and I hope not. But only literally. Metaphorically, I hope we *did* rape. For metaphorically we had every right to. It is not after all on Northern soldiers that the corpses of six hundred thousand American soldiers should be draped. When mourning the stolen jewels and axed pianos of plundered Georgia, mourn them too.[69]

This is the Sherman who did what he had to do to end the war, who believed that he and his men operated within the bounds of legitimate warfare. He is gruff, does not suffer fools, but cares about his men—the Uncle Billy of song and legend. Haunted by memories of his son Willie, he writes "the order that altered the face of modern warfare," in order to "make war so terrible—so terrible its memory stops even the concept of future wars."[70] But other fathers' sons will have to die to avenge Willie.

One of these is Nick Whiteman, history buff turned Army captain, the somewhat stereotypical decent man caught up in indecent circumstances. He takes no pleasure in foraging, no joy in frightening civilians, perhaps a grim enjoyment in freeing slaves. Mostly he worries, fearful that "history could not possibly let the South get away with slavery; history would not possibly let us get away with what we were doing to the South. Somehow or other, we'd both have to pay." Nick buries foraging details killed by Confederates and witnesses Sherman ordering prisoners to clear the minefield outside of Sandersville, an event that he finds both horrifying and banal: "Half of us thought it war. Half of us thought it murder." He has no confusion, however, when he witnesses the debacle at Ebenezer Creek. "It was inexcusable," he recalled wearily, "and it was even more inexcusable that nobody offered any excuses."[71] These two moments of the March—Sandersville and Ebenezer Creek—come to stand for all of the horrible things, the morally indefensible things, soldiers are asked to do and witness during war. There centrality to Nick's experience marks this, I think, as a post-Vietnam sort of book. *Jubilee*, for example does not allow its soldiers the same ethical questioning.

The third narrator is Annie Baker, a young widow alone in her home. She tries to hide some food and valuables from the foragers who come, but they discover everything, and a relatively peaceful encounter turns ugly. She realizes that seeing her home violated (even though her body was not) means that she will never be able to live there again, and she takes to the roads. She pairs up with other refugees—women, children, Confederate deserters—but mostly she just walks. She finds an abandoned house in which to hide, and then meets Nick. And shoots him.

The final act takes place inside the abandoned house. A Confederate Major Lindley keeps Annie from killing Nick, explaining that it will not give her life and suffering any more meaning. Lindley and Nick are allies, examples of the adage that by the end of the war soldiers from opposite sides have more in common with each other than with civilians. Sherman has the final words, defending the March, justifying it, accepting that he will always be bound up with its destruction. In the end this seems to be Bass's message, and one that resonated in the late twentieth century.

Far and away the most ambitious Sherman's March novel is E. L. Doctorow's *The March* published in 2005. This multi-award-winning work takes on the entire March—Georgia, South Carolina, North Carolina—from a veritable kaleidoscope of perspectives.[72] His main characters are Sherman himself; Pearl, a newly freed girl; Emily Thompson, an elite Southern woman; Arly and Will, hapless Confederate stragglers; the cynical physician Wrede Sartorius, and Stephen Walsh, a Union soldier. In some ways, this assortment of personalities evokes a combination of Jakes *Savannah* and Bass's *Sherman's*

March, and certain of the same themes come through Doctorow's work as well. Southern aristocrats' world is turned upside down as Emily loses her identity as "Judge Thompson's daughter." Men learn what they are made of, if they are able to live by their internal compasses. African Americans test their freedom, only to run up against the limits of Northern racism.

Doctorow's plot is really multiple plots, the characters intersecting briefly with each other before inexorably moving on. At times, he strains credulity as with Pearl. A light-skinned runaway, she disguises herself as a drummer boy, is taken under Sherman's wing, saves her once-cruel mistress, and ultimately decides to live her life passing as white. Doctorow includes many of the signal events of the March: the prisoners being freed in exchange for futile service in Milledgeville, enraged Union troops burning Millen in retaliation for the conditions at Camp Lawton, Ebenezer Creek, murdered foragers, Sherman ordering the prisoners to clear the road of mines, Savannah.[73] But still they keep moving—through the swamps, past the villages burned by Kilpatrick, and into the flames of Columbia. They cross the Pee Dee and enter North Carolina, with more foraging, more violence, more dead soldiers. In Fayetteville the river is clogged with the carcasses of used-up mules and horses, but the men keep going, fighting at Averasboro and Bentonville, and finally to the surrender and the Grand Review in Washington.

Doctorow's strength is in his evocation of the army as an organism, ever alive, leaving nothing undisturbed. It appears first as a cloud, then the sound, "not fearsomely heaven-made, like thunder or lighting or howling wind, but something felt through their feet, a resonance, as if the earth was humming." It is later described as a sort of centipede or snake:

> Imagine a great segmented body moving in contractions and dilations at a rate of twelve or fifteen miles a day, a creature of a hundred thousand feet. It is tubular in its being and tentacled to the roads and bridges over which it travels. It sends out as antennae its men on horses. It consumes everything in its path. It is an immense organism, this army, with a small brain. That would be General Sherman.[74]

This metaphor of the March as one creature is the opposite of the ones used so often—of swarms of locusts or other insects, for example, that emphasize the numbers of men, as opposed to the vastness of its size. The complexity of the plot and its relentless forward motion seem to mirror that of the March.

Doctorow's Sherman is very much of a piece with the conventional wisdom. He is both dedicated and difficult, even unstable at times. He's "Uncle

Billy" at points, exasperated and exhausted at others. He mourns his lost children—Willie and the baby who dies over the course of the March. He might be the only person who truly understands the March and its ultimate significance. When it is all over, and he sits on the reviewing stand in Washington and reflects that he longs for the March: "not for its blood and death but for the bestowal of meaning to the very ground trod upon, how it made every field and swamp and river into something of moral consequence."[75] It is in exploring the multitudinous moral consequences that this novel excels.

In 2012 the Steppenwolf Theater Company in Chicago brought an adaptation of the book to the stage. While simplified, it still featured more than twenty-five characters and ran almost three hours. Frank Galati, the company member who wrote the adaptation, described it as a "quest for meaning," trying to make sense of the mysteries of war and remembrance. Reviews were mixed, mostly because of the difficulty in following so many storylines. It remains to be seen whether the play will be staged elsewhere.[76]

Cinematic March

The scope and scale of Sherman's March have conspired against it being the subject of many films. There are few true battles, and the idea of filming endless foraging leaves a scriptwriter with few heroes on which to focus. Historian Bruce Chadwick has noted that relatively few films portray Civil War generals, although John Wayne did play Sherman in *How the West Was Won*. The March was featured in some silent films: *Hearts and Flags* (1912), *When Sherman Marched to the Sea*, (1913) and the epic *Birth of a Nation* (1915).[77]

D. W. Griffith used Sherman's March to advance his Lost Cause rendering of the war. "While the women and children weep, a great conqueror marches to the sea" explains the title card. He personalizes the action by having the audience identify with a terrified Southern family cowering as scores of men march by. The screen glows red as "the torch of war" is put to Atlanta, and confusion ensues. Then we see dozens of white refugees. His is not the story of liberators bringing freedom to grateful slaves, but of terror and fear.[78]

Although Sherman's March takes only a couple of minutes of screen time, and is in fact entirely incidental to the plot of the movie, *Birth of a Nation* played an outsize role in perpetuating the image of the March as pure, wanton, devastation. Griffith manages to do this without ever showing Sherman on screen—he appears only as a name on the title card.[79] Perhaps that made him all the more terrifying and turned the March into a faceless entity. Because the movie itself was such a spectacle, and because it bore the imprimatur of no less than President Woodrow Wilson, it was more important than just any other film.[80]

Surprisingly, given the astronomical success of *Gone with the Wind*, the March has rarely been the focus of other feature films. *Raintree County* (1957), a pale imitation of *Gone with the Wind* starring Elizabeth Taylor, did feature its hero, Johnny Shawnessy (played by Montgomery Clift) marching along with Sherman in order to find his runaway Southern wife. But the movie was not terribly well received, perhaps because of its convoluted plot, perhaps because of its Union perspective.[81] It would be documentaries that took up the mantle of bringing the March to a new generation.

In 1981 Ross McElwee, a Southern-born documentary filmmaker, planned to make a movie not unlike this book: a study of the legacy of Sherman's March in the 1980s American South. He had grown up with an aunt who had a sofa laced with puncture wounds, caused, so the story went, by Union bayonets in search of hidden treasures. But then his girlfriend broke up with him, one in a long line of failed relationships, and his film took a turn. *Sherman's March: A Meditation upon the Possibilities of Romantic Love in the South during an Era of Nuclear Weapons Proliferation* was the improbable result, blending McElwee's search for romantic answers, his anxieties about nuclear war, and his search for Sherman. In many ways, McElwee's bizarrely compelling journey of self-discovery echoes those of fellow searchers like James Reston Jr. and Jerry Ellis.

McElwee flirts with possible girlfriends and visits past ones, never succeeding in finding the magic formula for lasting love. Along the way he encounters Southern belles and survivalists, attends antinuclear and pro–Equal Rights Amendment rallies, and semistalks Burt Reynolds, an icon of twentieth-century Southern white masculinity. Periodically he stops in the stations of the Sherman's March cross: Peachtree Creek and the Cyclorama, Stone Mountain and Ossabaw Sound, Charleston and Columbia, and finally Bentonville. Ironically, McElwee seems to identify most closely with Sherman, rather than with his Southern victims. Sherman had failed in business before the March and had struggled early in his military career; McElwee too was failing in filmmaking. Plus, as McElwee points out, they both have red beards.[82]

Certainly, the March made Sherman, just as *Sherman's March* made McElwee. The film was critically acclaimed, an enormous success and suddenly McElwee was famous. While the movie itself tells us very little about Sherman's March specifically, it tells us a lot about the place of the March in

American culture. It is hard to imagine framing a romantic journey around Antietam or Grant's overland campaign.

In the fall of 1990, PBS made television history when it broadcast Ken Burns's massive nine-episode, eleven-hour documentary *The Civil War*. Almost 40 million people watched the initial airing of it, and over the years it has become an evergreen performer for PBS. It is arguably the most influential account of the Civil War in American History. As such, it has come in for its fair share of criticism, in terms of both emphasis on certain aspects of the war (particularly the eastern theater at the expense of the western, and the relatively limited attention paid to women and African Americans) and its style. Burns is not a historian, and he consciously manipulates his viewers' emotions, every bit as cannily as a D. W. Griffith or a David O. Selznick. Too, Burns is clearly pushing the argument that the war was a necessary thing for America, almost a ritual purification after the sin of slavery.[83]

Burns discusses Sherman's March in Episode 8, "War Is All Hell," and all together devotes about twenty-five minutes to it. In many ways Burns presents a fairly standard interpretation of Sherman and the March. He overstates the degree to which the March represented a radical departure from prior Union policy (as opposed to an evolution in "hard handedness"), claiming that Sherman was the first general to understand the need to target civilians. He quotes liberally from Sherman's *Memoirs*, as well as from the diaries of Theodore Upson, Dolly Lunt Burge, and Mary Chesnut (who, of course, never witnessed the March directly but reported the news she heard from afar). Much of the "talking head" commentary came from Shelby Foote, whose folksiness helps to convey both the pleasure of the soldiers and the anger and resentment of white Southerners. We hear about Sherman's neckties, and see lurid flames, stop briefly in Milledgeville, and are suddenly in Savannah. Overall the impression of the March is as an unstoppable force of destruction, sweeping aside everything in its path.

Burns includes a brief section on the March as an army of liberation, entitling it "The Breath of Emancipation," but strangely omits any mention of the tragedy that unfolded at Ebenezer Creek. He describes the anger unleashed on South Carolina, and the difficulties the men had making their way through the swamps. But then, rather than discuss the bombardment and burning of Columbia, Burns shifts his attention to the devastation and evacuation of Charleston. He leaves viewers with the distinct impression that this was also Sherman's doing, when it was not. We see the ruins of Charleston and learn that few houses were left standing, but nothing of the fate of Columbia, or, for that matter, the rest of the Carolinas campaign. This odd omission serves to intensify the portrait of the March as one of pure devastation, without the recognition that the Marchers backed off again in North Carolina. Too, it reinforces the Georgia-centric view of the March that has predominated.

Our last glimpse of Sherman in this episode comes when he meets with Grant and Lincoln on the *River Queen* in March, where Sherman learns of Lincoln's hopes for a relatively lenient peace. The final episode, "The Better Angels of Our Nature" dispenses with the surrender at the Bennett place in a single sentence. Burns seems to be far more interested in the details of Lee's surrender to Grant, and the impact of Appomattox, with its themes of honor and reunion, then in the continuing conflict further South.

One could argue that Burns could not give equal weight to every campaign and event, even in an eleven-hour opus. The same cannot be said of the History Channel's 2007 vividly titled documentary "Sherman's March: The Shocking Campaign That Ended the Civil War."[84] If Ken Burns signature is sepia tones and violins, this documentary features live-action reenactments and computer generated smoke and flames. Despite its lurid promos, promising that Sherman would "ravage" the South and asking whether Sherman would prove to be "terrorist or savior," the film itself makes a surprisingly nuanced argument. It uses many of the same familiar sources—Theodore Upson's, Henry Hitchcock's, and Dolly Lunt Burge's diaries, Sherman's memoirs. Of course, the documentary lavishes attention on the destruction and devastation that accompanied the March, but it also looks at the affection and trusting relationship built between "Uncle Billy" and his loyal men, and at the tensions between the marchers and African Americans. Sherman is shown in his full complexity, as both an opponent of racial equality and a man who enjoyed being hailed as Moses.

The first hour of the ninety-minute film is devoted to the March to the Sea, but the last section deals with the Carolinas campaign. Emma LeConte describes the burning of Columbia, the soldiers march into North Carolina, and the war is finally over. Strangely, the documentary jumps from Grant, Lincoln, and Sherman meeting (inexplicably they are walking through a field, rather than sitting on a boat) to the Grand Review. It appears that the negotiations over a lenient peace were too far from the story they wanted to tell.

What is most striking about this documentary is the mismatch between its content and its presentation and promotion. A transcript would include much of the contemporary understanding of the March, and a discussion of the reasons that Southern whites created and perpetuated the myth of

Sherman as a devil. But the producers, mindful of popular opinions, felt the need to up the melodrama and the kitsch with fake flames and dramatic music. The companion website features a map that allows you to follow the path of the March. And when it loads, it traces it in flames.[85] It is truly a lost opportunity, and a sign that there is much to be done to adjust public understanding of the March. Yes, there were flames, but there was so much more.

CONCLUSION

Rubin's March

On a clear March day I drove out of the Atlanta airport and headed south, toward Jonesboro, Georgia. Twenty minutes later I turned onto Tara Boulevard, and a few minutes after that arrived at the Road to Tara Museum, Jonesboro's signature attraction. Two women in hoopskirts and shawls stood outside, waiting for two busloads of tourists who were about to arrive. Welcome to the land of Sherman's March, circa 2008.

I retraced most of the March over the course of two trips: from Atlanta to Savannah in March 2008 and North and South Carolina in June 2009. I am not sure what I expected to find, but I wanted to see what remained, what was memorialized, and what was forgotten. I wanted to try to get a feel for the places the March went through, to see the landscape and understand the terrain. I thought briefly about bringing a GPS with me, about marking definitively the latitude and longitude of locations burned or spared, of trying to measure and capture and codify the impact of the March. And then I thought better of it. After all, I reasoned, Sherman did not carry a GPS. Better to capture impressions.

I spent my first day in Clayton, Henry, and Newton Counties, the places that the March moved through on its first few days. The Road to Tara Museum had a lot of *Gone with the Wind* and almost no Sherman, except for one twisted Sherman's necktie. On the drive to McDonough and Covington, I was struck by the proliferation of new subdivisions and megachurches scraped out of the red Georgia clay. As I drove around the square in Covington, I thought that it looked remarkably like Hazzard, the setting for the old *Dukes of Hazzard* television show. Then I laughed and thought that all sleepy Southern towns must look alike. Imagine my delight when I discovered that Covington had been used for the exterior shots of Hazzard, and for the series *In the Heat of the Night* as well as about two dozen movies.[1] Each town had the requisite Civil War soldier monument, but I didn't find mentions of Sherman or the March. In Oxford, just a few miles outside of Covington, I followed the directions to Zora Fair's cottage, now a private home. I stood outside and tried, rather unsuccessfully, to imagine the "girl spy of the Confederacy."

I researched for a couple of days at the Atlanta History Center. Among the items that I looked at were the scrapbooks for the legendary Atlanta Civil War Roundtable. It had been founded in 1949, and its past presidents included Civil War historians Richard B. Harwell and Bell Irvin Wiley, and the Atlanta historian Franklin M. Garrett. The scrapbooks covered the years from 1960 to 1989 and were filled with photographs of historians and accounts of their many talks. Every year the roundtable took a trip to a battlefield or civil war site. Not once in those twenty-nine years did the Atlanta Civil War Roundtable host an event focusing on the March to the Sea. Not once did the participants take a trip retracing the March.[2] Apparently, they subscribed to the view that the March was to be forgotten, not celebrated.

I resumed my search for Sherman at the Atlanta Cyclorama, the massive painting of the Battle of Atlanta. But, because it was painted to boost General John A. Logan's political prospects, Sherman is literally hard to find, tucked into the background. That afternoon I reach Madison, Georgia, about sixty miles from Atlanta, and I have finally found references to the March. Madison calls itself "The Town Sherman Refused to Burn," and prides itself on having preserved much of its antebellum grandeur. Once called "the most aristocratic stop on the stagecoach route from Charleston to New Orleans," it now claims to stand as an architectural monument "to the time when cotton was king."[3] Madison survives on tourism, and its quaint streets are lined with boutiques and restaurants. At least it comes by its salvation pedigree honestly. Fifty miles southwest of Atlanta, the towns of the "Southern Loop" beckon visitors to "Come discover our unique shops in the quaint and nostalgic towns that Sherman missed." The implication seems to be that he spared them by design; the reality is that the March was nowhere near there. But any association with Sherman, however tenuous, seems to be good for business.[4]

Eatonton Georgia is most proud of being the birthplace of Joel Chandler Harris, and in addition to the usual Confederate soldier, the center of town also boasts a small statue of Brer Rabbit. The self-guided architectural tour notes that residences in Eatonton and Putnam County were spared, but that the loss of factories, mills, gins, barns, and warehouses meant that recovery during Reconstruction was slow.[5] I get lost trying to find Turnwold Plantation, where Joseph Addison Turner (with assistance from the young Joel Chandler Harris) published *The Countryman*, but I eventually find it. Like many plantation houses, it is not terribly large or impressive, but its slightly shabby air feels more authentic than the impeccably restored homes of Madison do.

As I drive toward Milledgeville, I cross over Lake Sinclair and Lake Oconee. The lakes were formed in 1953 and 1979, respectively, by damming the Oconee River. I find myself wondering how much they altered the landscape that the marchers would have seen, remembering again how hard it is to recapture the past and how subjective memory is.

In Milledgeville I finally find a place that embraces its experiences during Sherman's March—perhaps because it has to. Elsewhere, the scores of roadside markers that were put up by the state in the 1950s are hard to find, casualties of car crashes and bad weather, but they are many and well maintained in Milledgeville. If, as discussed in chapter 1, the stories Southern civilians told emphasized either victimization or defiance, Milledgeville exemplifies both. Outside the Old State Capitol the bricks from the destroyed Armory now make two elegant archways. Inside the building, a few chairs survived not only Sherman's soldiers' legislative session but the fires that periodically swept through the building in the intervening years. The old courthouse grounds feature not one but two markers commemorating the successful hiding of the Great Seal. The former Governor's Mansion has a small framed photograph of Sherman, tucked into a corner as a little wink to visitors. Not all of them think it's funny.

Griswoldville receives disproportionate attention in recountings of Sherman's March, perhaps because it was the only significant battle on the March to the Sea. Given that, I was surprised by how little was there: a flagpole, a marker, and an open field. If you did not know it was there, you would never find it. (A new monument to the Georgians who died there was dedicated in December 2012.)[6] About 130 miles away, Magnolia Springs State Park and the Bo Ginn National Fish Hatchery, built on what was briefly the site of the Confederacy's largest prison camp, is busier, but that's because almost nothing remained of the prison camp itself. When I visited, the exact location of the stockade was still a mystery; in 2010 archaeologists from Georgia Southern University uncovered dozens of artifacts from the camp. Work there continues, bringing the Camp Lawton story to the public.[7]

I visited Ebenezer Creek twice—once on my own in 2008 and then again in March 2009 with my digital project collaborator Kelley Bell. The first time I was struck by its isolation, and the fact that the state had just installed a historical marker there, as part of its new March to the Sea Trail. The marker is by a boat ramp that people use to go fishing in the cypress swamp. It is not a particularly reverential place—a little muddy and grubby, to be honest. When Kelley and I were there, a man named James Dailey struck up a conversation with us and told us that the marker was in the wrong place. The site of the crossing and horrible aftermath was deeper into the swamp. Then he offered to get his boat and take us there. We accepted. While we waited for Mr. Dailey, we started talking to another fisherman and explained what we were doing. He laughed, and then said "Oh, sure—there's a spot called Dead Nigger." Perhaps he noticed our shocked expressions, because he then clapped his hands, announced "Enough talk. Time to fish," and jumped into his boat. A few minutes later we too went out into the swamp, moving quietly through the deep, dark, waters until we came to a secluded wide spot. And it began to make sense. The folk memory of the March still runs deep in Georgia.

Savannah, like Milledgeville, emphasizes its Civil War past. Tour guides at the Green-Meldrim House, which Sherman used as his headquarters, joke about how Sherman was or was not received in polite society. The tour ends with mention of the ultimate in reunion narratives: in 1981, St. John's Episcopal Church (the house is now the church's rectory) hosted the wedding of a local woman, Helen Harris, daughter of the local UDC chapter president, to William Tecumseh Sherman IV.[8] The generally good-natured tone of Civil War remembrance in Savannah (after all, while white residents might have resented occupation, their homes and businesses were left intact) gives way in one place: Colonial Park Cemetery. Sherman's soldiers camped there, pitching tents among the mausoleums, breaking into vaults, and vandalizing tombstones. When they left, dozens of headstones lay scattered on the ground. Those whose graves could not be found were cemented into the walls of the cemetery, remaining as mute testimony to what the soldiers did.

My personal march to the sea left me with a few distinct impressions. I found fewer markers than I expected to, and most of the roadside markers put up by the state of Georgia discussed troop movements or skirmishes, as opposed to the more nebulous encounters between civilians and soldiers. In many towns there was a tension between celebrating antebellum homes and complaining that the March had cut a swath. After all, if it had really destroyed everything, these homes would be gone too. Finally, the narrative of the March that I found was almost entirely that of Southern whites. It is the story of destruction and violence, rather than liberation and jubilee. The only place that African Americans take center stage is at Ebenezer Creek, arguably the nadir of their experience.

PHASE TWO OF MY EXPLORATION of the March took place in reverse.[9] For a few days in June 2009 I worked my way from the Bennett Place in Durham,

*Tombstones vandalized by Sherman's men in Savannah's
Colonial Park Cemetery. (Photograph by the author)*

North Carolina, to Columbia, South Carolina, and then as far south as Barnwell, South Carolina. As in Georgia, I realized that what we see today are the exceptions, the structures and landscapes that have survived for almost 150 years. Where Sherman's men once saw plantation homes and broad fields, I saw tangles of timber interspersed with dollar stores and gas stations. Similarly, the places that are highlighted on Civil War trails and set off with historic markers are disproportionately sites of military importance—clashes of troops, rather than places were civilians and soldiers interacted for a moment in time.

With all of this in mind, we can begin at the end: the Bennett Place State Historic Site, in Durham, North Carolina, which bills itself as the "location of the largest surrender of the American Civil War." The surrender at the Bennett place, which officially took place on April 26, 1865 (after several days of negotiations), is often overshadowed by the surrender at Appomattox, and what is striking about the Bennett Place is the degree to which its small museum and reconstructed farm buildings seem to acknowledge that. The most notable feature at the site is the Unity Monument, erected in 1923 by the Morgan family (members of whom eventually dedicated the land that became the park). The monument describes the surrender on a low tablet, literally overshadowed by two pillars (representing North and South) supporting a crosspiece reading UNITY. Thus, it would seem, the significance of the Bennett Place lies in it not as a commemoration of the end of the war, with winners and losers, but as the beginning of peace.

The other places I visited, in both North and South Carolina were much less about reunion, and much more about emphasizing white Southern resistance or defiance. The battlefields of Bentonville and Averasboro in North Carolina and Rivers Bridge in South Carolina all stress military history—troops movements and the like—while downplaying the causes and results of the war, the people of the area, and Sherman's destructive ways. Interpretations at all three sites, to varying degrees, emphasize the degree to which Confederates were able to slow Sherman's men, though in the end never for long. Bentonville and Averasboro both have several monuments to fallen troops. I found the small Chicora Cemetery at Averasboro to be a poignant spot, with the expected monument to the Confederate dead flanked by rows of markers to unknown soldiers, identified only by their states. Averasboro has a monument to Union troops, listing the regiments in the XX Corps, but set so far back from the road as to be virtually invisible.

I found very few sites, or even historical markers, attesting to the destructiveness of the March. Perhaps it was naïve to expect to find ruins still standing so many years later. Certainly very few destroyed private homes have been left as reminders or testaments. Two sets of striking ruins remain however: the remains of the Fayetteville Arsenal, in Fayetteville, North Carolina, and the ruins of the Saluda Factory and Saluda River Bridge in Columbia. The Fayetteville site (part of the Museum of the Cape Fear complex) is bisected by a highway now, but piles of rocks and some foundations can still be seen, along with a metal "ghost tower," erected to give some scale to the ruins. They reminded me of an ancient civilization, for the layout of the actual building can still be seen. All that remains of the Saluda River Factory are some walls and stones that made up part of the millrace. It is deep in the woods of Columbia's Riverbank Zoo and Botanical Garden, and it was an unusual experience to have to turn left at the baboon cage in order to do my research! Here the feeling was less of an enduring civilization as one slowly being retaken by nature.

The further south I went, the greater the emphasis on the devastation Sherman's men left in their wake. In part, this may be a function of the claim that Sherman's men took the gloves off in South Carolina and put them back on again when they entered North Carolina. Certainly, those sites that I visited in South Carolina seemed to take the war, and Sherman's part in it, a bit more personally. The displays in the Cheraw Lyceum museum, complete with tiny dioramas, described the Cheraw region as having been "ravished" by Sherman's men but conceded that the explosion that destroyed the business district was a pure accident. Indeed, places that survived, whether a town like Cheraw or an individual home or church along the way, seem to take pains to explain why they were spared: a Masonic emblem left out, a church used as a stable (in Barnwell, South Carolina), or a shared last name.

The city of Columbia, at least immediately after the March, seemed to take a perverse pride in having been the target of so much Yankee wrath, and the question of exactly who set off the fire that burned the town has never quite been settled. Like many places through which the March passed, Columbia has a bit of a contradictory identity as far as Sherman is concerned. On the one hand, there is the sense of victimization because the city had been bombarded and burned. On the other hand, there is an element of pride or defiance in having survived and thrived. This juxtaposition can best be seen on the grounds of the South Carolina State House. You can see a marker commemorating the original state house (being replaced now by a new building) that was "burned by Sherman's troops." But turn around and you can see six stars on the walls of the state house, marking dents in the stone from Union cannonballs. Devastation and survival coexisting in the same spot. Perhaps the lesson we should take from the remains of Sherman's March is that the past cannot be completely erased.

I WRITE ALL OF THIS IN 2013, in the thick of the Civil War sesquicentennial. The commemorations of Emancipation have just begun; the bulk of the war's major battles are still ahead. "Sherman's March" as a metaphor still lives on, featured prominently as a symbol of scorched earth and destruction. One can only hope that the next generation remembers that it was not quite that simple.

NOTES

Introduction

1. "Atlanta Flames (1972–1980)," http://www.sportsecyclopedia.com/nhl/atlflames/ aflames.html, September 19, 2013; "Calgary Flames," http://flames.nhl.com, September 19, 2013. The Atlanta Flames are not the only Civil War–related NHL franchise. In 1997 the Columbus Blue Jackets, named for Ohio's many Civil War regiments and generals, began playing.

2. On arson in the South Bronx, see "Diary of an Urban Priest," *New York Times*, November 27, 1994, and "Church's Faith in the Bronx Survives Fire," *New York Times*, June 25, 1997; on gerrymandering in the now-disallowed Georgia 11th Congressional District, see Peter Applebome, "Suits Challenging Redrawn Districts," *New York Times*, February 14, 1994.

3. Claire Smith, "Baltimore Is Close to Home for Yanks," *New York Times*, October 13, 1996.

4. "Senate Outlaws Video Gambling," *Atlanta Constitution* March 7, 2001.

5. John Yow, "Pestilence," *Atlanta Journal-Constitution*, August 8, 1993; Mike Toner, "Tiny, Deadly Fire Ants Creep into Four More Georgia Counties," *Atlanta Constitution*, August 15, 1991; Aiken, *The Cotton Plantation South since the Civil War*, 78; Thomas, *A History of Marlboro County*, n.p.

6. "The Daisy in the South," *Washington Post*, October 10, 1897; "Cracker Corner: There Was Something about It. . . . ," *Georgia Historical Quarterly* 58 (Spring 1974): 117; "Black Is . . . Our New Year Traditions," http://www.blackisonline.com/2011/01/black-is-our-new-year-traditions/, January 2, 2011.

7. "General Sherman Tree, Sequoia National Park, California," *Time*, July 28, 2010, http://www.time.com/time/specials/packages/article/0,28804,2006404_2006095_200611_0,00.html, June 15, 2012.

8. On the ecological impact of the March, see Brady, *War upon the Land*, 122–26; "Historical March of Civil War General Had No Large Scale Environmental Impact," May 29, 1996, Press Release from University of Georgia Savannah River Ecology Laboratory.

9. The number of counties is based on my count: thirty-one in Georgia, eighteen in South Carolina, and fourteen in North Carolina.

10. William T. Sherman to Ulysses S. Grant, November 6, 1864, in Simpson and Berlin, *Sherman's Civil War*, 749–52.

11. Grimsley, *The Hard Hand of War*.

12. Sherman's March, also known as the Georgia and Carolinas campaign has a rich and detailed historiography. For overviews, see Rubin, "The Georgia and Carolinas Campaign"; Lucas, "William Tecumseh Sherman vs. the Historians." I found several works to be indispensable in informing my thinking and in writing this book: Bailey, *War and Ruin*; Campbell, *When Sherman Marched North from the Sea*; Davis, *Sherman's March*; Fellman, *Citizen Sherman*;

Glatthaar, *The March to the Sea and Beyond*; Miles, *To the Sea*; Royster, *The Destructive War*; Trudeau, *Southern Storm*.

13. I am not the first historian to explore aspects of the mythic and the legendary in Sherman's March. See Reardon, "William T. Sherman in Postwar Georgia's Collective Memory, 1865–1914"; Caudill and Ashdown, *Sherman's March in Myth and Memory*; Moody, *Demon of the Lost Cause*.

14. Blight, *Race and Reunion*; Brundage, *The Southern Past*; Janney, *Remembering the Civil War*.

Chapter 1

1. On the Atlanta campaign generally, see Castel, *Decision in the West*.

2. Bailey, *War and Ruin*, 23–25; Davis, *What the Yankees Did to Us*.

3. Sherman, *Memoirs*, 170–71; Inscoe, *The Civil War in Georgia*, 93–94; Bailey, *War and Ruin*, 28–31.

4. U.S. War Department, *The War of the Rebellion,* ser. I, vol. 39, part 3, 713–14; Sherman, *Memoirs*, 175–76.

5. Marszalek, *Sherman's March to the Sea*, 41, 43; Morgan, *Planters' Progress*, 98.

6. Siddali, "Babylon Is Fallen; van Tuyll, "Two Men, Two Minds: Coverage of Sherman's March to the Sea by Augusta and Savannah Newspapers."

7. The basic structure of this narrative is drawn from a combination of secondary sources, including Glatthaar, *The March to the Sea and Beyond*; Campbell, *When Sherman Marched North from the Sea*; Trudeau, *Southern Storm*; Miles, *To the Sea*; Kennett, *Marching through Georgia*; Schwabe, "Sherman's March through Georgia: A Reappraisal of the Right Wing."

8. Wood, *Clayton County*, 33; Kilgore, Smith, and Tuck, *A History of Clayton County, Georgia, 1821–1983*, 35.

9. Wills, *Army Life of an Illinois Soldier*, 321.

10. Osborn, *The Fiery Trail*, 54–55; Johnson account in McMichael, *History of Butts County*, 399, 409–10.

11. Miles, *To the Sea*, 180–81; *Monroe County, Georgia: A History*, 91–92, 155; Jasper County Historical Foundation, *History of Jasper County, Georgia*, 4, 28, 31–32; Williams, *History of Jones County Georgia for One Hundred Years*, 135.

12. Bragg, *Griswoldville*; Trudeau, *Southern Storm*, 193–215.

13. Wills, *Army Life of an Illinois Soldier*, 324.

14. Miller, *A Guide into the South*, 43–44.

15. Davidson, *History of Wilkinson County*, 263–64.

16. Bailey, *War and Ruin*, 77; Osborn, *The Fiery Trail*, 61.

17. Brannen, *Life in Old Bulloch*. Williams's story came from a 1934 *Savannah Morning News* article.

18. Brannen, *Life in Old Bulloch*, 54. From the recollections of a survivor, W. H. Cone.

19. Hitchcock, *Marching with Sherman*; Nichols, *The Story of the Great March*.

20. DeKalb Historical Society, *Vanishing DeKalb*, 16.

21. Sherman, *Memoirs*, 180–81.

22. Trudeau, *Southern Storm*, 140–41, 145; Miles, *To the Sea*, 74–76; Bailey, *War and Ruin*, 55–56; Camp, *Morgan County, Georgia*, 8; Hickey, *Rambles through Morgan County*, 13–14, 47, 74.

23. Lunt, *The Diary of Dolly Lunt Burge*, 158–61.

24. Ibid., 161–65.

25. Little, *Reminiscent: A Pictorial History of Eatonton/Putnam County, Georgia*; Inscoe, *The Civil War in Georgia*, 252–53.

26. Marszalek, *Sherman's March to the Sea*, 62; *Milledgeville and Baldwin County Civil War Centennial*, 45; Bonner, *Milledgeville*, 190–92.

27. Bonner, *Milledgeville*, 183–84; Sherman *Memoirs*, 185–86; Miles, *To the Sea*, 80.

28. Connolly, *Three Years in the Army of the Cumberland*, 317.

29. Bonner, *Milledgeville*, 187; Harrington, *Civil War Milledgeville*, 95–96; *Sesqui-Centennial of Milledgeville and Baldwin County Georgia, 1803–1953*; Hines, *A Treasure Album of Milledgeville and Baldwin County, Georgia*, 11. The inscription on Kane's headstone reads "IN MEMORY OF PATRICK KANE. He was an orderly, industrious and respected citizen—a native of Ireland aged about 50 years at the time of his death and shot down by a Federal Soldier on the 30th day of Nova. 1864, on the advance of Gen. Sherman's Army on Milledgeville."

30. Bonner, *Milledgeville*, 187–88; Harrington, *Civil War Milledgeville*, 51–52; Miller, *Fighting for Liberty and Right*, 281.

31. Connolly, *Three Years in the Army of the Cumberland*, 318–19.

32. Andrews, *The War-Time Journal of a Georgia Girl, 1864–1865*, 38.

33. Hitchcock, *Marching with Sherman*, 106.

34. Jordan, *Cotton to Kaolin*, 29; Mitchell, *History of Washington County*, 60–65.

35. Sherman, *Memoirs*, 191.

36. Knight, *Georgia's Landmarks, Memorials and Legends*, 2:1023; Jordan, *Cotton to Kaolin*, 30; Mitchell, *History of Washington County*, 66–67.

37. Mitchell, *History of Washington County*, 67.

38. Ibid., 27–28, 43; Washington County Historical Society, *Washington County*, 7.

39. Connolly, *Three Years in the Army of the Cumberland*, 325–28; Miller, *Fighting for Liberty and Right*, 282; Trudeau, *Southern Storm*, 259–60.

40. Townsend, "Camp Lawton Magnolia Springs State Park"; "Camp Lawton Stockade, Millen, Georgia," in Rogers and Saunders, *Swamp Water and Wiregrass*, 93–108.

41. Knight, *Burke County Folks*, 56; Bailey, *War and Ruin*, 91.

42. Hillhouse, *History of Burke County*, 131; Hillhouse, *Nuggets and Other Findings in Burke County*, 261.

43. Hillhouse, *History of Burke County*, 29; Knight, *Burke County Folks*, 145.

44. Shivers, *The Land Between*.

45. Hillhouse, *History of Burke County*, 81.

46. Thomas, *The Secret Eye*, 246–47, 253–54.

47. Marszalek, *Sherman's March to the Sea*, 94–96; Bailey, *War and Ruin*, 93–94.

48. Connolly, *Three Years in the Army of the Cumberland*, 354–55, 367, 373.

49. Sherman, *Memoirs*, 194; Marszalek, *Sherman's March to the Sea*, 96.

50. Hollingsworth, *The History of Screven County*, 38–39.

51. Marszalek, *Sherman's March to the Sea*, 98–104; Durham, *Guardian of Savannah*.

52. Marszalek, *Sherman's March to the Sea*, 104–6.

53. Miller, *Fighting for Liberty and Right*, 289–92.

54. Cram, *Soldiering with Sherman*, 151–52.

55. Mrs. Mary Jones to Mrs. Susan M. Cumming, in Myers and Jones, *The Children of Pride*, 2:1217.

56. Mrs. Laura E. Buttolph to Mrs. Mary Jones, in ibid., 1218–19.

57. Ibid., 1220–21, 1223–26.

58. Pond, *Recollections of a Southern Daughter*, 75.

59. Myers and Jones, *The Children of Pride*, 1227–1237. For more on Sherman's men in Liberty County, Georgia, see Monroe, "Men without Law: Federal Raiding in Liberty County, Georgia"; Rogers and Saunders, "The Scourge of Sherman's Men in Liberty County, Georgia."

60. A transcription of the telegram and Lincoln's reply dated December 26, 1864, can be found at http://myloc.gov/Exhibitions/lincoln/presidency/CommanderInChief/EndInSight/ExhibitObjects/GiftToLincoln.aspx, September 24, 2013.

61. Table in Sherman, *Memoirs*, 221.

62. For a Confederate account, see Jones *The Siege of Savannah in December, 1864*. For a recent study of Civil War Savannah, see Jones, *Saving Savannah*.

63. Godley and Bragg, *Stories of Old Savannah*, 41.

64. Sherman, *Memoirs*, 247–48.

65. Jones, *Saving Savannah*, 213–32; Marszalek, *Sherman's March to the Sea* 117–18. Hitchcock, *Marching with Sherman*, 202.

66. Jones, *Saving Savannah*, 219–20, 225; Marszalek, *Sherman's March to the Sea*, 119–20.

67. The reports from the Savannah campaign are all contained in U.S. War Department, *The War of the Rebellion*, ser. I, vol. 44.

68. Marszalek, *Sherman's March to the Sea*, 112; Knight, *Georgia's Landmarks, Memorials, and Legends*, 2:276, 286; Connolly, *Three Years in the Army of the Cumberland*, 375.

69. Sherman, *Memoirs*, 252–53.

70. Barrett, *Sherman's March through the Carolinas*, 44–45; Sherman, *Memoirs*, 253.

71. Barrett, *Sherman's March through the Carolinas* 40; Crabb, *Facing Sherman in South Carolina*, 22–25; Miles, *To the Sea*, 313–14.

72. Sherman, *Memoirs*, 254.

73. Connolly, *Three Years in the Army of the Cumberland*, 384.

74. Barrett, *Sherman's March through the Carolinas*, 52–53.

75. The Episcopal Church of the Holy Apostle, http://www.bcvm.org/churches/HolyApostles/index.htm, September 24, 2013.

76. Crabb, *Facing Sherman in South Carolina*, 24–25; Barrett, *Sherman's March through the Carolinas*, 53.

77. "These Honored Dead: The Battle of Rivers Bridge and Civil War Combat Casualties," http://www.nps.gov/history/NR/twhp/wwwlps/lessons/94rivers/94rivers.htm, September

24, 2013. A very detailed account can be found in Crabb, *Facing Sherman in South Carolina*, 48–59.

78. Crabb, *Facing Sherman in South Carolina*, 90–91.

79. Sherman, *Memoirs*, 276–77.

80. Lizzie P. Smith to Isabella Middleton Smith, January 19, 1865, in Smith, Smith, and Childs, *Mason Smith Family Letters*, 163; Chesnut, *Mary Chesnut's Civil War*, 715; Elmore, *A Heritage of Woe*, 98.

81. Sherman, *Memoirs*, 277.

82. Poet William Gilmore Simms published an account of his experiences in Columbia during the burning (*A City Laid Waste*); a classic account by a historian is Lucas, *Sherman and the Burning of Columbia*.

83. Miles, *To The Sea*, 315–17.

84. Wills, *Army Life of an Illinois Soldier*, 350.

85. Buck, *The Road to Reunion*, 49–50.

86. Loewen, *Lies across America*, 279–80, 285.

87. Osborn, *The Fiery Trail*, 129–31.

88. LeConte, *When the World Ended*, 30–31.

89. Ibid., 42–46.

90. Chesnut, *Mary Chesnut's Civil War*, 747.

91. Smith, Smith, and Childs, *Mason Smith Family Letters*, 181, 183.

92. Clemson, *A Rebel Came Home*.

93. Loewen, *Lies across America*, 281; Sherman, *Memoirs*, 287.

94. Sherman *Memoirs*, 208; Davis, *Sherman's March*, 185–86.

95. These allegations appear in both Miles, *To the Sea*, and Davis, *Sherman's March*. However, neither book includes footnotes or any attribution for these claims.

96. Miles, *To the Sea*, 318; Davis, *Sherman's March*, 187. Charles W. Wills also mentions this, though in his account the placard read "Fate of foragers." Wills, *Army Life of an Illinois Soldier*, 352.

97. Sherman to Kilpatrick, February 23, 1865. He wrote a similar letter to General Howard as well. *Report of Major General William T. Sherman*, 329–30.

98. Sherman to Hampton, February 24, 1865, *Report of Major General William T. Sherman*, 331–32; Davis, *Sherman's March*, 187–88; Barrett, *Sherman's March through the Carolinas*, 104–5.

99. Barrett, *Sherman's March through the Carolinas*, 109–10; Nelson, "Sherman at Cheraw."

100. Sherman to Slocum, March 6, 1865, *Report of Major General William T. Sherman*, 339.

101. Sherman to Kilpatrick, March 7, 1865, ibid., 340.

102. Barrett, *Sherman's March through the Carolinas*, 119.

103. Ibid., 121–22.

104. Ibid., 133–37.

105. Ibid., 141–42; Bradley, *This Astounding Close*, 14–15.

106. Miller, *Fighting for Liberty and Right*, 319, 321.

107. Edmondston, *Journal of a Secesh Lady*, 679–80.

108. Barrett, *Sherman's March through the Carolinas*, 148–49.

109. North Carolina Historic Sites: Bentonville Battlefield, http://www.nchistoricsites.org/Bentonvi/campaign.htm, September 24, 2013; Bradley, *This Astounding Close*, 15–18.

110. Bentonville has been the subject of several monographs, including Broadwater, *Battle of Despair*; Hughes, *Bentonville*; Bradley, *Last Stand in the Carolinas*. Other books devote considerable space to it, including, Barrett, *Sherman's March through the Carolinas*, 159–85; Davis, *Sherman's March*, 233–40; Bradley, *This Astounding Close*, 20–27.

111. Quoted in Barrett, *Sherman's March through the Carolinas*, 187.

112. Ibid., 191–92.

113. Sherman, *Memoirs*, 325–27.

114. Ibid., 344.

115. Barrett, *Sherman's March through the Carolinas*, 219–25.

116. Sherman, *Memoirs*, 346–47.

117. Bradley, *This Astounding Close*, 157–83; Barrett, *Sherman's March through the Carolinas*, 234–35; Pfanz "The Surrender Negotiations between General Johnston and General Sherman, April 1865."

118. The full text can be found in Bradley, *This Astounding Close*, 268–69.

119. Ibid., 206–22; Davis, *Sherman's March*, 278.

120. Davis, *Sherman's March*, 279.

Chapter 2

1. Lovett, *Grandmother Stories*, 162–66: Zora Fair's story can also be found in Perkerson, *White Columns in Georgia*, 25; Knight, *Georgia's Landmarks, Memorials and Legends*, 2:921; Historic Oxford pamphlet in Atlanta Civil War Roundtable Scrapbooks, MSS 808, Kenan Research Library, Atlanta History Center; Kaemmerlen, *General Sherman and the Georgia Belles*, 31–33.

2. Lovett, *Grandmother Stories*, 166–69.

3. Ibid., 171.

4. The cottage is at 1005 Asbury Street, Oxford, Georgia. The Oxford and Emory College State Historical Marker is at the intersection of West Pierce and Whatcoat Streets in Oxford. The text can be found at http://georgiainfo.galileo.usg.edu/gahistmarkers/oxfordhistmarker.htm, September 24, 2013.

5. Henken, "Taming the Enemy: Georgian Narratives about the Civil War"; Koppes, "Folklore: Where Fact Meets Fiction."

6. Undated Clipping: "Costumes of Gay 90's Highlight UDC Jubilee," United Daughters of the Confederacy Collection, MSS 765, box 4, folder 15, Kenan Research Library, Atlanta History Center.

7. Reston, *Sherman's March and Vietnam*, 64.

8. "A Civil War Reminiscence by Mrs. Rosa T. Lane," in McMichael, *History of Butts County*, 583.

9. Jones, *When Sherman Came*.

10. Campbell, *When Sherman Marched North from the Sea*; Frank, "To 'Cure Her of Her Pride and Boasting'"; Frank, "Bedrooms as Battlefields: The Role of Gender Politics in Sherman's March," in Whites and Long, *Occupied Women*; Schultz, "Mute Fury," 61.

11. Schultz, "Mute Fury," 63, 71.

12. Reston, *Sherman's March and Vietnam*, 75.

13. Schultz, "Mute Fury," 63.

14. Kaemmerlen, *General Sherman and the Georgia Belles*. This is book published for a general audience—in fact, I picked up my copy at the Road to Tara Museum in Jonesboro, Georgia. It generally reprints stories from other sources.

15. Simkins and Patton, *The Women of the Confederacy*.

16. For a look at the transmission of survival stories, see Hume and Roessner, "Surviving Sherman's March: Press, Public Memory, and Georgia's Salvation Mythology."

17. Lee, *Burke County, Georgia*, 24; Knight, *Burke County Folks*, 55, 139.

18. Campbell, *When Sherman Marched North from the Sea*, 88.

19. Fellman, *Citizen Sherman*, 226.

20. Feimster, "General Benjamin Butler and the Threat of Sexual Violence"; Schultz, "Mute Fury," 71–72; Campbell, *When Sherman Marched North from the Sea*, 45–48; Barber and Ritter, "'Physical Abuse . . . and Rough Handling': Race, Gender, and Sexual Justice in the Occupied South," in Whites and Long, *Occupied Women*.

21. Bonner, *Milledgeville*; Harrington, *Civil War Milledgeville*, 53–54.

22. Harrington, *Civil War Milledgeville*, 53–54.

23. Diane Miller Sommerville, personal communication with the author, describing records from the Georgia State Asylum.

24. Underwood, *The Women of the Confederacy*, 172.

25. Feimster, "General Benjamin Butler and the Threat of Sexual Violence."

26. James C. Bonner, in conversation with James Reston. Quoted in *Sherman's March and Vietnam*, 73.

27. Davidson, *History of Wilkinson County*, 263.

28. Miller, *A Guide into the South*, 45.

29. Cornelius Cadle, "An Adjutant's Reflections," MOLLUS 5, OH, 391–92; Belknap, "Recollections of a Bummer," 7.

30. Trowbridge *The South*, 478, 564.

31. McMichael, *History of Butts County*, 403–4.

32. Miller, *A Guide into the South*, 44.

33. Spalding, "Cracker Corner," 117.

34. Smith Atkins, "With Sherman's Cavalry," MOLLUS 11, IL, 390.

35. King, "Santa Was a Yankee," in *Sound of Drums*, 437–38.

36. Rainer, *Henry County, Georgia: Landmark Houses*, 46–47. For other examples, see Hollingsworth, *The History of Screven County, Georgia*, 39.

37. Jasper County Historical Foundation, *History of Jasper County, Georgia*, 51, 296.

38. Ibid., 208.

39. Atkins, "With Sherman's Cavalry," 387.

40. Sams, *Wayfarers in Walton*, 189.

41. McMichael, *History of Butts County*, 399.

42. Emanuel County Historic Preservation Society, *Emanuel County Georgia*, 9; Dorsey, *Footprints along the Hoopee*, 108–9.

43. Davidson, *History of Wilkinson County*, 269–70.

44. McGowen and McGowen, *Flashes of Duplin's History and Government*, 241–42. The date of the baby's birth is given as February 12, 1865, which is a bit early for soldiers to have been in North Carolina and present for the birth, but the general outlines of the story seem believable.

45. Email from Michael Fellman to author, July 6, 2011. Sherman's father, Charles, was a Mason, but given that he died when Sherman was so young, his impact is unlikely. http://www.freemason.com/past-grand-masters/98–1824-charles-r-sherman.html, July 6, 2011.

46. Jasper County Historical Foundation, *History of Jasper County*, 51–52.

47. McMichael, *History of Butts County*, 409–10. Similar stories are told about the survival of the Masonic temple in Chambersburg, Pennsylvania, the only Northern town burned by Confederate troops.

48. Hollingsworth, *The History of Screven County*, 39.

49. Story quoted in Reston, *Sherman's March and Vietnam*, 71.

50. Erlich, *Mrs. Beall's Mill: Georgia Historical Marker Program*.

51. Miller, *A Guide into the South*, 42–44.

52. Jordan, *Cotton to Kaolin*, 30.

53. "Four Familiar North DeKalb Sights on Historical Society Tour" *The News/Sun* October 15, 1980. In Civil War Roundtable of Atlanta Scrapbooks, volume 4.

54. Davidson, *History of Wilkinson County*, 262.

55. Stancil, *Vanishing Gwinnett*, 48.

56. Rozier, *The Houses of Hancock, 1785–1865*, 197.

57. Daniel, "Georgia Woman Tells Vividly of Seeing Battle of Atlanta," in Brannen, *Life in Old Bulloch*, 49.

58. Emanuel County Historic Preservation Society, *Emanuel County Georgia*, 20.

59. Hollingsworth, *The History of Screven County*, 39.

60. Knight, *Burke County Folks*, 57, 147.

61. L. C. Varnadoe, "What the Yankees Did to Us," *Confederate Veteran* 26 (October 1918), 438.

62. McMichael, *History of Butts County*, 41.

63. Bonner, *Milledgeville*, 188.

64. Ibid., 188; Cook, *History of Baldwin County Georgia*, 54; Knight, *Georgia's Landmarks, Memorials and Legends*, Vol. 2, 96; Kaemmerlen, *General Sherman and the Georgia Belles*, 65–66. Kaemmerlen also claims that the Barnetts hid the seal a second time, during Radical Reconstruction.

65. Lovett, *Grandmother Stories*, 170.

66. Brown, "The Monumental Legacy of Calhoun," 142.

67. Ibid., 140.

68. Ibid., 140–41.

69. Ladies Calhoun Monument Association, *A History of the Calhoun Monument at Charleston S. C.*, 13–14. See also Holmes, *Memorials to the Memory of Mrs. Mary Amarinthia Snowden*, 31, 33, 34.

70. "A Case of Stolen Bonds," *Washington Post*, August 12, 1880; "Those Stolen Southern Bonds," *New York Times*, August 12, 1880.

71. "Eulogy on Confederate Women," and "Sherman's 'Tough Set,'" in Underwood, *The Women of the Confederacy*, 46, 33. On the image of the unreconstructed Southern white woman, see Rubin, *A Shattered Nation*.

72. "The Belligerent Sex" in King, *Sound of Drums*, 447.

73. Ibid.

74. "Georgia Girls and Federal Lieutenants," in Kirkland, *The Pictorial Book of Anecdotes of the Rebellion; or, The Funny and Pathetic Side of the War*, 496.

75. McMichael, *History of Butts County*, 402.

76. "Johnstonville District: By Mrs. Eliza F. Hill Manry," United Daughters of the Confederacy, Georgia Division, Willie Hunt Smith Chapter, Barnesville. *History of Lamar County*.

77. Melton, "'The Town That Sherman Wouldn't Burn': Sherman's March and Madison, Georgia, in History, Memory, and Legend."

78. Reston, *Sherman's March and Vietnam*, 29. On Sherman as a ladies man, see Fellman, *Citizen Sherman*, 352–70.

79. *Georgia Landmarks and Legends*, 1:31–32. In *General Sherman and the Georgia Belles*, Cathy Kaemmerlen relates the same story, although she mistakenly refers to Shellman as Stelman, 71–72.

80. Avary, *Dixie after the War*, 118–19.

81. Soldiers often missed their own families and doted on the children they met along the way. Marten, *The Children's Civil War*, 74–75, 141–42.

82. Quoted in Emily Weil, *After Sherman's March*, 60.

83. McMichael, *History of Butts County*, 402.

84. Dorsey, *Footprints along the Hoopee*, 109.

85. Jasper County Historical Foundation, *History of Jasper County*, 291–92.

86. King, "Santa Was a Yankee," in *Sound of Drums*, January 5, 1964, 438–39.

87. McMichael, *History of Butts County*, 406–7.

88. Ibid., 407–8.

89. Ibid., 408–9.

90. Ibid., 408.

91. Silber, *The Romance of Reunion*.

92. "A Pretty War Story," *New York Times*, March 14, 1886, reprinted from *Louisville Courier Journal*. The story also appeared in the *Atlanta Constitution*, March 10, 1886.

93. Williams, *History of Jones County, Georgia*, 153–54.

Chapter 3

1. Slave narratives, a folk history of slavery in the United States from interviews with former slaves, South Carolina Narratives, vol. XIV, part 3, Henry D. Jenkins, ex-slave, eighty-seven

years old, 23, 26. I used the Library of Congress on-line versions of these narratives, all of which can be found at Born in Slavery: Slave Narratives from the Federal Writers' Project, 1936-1938. http://memory.loc.gov/ammem/snhtml/.

2. On the rocky transition to emancipation in general, see Litwack, *Been in the Storm So Long*, and Glymph, *Out of the House of Bondage*.

3. Few historians have dealt with African Americans along the route of the March in great depth. Exceptions include Drago, "How Sherman's March through Georgia Affected the Slaves"; Campbell, *When Sherman Marched North from the Sea*; Glatthaar, *The March to the Sea and Beyond*; Trudeau, *Southern Storm*.

4. There is an excellent introduction to the Works Progress Administration (WPA) narratives on the Library of Congress website. See http://memory.loc.gov/ammem/snhtml/snintro00.html.

5. A sample questionnaire can be found in Rawick, *The American Slave*, series I, vol. 1, 173–76.

6. Slave narratives, Arkansas Narratives, vol. II, part 5 [interview with Frank A. Patterson], 278. Patterson also claimed to have been present in Georgia for the capture of Jefferson Davis, for he was moved there late in the war.

7. Slave narratives, South Carolina Narratives, vol. XIV, part 4, Stories from Ex-slaves, 6.

8. "Woman Dies Who Saw Sherman March to the Sea," *Chicago Defender*, October 29, 1927.

9. Slave narratives, North Carolina Narratives, vol. XI, part 2, Dilly Yelladay, 426.

10. Ibid., North Carolina Narratives, vol. XI, part I, A Slave Story, 59–60, 62.

11. For a powerful visual representation of the connections between emancipation and the presence of the Union army, see *Visualizing Emancipation*, http://dsl.richmond.edu/emancipation/, accessed September 24, 2013.

12. Slave narratives, North Carolina Narratives, vol. XI, part 2, Tina Johnson, Ex-slave Story, 21.

13. Ibid., South Carolina Narratives, vol. XIV, part 4, Stories from Ex-slaves, 12.

14. Ibid., Georgia Narratives, vol. IV, part 4, Phil Towns, Old Slave Story, 45–46.

15. Ibid., South Carolina Narratives, vol. XIV, part 4, Stories from Ex-slaves, 12.

16. Ibid., Georgia Narratives, vol. IV, part 3, Plantation Life, 86.

17. Ibid., Arkansas Narratives, vol. II, part 3 [Interview with Hopkins, Elijah Henry], 312. Hopkins also claimed that when Jefferson Davis was captured near his father's home, he had one thousand wagons of Confederate silver with him.

18. North Carolina Narratives, vol. XI, part I, John C. Bectom, 96.

19. Ibid., Alabama Narratives, vol. I, "When Sherman Passed Through," 241.

20. Ibid., Georgia Narratives, vol. IV, part 4, An Account of Slavery Related by William Ward, 128–30. Ward was interviewed by one of the few documented African American interviewers, Edwin Driskell. http://memory.loc.gov/ammem/snhtml/snintro19.html, accessed September 24, 2013.

21. Ibid., South Carolina Narratives, vol. XIV, part 4, Julia Woodberry, ex-slave, age —. This narrative was miscataloged—story is actually Willis Williams, 210.

22. Ibid., Texas Narratives, vol. XVI, part 2—Ex-slave Stories (Texas) [Lorenza Ezell], 28–29.

23. Ibid., 28.

24. Maryland Narratives, vol. VIII, Alice Lewis, 37.

25. Arkansas Narratives, vol. II, part 5, interview with Moss, Claiborne, 158–59.

26. Ibid., 159.

27. Ibid., Georgia Narratives, vol. IV, part 3, Lewis Ogletree, ex-slave, 146.

28. Ibid., South Carolina Narratives, vol. XIV, part 3, Amie Lumpkin, ex-slave, 88 years old, 131–32.

29. Ibid., South Carolina Narratives, vol. XIV, part 3, interview with Sarah Poindexter, ex-slave, eighty-seven years old, 269.

30. Ibid., part 2, John Franklin, ex-slave, eighty-four years old, 85–86.

31. Ibid., part 1, Stories from Ex-slaves [George Briggs], 86–87.

32. The narrative mentions "Jools" and "Jewels," but there are no towns by that name in Georgia. There is a town "Jewell," near White Plains and Union Point, both of which are mentioned in the narrative. Too, Kilpatrick's story is very similar to one included in the finding aid for the Jewell's Mill records. MS 3312, Hargrett Rare Book and Manuscript Library, University of Georgia Libraries, http://hmfa.libs.uga.edu/hmfa/view?docId=ead/ms3312-ead.xml, accessed September 24, 2013.

33. Slave narratives, Georgia Narratives, vol. IV, part 3, Emmaline Kilpatrick, 11.

34. Ibid., South Carolina Narratives, vol. XIV, part 4, Alfred Sligh, ex-slave, one hundred years old, 92–93.

35. Ibid., Rev. James H. Johnson, ex-slave, eighty-two years old, 45.

36. Ibid., Georgia Narratives, vol. IV, part 4, "Slavery as Seen through the Eyes of Henry Wright," 203.

37. Ibid., North Carolina Narratives, vol. XI, part 1, John C. Bectom, 96–97.

38. Badeau, "Sherman's March to the Sea,"197; Ellis, *Marching through Georgia*, 71, 97.

39. Slave narratives, Florida Narratives, vol. III, slave Interview, 294–96.

40. Ibid., Georgia Narratives, vol. IV, part 2 [Shang Harris], 122.

41. Ibid., part 4, "An Account of Slavery Related by William Ward," 130–31.

42. Ibid., Phil Towns, "Old Slave Story," 46.

43. Paul Escott claimed that he found fifty Georgia accounts with negative impressions, versus ten positive ones. Escott, "The Context of Freedom: Georgia's Slaves during the Civil War."

44. Slave narratives, South Carolina Narratives, vol. XIV, part 4, Stories from Ex-slaves, 13.

45. Ibid., Georgia Narratives, vol. IV, part 3, Aunt Ferebe Rogers, 216.

46. Ibid., part 2, "Slavery Days as Related by Snovey Jackson," 306. Also quoted in Harrington, *Civil War Milledgeville*, 13–14.

47. Slave narratives, North Carolina Narratives, vol. XI, part 2, Frank Magwood, 92.

48. Ibid., "Uncle" George G. King,. eighty-three years old, Tulsa, Oklahoma, 167.

49. Clarke, *Dwelling Place*, 438–40.

50. Dennett, *The South as It Is*, 177.

51. See Glymph, *Out of the House of Bondage*; Mohr, *On the Threshold of Freedom*; O'Donovan, *Becoming Free in the Cotton South*.

52. Reidy makes a similar argument in *From Slavery to Agrarian Capitalism*, 128.

53. Ibid., 133.

54. Mohr, *On the Threshold of Freedom*, 95.

55. "Sherman's March to the Sea Recalled by Ancient Darkey," *Atlanta Constitution*, January 20, 1929.

56. Escott, "The Context of Freedom: Georgia's Slaves during the Civil War," 93.

57. Gibson, *Scotland County*, 139.

58. Lovett, *Grandmother Stories*, 170.

59. Powers, *Afoot and Alone*, 60–62.

60. Data compiled from 1860 census, Historical U.S. Census Browser, http://mapserver.lib .virginia.edu.

61. Drago, "How Sherman's March through Georgia Affected the Slaves," 363; Escott, "The Context of Freedom: Georgia's Slaves during the Civil War," 84–85.

62. Drago, "How Sherman's March through Georgia Affected the Slaves," 366.

63. Loewen, *Lies across America*, 283.

64. Mitchell, *History of Washington County*, 68.

65. Lee, *Burke County, Georgia*, 131. The same story is told in Clark, *Lost Arcadia; or, the Story of My Old Community*, 103–5.

66. Jasper County Historical Foundation, *History of Jasper County, Georgia*, 52.

67. "Eulogy on Confederate Women," in Underwood, *The Women of the Confederacy*, 60.

68. Trowbridge, *The South*, 549.

69. McMichael, *History of Butts County*, 440–43.

70. Ibid., 437–38.

71. "A Woman's Ingenuity," in King, *Sound of Drums*, 453–54.

72. Trowbridge, *The South*, 478–79.

73. Davidson, *History of Wilkinson County*, 265–66.

74. McMichael, *History of Butts County*, 436.

75. Thomas, *History of Jefferson County*, 52–53.

76. Hickey, *Rambles through Morgan County*, 28.

77. Robert Hunt finds a distinct emancipationist strain in the memories of members of the Army of the Cumberland; I found much less among Sherman's veterans. Hunt, *The Good Men Who Won the War*.

78. "Marching through Georgia . . . P. R. McWilliams, 116th Illinois," in Hinman, *Camp and Field*, 461–62.

79. Fellman, *Citizen Sherman*, 150, 154.

80. Special Field Orders No. 15, U.S. War Department, *The War of the Rebellion*, ser. 3, vol. 4, 434; Fellman, *Citizen Sherman*, 157–61; Murray, "General Sherman, the Negro, and Slavery: The Story of an Unrecognized Rebel," 125–30.

81. Mohr, *On the Threshold of Freedom*, 93–94.

82. Reidy, *From Slavery to Agrarian Capitalism*, 132–33.

83. Reston, *Sherman's March and Vietnam*, 78. Fellman, *Citizen Sherman*, 243, 255. Fellman argued that Sherman's initial peace terms showed his interest in maintaining the South's racial (and electoral) caste systems.

84. Reston, *Sherman's March and Vietnam*, 81.

85. Ellis, *Marching through Georgia*, 96.

86. Garrett, *Atlanta and Environs*, 2:26. See also Dorsey, *To Build Our Lives Together*, 35–36.

87. Major Henry O. Marcy, "Sherman's Campaign in the Carolinas," MOLLUS 53, MA, 337.

88. Drago, "How Sherman's March through Georgia Affected the Slaves," 364–65.

89. Marcy, "Sherman's Campaign in the Carolinas," 343–44.

90. Reston, *Sherman's March and Vietnam*, 64–65.

91. "Foraging. An interesting Trip after Rations in the Heart of South Carolina by Fred Reitz, Company I, 21st Wisconsin," in King and Derby, *Camp-Fire Sketches and Battle-Field Echoes of the Rebellion*, 294.

92. Oake, *On the Skirmish Line*, 320–21.

93. Mohr, *On the Threshold of Freedom*, 93; Escott, "The Context of Freedom," 91–93; Drago, "How Sherman's March through Georgia Affected the Slaves," 371; Rogers and Saunders, *Swamp Water and Wiregrass*, 67.

94. Charles A. Hopkins, "The March to the Sea," MOLLUS 36, RI, 62–63.

95. Charles D. Kerr, Col., "From Atlanta to Raleigh," MOLLUS 26, MN, 216; Trudeau, *Southern Storm*, 380–83.

96. Kerr, "From Atlanta to Raleigh," 216.

97. Ellis, *Marching through Georgia*, 249–50.

98. Ghosts of Ohio, http://www.ghostsofohio.org/lore/elsewhere_lore_8.html, accessed July 11, 2012.

99. For a transcript of the meeting, see Frazier, "Colloquy with Colored Ministers." For African Americans in wartime Savannah, see Byrne, "'Uncle Billy' Sherman Comes to Town: The Free Winter of Black Savannah," and Jones, *Saving Savannah*.

100. Special Field Orders No. 15, Headquarters Military Division of the Mississippi, 16 Jan. 1865, Orders & Circulars, ser. 44, Adjutant General's Office, Record Group 94, National Archives, http://www.history.umd.edu/Freedmen/sfo15.htm, accessed July 11, 2012.

101. Fellman, *Citizen Sherman*, 165.

102. Ibid., 169.

103. Gerteis, *From Contraband to Freedman*, 57.

104. Conwell, *Magnolia Journey*, 80–82.

105. Drago "How Sherman's March through Georgia Affected the Slaves," 373.

106. Blight, *Frederick Douglass' Civil War*; Blight, *Race and Reunion*.

107. Janney, *Remembering the Civil War*, 111–26.

108. Brundage, *The Southern Past*, 10, 138–82.

109. Blight, *American Oracle*, 11–21; Cook, *Troubled Commemoration*, 185–91.

110. Lewis, *Walking with the Wind*, 216, 218–19. See also Fairclough, "Civil Rights and the Lincoln Memorial: The Censored Speeches of Robert R. Moton (1922) and John Lewis (1963)," 408–10.

111. Lewis, *Walking with the Wind*, 222–26.

112. Ibid., 226–27.

Chapter 4

1. "'Bummers' in Sherman's Army," 5–6.

2. Ibid., 6.

3. Ibid., 8–11.

4. Ibid., 12–13.

5. Ibid., 14.

6. Caputo, *A Rumor of War*; Fussell, *Wartime*.

7. Lynette Alvarez, "Nearly a Fifth of War Veterans Report Mental Disorders, a Private Study Finds," *New York Times* April 18, 2008.

8. Reston, *Sherman's March and Vietnam*, 170–71. On the idea of destructiveness and the degree to which the Civil War represented a change in the nature of warfare, see Royster, *The Destructive War*, and Neely, *The Civil War and the Limits of Destruction*.

9. In *Shook Over Hell*, Eric T. Dean Jr. argues that while it is difficult to quantify post-traumatic stress disorders in Civil War veterans, "such problems—frequently severe in magnitude—existed and do not appear to have been isolated," 211.

10. This is not to say that every veteran fit the stereotype of the happy GAR or MOLLUS member. For analysis of the darker sides of veteran life, see Marten, *Sing Not War*.

11. There are no secondary sources on the Society of Army of the Tennessee exclusively. For the GAR, see McConnell, *Glorious Contentment*, and Dearing, *Veterans in Politics*. On the more sentimental aspects of veterans writings, see David W. Blight, "Quarrel Forgotten or a Revolution Remembered?," in Logue and Barton, *The Civil War Veteran*, 407–23.

12. "News of the Day," *New York Times*, July 25, 1866.

13. Keim, *Sherman*, 104; Society of the Army of the Tennessee, *Report of the Proceedings of the Society of the Army of the Tennessee at the Twentieth Meeting Held at Detroit, MICH, September 14th and 15th, 1887*, 131–33. The society published detailed reports of each reunion, initially in pamphlet form, but later in collected bound volumes. I have drawn much of this discussion from the bound volumes and cite the reports accordingly. The overall title is *Report of the Proceedings of the Society of the Army of the Tennessee*.

14. *Report of the Proceedings of the Society of the Army of the Tennessee at the Third Annual Meeting Held at Chicago, Illinois, December 15th and 16th 1868*, 290.

15. *Report of the Proceedings of the Society of the Army of the Tennessee at the Sixteenth Annual Meeting Held at Cleveland OH, October 17th and 18th, 1883* in bound volume 4, 538.

16. The menu and toasts come from *Report of the Proceedings of the Society of the Army of the Tennessee at the Thirty-First Annual Meeting Held at Chicago, Illinois, October 10th and 11th, 1899*, 98–100. Other song lists can be found in *Report of the Proceedings of the Society of the Army of the Tennessee at the Tenth Annual Meeting Held at Washington DC, October 18th and 19th, 1876*, bound volume 2, 532–36.

17. *Report of the Proceedings of the Society of the Army of the Tennessee at the fifth Annual Meeting Held at Cincinnati Ohio, April 6th and 7th 1871*, 510.

18. *Report of the Proceedings of the Society of the Army of the Tennessee at the Fourth Annual Meeting Held at Louisville, Kentucky, November 17th and 18th 1869*, 359.

19. Hunt, *The Good Men Who Won the War*, explores the ways that soldiers in the Army of the Cumberland recalled their role in emancipation, but the members of the society seem to be much less interested in that aspect of the March.

20. *Report of the Proceedings of the Society of the Army of the Tennessee at the Sixteenth Annual Meeting Held at Cleveland, Ohio, October 17th and 18th, 1883*, bound volume 4, 508–10.

21. *Report of the Proceedings of the Society of the Army of the Tennessee at the Second Annual Meeting Held at St. Louis Missouri, November 13th and 14th, 1867*.

22. "General Sherman's Address," *New York Times*, November 17, 1867.

23. "Oration of General Cogswell," *The Army Reunion: With Reports of the Meetings of the Societies of the Army of the Cumberland; the Army of the Tennessee; the Army of the Ohio; and the Army of Georgia, Chicago, December 15 and 16, 1868*, 91–103.

24. *Report of the Proceedings of the Society of the Army of the Tennessee at the Twenty-First Annual Meeting Held at Toledo OH, September 5th and 6th, 1888*, bound volume 6, 97–99.

25. "Bummer," *Oxford English Dictionary Online*, http://www.oed.com accessed April 15, 2008. In his article "Recollections of a Bummer," Charles Belknap claimed that the name derived from "Boomer," a reference to the guns bombarding Savannah, but this seems rather unlikely. Belknap, "Recollections of a Bummer," 5.

26. Glatthaar, *The March to the Sea and Beyond*, 121–22.

27. Special Field Orders No. 120, November 9, 1864, http://www.cviog.uga.edu/Projects/gainfo/order2.htm, accessed November 6, 2007.

28. Porter, "General Sherman.".

29. P. R. McWilliams, "Marching through Georgia: "'So We Sang the Chorus from Atlanta to the Sea'; A Sketch of the Great March by One Who Tramped All The Way," in Hinman, *Camp and Field*, 463.

30. Belknap, "Recollections of a Bummer," 5.

31. Belknap, "Bentonville: What a Bummer Knows about It," 4–5.

32. Major Samuel Mahon, "The Forager in Sherman's Last Campaigns," MOLLUS 56, IA, 198; Charles A. Hopkins, "The March to the Sea," MOLLUS 36, RI, 56.

33. Belknap, "Recollections of a Bummer," 5.

34. Manning F. Force, "Marching across Carolina," MOLLUS 1, OH, 14–15.

35. Belknap, "Bentonville: What a Bummer Knows about It," 4.

36. Lt. Marcus Bates, "The Battle of Bentonville," MOLLUS 30 MN, 137.

37. Badeau, "Sherman's March to the Sea,"188, 197, 201.

38. Trowbridge, *The South*, 561–62.

39. Col. Charles D. Kerr, "From Atlanta to Raleigh," MOLLUS 26, MN, 208.

40. "From Atlanta to the Sea," *New York Times*, December 17, 1890. For another reference to the March as a picnic, see P. R. McWilliams, "Marching through Georgia," in Hinman, *Camp and Field*, 464.

41. Charles A. Hopkins, "The March to the Sea," MOLLUS 36, RI, 49.

42. Duncan, "The Army of the Tennessee" 167.

43. Force, "Marching across Carolina," 10–11.

44. Kerr, "From Atlanta to Raleigh," 210–11.

45. Mahon, "The Forager in Sherman's Last Campaigns," 192–93.

46. Ibid., 190, 194.

47. Adj. H. H. Rood, "Sketches of the Thirteenth Iowa," MOLLUS 55, IA, 128.

48. Hopkins, "The March to the Sea," 50–51.

49. Major Henry O. Marcy, "Sherman's Campaign in the Carolinas," MOLLUS 53, MA, 342.

50. Waters, *The Army Bummer and Good Night*, 3–5.

51. Ibid., 4–5; Belknap "Bentonville: What a Bummer Knows about It," 5.

52. Marcy, "Sherman's Campaign in the Carolinas," 340.

53. Hopkins, "The March to the Sea54–55.

54. Davis, *Camp-Fire Chats of the Civil War*, 316; Marcy, "Sherman's Campaign in the Carolinas," 343.

55. Brockett, *The Camp, the Battle Field, and the Hospital*, 378.

56. Marcy, "Sherman's Campaign in the Carolinas," 343.

57. On the history of the charivari, particularly in the American South, see Wyatt-Brown, *Southern Honor*, 435, 440.

58. Kerr, "From Atlanta to Raleigh," 212.

59. Marcy, "Sherman's Campaign in the Carolinas," 340.

60. Force, "Marching across Carolina," 12; Belknap, "Recollections of a Bummer," 6.

61. General Horace Porter, "General Sherman," *Harper's Weekly*, February 21, 1891.

62. Sullivan, *My Folks and the Civil War*, 79.

63. Force, "Marching across Carolina," 14.

64. William H. Duncan, "Through the Carolinas with the Army of Tennessee," MOLLUS 29, MN, 330–31; Marcy, "Sherman's Campaign in the Carolinas," 336–37.

65. Frank H. Putney, "Incidents of Sherman's March through the Carolinas," MOLLUS 48, WI, 381.

66. Ibid., 384–86.

67. Oake, *On the Skirmish Line*, 296.

68. Ibid., 301.

69. Ibid., 308.

70. Ibid., 317.

71. "Slocum, Soldier and Man," *New York Times*, May 5, 1894.

72. Belknap, "Recollections of a Bummer," 3–4, 5.

73. Mahon, "The Forager in Sherman's Last Campaigns," 199.

74. Kerr, "From Atlanta to Raleigh," 211.

75. Marcy, "Sherman's Campaign in the Carolinas," 340.

76. Mahon, "The Forager in Sherman's Last Campaigns," 191.

77. Oake, *On the Skirmish Line*, 273.

78. Mahon, "The Forager in Sherman's Last Campaigns," 200.

79. Davis, *Camp-Fire Chats of the Civil War*, 301.

80. Belknap, "Recollections of a Bummer," 4.

81. Ibid., 8.

82. Hopkins, "The March to the Sea," 57.

83. Force, "Marching across Carolina," 15.

84. Hickenlooper, *Sherman*.

85. Campbell, *When Sherman Marched North from the Sea*, 45–48.

86. Marcy, "Sherman's Campaign in the Carolinas," 345.

87. Putney, "Incidents of Sherman's March through the Carolinas," 386–87.

88. "From Atlanta to the Sea," *New York Times*, December 7, 1890.

89. Cornelius Cadle, "An Adjutant's Recollections," MOLLUS 5, OH, 391–92.

90. Duncan, "Through the Carolinas with the Army of the Tennessee," 331–32.

91. "Foraging. An interesting Trip after Rations in the Heart of South Carolina by Fred Reitz, Company I, 21st Wisconsin," in King and Derby, *Camp-Fire Sketches and Battle-Field Echoes of the Rebellion*, 296.

92. Putney, "Incidents of Sherman's March," 339.

93. Belknap, "Recollections of a Bummer," 9–10.

94. Ibid., 14–15.

95. Putney, "Incidents of Sherman's March," 339.

96. "Hiding Their Infant Moses," in Kirkland, *The Pictorial Book of Anecdotes*, 538–39.

97. E. J. Hale, "Sherman's Bummers," in Underwood, *The Women of the Confederacy*, 162.

98. Tourgée, *The Veteran and His Pipe*, 114–15.

99. Hickenlooper, *Sherman*.

100. "Soldiers at the Banquet," *New York Times*, November 18, 1892.

Chapter 5

1. William T. Sherman has also been the subject of countless biographies, including Walters, *Merchant of Terror*; Marszalek, *Sherman*; Fellman, *Citizen Sherman*; Hirshson, *The White Tecumseh*; and Woodworth, *Sherman*.

2. My discussion of the Grand Review in this paragraph comes from Royster, *The Destructive War*, 405–17. The Walt Whitman quote is on p. 411.

3. Sherman, *Memoirs*, 378.

4. Royster, *The Destructive War*, 410–11.

5. Sherman's address to his army, Headquarters Military division of the Mississippi, in the field, Washington, D.C., May 30, 1865, Special Field Orders No. 76. [Signed] W. T. Sherman, Major General. [Washington, D.C. 1865.]. http://hdl.loc.gov/loc.rbc/rbpe.20406o10a.

6. William M. Ferraro, "Creating Memory at the End of the Civil War."

7. Sherman, *Memoirs*, xvii–xviii.

8. Ibid., 180–83, 185, 190.

9. Ibid., 191–93.

10. Ibid., 194, 220–21, 236.

11. Ibid., 221, 254, 306–7.

12. Ibid., 284–85, 287.

13. Ibid. 287. In his report Sherman wrote: "Before one single public building had been fired by order, the smoldering fires, set by HAMPTON's order, were rekindled by the wind, and

communicated to the buildings around. About dark they began to spread, and got beyond the control of the brigade on duty within the city. . . . without hesitation I charge Gen. WADE HAMPTON with having burned his own City of Columbia, not with a malicious intent, or as the manifestation of a silly "Roman stoicism," but from folly and want of sense, in filling it with lint, cotton, and tinder. Our officers and men on duty worked well to extinguish the flames; but others not on duty, including the officers who had long been imprisoned there, rescued by us, may have assisted in spreading the fire after it had once begun, and may have indulged in unconcealed joy to see the ruin of the capital of South Carolina." "Report of Major General William T. Sherman, commanding General of the Mississippi, Goldsborough NC, April 4, 1865," U.S. War Department, *The War of the Rebellion*, ser. I, vol. 47, part 1, pp. 21–22.

14. Sherman, *Memoirs*, 324, 330.

15. Ibid., 180–81, 185.

16. Ibid., 244–45.

17. Ibid., 247–49.

18. Boynton, *Sherman's Historical Raid*, 8–9.

19. Historian Albert Castel went back to the official records for four sample chapters of Sherman's memoirs (those dealing with the Atlanta campaign) and he found them riddled with errors, exaggerations, and misstatements, leading him to conclude that many of Boynton's criticisms were fair, regardless of his reasons for writing them. Castel, "Prevaricating through Georgia: Sherman's Memoirs as a Source on the Atlanta Campaign."

20. Moulton, *The Review of General Sherman's Memoirs Examined*. See also General Judson Kilpatrick's multipart defense in the *New York Times*, January 20and 24, 1876; March 6, 1876. Trefousse, "Civil Warriors in Memory and Memoir: Grant and Sherman Remember," 550, 555–56.

21. Davis, *The Rise and Fall of the Confederate Government*, 2:563–64, 570.

22. Ibid., 627, 685–86.

23. Grant, *Personal Memoirs of Ulysses S. Grant* (1885), http://www2.hn.psu.edu/faculty/jmanis/poldocs/Personal-Memoirs-Grant.pdf, 492–93.

24. Ibid., 519, 572, 580.

25. Fellman, *Citizen Sherman*, 300, 303.

26. "General Sherman: Speech at Salem Illinois," *New York Times*, July 10, 1866.

27. "Proud of Plymouth Rock," *New York Times*, December 22, 1886.

28. "Gen. Sherman's Memories," *New York Times*, December 23, 1886.

29. Shurter, *The Complete Orations and Speeches of Henry W. Grady*, 14, 18.

30. Marszalek, "Celebrity in Dixie," 368–69, 371.

31. Ibid., 373–74; Garrett, *Atlanta and Environs*, 1:953.

32. Garrett, *Atlanta and Environs*, 1:953.

33. *Atlanta Constitution*, January 30 and 31, 1879.

34. *Atlanta Constitution*, January 31, 1879.

35. Marszalek, "Celebrity in Dixie," 376–78.

36. Newman, *Southern Hospitality*, 32; Doyle, *New Men, New Cities, New South*, 155.

37. Fellman, *Citizen Sherman*, 304; Garret, *Atlanta Environs* 2:32–33.

38. Fellman, *Citizen Sherman*, 304–5; Kimball, *International Cotton*, 212; "Mexican Veterans at Atlanta," *New York Times*, November 16, 1881.

39. *Atlanta Constitution*, November 19, 1881; reprinted in *New York Times*, November 23, 1881.

40. Marszalek, "Celebrity in Dixie," 382–83; Reston, *Sherman's March and Vietnam*, 52–53.

41. "Jeff Davis on Sherman: The Vanquished," *New York Times*, June 12, 1881.

42. Fellman, *Citizen Sherman*, 304.

43. Theodore Rosengarten, "New Views on the Burning of Columbia."

44. Jack Avery, "Reconstruction in Georgia," undated, in United Daughters of the Confederacy Collection, box 4, folder 16, Kenan Research Library, Atlanta History Center.

45. Fellman, *Citizen Sherman*, 148.

46. Maj. David F. Boyd, "Gen. W. T. Sherman: His Early Life in the South and His Relations with Southern Men," *Confederate Veteran* 18 (September 1910): 409.

47. Ibid., 413–14.

48. "Gushing Tribute to Gen W. T. Sherman," *Confederate Veteran* 18 (September 1910): 408; "Did Sherman 'Love' Southerners?," *Confederate Veteran* 18 (December 1910): 554; "Sherman's Love (?) for the South," *Confederate Veteran* 19 (May 1911): 223–24.

49. Steed, *Georgia*, 136.

50. Ibid., 136–37.

51. Mohr, *On the Threshold of Freedom*, 93–94; Reston *Sherman's March and Vietnam*, 81.

52. John C. Stiles, "Sherman in War and Peace," *Confederate Veteran* 24 (July 1916): 295–96.

53. Major Henry O. Marcy, "Sherman's Campaign in the Carolinas," MOLLUS 53, MA, 334.

54. "Slocum, Soldier and Man," *New York Times*, May 5, 1894.

55. Colonel Charles D. Kerr, "General William T. Sherman," MOLLUS 28, MN, 505; Hickenlooper, *Sherman*.

56. Sherman, "General Sherman in the Last Year of the War," 10–11, 18.

57. "A Look Back: General Sherman's Funeral in 1891 Drew Thousands," *Stltoday.com*, February 20, 2011.

58. Peter Schjeldal, "High and Low Relief: Augustus Saint-Gaudens at the Met," *New Yorker*, August 24, 2009. http://www.newyorker.com/arts/critics/artworld/2009/08/24/090824craw_artworld_schjeldahl?currentPage=1.

59. Elihu Root, *Speech By the Secretary of War Mr. Root upon the Unveiling of St. Gaudens' Statue of General Sherman in the City of New York, May 30, 1903.*, 6–7.

60. Grand Army Plaza, http://www.nycgovparks.org/parks/M062/highlights/13127.

61. Hagans, "Saint-Gaudens, Zorn, and the Godesslike Miss Anderson," 81.

62. New York City Public Art Curriculum, http://www.blueofthesky.com/publicart/works/sherman.htm. The statue has suffered over the years from constant exposure to the elements. It was re-gilded in 1989, but the gold leaf was deemed too bright and even "vulgar" or "tacky." In 1996 tinted wax was applied to the statue to tone down its brilliance and it is annually recoated. But the pigeons in the plaza claw at the wax, and their acidic droppings have been eating away at it, and the statue itself. In 2013 the Central Park Conservancy began a new restoration, which included regilding (with a darker patina) and a protective polyurethane

coating. "Restored Plaza Hailed (but Turn Down That General!)," *New York Times*, June 7, 1990; "It's General Sherman's Time to Shine, but Not Too Much," *New York Times* June 18, 2013.

63. Schjeldal, "High and Low Relief: Augustus Saint-Gaudens at the Met."

64. Henry Van Dyke, "The Statue of Sherman by St. Gaudens," in *The Poems of Henry Van Dyke*, 166.

65. Report of the Proceedings of the Society of the Army of the Tennessee at the Twenty-Third Annual Meeting Held at Chicago IL, October 7th and 8th, 1891, 389.

66. Ibid., 418; Keim, *Sherman*, 13.

67. Keim, *Sherman*, 14–15, 18–19; Jacob, *Testament to Union*, 12, 92–93.

68. Keim, *Sherman*, 21–22, 25–26. Jacob, *Testament to Union*, 95.

69. Keim, *Sherman*, 28; Jacob, *Testament to Union*, 95, 5–6.

70. Keim, *Sherman*, 33–55.

71. Ibid., 70–71, 78, 88.

72. Ibid., 67–68.

73. Reaves, *Historic Henry County*, 20.

74. Reston, *Sherman's March and Vietnam*, 92–93.

75. Förster and Nagler, *On the Road to Total War*, 8. Mark A. Smith has argued that Sherman did not stray far from the teachings of Jomini and Clausewitz on the March, in Smith, "Sherman's Unexpected Companions: Marching through Georgia with Jomini and Clausewitz." Several historians have explored the question of whether Sherman's March qualified as a "total war" or not, including Grimsley, "Modern War/Total War,", 379–89; Neely, "Was the Civil War a Total War?"; Hsieh, "Total War and the American Civil War Reconsidered: The End of an Outdated 'Master Narrative.'"

76. For an exhaustive look at the Lieber Code, see Witt, *Lincoln's Code*. Witt deals specifically with the March on pp. 276–84.

77. David Bosco, "Moral Principle vs. Military Necessity"; Carnahan, "Lincoln, Lieber, and the Laws of War."

78. "General Orders No. 100: The Lieber Code," http://avalon.law.yale.edu/19th_century/lieber.asp.

79. Ibid.

80. Sutherland, "Abraham Lincoln, John Pope, and the Origins of Total War," 577, 580, 584.

81. Carnahan, "Lincoln, Lieber, and the Laws of War," 218, 228.

82. Bosco, "Moral Principle vs. Military Necessity."

83. Lippitt, *Field Service in War*, 115–18.

84. Ibid., 130, 135.

85. Ibid., 138–39.

86. Towns, *Enduring Legacy*, 93–94; General Orders No. 73, http://www.sewanee.edu/faculty/willis/Civil_War/documents/LeeGenOrders73.html; Mrs. Elizabeth Wysor Klingberg, "Campaigns of Lee and Sherman," *Confederate Veteran* 24 (August 1916): 357–59.

87. William T. Sherman to James M. Calhoun et al., September 12, 1864; William T. Sherman to John Bell Hood, September 12, 1864; William T. Sherman to John Bell Hood, September 14, 1864, all in Simpson and Berlin, *Sherman's Civil War*, 708, 710–11.

88. Fellman, *Citizen Sherman*, 171, 179; Michael Fellman, "At the Nihilist Edge: Reflections on Guerrilla Warfare during the American Civil War" in Förster, and Nagler, *On the Road to Total War*, 535.

89. Fellman, *Citizen Sherman*, 182–83.

90. Ibid., 225–26.

91. Cornelius Cadle, "An Adjutant's Recollections," MOLLUS 5, OH, 397–99.

92. "Mr. Larrabee Defends the Army," *New York Times*, May 11, 1902.

93. "Fifteen Billion Human Lives Have Been Sacrificed in War since the Beginning of Authentic History . . . ," *New York Times*, September 13, 1914.

94. "Prof. Sloane Warns America against War," *New York Times*, September 20, 1914.

95. Yandell Henderson, "Ourselves as Germans See Us," *New York Times*, May 21, 1915.

96. Mary Cadwalader Jones, "What Sherman's Men Did," *New York Times*, May 26, 1915.

97. George Haven Putnam, "War as We Made It," *New York Times*, June 4, 1915.

98. John A. Bigelow, "Nothing but Their Eyes to Weep With," *New York Times*, June 13, 1915. Bigelow was the author of *The Principles of Strategy* (Philadelphia: Lippincott, 1894). Bigelow's letter was also reprinted in the *William and Mary Quarterly* under the title "Did Grant, Sherman and Sheridan Teach Militarism to Germany?," *William and Mary College Quarterly Historical Magazine* 24 (July 1915): 66–72.

99. "Georgia Was Not Belgium," *New York Times*, June 15, 1915.

100. Frank Jewett Mather Jr., "The Degree of War," *New York Times*, June 15, 1915.

101. John Bigelow, "Georgia and Belgium," *New York Times*, June 19, 1915.

102. Some contributors to *Confederate Veteran* complained about this new silence. See Dr. Henry E. Shepherd, "Historic Ironies—Sherman and German," *Confederate Veteran* 26 (January 1918): 17–19; Will T. Hale, "Historic Exposures Commended," *Confederate Veteran* 26 (February 1918): 91.

103. "Tells of German Insurance Scheme," *New York Times*, January 10, 1919; "Tells of Horrors Seen in Belgium," *New York Times*, January 16, 1919.

104. Ford, *Great Trade Route*, 243.

105. Ibid., 299–302.

106. Discussed in Reston, *Sherman's March and Vietnam*, 72.

107. "Many Protests Boost Sherman Stamp Sales," *Reading Eagle*, April 7, 1937.

108. See John F. Marszalek, "Philatelic Pugilists," in Hattaway and Rafuse, *The Ongoing Civil War*, 127–38; "Sherman's Picture on U.S. Postage Stamps," *Confederate Veteran* 19 (June 1911): 272.

109. Rosengarten, "New Views on the Burning of Columbia."

110. Reston, *Sherman's March and Vietnam*, 6.

111. Ibid., 7–8.

112. Ibid., 15–16.

113. Rosengarten, "New Views on the Burning of Columbia."

Chapter 6

1. Conwell, *Magnolia Journey*, 92.

2. McPherson, *Reconstructing Dixie*, 99; Schmeller, *Perceptions of Race and Nation in English and American Travel Writers, 1833–191*. See Cox, *Traveling South*, 15, for a discussion of the ways that antebellum travel writers helped to shape American national identity. See McIntyre, *Souvenirs of the Old South*, 4, for changing notions of region after the Civil War. Stanonis's introduction to *Dixie Emporium* suggests that even today travelers are still seeking some kind of "authentic" experience.

3. Nelson, *Ruin Nation*, 2–3, 5, 9.

4. Dennett, *The South as It Is*, 201; Ferguson, *America During and After the War*, 219.

5. Andrews, *The South since the War*, 215. For other descriptions of twisted ties, see Andrews, 31–32; Ferguson, *America During and After the War*, 221.

6. Dennett, *The South as It Is*, 267.

7. Trowbridge, *The South*, 501, 571.

8. King, *The Great South*, 363; Somers, *The Southern States since the War*, 72; Trowbridge, *The South*, 506–7. Somers attributes this to the Georgia Central investing its money in London right before the war.

9. Trowbridge, *The South*, 475, 502.

10. Ibid., 476–77, 481; Dennett, *The South as It Is*, 260.

11. Somers, *The Southern States since the War*, 70–71; Powers, *Afoot and Alone*, 47.

12. Conwell, *Magnolia Journey*, 92–93.

13. Kennaway, *On Sherman's Track*, 119.

14. Ferguson, *America During and After the War*, 221–22.

15. Dennett, *The South as It Is*, 233–34, 260.

16. Andrews, *The South since the War*, 32. Andrews's entry is dated September 12, 1865; Dennett's are from December 11 and December 23, 1865.

17. Powers, *Afoot and Alone*, 22–23.

18. On faithful slaves, see Trowbridge, *The South*, 478–49, 549. For white Southern resentment, see Powers, *Afoot and Alone*, 60–62, and Dennett *The South as It Is*, 183.

19. See Erik S. Schmeller's discussion of Henry Latham in particular. Schmeller, *Perceptions of Race and Nation in English and American Travel Writers, 1833–1914*, 64–67, 92.

20. Trowbridge, *The South*, 455, 464. See O'Donovan, *Becoming Free in the Cotton South* on the challenges facing the Freedmen's Bureau as a labor organizer.

21. Conwell, *Magnolia Journey*, 93.

22. Dennett, *The South as It Is*, 183.

23. Kennaway, *On Sherman's Track*, 117.

24. Trowbridge, *The South*, 576. On white anger and resentment during Reconstruction, see Rubin, *A Shattered Nation*.

25. Trowbridge *The South*, 478.

26. Ferguson, *America During and After the War*, 212, 222–23.

27. Trowbridge, *The South*, 456.

28. Ibid., 552.

29. Andrews, *The South since the War*, 7.

30. Trowbridge, *The South*, 456–57.

31. "The March of Sergeant Bates," *New York Times*, March 5, 1868.

32. The basic contours of Sergeant Bates's story are drawn from Lomask, "Carrying the Stars and Stripes Unfurled, from Vicksburg to Washington"; Bates, *Sergeant Bates' March*.

33. "Mark Twain's Letter from Washington," *Territorial Enterprise*, February 27, 1868, http://www.twainquotes.com/18680227t.html, accessed July 16, 2012.

34. Bates, *Sergeant Bates' March*, 13–14; Harrington, *Civil War Milledgeville*, 27–28.

35. Bates, *Sergeant Bates' March*, 15.

36. Ibid., 17.

37. Ibid., 16.

38. Coulter, "Father Sherman's 'March to the Sea,'" 377–78.

39. "A Sherman 'March' That Georgia Stopped," *Literary Digest*, May 19, 1906, 748–49; Coulter, "Father Sherman's 'March to the Sea,'" 378–82.

40. "Sherman's March Over," *New York Times*, May 4, 1906; Coulter, "Father Sherman's 'March to the Sea,'" 384–85.

41. "Father Sherman's March," *Los Angeles Times*, May 16, 1906.

42. "Comment," *Harper's*, May 12, 1906.

43. Coulter, "Father Sherman's 'March to the Sea,'" 388–92.

44. On Atlanta's rising from the ashes, see Link, *Atlanta, Cradle of the New South*, 53–60.

45. Kennaway, *On Sherman's Track*, 115–16. On speed of rebuilding, see also Latham, *Black and White*, 129.

46. Ferguson, *America During and After the War*, 228.

47. Andrews, *The South since the War*, 339–40.

48. Reid, *After the War*, 355.

49. Ibid., 356; Trowbridge, *The South* 453.

50. King, *The Great South*, 350.

51. Andrews, *The South since the War*, 29; Dennett, *The South as It Is*, 230.

52. Andrews *The South since the War*, 33–34.

53. Ibid., 31.

54. Dennett, *The South as It Is*, 230, 242.

55. Trowbridge, *The South*, 555–56.

56. Ibid., 559.

57. Pike, *The Prostrate State*, 114–15. Englishman George Campbell made much the same argument in *White and Black*, 331.

58. Brown, *I Travel by Train*, 60.

59. Branston, *Let the Band Play "Dixie,"* 240.

60. Price, *America after Sixty Years*, 208.

61. Steed, *Georgia*, 15.

62. Graves, "Marching through Georgia Sixty Years After," 259.

63. Graham, "Marching through Georgia: Following Sherman's Footsteps To-Day (Part I)," 614–20.

64. Graham, "Marching through Georgia: Following Sherman's Footsteps To-Day (Part II)," 813–23.

65. Steed, *Georgia*, 41; Price, *America after Sixty Years*, 211–12.

66. Perkerson, *White Columns in Georgia*, 7, 61–62.

67. Price, *America after Sixty Years*, 203.

68. Brown, *I Travel by Train*, 62–63.

69. De Laubenfels, "Where Sherman Passed By," 381–95; de Laubenfels, "With Sherman through Georgia: A Journal," 288–300. The *Geographical Review* appears to have been written for a more specialized, scholarly audience. The *Georgia Historical Quarterly* article contains a transcription of the brief journal. The articles contain largely the same information, and the argument is essentially the same in both.

70. De Laubenfels, "With Sherman through Georgia," 291.

71. Ibid., 291–92.

72. Examples of the phoenix metaphor can be found in Derry, *Georgia*, 32; Field, *Bright Skies and Dark Shadows*, 101–2. Adoption of new seal in Garrett, *Atlanta and Environs*, 2:131.

73. Derry, *Georgia*, 41; Ralph, *Dixie; or, Southern Scenes and Sketches*, 242; McClure, *The South*, 58–59.

74. McClure, *The South*, 58–59, 70.

75. Ibid., 40–41.

76. Graham, "Marching through Georgia: Following Sherman's Footsteps To-Day (Part I)."

77. Branston, *Let the Band Play "Dixie,"* 244–45.

78. Field, *Bright Skies and Dark Shadows*, 106.

79. *The Civil War Centennial, a Report to the Congress* (Washington: [For sale by the Supt. of Docs., U.S. Govt. Print. Off.], 1968), 3; Cook, *Troubled Commemoration*.

80. *The Civil War Centennial, a Report to the Congress*. See highlights from the individual state reports, 51–62.

81. Cook, *Troubled Commemoration*, 69, 72–74; Georgia Civil War Centennial Commission, "Civil War Centennial Manual for Georgians," 9, 12.

82. Georgia Civil War Centennial Commission, "Civil War Centennial Manual for Georgians," 13.

83. Georgia Civil War Centennial Commission, "Report of the Georgia Civil War Centennial Commission." On a general decline of Southern interest in the Centennial once the Confederacy started losing, see Cook, *Troubled Commemoration*, 206.

84. Quoted in Cook, *Troubled Commemoration*, 60.

85. "Rivers Bridge Fight Recalled," *News and Courier* (Charleston), May 12, 1960. Thanks to Dan Bell of the South Carolina State Parks Department for telling me about this.

86. "The North Carolina Confederate Centennial Commission," http://www.history.ncdcr.gov/centennial/features/confederate.htm.

87. Naipaul, *A Turn in the South*, 99.

88. Ibid., 100–101.

89. Reed, *Whistling Dixie*, 31.

90. Reston, *Sherman's March and Vietnam*, 41, 87.

91. Ibid., 67.

92. Horwitz, *Confederates in the Attic*, 283.

93. Ibid., 76, 284,

94. Ibid., 312–13.

95. The theme of self-discovery is a powerful one. Even a guide to retracing the March by bicycle encouraged riders to "transcend its Civil War theme," on the road to finding themselves. Bailey and Bailey, *Cycling through Georgia*, x.

96. Reston, *Sherman's March and Vietnam*, 5–6, 196–97.

97. Ellis, *Marching through Georgia*, 5.

98. Ibid., 3, 71, 124.

99. Ibid., 109.

100. Ibid., 302.

101. North Carolina Historic Sites, Bentonville Battlefield, http://www.nchistoricsites.org/bentonvi/.

102. "Southerners Resist Monument to Sherman," *Fayetteville Observer-Times*, July 10, 1994; Loewen, *Lies across America*, 288–89; Martinez and Harris, "Graves, Worms, and Epitaphs: Confederate Monuments in the Southern Landscape," 282.

Chapter 7

1. Connelly, *Will Success Spoil Jeff Davis?*, 12, 125. The author T. Lawrence Connelly is actually Thomas L. Connelly, a noted Civil War historian.

2. Overviews of the intersection of the Civil War and American popular culture can be found in Cullen, *The Civil War in Popular Culture*; Fahs and Waugh, *The Memory of the Civil War in American Culture*; Kaufman, *The Civil War in American Culture*. Sherman and popular culture specifically can be found in Caudill and Ashdown, *Sherman's March in Myth and Memory*.

3. S. H. M. Byers, "A Historic War Song: How and Where I Wrote 'Sherman's March to the Sea,'" MOLLUS 55, IA, 393–95; McWhirter, *Battle Hymns*, 169–70.

4. Byers, "A Historic War Song," 400.

5. Ibid., 396–400; Sherman, *Memoirs*, 282.

6. Byers, "A Historic War Song," 398–99.

7. The chorus goes as follows: "Then sang we a song to our chieftain, / That echo'd o'er riv-er and lea, / And the stars in our banners shone brighter / When Sherman march'd down to the sea." This transcription comes from "When Sherman Marched Down to the Sea; Marching Song of Sherman's Army" (Cincinnati and St Louis: A. C. Peters & Bro.; J. L. Peters & Bro., 1865), http://scriptorium.lib.duke.edu/sheetmusic/b/b20/b2047/; Sherman, *Memoirs*, 282–83; Byers, "A Historic War Song," 398–99. Two other versions, one attributed to an entirely different author, can also be found in the Library of Congress's Historic American Sheet Music collections. See "Sherman's March to the Sea. Air: Kitty Tyrrell," published by Randolph, 770

Broadway, N.Y. [n.d.], and "Sherman's March to the Sea. Words (in part) and music by David A. Warden," published by the composer, 311 German Street, [n.d.], http://memory.loc.gov/ ammem/amsshtml/amsshome.html.

8. Pat Padua, "Sherman's March to the Sea," *In the Muse Performing Arts Blog* from the Library of Congress, http://blogs.loc.gov/music/2010/08/sherman. The YouTube link is embedded in the blog post.

9. Tribble, "Marching through Georgia," 425–26.

10. Henry Clay Work, "Marching through Georgia, in Honor of Maj. Gen. Sherman's Famous March 'from Atlanta to the sea'" (Chicago: Root and Cady, 1865), http://scriptorium.lib .duke.edu/sheetmusic/b/b20/b2018/.

11. Tribble, "Marching through Georgia," 423.

12. Ibid., 428; Royster, *The Destructive War*, 364–65.

13. "Girl Tabooes Northern Song," *Atlanta Constitution*, June 12, 1902; "Wouldn't Sing 'Marching through Georgia,'" *New York Times*, June 12, 1902; "Southern Girl Refuses to Sing Northern Song," *Chicago Daily Tribune*, June 13, 1902; Cox, *Dixie's Daughters*, 118–19.

14. Marshall, *Creating a Confederate Kentucky*; Cox, *Dixie's Daughters*, 118–19.

15. "An Unreconstructed Rebel," *Chicago Daily Tribune*, June 15, 1902.

16. "Partisan Teaching in Public Schools," *Atlanta Constitution*, June 17, 1902.

17. "Wouldn't Sing Marching through Georgia," *Confederate Veteran* 9 (July 1902): 291.

18. "Miss Laura Galt Is Given Medal," *Atlanta Constitution*, August 2, 1902; "Gold Medal for Miss Galt," *Atlanta Constitution*, August 2, 1902.

19. "Laura Galt Honored in the Far West," *Confederate Veteran* 11 (January 1903): 5–6. UCV Camp John Morgan (no. 448), in De Queen, Arkansas, passed a similar, though shorter, resolution celebrating Galt in September 1902; see *Confederate Veteran* 11 (March 1903): 147.

20. Caroline Janney makes a similar argument about the distinctions between reunion and reconciliation in *Remembering the Civil War*.

21. "Augusta's Social Side," *Atlanta Constitution*, November 15, 1903.

22. "Prominent People," *Los Angeles Times*, February 21, 1904.

23. "United Daughters at Charleston," *Confederate Veteran* 12 (February 1904): 61-64; "Kentucky in the Southern Confederacy," *Confederate Veteran* 14 (August 1906): 360; "The Virginia Division," *Confederate Veteran* 26 (August 1918): 369.

24. Jimmy Carter, "Washington Press Club Dinner Remarks at the Annual Dinner Honoring New Members of Congress," January 26, 1977, http://www.presidency.ucsb.edu/ws/index .php?pid=7178.

25. Boller, *Presidential Anecdotes*, 344.

26. H. E. Hagenbach, "Sherman's Advance on Savannah," Cincinnati, 1864, http://lcweb2 .loc.gov/diglib/ihas/loc.natlib.ihas.200000213/default.html; "Confederate Songs and Sheet Music," *Confederate Veteran* 39 (October 1931): 392–93.

27. "Sherman's March," Air: Ginger blue, by Michael Fee (H. De Marsan, No. 54 Chatham Street, N.Y., n.d.), http://memory.loc.gov/ammem/amsshtml/amsshome.html. On the evolution of minstrelsy during the Civil War, see McWhirter, *Battle Hymns*, 137–45.

28. David Warden, "When Sherman's On De Track," ([Philadelphia?], Pennsylvania, Wm. R. Smith, 1865), http://scriptorium.lib.duke.edu/sheetmusic/b/b20/b2046/.

29. "A New Song for Sherman & Sheridan. Air-'Villikins and His Dinah'" (n.p., n.-d., http://memory.loc.gov/ammem/amsshtml/amsshome.html.

30. Thomas Fanning, "The Sherman Bummers" (Cincinnati: Helmick, 1881), http://hdl.loc.gov/loc.music/sm1881.08878.

31. "Sherman's Raid through Georgia," *Confederate Veteran* 12 (March 1904): 103.

32. Ibid.

33. Steven Hull's White Mansions Page.

34. Ibid.

35. On other 1970s popular music influenced by the Civil War, and the Confederacy in particular, see Cullen, *Civil War in Popular Culture*, 108–38.

36. Steven Hull's White Mansions Page; Ballad of White Mansions.

37. Barnard, *Photographic Views*; "George Barnard's Patriotic Views of Sherman's Campaign," Wisconsin Historical Society, http://www.wisconsinhistory.org/whi/feature/barnard/.

38. Davis, *George N. Barnard*, 85.

39. Barnard, *Photographic Views*, vii, xviii; Davis, *George N. Barnard*, 89, 170; Bailey and Fraser, *Portraits of Conflict*, 5–7.

40. Davis, *George N. Barnard*, 90–91, 93; Bailey and Fraser, *Portraits of Conflict*, 7.

41. Davis, *George N. Barnard*, 170.

42. I am very grateful to Tom Beck of University of Maryland Baltimore County Special Collections for allowing me to see and touch UMBC's copy of *Photographic Views*.

43. Davis, *George N. Barnard*, 171.

44. Timothy Sweet, *Traces of War*, 138–40, 143, 192; Davis, *George N. Barnard*, 177; Bailey and Fraser, *Portraits of Conflict*, 7.

45. Sweet, *Traces of War*, "Destruction of Madison Station, Georgia, December 3, 1864," and "Destruction of Millen Junction, Georgia, December 3, 1864," *Harper's Weekly*, January 7, 1865; "Winnsborough, South Carolina," "Foragers 'Starting Out' in the Morning," and "Foragers Returning at Night," *Harper's Weekly*, April 1, 1865.

46. The *Frank Leslie's* images were collected into a two-volume set during the 1880s and republished as Leslie, Mottelay, and Campbell-Copeland, *The Soldier in Our Civil War*. All of the following page citations are to volume 2: "Burning the Railroad Roundhouse, Atlanta," 329; "Sherman's 'Bummers' Foraging in South Carolina," 360; "Federal Troops Foraging in Georgia," 41.

47. Sweet, *Traces of War*, 146–47; "General News," *New York Times*, October 3, 1865; "Doyle News."

48. Gallagher, *Causes Won, Lost, and Forgotten*, 136–40, 184–87.

49. "Don Troiani: Historical Art Prints."

50. Gallon Historical Art, Inc.

51. Official Mort Küntsler Website.

52. Melville, "The March to the Sea," in *Battle-Pieces*, 128–32.

53. Sweet, *Traces of War*, 193–94.

54. Milder, "The Rhetoric of Melville's *Battle-Pieces*," 185–86.

55. Melville, "The Frenzy in the Wake," in *Battle-Pieces*, 133–34.

56. "Ethiopia Saluting the Colors," The Walt Whitman Archive. There is something about this poem that reminds me of Winslow Homer's painting *Near Andersonville*, which has been compellingly analyzed by Peter Wood. Wood, *Near Andersonville*.

57. George Hutchinson and David Drews, "Racial Attitudes," in J. R. LeMaster and Donald D. Kummings, *Walt Whitman: An Encyclopedia* (New York: Garland Publishing, 1998), http://whitmanarchive.org/criticism/current/encyclopedia/entry_44.html; "About Ethiopia Saluting the Colors," The Library of Congress Song of America Project, http://www.loc.gov/creativity/hampson/about_ethiopia.html.

58. Holmes, *The Poetical Works of Oliver Wendell Holmes in Three Volumes*, 2:35–36. The first three stanzas (excluding "Soon shall Richmond's . . . ") were also included, without attribution in Moore, *The Civil War in Song and Story*, 194.

59. J. Ward Childs, "The 15th Veteran Corps," in King, and Derby, *Camp-Fire Sketches and Battle-Field Echoes of the Rebellion*, 103. Childs served as a private in the 53rd Regiment, Massachusetts Infantry, National Park Service Soldiers and Sailors Database, http://www.nps.gov/civilwar/soldiers-and-sailors-database.htm.

60. Charles G. Halpine, "Song of Sherman's Army," in Browne, *Bugle-Echoes*, 268–70.

61. Brooks, "Sherman's March," in *Old Ace and Other Poems*, 37–41; "Sherman's March," *Los Angeles Times*, October 22, 1892.

62. Brigadier General John Tilson, "The March to the Sea," in Report of the Proceedings of the Society of the Army of the Tennessee at the Eighth Annual Meeting Held at Springfield, Illinois, October 14th and 15th, 1874, 250–59.

63. Lawrence, "Resting Place," in *Memory Hill*, 52–53.

64. Spivey, "Sherman," "Up from Underground," "Worthies in Bronze," in *To Die in Atlanta*, 9–12.

65. Spivey, "A Man of War," "This Tropic City Savannah," in ibid., 26, 32.

66. Spivey, "A Burning House," in ibid., 27; Jim Miles, *To The Sea*, 227.

67. Spivey, "Mrs. Brown Cooking Turnips," in *To Die in Atlanta*, 28–29.

Chapter 8

1. Silber, *The Romance of Reunion*.

2. Peck, *The M'Donalds*, 5.

3. Ibid., 11–12, 18–19, 22, 30, 62, 103, 175, 186–87.

4. Ibid., 52, 58, 108, 177, 180, 183.

5. Ibid., 114–21; *Report of Major General William T. Sherman to the Hon. Committee on the Conduct of the War*.

6. Peck, *The M'Donalds*, 175, 177, 180, 182–83.

7. Bird, *Sherman's March to the Sea*.

8. "Joel Chandler Harris, (1845–1908)," *New Georgia Encyclopedia*, http://www.georgiaencyclopedia.org/nge/Article.jsp?id=h–525; Inscoe, "The Confederate Home Front Sanitized," 664–65.

9. Harris, *On the Plantation*.

10. Ibid., 224–26; Inscoe, "The Confederate Homefront Sanitized," 664–66; King, *Sound of Drums*, 155–57.

11. Harris, *On the Plantation*, 228–29.

12. Ibid., 230.

13. Ibid., 223–24.

14. Ibid., 231–32.

15. Inscoe, "The Confederate Home Front Sanitized," 669.

16. Kennedy, *Cicely*, 57–60, 62.

17. Ibid., 85.

18. Ibid., 140–43, 199–200.

19. Ibid., 95–96.

20. Ibid., 304–5.

21. Gardner, *Blood & Irony*, 182.

22. Margaret Mitchell and *Gone with the Wind* have been the subjects of scores of books and articles. A sample would include Farr, *Margaret Mitchell of Atlanta*; Harwell (ed.), *Gone with the Wind as Book and Film*; Mitchell and Harwell, *Margaret Mitchell's Gone with the Wind Letters, 1936–1949*; Haskell, *Frankly My Dear*; *Margaret Mitchell: The Book, the Film, the Woman*; Pyron, *Recasting: Gone with the Wind in American Culture*; Pyron, *Southern Daughter*.

23. Pyron, *Southern Daughter*, 240; Taylor, *Scarlett's Women*, 46, 52; Farr, *Margaret Mitchell of Atlanta*, 13, 15–17.

24. William S. Howland, "Margaret Mitchell, Romantic Realist," in *Margaret Mitchell: The Book, the Film, the Woman*, 1996; Farr, *Margaret Mitchell of Atlanta*, 15.

25. Kilgore, Smith, and Tuck, *A History of Clayton County, Georgia*, 198.

26. Mitchell and Harwell, *Margaret Mitchell's Gone with the Wind Letters*, 2–3, 43, 55–57. Mitchell continued to respond to challenges to her research after the film came out. See 307–10.

27. Pyron, *Southern Daughter*, 240–43; Norman S. Berg, "The Real Story of Gone with the Wind," in *Margaret Mitchell: The Book, the Film, the Woman*, n.p.

28. Malcolm Cowley, "Going with the Wind," in Pyron, *Recasting: Gone with the Wind in American Culture*, 19.

29. Mitchell, *Gone with the Wind*, 391–92.

30. Ibid., 417–23.

31. Ibid., 435–40.

32. Ibid., 440.

33. Ibid., 440–43.

34. Ibid., 391, 441–42.

35. Howard, *Gone with the Wind: The Screenplay*, 7.

36. Wilbur G. Kurtz, "How Hollywood Built Atlanta," Harwell, *Gone with the Wind as a Book and Film*, 139–43.

37. Harwell, *Gone with the Wind as a Book and Film*, 170; Catherine Clinton, "Gone with the Wind," in Carnes, *Past Imperfect*, 132.

38. Howard, *Gone with the Wind: The Screenplay*, 87, 138.

39. Chadwick, *The Reel Civil War*, 194–97, 204; Clinton, "Gone with the Wind," 132.

40. Harmetz, *On the Road to Tara*, 106.

41. "Another Yankee Invasion: Auditioning for Scarlett Created Chaos in Alabama," *Atlanta Journal and Constitution*, October 19, 1975.

42. Farr, *Margaret Mitchell of Atlanta*, 11.

43. Nell Battle Lewis, "Scarlett Materializes," in Harwell, *Gone with the Wind as Book and Film*, 172.

44. This section deals with about a dozen novels or plays that engage substantially with Sherman's March. Of course, countless other books include mention of the March, or a few scenes. There is simply not space to discuss them all. Two books that fall into this category are Price, *New Moon Rising* (this is volume 2 of her popular St. Simon's trilogy), and Crane, *Freedom's Banner*.

45. Brick, *Jubilee*.

46. Ibid., 267.

47. Ibid., 282–93.

48. Ibid., 305–6.

49. Lon Tinkle, "No Time for Love," *New York Times*, March 4, 1956.

50. Haeger, *My Dearest Cecelia*.

51. Ibid.; "Georgia Mysteries: Sherman's Girlfriend," http://georgiamysteries.blogspot .com/2009/05/shermans-girlfriends.html.

52. Rawl, *From the Ashes of Ruin*, 44, 111.

53. Ibid., 107, 117–19.

54. Ibid., 143.

55. Ibid., 153, 160–61.

56. Bowne, *Louisa: A Southern Girl's Escape in 1864*.

57. Babe, *Rebel Women*.

58. Ibid., act 1, p. 17.

59. Ibid., act 3, p. 49.

60. Alan Rich, "Wringing the Belles," *New York Magazine*, June 21, 1976, 64; Clive Barnes, "Stage: Rebel Women," *New York Times*, June 4, 1976.

61. Walter Kerr, "From Brilliance, to Bewilderment, to a Blunder," *New York Times*, June 13, 1976.

62. Howel, *Black Heritage*.

63. Ibid., 44–45, 49, 51.

64. Ibid., 56.

65. Barnes, *Sherman's Fifth Corps*.

66. Ibid., location 1253 of 4312.

67. Jakes, *Savannah*.

68. Ibid., 109, 163.

69. Bass, *Sherman's March*, 13.

70. Ibid., 56, 67.

71. Ibid., 134, 139.

72. Doctorow, *The March*. It won the 2005 National Book Critics Circle Award, the 2006 PEN/Faulkner fiction award, and the 2006 Michael Shaara Award for Excellence in Civil War fiction. It was also a finalist for the 2005 National Book Award and the 2006 Pulitzer Prize.

73. Ibid., 18–19, 66–67, 70–73, 114–20.

74. Ibid., 9, 61–62.

75. Ibid., 358–59.

76. "The March: Steppenwolf Theater Company," http://www.steppenwolf.org/Plays-Events/productions/index.aspx?id=530; Hedy Weiss, "Steppenwolf Tackles Doctorow's 'The March,' in World-Premiere Production," *Chicago Sun Times*, April 11, 2012.

77. Chadwick, *The Reel Civil War*, 74–76.

78. D. W. Griffith, *The Birth of a Nation*, 1915; Gallagher, *Causes Won, Lost, and Forgotten*, 44–45.

79. Caudill and Ashdown, *Sherman's March in Myth and Memory*, 130–31; Rogin, "'The Sword Became a Flashing Vision': D. W. Griffith's *The Birth of a Nation*."

80. Kaufman, *The Civil War in American Culture*, 30–33.

81. Gallagher, *Causes Won, Lost, and Forgotten*, 93–95; Caudill and Ashdown, *Sherman's March in Myth and Memory*, 133–34.

82. Ross McElwee, *Sherman's March*; McPherson, *Reconstructing Dixie*, 132–33.

83. Kaufman, *The Civil War in American Culture*, 116–20. For a detailed critique of Burns's series, see Toplin, *Ken Burns's the Civil War*.

84. "Sherman's March. the Shocking Campaign That Ended the Civil War," documentary, History Channel (2007).

85. http://www.history.com/interactives/shermans-march.

Conclusion

1. "On Location in Covington, Newton County, Georgia," brochure.

2. Atlanta Civil War Roundtable Scrapbooks, MSS 808, Kenan Research Center, Atlanta History Center.

3. Madison Georgia brochure.

4. "The Southern Loop" brochure. The towns are Fairburn, Palmetto, Newnan, Hogansville, Sharpsburg, and Senoia.

5. "Welcome to Historic Eatonton, Georgia, USA. Self-Guided Tour Brochure."

6. "Griswoldville Monument set for Dedication Saturday," *Macon.com*, December 1, 2012.

7. "US Fish and Wildlife Service, Camp Lawton Archaeological Site," http://www.fws.gov/camplawtonsite/index.html.

8. Reston, *Sherman's March and Vietnam*, 96.

9. This section is adapted from "Anne Rubin Follows the Traces of Sherman's March," http://uncpressblog.com/2009/06/24/anne-rubin-follows-the-traces-of-shermans-march/.

BIBLIOGRAPHY

Primary Sources

Manuscript Collections

Kenan Research Library, Atlanta History Center, Atlanta, Ga.

    Civil War Roundtable of Atlanta Scrapbooks, 1960–89.

    United Daughters of the Confederacy Collection

Published Works

Anderson, Jean Bradley. *Durham County: A History of Durham County, North Carolina.* Durham: Duke University Press, 1990.

Andrews, Eliza Frances. *The War-Time Journal of a Georgia Girl, 1864–1865.* Lincoln: University of Nebraska Press, 1997.

Andrews, Sidney. *The South since the War: As Shown by Fourteen Weeks of Travel and Observation in Georgia and the Carolinas.* Boston: Ticknor & Fields, 1866.

The Army Reunion: With Reports of the Meetings of the Societies of the Army of the Cumberland; the Army of the Tennessee; the Army of the Ohio; and the Army of Georgia, Chicago, December 15 and 16, 1868. Chicago: S. C. Griggs and Company, 1869.

Asch, Nathan. *The Road: In Search of America.* New York: W. W. Norton, 1937.

Avary, Myrta Lockett. *Dixie after the War: An Exposition of Social Conditions Existing in the South, during the Twelve Years Succeeding the Fall of Richmond.* Freeport, N.Y.: Books for Libraries Press, 1906.

Babe, Thomas. *Rebel Women.* New York: Dramatists Play Service, 1977.

Badeau, General Adam. "Sherman's March to the Sea." In *Civil War Stories, Retold from St. Nicholas,* 188–201. New York: Century, 1905.

Bailey, Sue C., and William H. Bailey. *Cycling through Georgia: Tracing Sherman's March from Chickamauga to Savannah.* Atlanta: Susan Hunter, 1989.

Barnard, George N. *Photographic Views of Sherman's Campaign.* With a new preface by Beaumont Newhall. New York: Dover, 1977.

Barnes, J. A. *Sherman's Fifth Corps: A Civil War Novel.* N.p: MRC Press, 2011.

Bass, Cynthia. *Sherman's March.* New York: Bantam, 1995.

Bates, Gilbert H. *Sergeant Bates' March, Carrying the Stars and Stripes Unfurled, from Vicksburg to Washington.* New York: B. W. Hitchcock, 1868.

Beeson, Leola Selman. *History Stories of Milledgeville and Baldwin County.* Macon, Ga.: J. W. Burke, 1943.

————. *The One Hundred Years of the Old Governors' Mansion, Milledgeville, Georgia, 1838–1938.* Macon, Ga.: J. W. Burke, 1938.

Belknap, Charles E. "Bentonville: What a Bummer Knows about It." Washington D.C.: Military Order of the Loyal Legion of the United States. *Commandery of the District of Columbia War Papers* 121893.

————. "Recollections of a Bummer." Washington D.C.: Military Order of the Loyal Legion of the United States. *Commandery of the District of Columbia War Papers* 28, 1898.

Bell, De Loss Ernest, ed. *De Loss Ernset Bell's Treasury of Civil War Humor.* Moreno Valley, Calif.: Jolly Publications, 1998.

Bird, E. G. *Sherman's March to the Sea; or, Fighting His Way through Georgia. A Realistic Romance.* New York: Munro's Pub. House, 1891.

Bizell, Oscar M., ed. *The Heritage of Sampson County, North Carolina.* Newton Grove, N.C.: Sampson County Historical Society, 1983.

Bonner, James C. *Milledgeville: Georgia's Antebelleum Capital.* Athens: University of Georgia Press, 1978.

Botume, Elizabeth Hyde. *First Days amongst the Contrabands.* New York: Arno Press, 1968.

Bowne, Elizabeth. *Louisa: A Southern Girl's Escape in 1864.* Westville, Fla.: New Hope Press, 1995.

Boyd, Kenneth W. *Georgia Historical Markers-Coastal Counties.* Marietta, Ga.: Cherokee Publishing Company, 1991.

Boynton, Henry V. *Sherman's Historical Raid: The Memoirs in the Light of the Record; A Review Based upon Compilations from the Files of the War Office.* Cincinnati: Wilstach, Baldwin, 1875.

Brannen, Dorothy. *Life in Old Bulloch: The Story of Wiregrass County in Georgia.* Gainesville, Ga.: Magnolia Press, 1987.

Branston, Ursula. *Let the Band Play "Dixie"! Improvisations on a Southern Signature Tune.* London: George G. Harrap, 1940.

Brick, John. *Jubilee.* Garden City, N.Y.: Doubleday, 1956.

Brockett, Linus Pierpont. *The Camp, the Battle Field, and the Hospital; or, Lights and Shadows of the Great Rebellion. Including Adventures of Spies and Scouts, Thrilling Incidents, Daring Exploits, Heroic Deeds, Wonderful Escapes, Sanitary and Hospital Scenes, Prison Scenes, Prison Experiences, Etc., Etc.* Philadelphia: National Pub. Co., 1866.

Brooks, Fred Emerson. *Old Ace, and Other Poems.* New York: Cassell, 1894.

Brown, Rollo Walter. *I Travel by Train.* New York: D. Appleton-Century, 1939.

Browne, Francis F. *Bugle-Echoes: A Collection of the Poetry of the Civil War, Northern and Southern.* New York: White, Stokes, & Allen, 1886.

"'Bummers' in Sherman's Army." *Soldiers' and Sailors' Half-Dime Tales of the Late Rebellion* 1, no. 1 (1868): 3–14.

Burns, Ken, Ric Burns, Geoffrey C. Ward, and David G. McCullough. *The Civil War.* Documentary film. PBS, 1990.

Camp, Lynn Robinson. *Morgan County, Georgia.* Charleston: Arcadia, 2004.

Campbell, George. *White and Black: The Outcome of a Visit to the United States.* London: Chatto and Windus, 1879.

Caputo, Philip. *A Rumor of War*. New York: Holt, Rinehart and Winston, 1977.

Chesnut, Mary Boykin Miller. *Mary Chesnut's Civil War*. Edited by C. Vann Woodward. New Haven: Yale University Press, 1981.

Chesterfield County South Carolina, 2005. Knoxville: Tennessee Valley Publishing, 2005.

Clark, Walter. *Lost Arcadia; or, the Story of My Old Community*. Augusta: Chronicle Job Print., 1909.

———. *When Sherman Came: Southern Women and the Great March*. Augusta: Chronicle Job Print., 1909.

Clayton, Sarah "Sallie" Conley. *Requiem for a Lost City: A Memoir of Civil War Atlanta and the Old South*. Edited by Robert Scott Davis Jr. Macon, Ga.: Mercer University Press, 1999.

Clemson, Floride. *A Rebel Came Home: The Diary of Florida Clemson Tells of Her Wartime Adventures in Yankeeland, 1863–64, Her Trip Home to South Carolina, and Life in the South During the Last Few Months of the Civil War*. Edited by Charles M. McGee Jr. and Ernest M. Lander Jr. Columbia: University of South Carolina Press, 1961.

Connelly, T. Lawrence. *Will Success Spoil Jeff Davis? The Last Book About the Civil War*. New York: McGraw-Hill, 1963.

Connolly, James Austin. *Three Years in the Army of the Cumberland: The Letters and Diary of Major James A. Connolly*. Edited by Paul M. Angle. Civil War Centennial Series. Bloomington: Indiana University Press, 1959.

Conwell, Russell H. *Magnolia Journey: A Union Veteran Revisits the Former Confederate States; Arranged from the Letters of Correspondent Russell H. Conwell to the Daily Evening Traveller (Boston 1869)*. Edited by Jospeh C. Carter. Tuscaloosa: University of Alabama Press, 1974.

Cook, Mrs. Anna Maria Green. *History of Baldwin County Georgia*. Spartanburg, S.C.: Reprint Company, 1978.

Cram, George Franklin. *Soldiering with Sherman: Civil War Letters of George F. Cram*. Edited by Jennifer Cain Bohrnstedt. DeKalb: Northern Illinois University Press, 2000.

Crane, Teresa. *Freedom's Banner*. New York: St. Martin's Press, 1994.

Daniels, Jonathan. *A Southerner Discovers the South*. New York: Macmillan, 1938.

Davidson, Victor. *History of Wilkinson County*. Macon, Ga.: J. W. Burke, 1930.

Davis, Jefferson. *The Rise and Fall of the Confederate Government*. Vol. 2. New York: Thomas Yoseloff, 1957.

Davis, Washington. *Camp-Fire Chats of the Civil War*. Detroit: W. H. Boothroyd, 1887.

DeKalb Historical Society. *Vanishing DeKalb: A Pictorial History*. Decatur, Ga.: DeKalb Historical Society, 1985.

de Laubenfels, David J. "Where Sherman Passed By." *Geographical Review* 47 (1957): 381–95.

———. "With Sherman through Georgia: A Journal." *Georgia Historical Quarterly* 41 (1957): 288–300.

Dennett, John Richard. *The South as It Is*. Edited by Henry Christman. Athens: University of Georgia Press, 1965.

Derry, J. T. *Georgia: A Guide to Its Cities, Towns, Scenery, and Resources*. Philadelphia: J. B. Lippincott, 1878.

Dickson, Frank A. *Journeys into the Past: The Anderson Region's Heritage*. Anderson, S.C.: Anderson Bicentennial Committee, 1975.

Doctorow, E. L. *The March: A Novel*. New York: Random House, 2005.

Dorsey, James E. *Footprints along the Hoopee: A History of Emanuel County, 1812–1900*. Spartanburg, S.C.: Reprint Company, 1978.

Edmondston, Catherine Ann Devereux. *Journal of a Secesh Lady: The Diary of Catherine Ann Devereux Edmondston, 1860–1866*. Edited by Beth G. Crabtree and James Welch Patton. Raleigh: Division of Archives and History, 1979.

Ellis, Jerry. *Marching through Georgia: My Walk with Sherman*. New York: Delacorte Press, 1995.

Elmore, Grace Brown. *A Heritage of Woe: The Civil War Diary of Grace Brown Elmore, 1861–1868*. Edited by Marli Frances Weiner. Southern Voices from the Past. Athens: University of Georgia Press, 1997.

Emanuel County Historic Preservation Society. *Emanuel County Georgia*. Charleston: Arcadia, 1998.

Erlich, Margaret. *Mrs. Beall's Mill: Georgia Historical Marker Program Dedication*. Eatonton, Ga.: Putnam County Historical Society, 1999.

Ferguson, Robert. *America During and After the War*. London: Longmans, Green, Reader, and Dyer, 1866.

Field, Henry Martin. *Bright Skies and Dark Shadows*. New York: Charles Scribner's Sons, 1890.

Flanigan, James C. *History of Gwinnett County, Georgia*. Hapeville, Ga.: Longino and Porter, 1943.

Ford, Ford Madox. *Great Trade Route*. New York: Oxford University Press, 1937.

Fowler, Malcolm. *They Passed This Way: A Personal Narrative of Harnett County History*. N.p.: Harnett County Centennial Inc., 1955.

Frazier, Garrison. "Colloquy with Colored Ministers." *Journal of Negro History* 16 (1931): 88–94.

Garrett, Franklin M. *Atlanta and Environs: A Chronicle of Its People and Events*. New York: Lewis Historical Publishing Company, 1954.

Gay, Mary A. H. *Life in Dixie during the War*. Edited by J. H. Segars. Macon, Ga.: Mercer University Press, 2001.

Gay, William, and J. H. Beale. *Picturesque Sketches of American Progress*. New York: Empire Manufacturing House, 1886.

Georgia Civil War Centennial Commission. *Civil War Centennial Manual for Georgians*. Atlanta: Georgia Civil War Commission, 1960.

———. *Report of the Georgia Civil War Centennial Commission*. Atlanta: Georgia Civil War Commission, 1965.

Georgia Division—United Daughters of the Confederacy. *Across the River: A Celebration of the Georgia Division's Centennial*. Atlanta: Georgia Division—United Daughters of the Confederacy, 1995.

Georgia Historical Commission. *Georgia Civil War Historical Markers*. Atlanta: Georgia Historical Commission, 1964.

Gibson, Joyce M. *Scotland County Emerging, 1750–1900: The History of a Small Section of North Carolina*. Laurel Hill, N.C.: Joyce M. Gibson, 1995.

Godley, Margaret Walton, and Lillian C. Bragg. *Stories of Old Savannah, Second Series*. [Savannah?]: n.p., 1949.

Granger, Mary, ed. *Savannah River Plantations*. Spartanburg, S.C.: Reprint Company, 1972.

Graham, Stephen. "Marching through Georgia: Following Sherman's Footsteps To-Day (Part I)." *Harper's Magazine* 140 (April 1920): 612–20.

———. "Marching through Georgia: Following Sherman's Footsteps To-Day (Part II)." *Harper's Magazine* 140 (May 1920): 813–23.

Grant, Ulysses S. *Personal Memoirs of Ulysses S. Grant*. 1885. State College: Penn State Electronic Edition, 2004.

Graves, Ralph A. "Marching through Georgia Sixty Years After: Multifold Industries and Diversified Agriculture Are Restoring the Prosperity of America's Largest State East of the Mississippi." *National Geographic Magazine* 50, no. 3 (1926): 259–311.

Haeger, Diane. *My Dearest Cecelia: A Novel of the Southern Belle Who Stole General Sherman's Heart*. New York: St. Martin's Press, 2003.

Hale, Edward Everett, ed. *Stories of War Told by Soldiers*. Boston: Roberts Brothers, 1879.

Hall, Edward H. *Appletons' Hand-Book of American Travel: The Southern Tour*. New York: D. Appleton, 1872.

Hamilton, Sylla. *Forsaking All Others: A Story of Sherman's March through Georgia*. New York: Neale Publishing Company, 1905.

Harrington, Hugh T. *Civil War Milledgeville: Tales from the Confederate Capital of Georgia*. Charleston: History Press, 2005.

Harris, Joel Chandler. *On the Plantation: A Story of a Georgia Boy's Adventures during the War*. Introduction By William C. Mcdonald, Ph.D. Fredericksburg, Va.: Sergeant Kirkland's, 1997.

Hedrick, John A. *Letters from a North Carolina Unionist: John A. Hedrick to Benjamin S. Hedrick, 1862–1865*. Edited by Judkin Browning and Michael Thomas Smith. Raleigh: Division of Archives and History, 2001.

Heyward, Pauline DeCaradeuc. *A Confederate Lady Comes of Age: The Journal of Pauline Decaradeuc Heyward, 1863–1888*. Edited by Mary D. Robertson. Columbia: University of South Carolina Press, 1992.

Hickenlooper, Andrew. *Sherman. General Andrew Hickenlooper's Address at the Twenty-Third Meeting of the Society of the Army of the Tennessee Chicago Ill. October 7th 1891*. Cincinnati: Press of F. W. Freeman, 1891.

Hickey, Louise McHenry. *Rambles through Morgan County: Her History, Century Old Houses and Churches, and Tales to Remember*. Madison, Ga.: Morgan County Historical Society, 1971.

Hillhouse, Albert M. *A History of Burke County, Georgia 1777–1950*. Swainsboro, Ga.: Magnolia Press, 1985.

———. *Nuggets and Other Findings in Burke County, Georgia*. Danville, Ky.: Prompt Printing, 1981.

Hines, Nelle Womack. *A Treasure Album of Milledgeville and Baldwin County, Georgia*. Macon, Ga.: J. W. Burke, 1936.

Hinman, W. F., ed. *Camp and Field: Sketches of Army Life Written by Those Who Followed the Flag, '61–'65*. Cleveland: N. G. Hamilton, 1892.

Hitchcock, Henry. *Marching with Sherman: Passages from the Letters and Campaign Diaries of Henry Hitchcock, Major and Assistant Adjutant General of Volunteers, November 1864–May 1865*. Edited by M. A. DeWolfe Howe. New Haven and London: Yale University Press, H. Milford, and Oxford University Press, 1927.

Hollingsworth, Dixon, ed. *The History of Screven County, Georgia*. Dallas, Tex.: Curtis Media, 1989.

Holmes, James G., ed. *Memorials to the Memory of Mrs. Mary Amarinthia Snowden Offered by Societies, Associations and Confederate Camps Published by the Ladies Memorial Association of Charleston S.C.* Charleston: Walker, Evans & Cogswell Co. Publishers, 1898.

Holmes, Oliver Wendell. *The Poetical Works of Oliver Wendell Holmes in Three Volumes*. New York: Houghton, Mifflin, 1891.

Horwitz, Tony. *Confederates in the Attic: Dispatches from the Unfinished Civil War*. New York: Vintage, 1998.

House, Ellen Renshaw. *A Very Violent Rebel: The Civil War Diary of Ellen Renshaw House*. Edited by Daniel E. Sutherland. Knoxville: University of Tennessee Press, 1996.

Howard, Sidney. *Gone with the Wind: The Screenplay*. Edited by Herb Bridges and Terryl C. Boodman. New York: Delta, 1989.

Howel, Terry K. *Black Heritage*. New York: Vantage Press, 1978.

Huneycutt, James E., and Ida C. *A History of Richmond County*. Rockingham, N.C.: James E. and Ida C. Hunneycutt, 1976.

Hutchinson, John. *No Ordinary Lives: A History of Richmond County, North Carolina, 1750–1900*. Virginia Beach: Donning, 1998.

Jacks, L. P. *My American Friends*. New York: Macmillan, 1933.

Jakes, John. *Savannah; or, a Gift for Mr. Lincoln*. New York: Dutton, 2004.

Jasper County Historical Foundation. *History of Jasper County, Georgia*. Monticello, Ga.: Jasper County Historical Foundation, 1984.

Johnson, Bob, and Charles S. Norwood, eds. *History of Wayne County North Carolina*. Goldsboro, N.C.: Wayne County Historical Society, 1979.

Jones, Charles C., Jr. *The Siege of Savannah in December, 1864, and the Confederate Operations in Georgia and the Third Military District of South Carolina During General Sherman's March from Atlanta to the Sea*. Albany, N.Y.: Joel Munsell, 1874.

Jones, Katharine M. *When Sherman Came: Southern Women and the "Great March."* Indianapolis: Bobbs-Merrill, 1964.

Jordan, Mary Alice, ed. *Cotton to Kaolin: A History of Walton County, Georgia, 1784–1989*. Sandersville, Ga.: Washington County Historical Society, 1989.

Kaemmerlen, Cathy J. *General Sherman and the Georgia Belles: Tales from the Women Left Behind*. Charleston: History Press, 2006.

Keim, DeB. Randolph. *Sherman: A Memorial in Art, Oratory and Literature by the Society of the Army of the Tennessee with the Aid of the Congress of the United States of America*. Washington, D.C.: Government Printing Office, 1904.

Kennaway, John H. *On Sherman's Track; or, the South after the War*. London: Seeley, Jackson, and Halliday, 1867.

Kennedy, Sarah Beaumont. *Cicely: A Tale of the Georgia March*. New York: Doubleday, Page, 1911.

Kilgore, Alice Copeland, Edith Hanes Smith, and Frances Partridge Tuck, eds. *A History of Clayton County, Georgia, 1821–1983*. Roswell, Ga.: Ancestors Unlimited, 1983.

Kimball, H. I. *International Cotton Exposition (Atlanta, Georgia, 1881) Report of the Director-General*. New York: D. Appleton, 1882.

King, Edward. *The Great South*. Edited by James M. McPherson. New York: Arno Press, 1969.

King, Spencer B. *Sound of Drums: Selected Writings of Spencer B. King from His Civil War Centennial Columns Appearing in the Macon (Georgia) Telegraph News, 1960–1965*. Macon, Ga.: Mercer University Press, 1984.

King, W. C., and W. P. Derby, eds. *Camp-Fire Sketches and Battle-Field Echoes of the Rebellion*. Springfield, Mass.: W. C. King, 1887.

Kirkland, Frazar. *The Pictorial Book of Anecdotes of the Rebellion; or, the Funny and Pathetic Side of the War*. St. Louis: J. H. Mason, 1889.

Knight, Jo Goodson, ed. *Burke County Folks, 1851–1900: The Events in Their Lives as Published in Early Newspapers Covering Burke and Neighboring Counties in Georgia*. Baltimore: Gateway Press, 2004.

Knight, Lucian Lamar. *Georgia's Landmarks, Memorials and Legends Complete in Two Volumes*. Atlanta: Byrd Printing Company, 1913.

Kohler, Mike. *200 Years of Progress: A Report of the History and Achievements of the People of Lenoir County*. Kinston, N.C.: Kinston-Lenoir County Bicentennial Commission, 1976.

Ladies Calhoun Monument Association. *A History of the Calhoun Monument at Charleston S.C.* Charleston: Lucas, Richardson & Co., 1888.

Latham, Henry. *Black and White: A Journal of Three Months Tour in the United States*. New York: Negro Universities Press, 1969.

Lawrence, Harold. *Memory Hill*. Atlanta: Cherokee, 1994.

Lee, Angela. *Burke County, Georgia*. Dover, N.H.: Arcadia, 1996.

LeConte, Emma. *When the World Ended: The Diary of Emma LeConte*. Edited by Earl Schenck Miers. New York: Oxford University Press, 1957.

Leigh, Frances Butler. *Ten Years on a Georgia Plantation since the War, 1866–1876*. Edited by and introduced by Charles E. Wynes. Savannah: Beehive Press, 1992.

Leslie, Frank, Paul Fleury Mottelay, and T. Campbell-Copeland. *The Soldier in Our Civil War: A Pictorial History of the Conflict, 1861–1865, Illustrating the Valor of the Soldier as Displayed on the Battle-Field*. New York: J. H. Brown Publishing Company, 1884.

Lewis, John, with Michael D'orso. *Walking with the Wind: A Memoir of the Movement*. New York: Harcourt Brace, 1998.

Lippitt, Francis J. *Field Service in War: Comprising Marches, Convoys, Camps and Contonments, Reconnaissances, Outposts, Foraging, and Notes on Logistics*. New York: D. Van Nostrand, 1869.

Little, Windee Allienor. *Reminiscent: A Pictorial History of Eatonton/Putnam County, Georgia*. Virginia Beach: Donning Company, Publishers, 1999.

Lovett, Howard Meriwether. *Grandmother Stories from the Land of Used-to-Be*. Spartanburg, S.C.: Reprint Company, 1974.

Lunt, Dolly Sumner. *The Diary of Dolly Lunt Burge, 1848–1879*. Edited by Christine Jacobson Carter. Southern Voices from the Past. Athens: University of Georgia Press, 1997.

McClure, A. K. *The South: Its Industrial, Financial, and Political Condition*. Philadelphia: J. B. Lippincott, 1886.

McElroy, John. *Andersonville*. New York: Arno Press, 1969.

McGowen, Faison Wells, and Pearl Candy McGowen. *Flashes of Duplin's History and Government*. Kenansville, N.C.: n.p., 1971.

McMichael, Lois. *History of Butts County, Georgia, 1825–1976*. Atlanta: Cherokee Publishing Co., 1978.

Medley, Mary Louise. *History of Anson County North Carolina, 1750–1976*. Wadesboro, N.C.: Anson County Historical Society, 1976.

Melville, Herman. *Battle-Pieces and Aspects of the War*. Amherst: University of Massachusetts Press, 1972.

Milledgeville and Baldwin County Civil War Centennial. Milledgeville, Ga.: Milledgeville and Baldwin County Chamber of Commerce, 1961.

Miller, J. D. *A Guide into the South: An Open Gate to the Laborer, Large Returns to the Investor, an Index for the Traveler, a Great Welcome to the Deserving*. Atlanta: Index Printing Company, 1911.

Miller, Willian Bluffton. *Fighting for Liberty and Right: The Civil War Diary of William Bluffton Miller, First Sergeant, Company K, Seventy-Fifth Indiana Volunteer Infantry*. Edited by Jeffrey L. Patrick and Robert J. Willey. Knoxville: University of Tennessee Press, 2005.

Mitchell, Ella. *History of Washington County*. Greenville, S.C.: Southern Historical Press, 2000.

Mitchell, Margaret. *Gone with the Wind*. New York: Macmillan, 1936.

Mitchell, Margaret, and Richard Barksdale Harwell, eds. *Margaret Mitchell's Gone with the Wind Letters, 1936–1949*. New York and London: Collier Macmillan, 1986.

MOLLUS. *Military Order of the Loyal Legion of the United States Sketches of War History*. 60 vols. Wilmington, N.C.: Broadfoot Publishing Company, 1991.

Monroe County, Georgia: A History. Forsyth, Ga.: Monroe County Historical Society, 1979.

Moore, Frank, ed. *Anecdotes, Poetry, and Incidents of the War: North and South, 1865*. Collected and Arranged by Frank Moore. New York: Publication Office, Bible House, 1867.

———. *The Civil War in Song and Story, 1860–1865*. New York: Johnson Reprint Company, 1970.

Morgan, Mrs. Irby (Julia). *How It Was; Four Years among the Rebels*. Nashville: Publishing House Methodist Episcopal Church, South, 1892.

Morton, Joseph W., Jr., ed. *Sparks from the Campfire; or, Tales of the Old Veterans*. Philadelphia: Keyston Publishing Co., 1895.

Moulton, C. W. *The Review of General Sherman's Memoirs Examined, Chiefly in the Light of Its Own Evidence*. Cincinnati: R. Clarke & Co., Printers, 1875.

Myers, Robert Manson, and Charles Colcock Jones. *The Children of Pride: A True Story of Georgia and the Civil War*. New Haven: Yale University Press, 1972.

Naipaul, V. S. *A Turn in the South*. New York: Alfred A. Knopf, 1989.

Nichols, George Ward. *The Story of the Great March*. 22nd ed. New York: Harper & Brothers, 1865.

Oake, William Royale. *On the Skirmish Line behind a Friendly Tree: The Civil War Memoirs of William Royal Oake, 26th Iowa Volunteers*. Edited by Stacy Dale Allen. Helena, Mont.: Farcountry Press, 2006.

Official South Carolina Historical Markers, a Directory. Columbia, S.C.: Confederation of South Carolina Local Historical Societies, 1978.

Osborn, Thomas Ward. *The Fiery Trail: A Union Officer's Account of Sherman's Last Campaigns*. Edited by Richard Barksdale Harwell and Philip N. Racine. Knoxville: University of Tennessee Press, 1986.

Parker, Roy, Jr. *Cumberland County: A Brief History*. Raleigh: North Carolina Division of Archives and History, 1990.

Peck, William Henry. *The M'Donalds; or, The Ashes of Southern Homes. A Tale of Sherman's March*. New York: Metropolitan Record office, 1867.

Perkerson, Medora Field. *White Columns in Georgia*. New York: American Legacy Press, 1982.

Phillips, Ulrich Bonnell. "Historical Notes of Milledgeville, Ga." *Gulf State Historical Magazine*, November 1903. Offprint.

Pike, James Shepherd. *The Prostrate State; South Carolina under Negro Government*. New York: D. Appleton, 1874.

Pinckney, Roger. "Church in the Woods." *Garden & Gun* 2 (July/August 2008): 46–47.

Pond, Cornelia Jones. *Recollections of a Southern Daughter: A Memoir by Cornelia Jones Pond of Liberty County*. Edited by Lucinda H. MacKethan. Athens: University of Georgia Press, 1998.

Powers, Stephen. *Afoot and Alone: A Walk from Sea to Sea by the Southern Route*. Hartford: Columbian Book Company, 1872.

Price, Eugenia. *New Moon Rising*. Philadelphia: J. B. Lippincott, 1969.

Price, Morgan Phillips, ed. *America after Sixty Years: The Travel Diaries of Two Generations of Englishmen*. New York: Arno Press, 1974.

Price, Vivian. *The History of DeKalb County, Georgia, 1822–1900*. Decatur, Ga.: DeKalb Historical Society, 1997.

Rainer, Vessie Thrasher. *Henry County, Georgia: The Mother of Counties*. 1971.

———. *Henry County, Georgia: Landmark Houses*. McDonough, Ga.: Dr. R. A. Rainer, Jr., 1986.

Ralph, Julian. *Dixie; or, Southern Scenes and Sketches*. New York: Harper and Brothers, 1896.

Rawick, George. *The American Slave: A Composite Autobiography*. Contributions in Afro-American and African Studies, no. 11. Westport, Conn.: Greenwood, 1972.

Rawl, Miriam Freeman. *From the Ashes of Ruin*. Columbia, S.C.: Summerhouse, 1999.

Reaves, Michael. *Historic Henry County*. San Antonio: Historical Publishing Network, 2004.

Reid, Whitelaw. *After the War: A Southern Tour, May 1, 1865 to May 1, 1866*. Cincinnati: Moore, Wilsatch, & Baldwin, 1866.

Report of Major General William T. Sherman to the Hon. Committee on the Conduct of the War. Millwood, N.Y.: Kraus Reprint Co., 1977.

Reston, James. *Sherman's March and Vietnam*. New York: Macmillan, 1984.

Root, Elihu. *Speech by the Secretary of War Mr. Root upon the Unveiling of St. Gaudens' Statue of General Sherman in the City of New York, May 30, 1903*. Washington, D.C.: Gibson Bros. Printers and Bookbinders, 1903.

Rozier, John. *The Houses of Hancock, 1785–1865*. Decatur, Ga.: Auldfarran Books, 1996.

Sams, Anita B. *Wayfarers in Walton*. Monroe, Ga.: General Charitable Foundation of Monroe, Georgia, 1967.

Sesqui-Centennial of Milledgeville and Baldwin County Georgia, 1803–1953. Milledgeville, Ga.: Old Capital Historical Society, 1953.

Sherman, P. Tecumseh. *General Sherman in the Last Year of the War: An Address Delivered at the Thirty-Eighth Reunion of the Society of the Army of the Tennessee at St. Louis, Missouri*. New York: Robert Grier Cooke, 1908.

Sherman, William T. *Memoirs of General William T. Sherman*. Bloomington: Indiana University Press, 1957.

Shivers, Forrest. *The Land Between: A History of Hancock County, Georgia to 1940*. Spartanburg, S.C.: Reprint Company, 1990.

Shurter, Edwin DuBois, ed. *The Complete Orations and Speeches of Henry W. Grady*. New York: Hinds, Noble & Eldredge, 1910.

Simms, William Gilmore. *A City Laid Waste: The Capture, Sack, and Destruction of the City of Columbia*. Edited by David Aiken. Columbia: University of South Carolina Press, 2005.

Simpson, Brooks D., and Jean V. Berlin, eds. *Sherman's Civil War: Selected Correspondence of William T. Sherman, 1860–1865*. Chapel Hill: University of North Carolina Press, 1999.

Smith, D. E. Huger, Alice R. Huger Smith, and Arney R. Childs, eds. *Mason Smith Family Letters, 1860–1868*. Columbia: University of South Carolina Press, 1950.

Society of the Army of the Tennessee. "Report of the Proceedings of the Annual Meeting of the Society of the Army of the Tennessee." Cincinnati: The Society, 1877– .

Somers, Robert. *The Southern States since the War, 1870–71*. Edited by Malcolm C. McMillan. Tuscaloosa: University of Alabama Press, 2004.

Spalding, Phinizy ed. "Cracker Corner: And More about Sherman's Nags . . . and Another Cemetery," *Georgia Historical Quarterly* 58 (Spring 1974): 117.

Spivey, Ted Ray. *To Die in Atlanta: Poems of the Civil War and After*. Atlanta: Oconee Press, 1987.

Stancil, W. Dorsey. *Vanishing Gwinnett, Gwinnett County, Georgia: Pictorial History of Bygone Days*. Lawrenceville, Ga.: Gwinnett Historical Society, 1984.

———. *Vanishing Gwinnett II, Gwinnett County, Georgia: More Scenes of Bygone Days*. Lawrenceville, Ga.: Gwinnett Historical Society, 2001.

Steed, Hal. *Georgia: Unfinished State*. Atlanta: Cherokee Publishing Company, 1971.

Sullivan, Marge Nichols, ed. *My Folks and the Civil War: A Treasury of Civil War Stories Shared by Capper's and Grit Readers*. Topeka: Capper Press, 1994.

Thomas, Ella Gertrude Clanton. *The Secret Eye: The Journal of Ella Gertrude Clanton Thomas, 1848–1889*. Edited by Virginia Ingraham Burr. Gender and American Culture. Chapel Hill: University of North Carolina Press, 1990.

Thomas, Mrs. Z. V. *History of Jefferson County*. Macon, Ga.: J. W. Burke, 1927.

Thomas, Rev. J. A. W. *A History of Marlboro County, with Traditions and Sketches of Numerous Families*. Baltimore: Regional Publishing Company, 1971.

Tourgée, Albion. *The Veteran and His Pipe*. Chicago: Belford, Clarke, 1886.

Trowbridge, J. T. *The South: A Tour of Its Battle-Fields and Ruined Cities*. New York: Arno Press, 1969.

Underwood, J. L. *The Women of the Confederacy*. New York: Neale Publishing Company, 1906.

United Daughters of the Confederacy, Georgia Division, Willie Hunt Smith Chapter, Barnesville. *History of Lamar County*. Barnesville, Ga.: Barnesville News-Gazette, 1932.

United States. War Department. *The War of the Rebellion: A Compilation of the Official Records of the Union and Confederate Armies*. Washington, D.C.: 1880–1901.

Van Dyke, Henry. *The Poems of Henry Van Dyke*. New York: C. Scribner's Sons, 1920.

Washington County Historical Society. *Washington County*. Charleston: Arcadia, 2003.

Waters, Joseph G. *The Army Bummer and Good Night by Captain Joseph G. Waters. Kansas Commandery F the Military Order of the Loyal Legion of the United States*. Leavenworth, Kans.: n.p., 1897.

Watkins, William L. *Anderson County: The Things That Made it Happen*. Anderson, S.C.: Privately printed, 1995.

Weil, Emily. *After Sherman's March: Goldsboro at the End of the Civil War*. Durham: BW&A Books, 2007.

Wheeler, Frank T. *Savannah River Plantations: Photographs From the Collection of the Georgia Historical Society*. Charleston: Arcadia, 1998.

Wills, Charles Wright. *Army Life of an Illinois Soldier: Including a Day-by-Day Record of Sherman's March to the Sea; Letters and Diary of Charles W. Wills*. Edited by Mary E. Kellogg. Shawnee Classics. Carbondale: Southern Illinois University Press, 1996.

Williams, Carolyn White. *History of Jones County Georgia for One Hundred Years, Specifically 1807–1907*. Macon, Ga.: J. W. Burke, 1957.

Wood, Chris. *Clayton County: Reflections of a Crescent Jewel*. Atlanta: Longstreet Press, 1993.

Wood, Edward J. *A Fierce, Wild Joy: The Civil War Letters of Colonel Edward J. Wood, 48th Indiana Volunteer Infantry Regiment*. Edited by Stephen E. Towne. Knoxville: University of Tennessee Press, 2007.

Periodicals

Atlanta Constitution	*Field and Post-Room*
Atlanta Journal-Constitution	*Los Angeles Times*
Chicago Daily Tribune	*New York Times*
Chicago Defender	*Washington Post*
Confederate Veteran	

Websites

"About Ethiopia Saluting the Colors," *Library of Congress Song of America Project*. http://www.loc.gov/creativity/hampson/about_ethiopia.html, December 1, 2012.

Allmusic.com. http://www.allmusic.com/album/white-mansions-mw0000268640, December 1, 2012.

Ballad of White Mansions. http://www.whitemansions.co.uk/index.html, December 1, 2012.

Born in Slavery: Slave Narratives from the Federal Writer's Project, 1936-1938. http://memory .loc.gov/ammem/snhtml/snhome.html

Don Troiani: Historical Art Prints. http://www.historicalartprints.com/viewgallist .php?id=159, June 20, 2013.

"Doyle News." http://www.doylenewyork.com/pr/american_art/07PT01/default.htm, September 25, 2013.

Gallon Historical Art, Inc. http://gallon.com/categories.asp, June 20, 2013.

"Georgia Mysteries: Sherman's Girlfriend." http://georgiamysteries.blogspot.com/2009/05/ shermans-girlfriends.html, December 1, 2012.

In the Muse Performing Arts Blog from the Library of Congress. http://blogs.loc.gov/ music/2010/08/sherman, August 15, 2010.

National Park Service Soldiers and Sailors Database. http://www.nps.gov/civilwar/soldiers- and-sailors-database.htm, December 1, 2012.

New Georgia Encyclopedia. http://www.georgiaencyclopedia.org/nge/Article.jsp?id=h–525, December 1, 2012.

Official Mort Küntsler Website. http://www.mortkunstler.com, June 20, 2013.

Steven Hull's White Mansions Page. http://www.ozarkdaredevilstabs.com/white_mansions .htm, December 1, 2012.

Walt Whitman Archive, http://whitmanarchive.org/published/LG/1871/poems/180, December 1, 2012.

Secondary Sources

Aiken, Charles S. *The Cotton Plantation South since the Civil War*. Baltimore: Johns Hopkins University Press, 1998.

Angley, Wilson, Jerry Cross, and Michael Hill, compilers. *Sherman's March through North Carolina*. Raleigh: North Carolina Division of Archives and History, 1995.

Bailey, Anne J. *War and Ruin: William T. Sherman and the Savannah Campaign*. Wilmington, Del.: Scholarly Resources, 2003.

Bailey, Anne J., and Walter J. Fraser Jr. *Portraits of Conflict: A Photographic History of Georgia in the Civil War*. Edited by Bobby Roberts and Carl Moneyhon. Portraits of Conflict Series. Fayetteville: University of Arkansas Press, 1996.

Barrett, John Gilchrist. *Sherman's March through the Carolinas*. Chapel Hill: University of North Carolina Press, 1956.

Baruch, Mildred J., and Ellen J. Beckman. *Civil War Union Monuments*. Washington, D.C.: Daughters of Union Veterans of the Civil War, 1861–1865 Inc., 1978.

Blight, David W. *American Oracle: The Civil War in the Civil Rights Era*. Cambridge, Mass.: Belknap Press of Harvard University Press, 2011.

———. *Frederick Douglass' Civil War: Keeping Faith in Jubilee*. Baton Rouge: Louisiana State University Press, 1989.

———. *Race and Reunion: The Civil War in American Memory*. Cambridge, Mass.: Belknap Press of Harvard University Press, 2001.

Bodenhamer, David J., John Corrigan, and Trevor M. Harris. *The Spatial Humanities: GIS and the Future of Humanities Scholarship*. Bloomington: Indiana University Press, 2010.

Bodnar, John. *Remaking America: Public Memory, Commemoration, and Patriotism in the Twentieth Century*. Princeton: Princeton University Press, 1992.

Boller, Paul F. *Presidential Anecdotes*. Rev. ed. New York: Oxford University Press, 1996.

Bosco, David. "Moral Principle vs. Military Necessity." *American Scholar* 77 (2008): 25–34.

Bradley, Mark L. *Last Stand in the Carolinas: the Battle of Bentonville*. Campbell, Calif.: Savas Publishers, 1996.

———. *This Astounding Close: The Road to the Bennett Place*. Chapel Hill: University of North Carolina Press, 2000.

Brady, Lisa M. *War upon the Land: Military Strategy and the Transformation of Southern Landscapes during the American Civil War*. Athens: University of Georgia Press, 2012.

Bragg, William Harris. *Griswoldville*. Macon, Ga.: Mercer University Press, 2000.

Bridges, Herb. *Gone with the Wind: The Three-Day Premiere in Atlanta*. Macon, Ga.: Mercer University Press, 1999.

Broadwater, Robert P. *Battle Despair: Bentonville and the North Carolina Campaign*. Macon, Ga.: Mercer University Press, 2004.

Brown, Thomas J. "The Monumental Legacy of Calhoun." In *The Memory of the Civil War in American Culture*, edited by Alice Fahs and Joan Waugh, 130–56. Chapel Hill: University of North Carolina Press, 2002.

Brundage, W. Fitzhugh. *The Southern Past: A Clash of Race and Memory*. Cambridge, Mass.: Belknap Press of Harvard University Press, 2005.

Bryan, Thomas Conn. *Confederate Georgia*. Athens: University of Georgia Press, 1953.

Buck, Paul H. *The Road to Reunion, 1865–1900*. Boston: Little Brown, 1938.

Byrne, William A. "'Uncle Billy' Sherman Comes to Town: The Free Winter of Black Savannah." *Georgia Historical Quarterly* 79 (1995): 91–116.

Campbell, Jacqueline Glass. *When Sherman Marched North from the Sea*. Chapel Hill: University of North Carolina Press, 2003.

Carnahan, Burrus M. "Lincoln, Lieber, and the Laws of War: The Origins and Limits of the Principle of Military Necessity." *American Journal of International Law* 92 (1998): 213–31.

Carnes, Mark C., ed. *Past Imperfect: History According to the Movies*. New York: Henry Holt, 1996.

Castel, Albert E. *Decision in the West: The Atlanta Campaign of 1864*. Lawrence: University Press of Kansas, 1992.

———. "Prevaricating through Georgia: Sherman's Memoirs as a Source on the Atlanta Campaign." *Civil War History* 40 (1994): 48–71.

Caudill, Edward, and Paul Ashdown. *Sherman's March in Myth and Memory*. American Crisis Series. Lanham: Rowman & Littlefield, 2008.

Chadwick, Bruce. *The Reel Civil War: Mythmaking in American Film*. New York: Vintage Books, 2001.

Churchill, Edward M. "Betrayal at Ebenezer Creek." *Civil War Times* 37 (October, 1998): 52–59.

Clark, Thomas D., ed. *Travels in the New South, a Bibliography*. 2 vols. Norman: University of Oklahoma Press, 1962.

Clarke, Erskine. *Dwelling Place: A Plantation Epic*. New Haven: Yale University Press, 2005.

Conn, Steven. "Narrative Trauma an Civil War History Painting; or, Why Are These Pictures So Terrible?" *History and Theory* 41 (December 2002): 17–42.

Cook, Robert. *Troubled Commemoration: The American Civil War Centennial, 1961–1965*. Making the Modern South. Baton Rouge: Louisiana State University Press, 2007.

Coulter, E. Merton. "Father Sherman's 'March to the Sea.'" *Georgia Review* 10 (1956): 375–93.

Cowdrey, Albert E. *This Land, This South: An Environmental History*. Rev. ed. Lexington: University Press of Kentucky, 1996.

Cox, John D. *Traveling South: Travel Narratives and the Construction of American Identity*. Athens: University of Georgia Press, 2005.

Cox, Karen L. *Dixie's Daughters: The United Daughters of the Confederacy and the Preservation of Confederate Culture*. New perspectives on the History of the South. Gainesville: University Press of Florida, 2003.

Crabb, Christopher G. *Facing Sherman in South Carolina: March through the Swamps*. Charleston, S.C.: History Press, 2010.

Cullen, Jim. *The Civil War in Popular Culture: A Reusable Past*. Washington, D.C.: Smithsonian Institution Press, 1995.

Davis, Burke. *Sherman's March*. New York: Random House, 1980.

Davis, Keith F. *George N. Barnard: Photographer of Sherman's Campaign*. Kansas City, Mo.: Hallmark Cards, 1990.

Davis, Stephen. *What the Yankees Did to Us: Sherman's Bombardment and Wrecking of Atlanta*. Macon, Ga.: Mercer University Press, 2012.

Dean, Eric T. *Shook Over Hell: Post-Traumatic Stress, Vietnam, and the Civil War*. Cambridge, Mass.: Harvard University Press, 1997.

Dearing, Mary R. *Veterans in Politics: The Story of the G. A. R.* Baton Rouge: Louisiana State University Press, 1952.

Diffley, Kathleen Elizabeth. *Witness to Reconstruction: Constance Fenimore Woolson and the Postbellum South, 1873–1894*. Jackson: University Press of Mississippi, 2011.

Dorsey, Allison. *To Build Our Lives Together: Community Formation in Black Atlanta, 1875–1906*. Athens: University of Georgia Press, 2004.

Doyle, Don H. *New Men, New Cities, New South: Atlanta, Nashville, Charleston, Mobile, 1860–1910*. Chapel Hill: University of North Carolina Press, 1990.

Drago, Edmund L. "How Sherman's March through Georgia Affected the Slaves." *Georgia Historical Quarterly* 57 (Fall, 1973): 361–74.

Durham, Roger S. *Guardian of Savannah: Fort Mcallister, Georgia, in the Civil War and Beyond*. Studies in Maritime History. Columbia: University of South Carolina Press, 2008.

Escott, Paul D. "The Context of Freedom: Georgia's Slaves during the Civil War." *Georgia Historical Quarterly* 58 (Spring 1974): 79–101.

Fahs, Alice, and Joan Waugh, eds. *The Memory of the Civil War in American Culture.* Civil War America. Chapel Hill: University of North Carolina Press, 2004.

Fairclough, Adam. "Civil Rights and the Lincoln Memorial: The Censored Speeches of Robert R. Moton (1922) and John Lewis (1963)." *Journal of Negro History* 82 (1997): 408–16.

Farr, Finis. *Margaret Mitchell of Atlanta: The Author of Gone with the Wind.* New York: William Morrow, 1965.

Feimster, Crystal N. "General Benjamin Butler and the Threat of Sexual Violence during the American Civil War." *Daedalus* 138 (2009): 126–34.

Fellman, Michael. *Citizen Sherman: A Life of William Tecumseh Sherman.* New York: Random House, 1995.

Ferraro, William M. "Creating Memory at the End of the Civil War: William Tecumseh Sherman's Special Field Orders, No. 76." *OAH Magazine of History* 8 (1993): 19–25.

Foote, Kenneth E. *Shadowed Ground: America's Landscapes of Violence and Tragedy.* Revised and updated. Austin: University of Texas Press, 2003.

Förster, Stig, and Jörg Nagler, eds. *On the Road to Total War: The American Civil War and German Wars of Unification, 1861–1871.* Cambridge: German Historical Institute and Cambridge University Press, 1997.

Frank, Lisa Tendrich. "To 'Cure Her of Her Pride and Boasting': The Gendered Implications of Sherman's March." Ph.D. dissertation, University of Florida, 2001.

Frazier, Garrison. "Colloquy with Colored Ministers." *Journal of Negro History* 16 (1931): 88–94.

Fussell, Paul. *Wartime: Understanding and Behavior in the Second World War.* New York: Oxford University Press, 1989.

Gallagher, Gary W. *Causes Won, Lost, and Forgotten: How Hollywood and Popular Art Shape What We Know about the Civil War.* Steven and Janice Brose Lectures in the Civil War Era. Chapel Hill: University of North Carolina Press, 2008.

Gardner, Sarah E. *Blood and Irony: Southern White Women's Narratives of the Civil War, 1861–1937.* Chapel Hill: University of North Carolina Press, 2003.

Gates, Paul W. *Agriculture and the Civil War.* Edited by Allan Nevins. The Impact of the Civil War [The Civil War Centennial Commission Series]. New York: Alfred A. Knopf, 1965.

Gelbert, Doug. *Civil War Sites, Memorials, Museums, and Library Collections: A State-by-State Guidebook to Places Open to the Public.* Jefferson, N.C.: McFarland, 1997.

Gerteis, Louis S. *From Contraband to Freedman: Federal Policy toward Southern Blacks, 1861–1865.* Westport, Conn.: Greenwood Press, 1973.

Glatthaar, Joseph T. *The March to the Sea and Beyond.* Baton Rouge: Louisiana State University Press, 1985.

Glymph, Thavolia. *Out of the House of Bondage: The Transformation of the Plantation Household.* Cambridge: Cambridge University Press, 2008.

Grimsley, Mark. *The Hard Hand of War: Union Military Policy toward Southern Civilians, 1861–1865.* Cambridge: Cambridge University Press, 1995.

———. "Modern War/Total War." In *The American Civil War: a Handbook of Literature and Research*, edited by Steven E. Woodworth, 379–89. Westport, Conn.: Greenwood Press, 1996.

Hagans, William E. "Saint-Gaudens, Zorn, and the Godesslike Miss Anderson." *American Art* 16 (2002): 66–90.

Harmetz, Aljean. *On the Road to Tara: The Making of Gone with the Wind*. New York: H. N. Abrams, 1996.

Harwell, Richard, ed. *Gone with the Wind as Book and Film*. Columbia: University of South Carolina Press, 1983.

Haskell, Molly. *Frankly, My Dear: Gone with the Wind Revisited*. New Haven: Yale University Press, 2009.

Hattaway, Herman, and Ethan Sepp Rafuse. *The Ongoing Civil War: New Versions of Old Stories*. Shades of Blue and Gray Series. Columbia: University of Missouri Press, 2004.

Heider, Karl G. "The Rashomon Effect: When Ethnographers Disagree." *American Anthropologist*, n.s., 90, no. 1 (Mar. 1988): 73–81.

Henken, Elissa R. "Taming the Enemy: Georgian Narratives about the Civil War." *Journal of Folklore Research* 40 (2003): 289–307.

Hill, Michael, ed. *Guide to North Carolina Highway Historical Markers*. Raleigh: North Carolina Division of Archives and History, 2001.

Hirshson, Stanley P. *The White Tecumseh: A Biography of General William T. Sherman*. New York: J. Wiley, 1997.

Hsieh, Wayne Wei-Siang. "Total War and the American Civil War Reconsidered: The End of an Outdated 'Master Narrative.'" *Journal of the Civil War Era* 1 (2011): 394–408.

Huddleston, John. *Killing Ground: Photographs of the Civil War and the Changing American Landscape*. Baltimore: Johns Hopkins University Press, 2002.

Hughes, Nathaniel Cheairs. *Bentonville: The Final Battle of Sherman and Johnston*. Civil War America. Chapel Hill: University of North Carolina Press, 1996.

Hume, Janice, and Amber Roessner. "Surviving Sherman's March: Press, Public Memory, and Georgia's Salvation Mythology." *Journalism and Mass Communication Quarterly* 86 (2009): 119–37.

Hunt, Robert Eno. *The Good Men Who Won the War: Army of the Cumberland Veterans and Emancipation Memory*. Tuscaloosa: University of Alabama Press, 2010.

Inscoe, John C. "The Confederate Home Front Sanitized: Joel Chandler Harris' *On the Plantation* and Sectional Reconciliation." *Georgia Historical Quarterly* 76 (Fall 1992): 652–74.

———, ed. *The Civil War in Georgia*. Athens: University of Georgia Press, 2011.

Jacob, Kathryn Allamong. *Testament to Union: Civil War Monuments in Washington, D.C.* Baltimore: Johns Hopkins University Press, 1998.

Janney, Caroline E. *Remembering the Civil War: Reunion and the Limits of Reconciliation*. Chapel Hill: University of North Carolina Press, 2013.

Jones, Jacqueline. *Saving Savannah: The City and the Civil War*. New York: Alfred A. Knopf, 2008.

Kaufman, Will. *The Civil War in American Culture*. BAAS Paperbacks. Edinburgh: Edinburgh University Press, 2006.

Kennett, Lee B. *Marching through Georgia: The Story of Soldiers and Civilians during Sherman's Campaign*. New York: HarperCollins, 1995.

———. *Sherman: A Soldier's Life*. New York: HarperCollins, 2001.

Klingberg, Frank W. *The Southern Claims Commission*. Berkeley: University of California Press, 1955.

Knowles, Anne Kelly, and Amy Hillier. *Placing History: How Maps, Spatial Data, and Gis Are Changing Historical Scholarship*. Redlands, Calif.: ESRI Press, 2008.

Koppes, Steven N. "Folklore: Where Fact Meets Fiction." *University of Georgia Research Magazine* (2000).

Link, William A. *Atlanta, Cradle of the New South: Race and Remembering in the Civil War's Aftermath*. Chapel Hill: University of North Carolina Press, 2013.

Litwack, Leon F. *Been in the Storm So Long: The Aftermath of Slavery*. New York: Knopf, distributed by Random House, 1979.

Loewen, James W. *Lies across America: What Our Historic Sites Get Wrong*. New York: New Press, 1999.

Logue, Larry M., and Michael Barton, eds. *The Civil War Veteran: A Historical Reader*. New York: New York University Press, 2007.

Lomask, Milton. "Carrying the Stars and Stripes Unfurled, From Vicksburg to Washington." *American Heritage* 16 (1965).

Lucas, Marion Brunson. *Sherman and the Burning of Columbia*. College Station: Texas A&M University Press, 1976.

———. "William Tecumseh Sherman vs. The Historians." *Proteus* 17 (2000): 15–21.

Margaret Mitchell: The Book, the Film, the Woman. Atlanta: Atlanta-Fulton Public Library Foundation, 1996.

Marshall, Anne E. *Creating a Confederate Kentucky: The Lost Cause and Civil War Memory in a Border State*. Chapel Hill: University of North Carolina Press, 2010.

Marszalek, John F. "Celebrity in Dixie: Sherman Tours the South, 1879." *Georgia Historical Quarterly* 66 (Fall 1982): 368–83.

———. *Sherman: A Soldier's Passion for Order*. New York: Free Press, 1993.

———. *Sherman's March to the Sea*. Abilene, Tex.: McWhiney Foundation Press, 2005.

Marten, James Alan. *The Children's Civil War*. Civil War America. Chapel Hill: University of North Carolina Press, 1998.

———. *Sing Not War: The Lives of Union and Confederate Veterans in Gilded Age America*. Civil War America. Chapel Hill: University of North Carolina Press, 2011.

Martinez, J. Michael, and Robert M. Harris. "Graves, Worms, and Epitaphs: Confederate Monuments in the Southern Landscape." In *Confederate Symbols in the Contemporary South*, edited by J. Michael Martinez, William D. Richardson, and Ron McNinch-Su, 130–92. Gainesville: University Press of Florida, 2000.

McConnell, Stuart. *Glorious Contentment: The Grand Army of the Republic, 1865–1900*. Chapel Hill: University of North Carolina Press, 1992.

McIntyre, Rebecca Cawood. *Souvenirs of the Old South: Northern Tourism and Southern Mythology*. Gainesville: University Press of Florida, 2011.

McPherson, Tara. *Reconstructing Dixie: Race, Gender, and Nostalgia in the Imagined South*. Durham: Duke University Press, 2003.

McWhirter, Christian. *Battle Hymns: The Power and Popularity of Music in the Civil War*. Chapel Hill: University of North Carolina Press, 2012.

Melton, Brian. "'The Town That Sherman Wouldn't Burn': Sherman's March and Madison, Georgia, in History, Memory, and Legend." *Georgia Historical Quarterly* 86 (2002): 201-231.

Melton, Jeffrey Alan. *Mark Twain, Travel Books, and Tourism*. Tuscaloosa: University of Alabama Press, 2002.

Milder, Robert. "The Rhetoric of Melville's *Battle-Pieces*." *Nineteenth Century Literature* 44 (1989): 173–200.

Miles, Jim. *To the Sea: A History and Tour Guide of Sherman's March*. Nashville: Rutledge Hill Press, 1989.

Mitchell, Reid. *Civil War Soldiers: Their Expectations and Their Experiences*. New York: Viking, 1988.

Mohr, Clarence L. *On the Threshold of Freedom: Masters and Slaves in Civil War Georgia*. Baton Rouge: Louisiana State University Press, 1986.

Monroe, Haskell. "Men without Law: Federal Raiding in Liberty County, Georgia." *Georgia Historical Quarterly* 44 (1960): 154–71.

Moody, Wesley. *Demon of the Lost Cause: Sherman and Civil War History*. Columbia: University of Missouri Press, 2011.

Moore, Niamh, and Yvonne Whelan, eds. *Heritage, Memory and the Politics of Identity: New Perspectives on the Cultural Landscape*. Heritage, Culture, and Identity. Aldershot: Ashgate, 2007.

Morgan, Chad. *Planters' Progress: Modernizing Confederate Georgia*. Gainesville: University Press of Florida, 2005.

Murray, Robert K. "General Sherman, the Negro, and Slavery: The Story of an Unrecognized Rebel." *Negro History Bulletin* 22 (1959): 125–30.

Neely, Mark E., Jr. *The Civil War and the Limits of Destruction*. Cambridge, Mass.: Harvard University Press, 2007.

———. "Was the Civil War a Total War?" *Civil War History* 50 (2004): 434–58.

Nelson, Larry E. "Sherman at Cheraw." *South Carolina Historical Magazine* 100 (1999): 328–54.

Nelson, Megan Kate. *Ruin Nation: Destruction and the American Civil War*. Athens: University of Georgia Press, 2012.

Newman, Harvey K. *Southern Hospitality: Tourism and the Growth of Atlanta*. Tuscaloosa: University of Alabama Press, 1999.

Nudelman, Franny. *John Brown's Body: Slavery, Violence, and the Culture of War*. Cultural Studies of the United States. Chapel Hill: University of North Carolina Press, 2004.

O'Donovan, Susan E. *Becoming Free in the Cotton South*. Cambridge, Mass.: Harvard University Press, 2007.

Penningroth, Dylan C. *The Claims of Kinfolk: African American Property and Community in the Nineteenth-Century South*. Chapel Hill: University of North Carolina Press, 2003.

Pfanz, Harry W. "The Surrender Negotiations between General Johnston and General Sherman, April 1865." *Military Affairs* 16 (1952): 61–70.

Pyron, Darden Asbury. *Southern Daughter: The Life of Margaret Mitchell and the Making of Gone with the Wind*. Athens: Hill Street Press, 1991.

———, ed. *Recasting: Gone with the Wind in American Culture*. Miami: Florida International University, 1983.

Ransom, Roger L., and Richard Sutch. *One Kind of Freedom: The Economic Consequences of Emancipation*. 2nd ed. Cambridge: Cambridge University Press, 2001.

Reardon, Carol. *Pickett's Charge in History and Memory*. Civil War America. Chapel Hill: University of North Carolina Press, 1997.

———. "William T. Sherman in Postwar Georgia's Collective Memory, 1865–1914." In *Wars within a War: Controversy and Conflict over the American Civil War*, edited by Joan Waugh and Gary W. Gallagher, 223–48. Chapel Hill: University of North Carolina Press, 2009.

Reed, John Shelton. *Minding the South*. Columbia: University of Missouri Press, 2003.

———. *Whistling Dixie: Dispatches from the South*. Columbia: University of Missouri Press, 1990.

Reed, John Shelton, and Dale Volberg Reed. *1001 Things Everyone Should Know about the South*. New York: Doubleday, 1996.

Reidy, Joseph P. *From Slavery to Agrarian Capitalism in the Cotton Plantation South*. Chapel Hill: University of North Carolina Press, 1992.

Robertson, James, ed. *Index-Guide to the Southern Historical Society Papers*. 2 vols. Millwood, N.Y.: Kraus International Publications, 1980.

Rogers, George A., and R. Frank Saunders, Jr. "The Scourge of Sherman's Men in Liberty County, Georgia." *Georgia Historical Quarterly* 60 (1976): 356–69.

———. *Swamp Water and Wiregrass: Historical Sketches of Coastal Georgia*. Macon, Ga.: Mercer University Press, 1984.

Rogin, Michael. "'The Sword Became a Flashing Vision': D. W. Griffith's *The Birth of a Nation*." *Representations* 9 (Winter 1985): 150–95.

Rosengarten, Theodore. "New Views on the Burning of Columbia." *University South Caroliniana Society: Fifty Sixth Annual Meeting* (1993): http://library.sc.edu/socar/uscs/1993/addr93.html.

Royster, Charles. *The Destructive War: William Tecumseh Sherman, Stonewall Jackson, and the Americans*. New York: Knopf: Random House [distributor], 1991.

Rubin, Anne Sarah. *A Shattered Nation: The Rise and Fall of the Confederacy, 1861–1868*. Civil War America. Chapel Hill: University of North Carolina Press, 2005.

———. "The Georgia and Carolinas Campaign." In *A Companion to the U.S. Civil War.*, edited by Aaron Sheehan-Dean. Hoboken, N.J.: Wiley-Blackwell, 2014.

Samuels, Shirley. *Facing America: Iconography and the Civil War*. New York: Oxford University Press, 2004.

Savage, Kirk. *Standing Soldiers, Kneeling Slaves: Race, War, and Monument in Nineteenth Century America*. Princeton: Princeton University Press, 1997.

Schein, Richard, ed. *Landscape and Race in the United States*. New York: Routledge, 2006.

Schmeller, Erik S. *Perceptions of Race and Nation in English and American Travel Writers, 1833–1914*. Edited by Kristi E. Seigel. Travel Writing across the Disciplines. New York: Peter Lang, 2004.

Schultz, Jane E. "Mute Fury: Southern Women's Diaries of Sherman's March to the Sea, 1864–1865." In *Arms and the Woman: War, Gender, and Literary Representation*, edited by Adrienne Auslander Munich, Helen M. Cooper, and Susan Merrill Squier, 59–79. Chapel Hill: University of North Carolina Press, 1989.

Schwabe, Edward, Jr. "Sherman's March through Georgia: A Reappraisal of the Right Wing." *Georgia Historical Quarterly* 69 (1985): 522–35.

Severeo, Richard, and Lewis Milford. *The Wages of War: When America's Soldiers Came Home— From Valley Forge to Vietnam*. New York: Simon and Schuster, 1989.

Shackel, Paul. *Memory in Black and White: Race, Commemoration and the Post-Bellum Landscape*. Walnut Creek, Calif.: AltaMira Press, 2003.

Siddali, Silvana R. "Babylon Is Fallen." *Civil War Monitor* 1 (2011): 62–69.

Silber, Nina. *The Romance of Reunion: Northerners and the South, 1865–1900*. Civil War America. Chapel Hill: University of North Carolina Press, 1993.

Simkins, Francis Butler, and James Welch Patton. *The Women of the Confederacy*. Richmond: Garrett and Massie, 1936.

Simpson, Brooks D. "Grant's Tour of the South Revisited." *Journal of Southern History* 54, no. 3 (August 1988): 425–48.

Smith, Mark A. "Sherman's Unexpected Companions: Marching through Georgia with Jomini and Clausewitz." *Georgia Historical Quarterly* 81 (1997): 1–24.

Smith, Stephen A. *Myth, Media, and the Southern Mind*. Fayetteville: University of Arkansas Press, 1985.

Snow, Rev. Amy L. *The Endless Tour: Vietnam, Ptsd, and the Spiritual Void*. Victoria, B.C.: Trafford Publishing, 2002.

Stanonis, Anthony J. *Dixie Emporium: Tourism, Foodways, and Consumer Culture in the American South*. Athens: University of Georgia Press, 2008.

Steadman, Jennifer Bernhardt. *Traveling Economies: American Women's Travel Writing*. Columbus: Ohio State University Press, 2007.

Sutherland, Daniel. "Abraham Lincoln, John Pope, and the Origins of Total War." *Journal of Military History* 56 (1992): 567–86.

Sweet, Timothy. *Traces of War: Poetry, Photography, and the Crisis of the Union*. Baltimore: Johns Hopkins University Press, 1990.

Taylor, Helen. *Scarlett's Women: Gone with the Wind and Its Female Fans*. New Brunswick, N.J.: Rutgers University Press, 1989.

Toner, Mike. "Clues Found to Civil War Prison Site." *Cox News Service*, February 19, 2007.

Toplin, Robert Brent. *Ken Burns's the Civil War: Historians Respond*. New York: Oxford University Press, 1996.

Towns, W. Stuart. *Enduring Legacy: Rhetoric and Ritual of the Lost Cause*. Tuscaloosa: University of Alabama Press, 2012.

Townsend, Billy. "Camp Lawton Magnolia Springs State Park." Recreation and Interpretive Programming Section, Parks and Historic Sites Division, Georgia Department of Natural Resources, 1975.

———. *History of the Georgia State Parks and Historic Sites Division*. http://gastateparks.org/content/georgia/parks/75th_Anniv/parks_history.pdf 2001.

Trefousse, Hans L. "Civil Warriors in Memory and Memoir: Grant and Sherman Remember." *Georgia Historical Quarterly* 75(Fall 1991): 542–56.

Treib, Marc. *Spatial Recall: Memory in Architecture and Landscape*. Abingdon: Routledge, 2009.

Tribble, Edwin. "Marching through Georgia." *Georgia Review* 21 (1967): 423–29.

Trudeau, Noah Andre. *Southern Storm: Sherman's March to the Sea*. New York: Harper, 2008.

van Tuyll, Debra Reddin. "Two Men, Two Minds: Coverage of Sherman's March to the Sea by Augusta and Savannah Newspapers." *Journal of the Georgia Association of Historians* 17 (1996): 84–109.

Walters, John Bennett. *Merchant of Terror: General Sherman and Total War*. Indianapolis: Bobbs-Merrill, 1973.

Warren, Craig A. *Scars to Prove It: The Civil War Soldier and American Fiction*. Kent, Ohio: Kent State University Press, 2009.

Whites, LeeAnn, and Alecia P. Long. *Occupied Women: Gender, Military Occupation, and the American Civil War*. Baton Rouge: Louisiana State University Press, 2009.

Wiley, Bell Irvin. *The Life of Billy Yank*. Baton Rouge: Louisiana State University Press, 1952.

Williams, Alfred M. "Folk-Songs of the Civil War." *Journal of American Folklore* 5 (Oct.–Dec. 1892): 265–83.

Witt, John Fabian. *Lincoln's Code: The Laws of War in American History*. New York: Free Press, 2012.

Wood, Peter H. *Near Andersonville: Winslow Homer's Civil War*. Cambridge, Mass.: Harvard University Press, 2010.

Woodworth, Steven E. *Sherman*. New York: Palgrave Macmillan, 2009.

Wright, Gavin. *Old South, New South: Revolutions in the Southern Economy since the Civil War*. Baton Rouge: Louisiana State University Press, 1986.

Wyatt-Brown, Bertram. *Southern Honor: Ethics and Behavior in the Old South*. New York: Oxford University Press, 1982.

Zierdan, Martha, and Linda F. Stine. "Introduction: Historical Landscapes through the Prism of Archaeology." In *Carolina's Historical Landscapes: Archaeological Perspectives*, edited by Martha Zierdan, Linda F. Stine, Lesly M. Drucker, and Christopher Drudge, xii–xv. Knoxville: University of Tennessee Press, 1997.

INDEX

Burge, Dolly Lunt, 16
Burke County, Ga., 21–22
Burns, Ken, 229–30
Buttolph, Laura, 25
Butts County, Ga., 11, 51, 58–59, 62, 83–85
Byers, Samuel Hawkins Marshall, 175–79
Byrne, Florence, 48–49

Cadle, Cornelius, 116
Calgary Flames (hockey team), 1
Calhoun, James, 9
Camden, S.C., 77
Camp Lawton, 19, 21, 191, 226, 234
Canoochee, Ga., 14, 53
Carolinas campaign, 3, 5, 29–44, 106
Carr, Bathsheba Mallard, 54
Carter, Jimmy, 182–83
Cartersville, Ga., 63–64
Cash's Depot, S.C., 50
Chaffee, Julius T., 107
Cheraw, S.C., 36, 37, 238
Chesnut, Mary, 32, 35
Children's experiences, 58, 65–66, 117–18
Children's literature about Sherman's March, 45–46, 94–97, 104, 220–21
Childs, J. Ward, 199
Christmas in Savannah, 66, 224
Cicely: A Tale of the Georgia March, 209–10
Civil rights movement, 92–93
The Civil War, 229–30
Civil War Centennial, 7, 91–92, 168–71
Clark, Prince, 88
Clayton County, Ga., 211, 232
Clemson, Floride, 35
Clinton, Ga., 11
Cobb, Howell, 17, 123
Cogswell, William, 101
Colonial Park Cemetery, 28, 235
Columbia, S.C., 32–36, 72, 112, 159–60, 170–72, 176–77, 237–38; surrendered to Sherman, 3; fire, 33–34, 76, 116, 124–25, 220; slow to rebuild, 162–63, 168
Congaree River, 51
Connolly, James A., 17, 18, 20, 23, 28, 29
Conwell, Russell, 152, 157

Courthouse records saved from Sherman's March, 14, 17, 58–59
Covington, Ga., 15–16, 80, 232
Cram, George F., 24
Cuck, Cooper, 74

Davis, Jefferson, 127
Davis, Jefferson C. (Union general), 9, 22–23, 89, 125
Davis, Theo, 191, 192
Decatur, Ga., 15
de Laubenfels, David J., 166–67
Denhamville, Ga., 16
Dennett, John, 80, 153, 162
Doctorow, E. L., 225–27
Duncan, William, 106, 110, 116
Duplin, N.C., 54

Eatonton, Ga., 16, 233
Ebenezer Creek, Ga., 22–23, 27, 89–90, 125–26, 165, 234–35; fictional depictions of, 209, 223–24, 225
Ellis, Jerry, 78, 172–73
Elmore, Grace, 32
Emancipation, 69, 77–80, 156–57, 208
Emanuel County, Ga., 57–58
Ezell, Lorenza, 73–75

Fair, Zora, 45–46, 232–33
Fairfield County, S.C., 76
Fayetteville, N.C., 35, 37, 38–39, 72, 80, 112, 237
Ferguson, Robert, 155, 157
Fiction about Sherman's March, 7, 45–46, 94–97, 204–14, 217–27
Field, Henry, 168
Field Service in War, 142–43
Films about Sherman's March, 7, 215–17
Foraging, 103–4, 106–7, 142–43; and foragers executed by Confederates, 19, 36, 37, 96–97, 103. *See also* Bummers; Sherman's March
Force, Manning, 106, 115
Ford, Ford Madox, 148–49
Forsyth, Ga., 68
Fort McAllister, Ga., 24
Fortville, Ga., 11

Southern civilians, 2, 5–6; evacuated from Atlanta, 8–9; recalling hardships, 13–14, 19, 79; salvation stories, 15–16, 19–20, 23, 47, 52–57, 233; describing foraging/raiding, 20, 25–26, 34–35, 50, 76; treated kindly by Union soldiers, 34–35, 40, 56, 63–68, 116–18; spy stories, 44–45; outsmarting Yankees, 46–47; stories of victimization, 46–47; traumatized by experiences, 50; feigning illness, 57–58; hiding property, 57–61, 73, 109–10; concealing valuables on their bodies, 60–61; attitudes toward African Americans, 69–70, 81–82, 157–58; amazed by size of Sherman's March, 72; hiding from Sherman's March, 72; rumors about Sherman's March, 118; postwar attitudes toward Sherman, 128–34, 157–58; complaints about Confederates, 157–58; postwar resentments, 162–63, 173–74; in poetry, 197–98, 201–3; in fiction, 205–27 passim; in drama, 221–22. *See also* African Americans; Women

Spalding County, Ga., 76
Spencer, George, 67
Spivey, Ted, 202–3
Squires, Grant, 148
Stanton, Edwin, 23, 27–28, 42, 44, 90, 122, 125–26
Stark, Ga., 53
Statesboro, Ga., 14
Steed, Hal, 165–66
Sumter County, S.C., 69
Swainsboro, Ga., 14

Tennille, Ga., 14, 20–21
Thaxton, D. J., 54
"They Laid Waste to Our Land," 189–90
Thomas, Gertrude, 22
Thomasville, Ga., 58
Tilson, John, 201
Tombsboro, Ga., 13, 56
Total war, 4, 141–43. *See also* Laws of war
Tourgée, Albion, 118
Towns, Phil, 72, 79
Travel accounts, 7, 152–74, 232–38; minimizing destruction, 155–56, 166–67; interest in African Americans, 156, 163–64, 165; as journeys of self-discovery, 172–73, 228–29

Treveleyan, G. M., 146–47
Troiani, Don, 193–95
Trowbridge, John, 51, 153, 156, 161, 162–63
Turnwold Plantation, 17, 233

Uncle Caesar (slave), 84
Uncle Ned (slave), 84
Unionists and Unionism, 14, 17, 38, 158, 171
United Daughters of the Confederacy, 59, 181–83, 210

Van Dyke, Henry, 137
Varnedoe, Louisa, 220–21
Veterans: pride in service, 6, 97–98, 100–101, 115–16; reunions, 98–102; lighthearted recollections, 100–110 passim; justifying destruction, 111–13; mocking Wheeler's cavalry, 114–15; feelings toward children, 117–18
von Mach, Edmund, 148

Walker, Jacob, 83
Walton County, Ga., 53
Ward, William, 72, 78
Washington County, Ga., 13
Waters, Joseph G., 107
Waynesboro, Ga., 21, 50, 83
Wheeler's Confederate cavalry, 9, 19, 21, 22, 36, 49–50, 89–90, 114
"When Sherman Marched Down to the Sea" (song). *See* "Sherman's March to the Sea"
"When Sherman's on de Track," 184–86
White Mansions, 188–90
Whitman, Walt, 122, 198
Wilkinson County, Ga., 13
Williams, Alpheus S., 9
Williams, Mrs. F. S., 14
Williams, Isabella Huske, 40
Williams, Willis, 73
Wills, Charles Wright, 10–11, 13, 33
Wilson, Mary Butrill, 67–68
Winnsboro, S.C., 36

Wisconsin regiments: 12th, 111; 21st, 116–17

Women, during Sherman's March, 2–3, 16, 22, 25–26, 45–48, 60–61, 66–68, 83; forced to entertain soldiers, 49; sexually or physically assaulted, 49–50, 115–16; praised for devotion to the Confederacy, 61–62; standing up to soldiers, 62–63, 83; portrayed in fiction, 205–6, 209–17. *See also* Southern civilians

Woodlands Plantation, 32, 111, 155

Work, Henry Clay, 179

Works Progress Administration (WPA) slave narratives, 69–81

Worth, Nellie, 49

Wright, Henry, 77

Yelladay, Dilly, 71

Yorkville, S.C., 72, 79